P9-BHT-156

CENTRAL ASIA

*The author and publishers have made every effort to ensure the accuracy of the information in this book
at the time of going to press. However they cannot accept any responsibility for any loss, injury or
inconvenience resulting from the use of information contained in this guide.*

Printed and bound in Great Britain by Redwood Books Ltd.

Please help us keep this guide up to date

We have done our best to ensure that the information in this book is correct at the time of
going to press. But Central Asia is in a state of transition: the infrastructure is changing
constantly as the old Soviet organizations are further broken up and privatized, and the names
of streets are continuing to change. We would be delighted to hear from any travellers in the
region with news of changes, or suggested improvements to the guide. Significant
contributions will be acknowledged in the next edition, and the authors of the best letters will
receive a copy of the Cadogan Guide of their choice.

This highly readable book offers a fascinating introduction to this vast area.

Times Literary Supplement

Indispensable.

The Observer

Extremely well-researched and enjoyably crafted... The history is sound, the fables and tales amusing, the details riveting.

Los Angeles Times

What makes this useful guidebook even more interesting is Whittel's knack for weaving various anecdotes from past travellers who have explored these lands... a very readable book for armchair travellers.

Travel Books Review

About the Author and Updaters

Giles Whittell grew up in Kenya, Nigeria and Algeria. He studied history at Cambridge and then wrote gripping articles about recycling and middle management for *The Daily Telegraph*. Revolutions in Eastern Europe in 1989 caught him in the wrong place at the right time, so he rode a bicycle from Berlin to Bucharest and described the trip in *Lambada Country* (published 1992). He has written a second volume on Central Asia, *Extreme Continental* (1994), and is now *The Times'* correspondent in Los Angeles.

Catherine Davies studied history at Oxford and spent many years moving backwards on rivers. After six years at ABC Television news, a persistent interest in Central Asia drove her East to the republics for 1995. In London she works freelance for ABC TV and radio.

Peter Neville-Hadley read philosophy at York, before moving to London and taking up arts marketing as a career and Mandarin Chinese as a hobby, having no idea that eventually the two would change places. In between varied projects, including work for the Royal Opera House and marketing the multi-million pound 1991 Japan Festival, he began to spend more and more time in China. He now lives in Vancouver with his Canadian-Chinese wife, Diane (Meijuan), and is currently preparing *China: The Silk Route* for Cadogan.

Acknowledgements

Giles Whittell's acknowledgements

This book would have been impossible without heroic help at a chaotic time from dozens throughout Central Asia, including, and especially, Nikolai Shchetnikov, Valery Denisov, Vica Timonova, Yusup Kamalov, Kolya Astafiev, Valentin Dyerevyanko, Chris Bowers and Raja Changez Sultan. Thanks to Suzan Kentli for the pictures, and to Dave, Mike, Chris, Paul, Donald for maps and fighting with fonts. Bill Colegrave's enthusiasm and the endless hours put in by Rachel Fielding, Chris Schuler and Katrina Burroughs at Cadogan were likewise completely indispensable.

Catherine Davies' acknowledgements

Many thanks to Ravshan Rasulev, Raisa Gareyeva and Nourilda Nourlibaeva for continuously checking details. With a tight schedule, the pointers from Andrew Rhodes, Jeff and Linda Ludlow, Daniel Prior and the US Peace Corps were invaluable; likewise the Tajikistan expertise from Monica Whitlock and Alan Johnston. For many hours wandering Urgench, thank you Svetlana Gaikovich, in Samarkand, Rosa Zyryanova and Elena Urikh, and in Namangan, Saodat Kholmatova. Much appreciated was the support and 'B+B' provided by Susie and Douglas Busvine and Monica Whitlock. Vera Nuritova's energy and ability to make the phones work was inspiring. Thank you. Finally, thank you Neil Taylor for patient advice on travel details.

Peter Neville-Hadley's acknowledgements

Thanks to Lufthansa for a comfortable and efficient trip from North America to Central Asia and back, with research stops in Europe; and to Eurostar for a smooth glide between London and Paris collections of artefacts from Xinjiang. At Cadogan, particular thanks to Justine Hardy who took time from worrying about her own book to make these arrangements. Thanks to Nick Laing and Paul Craven of Steppes East for a useful pre-departure Central Asia briefing; to Dr. Nikolai Chtchetnikov and his staff at Dostuk Trekking for much practical assistance in Kyrgyzstan; to Iain McNeill in Almaty for help and advice and to Mr Dauren Valiev of Kan Tengri for vital visa support. In Pakistan the proprietors of the Hunza Inn in Gilgit, and the Gulmit Tourist Cottage, all freely gave of their time and vast stores of information. In Kashgar John Two and John Hu of Information Café fame loaned a bicycle and sorted out a number of confusions in the constantly changing problems of crossing the China–Kyrgyzstan border.

Publisher's acknowledgements

The publishers would like to thank all those from around the world who took the time to write and provide updated information, including: Michael H. Asher, Gavin Hellier, Judith and David Peez, Andrew Harper, Ruth O'Neill and Mark Coote, Guido Schöpping, Leigh Marconi and Ettore Marchetti, Caroline and Rupert Douglas Pennant, Leela Sasaki and Paul Certa, John Broome, Peter Bishop, Stephen Brook, Ron Fennell, Ross Weinstein.

Contents

Maps

Pack a broad-brimmed hat and a stout pair of boots. Bring a large water bottle and a thirst for adventure. You are heading, as Nikolai Przhevalski might have said, for the last frontier.

Introduction

'*Where?*', they will ask. Central Asia. South of Siberia, north of Pakistan, east of the Caucasus, west of China. In parts of this vast, addictive wilderness you are less likely to meet another tourist than you are in Antarctica.

When the Soviet Union broke up, it was the Baltic and Caucasian states that made the headlines. Further east, barely noticed, five new countries crept onto the international scene. Uzbekistan, Kazakhstan, Kyrgyzstan, Tajikistan and Turkmenistan share with the rest of the CIS racing inflation and a general bewilderment about where to go, and with whom, politically.

The great Silk Route oases of Uzbekistan are more accessible now than ever in their histories; you can even take a public bus along the golden road to Samarkand. Here, at the junction of ancient caravan routes, the colossal blue domes of Tamerlane's imperial capital dwarf the oblongs of a modern Uzbek town. In Khiva and Bukhara, legendary mazes of mosques and madrasas draw visitors from half way round the world much as they lured the players of the Great Game into life-or-death desert crossings in the 19th century.

The mountains of Tajikistan and Kyrgyzstan are as wild and beautiful as any in the world—and almost as high. The Tian Shan and the High Pamirs are territories virtually unseen by foreigners since before the Russian Revolution. They are inhabited by wild sheep and marmots, and by livestock rearers whose grandparents were among the last true nomads. To take a bus from Bishkek to Lake Issyk-Kul or hitch from Khorog to Sary Tash is not mere travel. It is exploration. Even in Kazakhstan, which took the full force of Russia's drive to assimilate Central Asia, you will still see the comforting, flattish cones of herdsmens' yurts as you trundle over the otherwise empty steppe along the TurkSib railway. And everywhere, the burdens of life are eased by age-old traditions of hospitality. The only sure way to offend in Central Asia is to decline an invitation to a feast.

Guide to the Guide

This book covers the five independent republics of former Soviet Central Asia, and the corridor leading to them through northern Pakistan and western China. Each of the Central Asian republics has its own chapter. Bear in mind that their convoluted borders reflect the political agenda of the old Soviet Union, not the lie of the land or its main transport arteries. The chapters are arranged to provide workable itineraries, and where readers are likely to stray across borders, the book does too.

The chapter on Uzbekistan includes those parts of northern Turkmenistan more easily reached from Bukhara than from Ashgabat, and the Kyrgyz and Tajik cities of the Fergana valley. The chapter on Kazakhstan begins in the south for the benefit of those approaching from Tashkent.

The final chapter covers the Karakoram Highway from Pakistan's Northwest Frontier Province to China's westernmost region, Xinjiang. It also includes the newly opened and still little-known passes from China into Kazakhstan and Kyrgyzstan.

Itineraries

The only overland journey that the Soviet authorities allowed in Central Asia remains the obvious one for lovers of **Islamic art and architecture**. By flying to Tashkent and continuing to Samarkand and Bukhara, you can take in the region's finest museums, mosques and madrasas without ever having to step outside Intourist-vetted tramlines. Given extra time, a side-trip from Samarkand to Shahrisabz gives glimpses of the Zerafshan mountains and of Tamerlane's most outrageous building project. Khiva, the most completely preserved/restored of Uzbekistan's Silk Route cities, is easily visited by plane or bus from Bukhara.

So much for sightseeing. With the demise of closed zones and the KGB, Central Asia offers Buchan-esque adventure as well. If you want **epic railway journies**, follow the czarist and Soviet railway builders in their bold sweep from the Caspian to the southern edge of Siberia. Start by taking the ferry from Baku to Turkmenbashy, where the Transcaspian railway was begun in 1881. It skirts the Kara-Kum desert, crosses the Amu Darya at the miserable town of Chardzhou, and continues via Bukhara and Samarkand to Tashkent. From here it heads north-east with the Tian Shan on the right for nearly 1000km. The TurkSib leaves the mountains at Almaty and trundles for another 1000 increasingly cold and lonely kilometres to Semipalatinsk.

The best starting points on this route for **trips into the mountains** are Samarkand and Bishkek. From Samarkand the western ends of the Zerafshan and Turkestan ranges are half a day's drive south-east. The road between them leads, when the Anzob pass is open, to Dushanbe. When it isn't, take the train via Termez and continue east into the Pamirs. Whether you take the spectacular and arduous Pamir highway via Khorog and Murgab or the more direct route via Daraut Kurgan, you will end up at the east end of the Fergana valley in Osh. Mountain junkies can traverse the Tian Shan from here to Bishkek, which is also the gateway to Lake Issyk-Kul and the start of the mountain route to China. Lowlanders can return by the valley floor to Samarkand or Tashkent.

Meanwhile, way beyond the serrated southern horizon, the **Karakoram Highway** struggles up the gorges of the Indus and the Hunza river to link Pakistan and China. At Kashgar the KKH ends and the now well-trodden route through Xinjiang to Ürümqi starts. You can branch off it into former Soviet Central Asia by crossing the Tian Shan from Kashgar to Bishkek via the Torugart Pass, or by bus or train from Ürümqi to Almaty.

A Note on Names

As Leningrad reverted to St Petersburg, so Leninabad is now Khŭjand and Tashkent's Prospekt Lenina is now Prospekt Sharaf Rashidov. The list of names that changed with the end of Soviet rule is long and lengthening. Every effort has been made to use the new ones, but if you spot one not incorporated here, please let us know.

Street names are changing more slowly than those of towns and cities, and the old ones tend to linger on in common usage. For this reason some Ulitsa Leninas and Karla Marxas have been identified as such even though their names may have changed by the time you go looking for them; people will still know where you mean when asking directions and taxi drivers often go by the old rather than the new.

Symbols Used on the Maps

☪ ☾	Mosque	🏛	Museum
🕌	Madrasa	⚚	Space centre
☉	Minaret	⊕	Airport
⚱	Mausoleum	🚌	Bus station
✡	Synagogue	T	Taxis
⛪	Cathedral	*i*	Tourist information
⛪	Church	✉	Post office
⛫	Fort	POL	Police
🐫	Caravanserai	ℝ	Restaurant
●	Bazaar	⊕	Hotel
⌐	Archaeological site	▲	Peak

Monuments

The Registan and Gur Emir, Samarkand; Kalyan minaret, Bukhara;
Tash Khauli palace, Khiva; Tash Rabat caravanserai, remotest Kyrgyzstan.

Museums

Tashkent (State Art Museum, Aybek Museum of the History of the Peoples of Uzbekistan); Almaty (Museum of Musical Instruments); Semipalatinsk (Dostoyevsky's house).

Mountain Lakes

Sary-Chelek, Son-Kul (Kyrgyzstan); Kara-Kul (Xinjiang).

Scenic Roads

Gilgit to Sost (Pakistan); Kara-Kol to Inylchek, north and south sides of
Lake Issyk-Kul (Kyrgyzstan); Pendzhikent to Dushanbe, Kalaichum to Khorog
(Tajikistan); Ust-Kamenogorsk to Rakhmanovski (Kazakhstan).

Flights

Dushanbe to Khorog (Tajikistan); Islamabad to Gilgit (Pakistan).

Soviet Engineering

Baikonur cosmodrome; Medeo ice rink, Almaty (Kazakhstan);
Toktogul hydro-electric dam, Kara-Kul (Kyrgyztan).

Bazaars

Samarkand

Belly Dancing

Hotel Sayor, Samarkand.

Skiing

Chimbulak (above Almaty).

Travel

PACK HORSES
IN THE TIANSHAN

Until 1991 the only way into former Soviet Central Asia for foreigners was by plane from Moscow with Aeroflot; a 4-hour flight over the Volga, the steppe and the desert, usually to Tashkent. Now there are direct flights to Tashkent and Almaty from at least 12 cities outside the CIS, by at least seven airlines. There are train, boat and road routes. The Karakoram Highway now links Pakistan to Kazakhstan and Kyrgyzstan as well as China. A gourd has turned into a collander.

By Air

From North America and Australasia

There are no direct flights from North America and Australasia to Central Asia. The easiest routes are via London, Europe, Moscow and Pakistan (*see* below). Uzbekistan Airways now flies twice a week from New York to Tashkent via Amsterdam, ✆ (212) 224 5682 (15 hours).

From Europe Direct

As flight schedules are in constant flux, it is worth seeking advice from a company which specializes in travel to the CIS, for example:

> **Alpha Omega Ltd**, 6 Beaconsfield Court, Garforth, Leeds LS25 1QH, ✆ (0113) 286 2121, ✉ 286 4964.
>
> **CIS Travel**, 7 Buckingham Gate, London SW1E 6JP, ✆ (0171) 828 7613, ✉ 630 8302.

Aeroflot's only direct flight to Central Asia is from Istanbul to Almaty.

Austrian Airlines, Swiss Centre, 10 Wardour Street, London W1V 4BJ, ✆ (0171) 434 7350, added Almaty to their schedule in 1995, providing London connections for two weekly flights from Vienna; £1114 rtn from London.

At the time of writing, **Europe Elite**, ✆/✉ (01753) 644 461 for information, ✆ (01293) 553 747 for reservations, are about to start operating three non-stop services a week from London Heathrow to both Alamaty and Tashkent. This is a new British airline using Boeing 757s which hopes to expand into Eastern Europe.

Kazakhstan Airways tickets can be bought from travel companies such as Aviamax, ✆ (0181) 893 5565, Sam Travel, ✆ (0171) 434 9561, and CIS Travel (*see* above). Flights leave once a week from Birmingham for Delhi via Atrau. There is no regularly scheduled connecting flight from Atrau to Almaty and the London Heathrow–Atrau service ceased to exist in early 1996. Charter flights are operated by a company in Delhi under the name Kazair. Beware, however—the company has a reputation for being extremely unreliable; flights are often cancelled at the last minute.

KLM, ✆ (0181) 750 9000, flies twice a week from Amsterdam to Almaty. Tickets bought in the UK (Heathrow office, terminal 4) and including a London–Amsterdam connection are cheaper than those bought in Amsterdam. Seasonal variations make them £899 (UK)/£924 (Netherlands) January to mid-June and October to November, £1041/£1045 mid-June to September and December.

Kyrgyz Airways are in the process of negotiating flights out of Europe to Bishkek.

Lufthansa, 10 Old Bond Street, London W1X 4EN, ✆ (0345) 737747, has four weekly flights to Almaty: flights from Frankfurt cost £738 (min. two weeks' stay), those with a London connection, £1132 (min. one week).

Turkish Airlines, 11–12 Hanover Street, London W1R 9HF, ✆ (0171) 499 4499, fly twice a week from Istanbul to Tashkent (£533 rtn) and on to Almaty (£567 rtn), once a week direct to Almaty, and direct to Ashgabat three times a week . London connections are regular and flexible. You can fly to one city and back from another. It's more expensive to buy the Istanbul–Central Asia portion of your ticket in Turkey, if starting elsewhere.

Turkmenistan Airways has two flights a week from London Heathrow, terminal 3 (£399), and one from Birmingham. At the time of writing all go via Kiev, but non-stop flights are planned for when Boeing 757s are added to the fleet in June 1996. Call CIS Travel or Sam Travel (*see* above).

Uzbekistan Airways, 72 Wigmore Street, London W1H 9DL, ✆ (0171) 935 1899, has four direct flights a week from London Heathrow, terminal 2, to Tashkent (6–7 hours) for about £375 o/w, £595 rtn. These prices are quotes from travel companies acting as general sales agents for the airlines and are cheaper than approaching the airline directly. Try HY Travel, ✆ (0171) 935 4775. Uzbek Airways flights also depart from Amsterdam, ✆ (20) 653 5200, and Frankfurt, ✆ (69) 2710 0265.

Via Moscow

This is the tried, tested and sometimes tiresome way to go. Moscow is served daily from London by:

> **Aeroflot**, 70 Piccadilly, London W1V 9HH, ✆ (0171) 355 2233 for reservations and ✆ (0171) 493 2410 for tickets.

> **British Airways**, 156 Regent Street, London W1R 5TA, ✆ (0345) 222111 for information and reservations.

> **SAS**, 52 Conduit Street, London W1R 0AY, ✆ (0171) 465 0535, via Stockholm.

Aeroflot usually has one flight a day from Moscow to Tashkent, and three a week from Moscow to Almaty. There are no Ashgabat, Dushanbe or Bishkek flights. For Tajikistan, fly to Tashkent and get a connection from there.

Aeroflot flights cost about $390 rtn Moscow–Almaty, $340 Moscow–Tashkent. They can be booked and paid for at any Aeroflot office worldwide; in Moscow they are sold at Intourist's central ticket office, Frunzenskaya Naberezhnaya 4, ✆ (095) 245 2750. Those booked at short notice may have only RQ (request) rather than OK status, but having paid in dollars you are almost sure of getting on.

Only accredited diplomats and journalists, and students enrolled in universities in the CIS, can save by paying in local currency inside the CIS.

Going via Moscow usually means changing airports from Sheremetevo II to Domodedovo or, occasionally, Vnukovo. By public transport this is cheap but takes time (allow 6 hours); change a few dollars into rubles at Sheremetevo II and take state bus 151 to *Rechnoy* (Речной) metro station. From here go down the green metro line to *Pavelet-skaya* (Павелецкая) station, where there are mainline trains to Domodedovo (1 hour). Taxi sharks ask up to $70 for airport transfers. Offer $40, refuse to go higher and pretend that you are just as happy going on a bus. Someone will eventually accept your price. At Domodedovo, Intourist handles all foreigners. Their reception is at the extreme left of the terminal, from where buses shuttle to a special check-in/departure lounge area.

Air China (CAAC), 41 Grosvenor Gardens, London SW1W 0BP, ✆ (0171) 630 0919, and 45 East 49th Street, New York, NY 10017, ✆ (212) 371 9898, toll free within US ✆ (1 800) 986 1985, flies between Moscow and Ürümqi; so does **Aeroflot**.

Transaero, ✆ (0171) 436 6767, is a recommended Russian airline which uses Boeing aircraft and Western-trained crews. Safety standards and comfort are better and prices reflect this. Moscow to Almaty economy class costs $450 rtn. Offices include: Moscow, ✆ (095) 151 4477; Berlin, ✆ (30) 4101 3432; and Frankfurt, ✆ (69) 6907 3229.

Via Minsk

Another reliable CIS airline is **Belavia.** There are twice-weekly (three from June 1996) direct flights to Minsk from London Gatwick (£286 rtn), and a twice-weekly service from Shannon Airport, Dublin (£258). From Minsk there are connections to Almaty (£187) and Tashkent (£200) but these are not timed to coincide with European flights; connections are better on some days of the week than on others. For reservations and information in London, ✆ (0171) 393 1201; in Minsk, ✆ (172) 250231; at Shannon Airport, ✆ (61) 472921.

From/Via Pakistan

Pakistan International Airlines (PIA), 45–46 Piccadilly, London, ✆ (0171) 734 5544 for reservations, ✆ 287 2582 for fare enquiries, has one flight a week from Islamabad to Tashkent (5 hours, about $250 o/w, $295 rtn) and to Almaty (4 hours, $415 o/w, $370 rtn); there is also a daily service, weather permitting, between Islamabad and Gilgit on the Karakoram Highway. It's cheaper to buy PIA Central Asian connections in Islamabad than to pay for the complete journey in London.

China Xinjiang Airways (CXA), a subsidiary of Air China (*see* above), operates a once-weekly service from Islamabad to Ürümqi.

PIA and **British Airways** each fly twice a week from London to Islamabad; PIA from Heathrow or Manchester direct (8 hours, £624 rtn), British Airways, ✆ (0345) 222111, from Gatwick via Manchester (from £742 rtn, depending on the season).

PIA has two flights a week from New York, ✆ (212) 370 9155, to Islamabad, one via Frankfurt ✆ (69) 273 9010, the other via Amsterdam ✆ (20) 626 4715.

other routes

Uzbekistan Airways has an impressive international network, with flights between Tashkent and Istanbul, Tel Aviv, Sharjah, Jeddah, Karachi, Bangkok, Kuala Lumpur and Beijing as well as London and Frankfurt. The aircraft mostly come from the part of Aeroflot's massive domestic fleet that was based at Tashkent, plus some recently purchased Airbuses.

Iran Air flies once a week from Tehran to Ashgabat but if on a connecting flight check on transit visa requirements. **CAAC** (*see* p.4) has frequent flights from Beijing to Ürümqi, while its subsidiary **CXA** and **Aeroflot** each have connections from Beijing to Almaty.

By Train

From forest through meadow, steppe and desert to oasis at a steady, clanking 60kmh; there is no slower, more romantic way of witnessing the transition from Europe to Asia than to take a train from Moscow to Tashkent. By the most direct route it takes two and a half days. This is the Saratov–Syr Darya mainline, one of three Herculean railway projects undertaken by the czarists to link Turkestan to Russia. The others are the Transcaspian railway and the Volgograd–Amu Darya line, although the latter ceased to operate in 1994. In the 1930s forced labour built the TurkSib railway, linking Tashkent and Kazakhstan to the Trans-Siberian; and in 1990 the Chinese at last opened their section of the Ürümqi–Almaty line, connecting Xinjiang to the Soviet Union.

Even then all these lines were closed to Westerners. Now they are open, cheap and unforgettable. A 3rd-class ticket from Moscow to Bishkek costs in the region of $58, and a 2nd-class kupe $95; you can travel 3rd class from Almaty to Irkutsk for $61. On trains between Moscow and the Central Asian capitals you usually have the choice of an open carriage with a hard seat which turns into a bunk at night; a berth in a four-person compartment (*kupe*); or a berth in a two-person compartment (*lyux*).

If possible, buy your tickets from Moscow's Orenburg Station at least one day before departure. Tickets are also available from Moscow's central Intourist ticket office at Frunzenskaya Naberezhnaya 4. English is spoken, but a surcharge of at least $5 in hard currency is added, and the queues may be worse than at the station.

All carriages have a *provodnik*, from whom you rent a bedding roll and clean sheets, and free boiling water for hot drinks. Bring your own mug, teapot, tea, coffee etc. Also bring provisions. Restaurant cars tend to leave Moscow spotless and efficiently run. For the first day or two they usually offer soup, bread, a choice of two main dishes and a change of scene, but by Tashkent the women in charge may be stirring only for bad-tempered vodka auctions.

In summer the desert sections of train journeys can be unbearably hot; compartment windows generally don't open unless broken. In fact that's increasingly how they'll be, since state subsidies are not as forthcoming as they were. Some trains board up their windows instead. Bring loose, light clothes.

Saratov–Syr Darya line: From Moscow's Kazan station, two trains a day leave for Tashkent (two and a half days), and one for Almaty and Bishkek (three days).

Volgograd–Amu Darya line: Trains leave Moscow's Paveletskaya station daily for Ashgabat (two and a half days) and Dushanbe (three and a half days). They all pass through Urgench (for Khiva) and Chardzhou (connections to Bukhara and Samarkand).

Transcaspian line: There are two trains a day along this line from Turkmenbashy to Ashgabat. Turkmenbashy can be reached by train and boat via Baku or, with luck and perseverance, via Astrakhan (*see* 'By Boat' below). Trains from Moscow to Baku (43 hours) leave from Moscow's Kursk station.

TurkSib line: This leaves the Trans-Siberian at Novosibirsk, from where there are daily through trains to Almaty and Tashkent. Novosibirsk is 43 hours by daily express from Moscow's Yaroslavl station.

All Moscow's mainline stations have their own metro stations.

Meshed–Sarakhs link: In May 1996 this stretch of track should open, linking Europe and Asia (*see* **Turkmenistan**, p.83).

For details of the **Ürümqi–Almaty line**, *see* p.288.

By Boat

It is possible to travel from Moscow to Turkmenbashy, the self-styled Gateway to Central Asia on Turkmenistan's barren Caspian coast, without setting foot on dry land.

The Volga

Start by joining a two-week cruise, most of it on the Volga, from Moscow to **Astrakhan**. Enquire at any Intourist office worldwide, or the Moscow office at Frunzenskaya Naberezhnaya 4; if you want to pay in rubles, the best place to ask is at Moscow's *Rechnoy Vokzal* ('River Station').

For those wanting to mix train and boat travel, the Volga is navigable along almost its entire length, with river stations in all major towns and several cabin steamers a day in either direction through the summer. These are filled mostly by Russians on package holidays but, space permitting, they act as river buses too. School-dinner type meals are generally included in the price of your ticket

The Volga has been dammed in so many places that over most of its length it is more lake than river. From Volgograd to Astrakhan, however, it flows unimpeded and serene between Russia and the Kazakh steppe—the true boundary between Europe and Asia. Volgograd–Astrakhan is a 19-hour boat journey; Volgograd is 24 hours by train from Moscow's Paveletskaya station. All passenger services on the Volga are run by **Rechflot**, a former Soviet monopoly.

The Caspian Sea

There are no scheduled passenger services from Astrakhan, on the Volga delta, to Turk-menbashy. However, Intourist at Astrakhan is reported to be extremely helpful in arranging *ad hoc* passages for foreigners (and their vehicles; in one case, a private bus) on cargo ships. They can be contacted via Andrei Malnshkin, an English-speaking guide at Astrakhan's museum (Sovietskaya Ulitsa 15). The crossing takes about four days.

In principle there is one sailing a day to Turkmenbashy by a large passenger- and car-ferry from Baku, the capital of Azerbaijan. In practice departures are erratic and tend to go only when full. Baku's ferry terminal is on the sea-front, two blocks east of the Hotel Azer-baijan. The ticket office is on the left-hand side as you face the sea. Go there as soon as you arrive in Baku and get your name on the list of passengers for the next sailing. If it is not possible to buy a ticket at once, establish when it will be possible and return at least half an hour before that time. There may be several false alarms; repeat the process until you have a ticket. The boat may not sail from this terminal, in which case you will be bussed to the point of departure. For more on this crossing, *see* 'Turkmenbashy', p.79.

By Road

From Russia

Until 1991, the roads from Moscow to Central Asia were strictly out of bounds to for-eigners. Nowadays it is technically possible to make the journey in your own vehicle, although the bureaucracy involved in bringing a car into the CIS means that it is easier—and in the long run probably cheaper—to buy your own vehicle on arrival in Central Asia (*see* p.20). Either way, the likely frequent police encounters should be built into your journey time and your budget.

For those who insist on making the trek, you leave Moscow on the M5 (the Ryazan road famous from Tolstoy's *War and Peace*) and head southeast for 1004km to Samara. From there you take the M32 across 2288km of steppe and desert to Tashkent.

From Pakistan and China

The Karakoram Highway from northern Pakistan to western China now forms part of an overland route to former Soviet Central Asia as well, thanks to two recently opened road crossings from China to the CIS. One is the Torugart pass, 3752m up in the Tian Shan on the Kyrgyz border and 160 very rough km from Kashgar (generally open only May–Sept). The 1992 Paris–Beijing rally came this way. Until recently there was no public transport on the Chinese side, but in late 1995 a new customs post was opened closer to Kashgar, accessible from there by local bus and with, in theory, two buses a day running up to the pass and the border. However, the road is often accessible only by jeep. Coming from Kyr-gyzstan, you may not be allowed to cross the border unless you have arranged to be met on the Chinese side. Coming the other way, the Chinese will not let you cross without a CIS visa, and sometimes insist on a Kyrgyz visa, whatever the current CIS regulations may be. Once you've entered Kyrgyzstan, you'll find jeeps and buses waiting to take you to Bishkek, but only for large sums in clean, 1990 or later $US cash. Asking prices may be as high as $200, negotiable to perhaps $60, depending on the circumstances (*see also* pp.265–8 and 343–4).

The other road crossing, used six days a week by international buses from Ürümqi to Almaty, is 600km north at Khorgos on the Kazakh border (*see also* pp.356–8).

There are plans to build a new road across the Roof of the World between Pakistan and Tajikistan, but the route has not yet been fixed. There are even rumours of plans to turn the jeep track that runs from Tashkurgan in China to Murgab in Tajikistan into an international highway. A more direct route to Osh opens in 1996, crossing the border at Irkeshtam, and sharing a customs post with the road to the Torugart crossing.

From Iran

The border crossing at Gaudan between the Iranian city of Meshed and the Turkmen capital, Ashgabat, is open to local traffic only. For some time following the break-up of the Soviet Union the Iranian embassy in London provided transit visas for entry into Turkmenistan by this route. These are no longer being issued, though transit visas are still available for overland travel between Turkey and Pakistan.

Specialist Holidays

Even those who would never dream of it anywhere else should at least consider joining a group in former Soviet Central Asia, especially if time for travelling—*and planning*—is short. Those involved in selling pre-paid trips to these countries tend to be enthusiasts; it's a more labour-intensive way of making money than sending plane-loads to Malaga, so it helps to enjoy the labour as well as the money. They also know as much as anyone about fast-changing entry formalities. They include:

In the UK

Exodus Expeditions (trekking), 9 Weir Road, London SW12 0LT, ✆ (0181) 675 5550.

Explore Worldwide (overland by coach, including Karakoram Highway), 1 Frederick Street, Aldershot, Hampshire GU11 1LQ, ✆ (01252) 319448.

Jamiesons (the Silk Route through the CIS and Asia), The Old Well House, Crossbush, nr Arundel, West Sussex BN18 9PT, ✆ (01903) 884666.

OTT Expeditions (mountaineering in the Pamirs and Tian Shan for those with some experience), 62 Nettleham Road, Sheffield S8 8SX, ✆ (01142) 588508.

Regent Holidays (travel arrangements for individual and group trips to Central Asia and China, including Tashkent/Almaty to Ürümqi), 15 John Street, Bristol BS1 2HR, ✆ (01179) 211711.

Steppes East (treks combined with tours of Samarkand and Bukhara, trekking on horseback in Kazakhstan, rafting and walking in the Altai), Castle Eaton, Swindon, Wiltshire SN6 6JU, ✆ (01285) 810267.

Tour de Force (occasional Silk Route tours with a botanist), 200–208 Tottenham Court Road, London W1P 9LA, ☎ (0181) 983 1487.

Voyages Jules Verne (upmarket Silk Route sightseeing with direct charter flights to Samarkand from London), 21 Dorset Square, London NW1 6QG, ☎ (0171) 723 5066.

In the USA

MIR (tours and travel arrangements, including visas and homestays, for visitors and foreign residents; member of ASTA), 85 Washington Street, Suite 210, Seattle, WA 98104, ☎ (206) 624 7289.

OTT Expeditions (*see* above), PO Box 2893, Ventura, CA 93002, ☎/⊚ (805) 641 0971.

REI Adventures (climbing, rafting and trekking), PO Box 1938, Summer, WA 98390, ☎ (206) 891 2631, toll free within US ☎ (1 800) 622 2236.

Red Tape—A Short Sermon

After the failed coup of August 1991, one of Gorbachev's reinstated aides was asked at a packed press conference whether old travel restrictions still applied to foreign journalists. The aide grinned, sighed and replied, 'Gentlemen, there are no rules here any more.'

There are no rules. This is worth remembering. Not quite true, but worth remembering. History's biggest, most expensive, most pervasive, most notorious bureaucratic monster had sunk to its knees. It is still dying, and will go on doing so for some time yet. Meanwhile new systems of controlling people—or empowering them—are tried, flung out, adopted and adapted all the time on every level across the CIS. Where rules are concerned, today's independent states are still in a state of flux.

There are no rules. None, at least, that everyone agrees on. None whose bluff is not worth calling. If a timid *apparatchik* refuses permission to visit to the former Aral port of Muynak, ask to see the minister. He may just as easily provide a limousine to take you there. If an Aeroflot ogress in Dushanbe's downtown ticket office declares there are no flights to Khorog for a month, nip down to the airport. You could be on the plane before you know it.

But there is not quite the same room for manoeuvre as there was in 1994. It's always worth a try, but don't be surprised if your efforts fail. Rules may change from place to place, day to day. But sometimes, some would argue increasingly, it is hard to circumvent them. If you do, success can be temporary, and they'll return to haunt you at a later, and probably less opportune, moment. Today's latitude is more often on the other side of the fence.

Independent travel is possible; it's part of the adventure. Be creative—have various options and test them all. Most importantly, pack a sense of humour.

Before 1991, bureaucratic hurdles had to be scrupulously cleared. In the confusion immediately following independence, many could be pushed aside. A few still can. It's true to say that if you seek out bureaucrats you will get bureaucracy. On the other hand, if they seek you out, be calm and friendly. Then be cooperative or dim as appropriate. Take this line and you will have a lot more fun and a lot less disappointment than if you don't. Just make sure you know the nature of the beast you're dealing with.

Entry Formalities

Visas

All non-CIS citizens need a visa to enter the CIS and, these days, one for each independent republic visited. A Russian one is insufficient. If a state lacks consular representation, the Russian Embassy will issue one on their behalf. In London, this still applies to Turkmenistan, Kyrgyzstan and Tajikistan. However, Turkmen visas may be purchased on arrival at Ashgabat airport and so, in theory, may Kazakh (business only) and Uzbek ones, providing you bring an invitation as well.

It is not necessary to have visas for all the republics on your wish list prior to departure, but it could save you hassle and expense later. Thanks to an agreement between all the republics except Turkmenistan, a visa from another state buys you 72 hours' leeway. If you intend to stay longer than those three days, you have to get the appropriate visa within that time. Otherwise claim to be 'in transit'. There are times when it is necessary to purchase so-called transit visas, for example for a day-trip into Turkmenistan; these are cheaper than regular visas ($10–15).

In November 1993, reciprocal freedom of movement was agreed between President Karimov and the UK and then the USA. For nationals of these countries, internal visas, which give permission to visit specified towns within Uzbekistan, are not required.

As a general rule, you will almost certainly need the local visa to stay in a hotel or buy another air ticket. You may never need it if you are disappearing into the mountains, transiting to a neighbouring republic by bus or train, or staying in a private apartment. If you stay in someone's home, however, consider your host, who will also pay the penalty if you are found lacking the necessary paperwork.

Russia

A Russian visa is essential for anyone travelling to Central Asia via Russia, and useful for those entering Central Asia by another route if they have been unable to obtain any other visa.

In the UK, Russian visas are issued by the **Russian Embassy** at 10 Kensington Palace Gardens, London W8, ✆ (0171) 229 8027 (consular section, closed Wed). If you get no joy here, it's well worth trying the consular department in Edinburgh, ✆ (0131) 225 7098, ✆ (0131) 225 9587. For addresses of Russian embassies in North America, Australia and New Zealand *see* pp.26–8.

For a **Russian tourist visa** (price £10, maximum duration three months), there are two options. Either pre-book and pre-pay some Russian hotel accommodation through Intourist (*see* pp.46–7), who will issue hotel vouchers, or make arrangements to procure a private invitation. The invitee has to take your details to their local police station, who may take between six weeks and three months to processs them. Once sanctioned, you will receive a green form. Allow a minimum of eight working days after submitting your application.

The alternative is a **business visa** (price £10 if applied for at least 10 days in advance, with a sliding scale up to £100 if travelling the following day; maximum duration three months). For this, they claim, you need an invitation from a 100% Russian-owned company, but pre-booked accommodation is not necessary.

You don't need Russian friends to get a Russian invitation. Some agencies sell invitations ('visa support') from Russian organizations of which you have never heard, and which you will never meet. They can be hard to find, however. In London the Russian Embassy has cracked down on companies providing what they consider 'spurious' invitations. In Holland, **Diek Reizeu** can provide invitations and arrange apartments in Moscow, ✆ (20) 682 5672.

To get either kind of visa you will need, in addition to proof of accommodation or an invitation, a Russian Embassy application form. Fill this in and present it, together with your actual passport (photocopies of the relevant pages are no longer accepted), at least two identical or nearly identical passport-size photos, and the payment in cash. If possible, ensure that your photos have a matt finish. A visa official frustrated by the ink stamp failing to stick to a gloss photo will not be inclined to be helpful.

Russian visas can be obtained by post (allow at least two weeks) or by queueing at the Russian Embassy on weekdays except Wednesdays, in which case be prepared for a long wait. You'll notice that visa agents gravitate towards the front of the queue. Should you decide to benefit from this, the agent handling fee is in the range of £20–30, including return registered post and VAT. Recommended agents are:

> **Visa and Passport Service**, 1 St Stephen's Mews, London W2, ✆ (0171) 229 1262.
>
> **Visa World**, 43 Elmgate Gardens, London W8, ✆ (0181) 959 6161.
>
> **P.V.S.**, 10 Parlaunt Road, Slough, Berkshire, ✆ (01753) 583 159.

A Russian visa is not a stamp in your passport but a separate form with your itinerary printed on it and the name of your host or host organization if you have been 'invited'. In Soviet times it had to be stamped by the police, or by Intourist on their behalf, every night of your trip. Intourist hotels still stamp visas, but no one checks that every night has been accounted for when you leave the CIS. Tourist visas are yellow, business ones purple. Whenever yours is inspected you will need to present your passport as well, and *you must have your visa to leave* as well as enter the CIS. Without it, an on-the-spot replacement will cost you dearly, and be issued only if the official in question is feeling indulgent.

Kazakhstan

Kazakh visas are available on arrival at Almaty airport, either transit only (approx $35) or, providing you have an invitation, single-entry, one-week visas ($30). Invitations can be gleaned from personal contacts or tourist/business organizations. Business ones are processed by the main consular department of the Foreign Ministry, and tourist ones by the visa section at the Ministry for Internal Affairs. At the end of the day the only difference this distinction makes is that 'tourists' will receive a copy of the invitation sent by their invitee.

If you apply for a tourist or business visa before you travel, an application form (plus invitation for tourist visa), passport and two passport-size photos should be taken to the Kazakh Consulate. Seven days for processing incurs a standard visa fee of £19/£32 for a one-/two-week visa. A shorter processing time costs more. You can opt to collect your visa from Almaty airport on arrival, but it's likely to be more expensive. You will need to list all the towns you wish to visit. Visa extension requires a letter explaining why, and a trip to OVIR, the local police office. It's easier and cheaper to be generous in your initial application.

If you intend to stay longer than three days, you must register with OVIR. Registration costs around $20–30. Hotels do this automatically for you, but private accommodation cannot. It's unlikely you'll get past a hotel receptionist without a visa, and you certainly won't get through the airport without a registration stamp. Take a chance if leaving Kazakhstan by any other form of transport.

In theory a new regulation demands an HIV certificate for anyone staying over three months. Tests made elsewhere are accepted if carried out within a month of the visa application.

Kyrgyzstan

Kyrgyzstan issues visas from its consulates in each of the Central Asian republics and from the growing number in Europe and the USA. The Kyrgyz Embassy in Washington has issued, in the past, a six-week visa without an invitation for $25. While this is not the norm, it is generally possible to get a one-month tourist visa with only a letter stating your reasons for the visit. However, Russian embassies acting on behalf of Kyrgyzstan still require an invitation. If travelling to Bishkek from another republic, the three-day transit rule will enable you to get a visa upon arrival ($25–50, depending on length of stay)—go to OVIR in the Foreign Ministry building (left-hand door), Kievskaya Ulitsa. If you have problems with the visa, try Intourist instead. OVIR has been known to send unlucky individuals to the Ministry of Foreign Affairs itself, ordering them to return afterwards to pay a fine for the privilege of their earlier direction. Alternatively try the Ministry of Tourism near the sports stadium, on the corner of Togolok Molko and Frunze. Anyone in need of 'visa support' (i.e. an invitation) should try Dostuk Trekking (*see* p.250) or Kyrgyz Concept (p.248). If your first port of call in Kyrgyzstan is not Bishkek, assure the officials that you'll obtain a visa as soon as you get to the capital. When Bishkek's airport is open, incoming foreigners are apparently required to register with the police there.

Whether you get your visa before or after arrival, you must obtain the registration stamp from OVIR. Go first to the Anim bank on Prospekt Chu. After waving your passport and parting with $3–4, you'll qualify for a receipt which you must take to OVIR. A travel agency in Bishkek providing visa support will take care of this for you.

Travelling in Kyrgyzstan is less likely to bring the frequent encounters with officialdom that occur elsewhere. Hotels do not always check your passport. There are, however, a few areas that require 'permission' to visit (*see* **Kyrgyzstan**, p.248). When getting your visa, make sure it states Kyrgyzstan and not only Bishkek, unless that is your sole destination. To avoid hassle later, it's worth asking OVIR to write on your visa the names of the towns that you want to visit.

Tajikistan

Get a Tajik visa from a Tajikistan embassy in Central Asia or from a Russian embassy before you leave home. A day trip from Samarkand to Pendzikent, just over the Tajik border, should not require a visa thanks to the three-day transit rule. However, regulations relating to Tajikistan are more fluid than those elsewhere. To avoid disappointment, check them before departure. If you enter Tajikistan from Osh without having Dushanbe or Khorog (the main town of the Pamir region) written on your visa you are, if questioned, in transit. In any event, you cannot travel to Khorog without permission, and this can only be obtained from the Ministry of Foreign Affairs in Dushanbe. Efforts to procure it in Osh will be fruitless.

Uzbekistan

With more consular representation now, it's not necessary to go via Moscow for an Uzbek visa or even to queue outside the Russian Embassy. But actually getting the visa in your hand can take a while. Visa instructions from the Uzbek consulate claim that the decision on a visa is taken during the 10 days after application. In practice it can take longer. In this vital respect Uzbekistan doesn't make things easy for an industry it's trying to promote.

Still, your trip will justify perseverence. Obtain an invitation or 'visa support' from business, personal or travel company contacts. They will apply to the Ministry of Foreign Affairs on your behalf. Ask for a copy of the invitation with your details on it. Some argue that this isn't strictly necessary since the Ministry should telex them to the appropriate consulate, but including a copy when you submit your application form, photos (3) and passport will avoid confusion and save time. Visa agents agree. Passports must be valid for at least 90 days more than the period of stay requested. Picking up the visa upon arrival at the airport (2nd floor, near Lufthansa office) is a sanctioned, if lengthy, process. For your own peace of mind, get it before.

Turn up at the airport without an invitation and prior arrangement and you'll be put on the first flight home. This is one of those rules that no amount of obsequious deference or belligerent bluster will change. If you arrive on 'transit time' from another republic, present that visa and your Uzbek invitation.

The minimum length of time for a visa application to be processed is seven days. A single-entry visa will cost $40 for a week, $60 for a month. Similarly business visas. Any visa required within three working days costs 50% extra. These times/costs can vary for the consulates in Central Asia.

In order to fly direct from London or Frankfurt to Tashkent by Uzbekistan Airways, you will need at least an invitation from Uzbekistan before you are sold a ticket. If you get a ticket without, you certainly won't be able to board unless you can show the relevant documentation.

Entering Uzbekistan by train or car is less officious. You still need an Uzbek invitation, which you must take within 72 hours to the Ministry of Foreign Affairs (across the road from the Opera House). First collect written confirmation, from a Western embassy, that you are a Westerner. This will cost a few dollars. Then be prepared to queue for 1–3 hours. Visas take up to four days to process.

Hotels check visas thoroughly. If staying in one town and in private accommodation for over three days, you must register with OVIR. There are numerous local offices; if unsure of the address, a list can be obtained from the consular section of an embassy. At the airport you will not be allowed to board any flight unless you have a registration stamp or paper. Attempting to get the appropriate stamp from a hotel where you are not resident is illegal and will be treated with contempt by all but the most unscrupulous receptionists. Registration costs around $20.

If you are travelling via Moscow, Uzbektourism, 3rd floor, Room 53, Ulitsa Polyanka 41, can arrange your visa. There may be a service charge of 15% for each night of pre-booked accommodation, with your visa issue conditional upon pre-booking, despite new diplomatic arrangements.

Turkmenistan

While Turkmenistan consulates are rare in Europe and the USA, you will be able to purchase a visa upon arrival at Ashgabat airport. In practice, however, this only applies if you arrive on an international flight. You cannot fly from Dashkhovuz (just across the Turkmen border from Uzbekistan) unless you already have a Turkmenistan visa. The three-day transit rule that helps in other Central Asian republics does not work here (*see* p.194 for solution). In theory you do not need an invitation to get a visa, but you do to extend it. In this case your sponsor must explain why you need to stay longer. Ten-day visas are issued and cost $20.

If you arrive in Ashgabat by any other form of transport and need a visa, go to the Ministry of Foreign Affairs (closed Wed).

To cross the border from Turkmenistan or Uzbekistan, pay a visit to the nearest regional (not city) *hakim* (mayor). In the future, the aim is to pass visa and registration responsibility from OVIR to the Ministry of Foreign Affairs. The appropriate departments will open at border points.

The fact that Turkmenistan doesn't acknowledge the three-day transit rule affects those leaving the country as well as arriving. Leaving Ashgabat for Uzbekistan by air is very difficult—to the point that you are unlikely to be able to board—without a valid Uzbek visa. At the very least you need an Uzbek invitation; and at best a letter from the Uzbek Ministry of Foreign Affairs guaranteeing that you will collect your visa upon arrival at Tashkent.

Re-entering the CIS

All Russian visas are single-entry unless otherwise requested and paid for. London's Russian Embassy will not issue double-entry visas for itineraries which involve leaving and re-entering the CIS via a Central Asian republic. This would affect anyone flying via Moscow who is planning a side-trip from Kazakhstan and/or Kyrgyzstan into Xinjiang, for example, or from Uzbekistan into Pakistan. Explain your plan to OVIR in Almaty or Bishkek, or at the Uzbek Foreign Ministry's office at Tashkent airport; you may be able to get a second single-entry visa for your return. All Central Asian republics issue multiple-entry visas.

China

All non-Chinese citizens need visas to enter the country. Available from Chinese embassies in all Western capitals (*see* pp.26–8 for addresses), they allow virtually unrestricted independent travel, and can be extended at Public Security Bureaus. The visa fee varies according to your nationality and place of application. Visas usually take five days to process, but this can be speeded up by the payment of extra fees. The Chinese frequently change the rules at short notice and are deaf to appeals if this ruins your plans. At times these have included requiring proof that you have £2000 or a return air ticket, and only accepting applications in your country of residence, although this is not the norm. You are asked on the visa form to list your itinerary, and a visa may be refused simply because your choices are not anodyne enough, or because the official you are dealing with is in a bad mood. Mentioning cities in Xinjiang should be avoided unless you are applying in Islamabad, Almaty or Bishkek. Visa validity varies between one and three months. Consulates, as opposed to full embassies, will only issue visas to residents of the immediate locality, and if you don't live in a city with a consulate, always apply to the embassy in your capital. In general, if your tour operator or travel agent offers a visa service, take advantage of it. You need to fill in an application form and provide a passport-size photo. Make sure your passport has at least two clean pages.

The embassies at Almaty, Bishkek and Islamabad rarely issue visas for more than one month, and the embassy at Bishkek stamps visas 'not good for entry via the Torugart Pass'.

Pakistan

Most foreigners, including citizens of all European and North American countries, need visas for Pakistan. The price varies according to nationality and type of visa, and both single- and multiple-entry visas are available. These are best bought in advance, although it is sometimes possible to enter Pakistan for 72 hours and then get a tourist visa in Islamabad following a long wrestle with bureaucracy. Get yours before leaving home or in Tashkent or Almaty. There is no Pakistan consulate in Ürümqi or anywhere near the Pakistan–Chinese border. For addresses of Pakistan embassies, *see* pp.26–8.

Customs and Currency

You have to fill in a joint customs and currency declaration on entering and leaving the CIS. The forms are in Russian. If incomprehensible, eavesdrop and ask. It's best at least to write 'no' rather than leaving a blank. On leaving, have receipts ready to show for major purchases and currency exchanges over $100. Don't take out more hard currency than you brought in unless you can prove you obtained it legally, and don't try exporting antiquities. Baggage is X-rayed and searched going in and out of CIS international airports; in Turkmenistan, it is searched thoroughly. Security is tight at Islamabad airport, where you will probably have to open your bags. Coming into the CIS, duty is payable on fax machines. Some cordless phones are confiscated because they use the same frequencies as CIS emergency services. The Chinese ask you to declare cameras and electronic items, and may want to see anything snazzy. At Moscow's Sheremetevo airport the 'red channel' and 'green channel' signs are meaningless. Join the shortest queue.

Getting Around Central Asia

By Air

In the CIS

In Central Asia, as in the rest of the CIS, Aeroflot was carved up into separate national airlines. This has not disrupted schedules; management of Aeroflot's domestic fleet had already been devolved to regional hubs, so the change consists mostly of complex leases and simple paint jobs. The exception is Turkmenistan, which bought a number of second-hand Boeing aircraft.

What has disrupted schedules is the shortage of fuel, reducing Aeroflot's Central Asian timetable to a shadow of its pre-1991 self. In Kyrgyzstan, the scheduled service is intermittent. When non-existent, the nearest airport to Bishkek is Almaty's, 4 hours away by bus. In Tajikistan, flights are at the mercy of Uzbek fuel embargoes and violence in Dushanbe. Uzbekistan, Turkmenistan and Kazakhstan have their own supplies or stable purchasing arrangements, but even here the price of fuel has risen so much faster than wages that the number of passengers—and therefore the number of flights—has fallen sharply. Domestic flights can be cancelled if the number of passengers doesn't justify the fuel.

Nevertheless, major routes are still well served, and even the dollar prices which most foreigners have to pay are low by international standards. Sample fares: Tashkent to Samarkand $51 (up to five flights a day); Tashkent to Almaty $86 (one flight a day). Most of these flights are unromantic time-savers, but a few, like the 45-minute hop over the western Pamirs from Dushanbe to Khorog, are white-knuckle rides worth building into your itinerary.

You can buy air tickets at most hotels run or used by Intourist; otherwise from Aeroflot ticket offices (*agenstva Aeroflota*) in city centres. Foreigners pay in dollars and have to show their passport. There's no point getting a CIS citizen to buy one for you in local currency.

Airport tax for international flights is $10–20, paid on departure. For domestic flights it's $5, paid either separately when you check in, as at Ashgabat airport, or else when you buy your ticket. Treat all your bags as hand luggage—the definition is as flexible as you'll need the cabin to be. Keeping everything with you will save time on arrival and protect you from everyone else's gear.

In Xinjiang and Pakistan

CXA has a Ürümqi–Kashgar service, and both **CXA** and **Kazakhstan Airways** fly Ürümqi–Almaty. There are no direct flights between Pakistan and Xinjiang. *See also* p.4.

By Helicopter

Soviet mountaineering in Central Asia was a competitive sport that began at around 4000m. Two-week approach marches from lush lowlands to base camps were laughed at; if you needed them to acclimatize you were a no-hoper. This part was done by helicopter. When foreign climbers provide the money, it still is.

Thus, with aeroplanes grounded, taxis running on gas and living standards in free fall, helicopter shuttle services still operate, for a few weeks each summer, between remote roadheads and even remoter mountaineering camps beneath the 7000m peaks of Kyrgyzstan and Tajikistan.

The main helicopter bases are Maidadir, near Inylchek in Kyrgyzstan, and the Karkara camp near Sary Dzhash in Kazakhstan, for the central Tian Shan; and Batken and Ashik Tash in southern Kyrgyzstan for the high Pamirs and the granite walls of the Alai range.

Chartering a helicopter costs from $400 an hour. Helicopters supplying big climbing expeditions often fly half empty, however, in which case heli-hitching is possible. Negotiate direct with the pilot, and open the bidding at $20.

By Train

In the CIS

This is the slowest and most sociable form of public transport in Central Asia. It is also, for Westerners, embarrassingly cheap. Daily trains in both directions between Moscow and each Central Asian capital, plus frequent local trains, mean that every station on the network, however small, is served by at least two trains a day.

On journeys which do not start or end in Moscow, the rolling stock tends to be older and grubbier, and there are usually no two-person *lyux* compartments. These lines include the Transcaspian between Turkmenbashy and Tashkent, the TurkSib from Tashkent to Novosibirsk, and the line from Bishkek through the Fergana valley to Dushanbe.

As rising air ticket prices force people off planes onto trains, ticket queues at stations lengthen. They can be exasperating. When a long wait is in prospect, people sometimes show their faces to establish their position in the queue, then disappear to eat or sleep. If they are recognized on their return they are generally let in. Thus the number of people between you and the ticket window can actually increase the longer you wait.

Check before queueing that your chosen ticket window sells tickets to your destination, and that the woman behind it is not about to go to lunch. Destinations and break times are usually painted on the window.

Bring your own food and drink. Summer temperatures in the sealed compartments of a Central Asian train can rise to over 45°C. Winter ones can fall below freezing.

Anyone travelling by train should be aware that crime on rail transport is increasing. Security is a big problem, and it's worth bringing a chain and locking the compartment door.

In Pakistan and Xinjiang

There are no trains in Pakistan's Northern Areas (though some 19th-century train freaks envisaged Gilgit as a major international railway junction). The Chinese government has plans to extend the Ürümqi–Korla line to Kashgar, but as yet Kashgar has no railway station.

By Bus

In the CIS

The tarmac spine of former Soviet Central Asia runs from Bukhara through Samarkand, Tashkent, Chimkent, Dzhambul and Bishkek to Almaty. By far the easiest way to travel along it is by bus. State and now some commercial or private buses ply its sections all day and much of the night. Those sections are: Bukhara to Samarkand (270km, 5 hours); Samarkand to Tashkent (289km, 6 hours); Tashkent to Chimkent (120km, 2–3 hours); Chimkent to Dzhambul (148km, 3–4 hours); Dzhambul to Bishkek (277km, 5 hours); Bishkek to Almaty (234km, 4 hours).

The main cities of the Fergana valley—Kokand, Fergana, Margilan, Namangan, Andizhan, Dzhalalabad and Osh—are similarly well-connected. However, buses between the valley and the rest of Uzbekistan pass through Khŭjand in Tajikistan, and can become unreliable at the first sign of unrest in that country.

Useful longer (overnight) bus routes include Samarkand to Nukus and Almaty to Ust-Kamenogorsk (one a day in each direction on both routes).

Buses tend to be crowded, and those on minor routes and in the mountains can be slow and infrequent as well; usually, though, the only alternatives are hitching and walking. Such routes include Bishkek to Naryn, Bishkek to Toktogul, Toktogul to Dzhalalabad, and the roads round Lake Issyk-Kul and into the Altai from Ust-Kamenogorsk. There are no buses on the Pamir highway from Dushanbe to Osh.

For overnight and mountain journeys it is advisable and sometimes essential to buy your ticket the day before. At least check. Otherwise turn up at the bus station and buy a ticket for the next bus to your destination. These days some buses won't actually sell tickets in advance; such is the effect of high fuel costs—unless 'worthwhile' they will not depart.

In all but the smallest bus stations particular ticket windows serve particular destinations. As in railway stations, avoid queueing at the wrong window or at one which is about to close for lunch. The relevant information is usually painted on the window. For tickets between major towns you seldom need queue more than 15 minutes. Sometimes you just buy your ticket on the bus. Whatever the routine, you'll soon be made aware of it.

Bus travel is slightly more expensive per kilometre than rail but, like all forms of state transport, it is feeling the effect of reduced investment. While departures are punctual, arrivals become estimates, dependent upon vehicle condition. Some break down. In general they are quickly repaired—just don't ask how. Breakdowns are greeted as a cheerful event, and they certainly offer another insight into Central Asian life. Those who haven't met their neighbour will soon do so. Join in and don't look at your watch.

In Pakistan and Xinjiang

In northern Pakistan, state-run NATCO buses compete with landslides and private vans along the Karakoram Highway between Rawalpindi and China. Although basic on the inside, the buses are hand-finished neo-baroque masterpieces in chrome and technicolour on the outside. Prices are higher than in the CIS republics, but still low (about $7 in rupees for the 16-hour trip from Rawalpindi to Gilgit).

China offers a similar service—without the decoration—along their portion of the Karakoram Highway. Between Kashgar and Ürümqi there is the luxury option of a sleeper bus.

Hitching

This is standard practice on roads not served by public transport. Wave vehicles down rather than stick out a thumb, and expect to pay the equivalent of a bus fare. *In extremis*, wave a dollar bill. Don't get in the back of an open truck for a high or winter journey unless you have serious winter clothing. People have been known to freeze to death doing this.

Short of chartering or buying your own vehicle, or walking, hitching is the only way to get to the remoter parts of Kyrgyzstan and Tajikistan.

Driving under your own steam is a good way of getting to those parts of Central Asia not served by public transport. The authorities are relatively relaxed about letting foreigners loose on their roads, and those roads are very beautiful. Be prepared, however, for fairly frequent encounters with traffic police, especially in Uzbekistan and Turkmenistan. You may have to share more than your enthusiasm for the scenery with them.

Buying a Vehicle

Buying a Russian-built vehicle in Central Asia need not cost more than the price of a few weeks' car hire in the West, and could cost much less. The place to buy is the *avtobazar* of any city or major town. Tashkent is reported to have a consistently wide choice, and Bishkek is also recommended. In most towns the *avtobazar* is next to the main bazaar, though Tashkent's is at the hippodrome near the city limits on the Samarkand road.

The time to buy is early on Sunday morning. Enlist someone whom you trust who knows a healthy Russian engine from an unhealthy one, and if necessary an interpreter. Good ways to find them would be through a private travel company like Dostuk Trekking in Bishkek or Kramds in Almaty, or through an Intourist service bureau.

Sunday morning motor markets are entirely secondhand affairs, and choice varies widely from week to week. Asking prices start at about $100 in local currency for motorbikes, $200 for motorbikes with sidecars and $500 for small cars. A Volga sedan would probably cost at least $1000. It is easier to pay with a wad of dollars than a bag of local notes. Dollars are a vendor's dream. They will ensure you get first refusal on a popular item; on the other hand they may lead the vendor to assume you are a millionaire and jack up the price.

An alternative to the *avtobazar* is simply to put the word about through employees at your hotel or anyone else you meet that you want to buy a car or motorbike and can pay in dollars. You'd be surprised what people have tucked away in their garages waiting for the right buyer.

Legal Requirements

Insist when buying that the vendor comes with you to the local headquarters of the traffic police (*GAI*) at the first opportunity, to play his part in registering the change of ownership. This process can take a day or two and it is probably wise to withhold some or all of your payment until it is completed.

The vehicle will be inspected for roadworthiness and, on payment of various fees, you will get a new number plate and a certificate of ownership. **Don't try driving/riding without these**. Random police checks are routine and all documents relating to both vehicle and driver (including passport) have to be produced every time.

No insurance of any kind seems to be required. International and even foreign driving licences are usually accepted as proof that you can drive/ride. All the CIS republics drive on the right-hand side.

Petrol

This is the main problem. Invest in as many jerry cans as is practical and fill them whenever possible. Kazakhstan and Turkmenistan are the only Central Asian republics with reasonably reliable petrol supplies. Elsewhere, petrol is often available only in major cities and then only at certain times in certain places—taxi drivers know where. It is sold by the state and by private operators who sell it straight from the tanker for up to twice as much.

By Boat

Short trips are possible along the river Irtysh in northeastern Kazakhstan in summer, and a pleasure steamer operates from Cholpan-Ata on Lake Issyk-Kul in Kyrgyzstan. The Amu Darya and Syr Darya rivers and the Aral Sea all used to be navigable, but so much water has been drawn off for irrigation that they are not any more.

By Horse

Horse is still a major form of transport in rural Kyrgyzstan and parts of Kazakhstan. The caretaker at Tash Rabat caravanserai (*see* p.268) can usually provide mounts and a guide to visit Lake Chatyr-Kul. **Steppes East** (*see* p.8), organizes treks on horseback in the Kara-Tau hills between Chimkent and Dzhambul in Kazakhstan. See other chapters for individual operators.

City Transport

Taxis

This is the easiest way to get around former Soviet cities. Though much more expensive than local public transport, it is still much cheaper than public transport in the West.

The post-independence economy means that many people have several jobs. A much-used form of transport in the city is the unofficial taxi. These are **private cars** whose drivers are happy to give someone a lift, often deviating from their own route. Cheaper than the recognizable state taxi, they can be hailed in the same way. If your destination doesn't appeal to the driver he'll tell you. While they're generally acknowledged as a safe form of transport, it's not advisable to use them after dark or, if they're already carrying passengers, on your own.

Public Transport

The alternatives are bus, trolleybus (electric bus), tram, *marshrutnoe* taxi and, in Tashkent, metro. Buses, trolleybuses and trams mostly follow numbered routes, but few towns have decent, readily available route maps (Bukhara is an exception). It is therefore more or less essential to master at least a few key phrases in Russian or the local language (*see* **Language**, pp.365–76). Dedicated monoglots will have to rely on detailed instructions from English-speakers. These can be surprisingly easy to come by; students of

English tend to thrust themselves upon you for practice, and all former Soviet citizens know their public transport systems backwards. Some buses are identified by their final destination. For these and all metro stations it helps to be able to make out place names in Cyrillic.

Marshrutnoe taxis are minibuses which follow set routes, picking up and setting down anywhere along them like Latin American *collectivos*. Like bus routes, these are usually numbered, but routes and numbers sometimes change faster than even locals can keep up with. If possible, check those given in this book before attempting a journey.

Tickets

On Tashkent's metro there is a flat fare of around 10 cents a ride. Tickets (or tokens for automatic barriers when available) are sold at stations. Bus, trolleybus and tram tickets are equally cheap and can be bought from kiosks near stops, from the driver, or from another individual who squeezes amoeba-like through the crowd. Inspectors wear plain clothes and levy on-the-spot fines. There is no such thing as a *marshrutnoe* taxi ticket; you pay the driver by passing your money to the front. Eventually the change, if required, makes its way back to you.

Problem Places

Special permission is required to visit Baikonur Cosmodrome and the Semipalatinsk nuclear test site in Kazakhstan, and the Pamir region (Badakhshan) in Tajikistan. Details of how to get permission are given in the chapters concerned.

The whole of Kyrgyzstan is officially open to foreigners, but some policemen manning the country's remoter checkpoints seem unaware of this. If possible, get OVIR in Bishkek (*see* p.248) to write your itinerary onto your (Russian) visa before heading for the mountains, especially if you are headed for Inylchek and Karakol.

Practical A–Z

TEA DRINKERS
CHAI-KHANA,
BUKHARA

Books

For a Western author, approval by Soviet censors meant vast sales and an avid, adoring readership from Leningrad to Vladivostok. Every last herdsman in Kyrgyzstan has heard of Jack London. Every last bookstall in Tashkent has Hemingway, Arthur Hailey and Agatha Christie—in translation.

Books in English are another matter. There are no foreign-language bookshops as such in the Central Asian republics. Those shops that stock some—only in the main cities— have a very limited supply, largely tourist guides. So bring all your own reading matter. If you are approaching up the Karakoram Highway, you can stock up on paperbacks in the bookshops of Rawalpindi and Islamabad, and in G. M. Beg's bookstore in Gilgit.

In London, try the **Russian, Central and East European Bookshop** at 28 Denmark Street, London WC2H 8NJ, ✆ (0171) 379 6253, 🖷 (0171) 240 6975, or **Arthur Prosthain** at 41 Great Russell Street, London WC1B 3PL, ✆ (0171) 636 1096. **Foyles**, on Charing Cross Road, has a small, politically orientated collection. For more main-stream options try the **Traveller's Bookshop**, 13 Blenheim Crescent, London W11 ✆ (0171) 229 5260. Secondhand books on the whole region form a much-collected genre served by several specialists, including:

Oxus Books, ✆ (0181) 870 3854 (phone for a catalogue).

Hosains Books, 25 Connaught Street, London W2 2AY, ✆ (0171) 262 7900.

A. C. Hall, ✆ (0181) 898 2638 (phone for a catalogue).

Fine Books Oriental, 46 Great Russell Street, London WC1B 3PA, ✆ (0171) 636 6068.

Books from these dealers can be very pricey. If all you want to do is read them, ask a good bookseller to find out about recent reprints; OUP and, sometimes separately, OUP Hong Kong have recently reprinted several famous turn-of-the-century titles on Central Asia. Alternatively, see if your local library can arrange an inter-library loan from a specialist, such as the India Office Library.

For suggested further reading, *see* pp.377–8.

Chai-khanas

The tea-house is a cornerstone of traditional Central Asian society. Providing shade, liquid, company if you want it, and somewhere to sit, it makes the summer endurable.

Chai-khanas are abundant only in Uzbekistan, and are at their grandest in the Fergana valley. Here they all have two storeys, and deep galleries on painted wooden columns. Smaller *chai-khanas* are often built over roadside streams or irrigation channels. The further a *chai-khana* is from Fergana, the more likely it is to be a concrete Soviet imitation. Real ones have daises instead of tables and chairs. Uzbeks take off their shoes (but not their socks) and sit cross-legged, resting against low balustrades at the ends of the dais.

You often need to scour the *chai-khana* for an unused teapot, or hover near someone who has nearly finished, before taking it to the samovar to be filled. The samovars are usually industrial-looking boilers set in cement rather than the shapely Turkish variety. There is a *chai-khana* or two in or near most bazaars, and it is quite normal to buy food in the bazaar to eat with your tea.

Climate and When to Go

Central Asia's climate is 'extreme continental'—cold in winter, very hot in summer, and very dry. This is as true of Gilgit, which has no monsoon, as of Kashgar and Samarkand. The further south you go the hotter it gets, and Almaty is noticeably cooler than Tashkent throughout the year.

Summer

From late June to early August, most of Uzbekistan bakes in the mid to high 40s. In southern Turkmenistan, midsummer temperatures can reach a staggering 50°C in the shade and 70° in the sun—the highest in the CIS. Very low humidity means you hardly sweat.

Winter

Winter in the lowland parts of the southern republics is mild, with average temperatures below freezing for only a few days in January and February. South of Tashkent, snow cover in the lowlands is light or non-existent. Even at 1600m, Kyrgyzstan's Lake Issyk-Kul is shallow because of low precipitation. In the mountains and north of Almaty, though, winters are harsh: areas above 3000m can receive up to 3m of snow a year, and January temperatures in Semipalatinsk *average* –23°C.

When to Go

Spring and autumn are the best seasons to visit lowland Central Asia. Turkmenistan is at its best when the Kara-Kum desert blooms briefly in May. Here, and in eastern Uzbekistan and western Tajikistan, fruit ripens and begins arriving in bazaars in August, but September and October are the pleasantest months.

June, July and August are the peak season for climbing and high-altitude trekking. The best months for travelling north up the Karakoram Highway are May and June; the best for travelling south are September and October.

Contraception

Bring your own. Although a brand of condom (*preservativ*) called 'Fantasy' is available in some pharmacies and Indian-manufactured versions can be bought from kiosks, the most widely used form of contraception in the former Soviet Union was abortion.

Crime

Theft in former Soviet Central Asia is increasing as living standards fall, but—contrary to the prevailing view in Russia that petty crime is rampant in Central Asia—levels are still way below those in Moscow (and big Western cities). Organized crime is another matter. Former Soviet Central Asia is thought to be a major new supplier of narcotics to the West, and rival mafia gangs operate sophisticated protection rackets in Tashkent's restaurants and private businesses. None of this should impinge on foreigners, except those foolish or unlucky enough to become involved in heroin smuggling. Never carry anything onto an aeroplane that you did not pack yourself.

In major tourist centres, especially Samarkand, valuables should be carried in money belts or pouches hidden beneath clothing, or left in a safe in a hotel—preferably an Intourist hotel. Do not leave them in hotel rooms.

The risk of physical assault is generally low. Crimes should, in principle, be reported to the police (*militsiya*) but for minor losses it may not be worth the trouble. You will have to write a detailed account of what happened, but the chances of prompt police action are slim. Do not try recovering stolen property yourself.

Drugs

It is rare to be offered illegal drugs in the former Soviet republics. Heroin poppies and apparently marijuana are grown in the mountains, but the end product is mostly for export. It is said that a giant marijuana plantation near the east end of Kyrgyzstan's Lake Issyk-Kul, patrolled by guard dogs and condoned by the Communist regime, was torched by the new government to launch a tough new anti-drugs policy.

Legal drugs are in critically short supply throughout the CIS. Bring your own (see 'Health' and 'Packing' below).

Electricity

The standard supply throughout Central Asia, including Xinjiang and northern Pakistan, is 220 volts 50 cycle AC. Plugs are two-pin, as in the USA and continental Europe. Shaver sockets are very rare.

Embassies and Consulates

Some of the former Soviet Central Asian republics are now opening embassies in Britain, North America and Australasia. Otherwise, the Russian Embassy will often issue CIS visas in English-speaking countries.

Austria

Embassy of Kyrgyzstan: 25 Naglerstrasse (Flat 5), 1010 Vienna, ✆ (1) 535 0379

Belgium

Embassy of Kazakhstan: 30 Avenue Vanbever, 1180 Brussels, ✆ (2) 374 9562

Embassy of Kyrgyzstan: 133 Rue de Tenbosch, 1050 Brussels, ✆ (2) 534 6502

Embassy of Uzbekistan: 166 Avenue Franklin Roosevelt, 1070 Brussels,
✆ (2) 649 0038

Canada

Russian Consulate: 52 Range Rd, Ottawa, Ontario K1N 8J5, ✆ (613) 236 7220

Russian Consulate: 3655 Ave. du Musée, Montréal, Québec H3G 2E1,
✆ (514) 842 5343

Embassy of the People's Republic of China: 515 St Patrick Street, Ottawa, Ontario
K1N 5H3, ✆ (613) 789 3404

Embassy of Pakistan: 151 Slater Street, Suite 608, Ottawa K1P 5H3,
✆ (613) 238 7881

France

Embassy of Uzbekistan: 3 Rue de Franklin Roosvelt, Paris 75008, ✆ (16 1) 53 83 80 70

Germany

Consulate of Uzbekistan: 3 Beethovenstrasse, 60325 Frankfurt, ✆ (69) 740554

Embassy of Kazakhstan: 5 Botschaft der Republik Kazakhstan, Schloss Marienfels,
53424 Remagen (Bonn), ✆ (2642) 93830

Embassy of Kyrgyzstan: 62 Koblenzstrasse, 51173 Bonn, ✆ (228) 365230

Embassy of Uzbekistan: 7 Deutschernstrasse, 53177 Bonn, ✆ (228) 9535717

UK

Consulate of Kazakhstan: 3 Warren Mews, London W1P 5DJ, ✆ (0171) 387 1047.
Open Mon–Fri 9am–12 noon, closed Wed.

Embassy of Iran: 5 Kensington Court, London W8 5DB, ✆ (0171) 937 5225;
visas ✆ (0171) 795-4901. *Open 9am–1pm.*

Embassy of Pakistan: 35 Lowndes Square, London SW1X 9JN, ✆ (0171) 235 2044.
*Embassy open Mon–Fri 9.30–5.30; visa and passport department Mon–Thurs
10am–1pm, Fri 10–12.30; visa collection Mon–Fri 4.30–5pm.*

Embassy of the People's Republic of China: 49–51 Portland Place, London W1N
3AH, ✆ (0171) 636 8845; consular/visa section, 31 Portland Place, W1N 3AG,
✆ (0171) 631 1430. *Open Mon–Fri 2–4pm.* There is a 24-hour visa information
service on ✆ (0891) 880808.

Embassy of Uzbekistan: 41 Holland Park, London W11 2RP, ✆ (0171) 229 7679);
consular department, 72 Wigmore Street, London W1H 9DL, (0171) 935 1899.
Open Mon–Fri 10am–11am, closed Thurs.

Russian Consulate General: 58 Melville Street, Edinburgh EH3 7HL, ✆ (0131) 225 7098.

Russian Embassy: 10 Kensington Palace Gardens, London W8 4QJ, ✆ (0171) 229 2666; consular section ✆ (0171) 229 8027. *Closed Wed.*

New Zealand

Russian Embassy: 57 Messines Road, Karori, Wellington, ✆ (4) 766742

USA

Consulate of Kyrgyzstan: Suite 707, 1511 K Street NW, Washington, DC 20005, ✆ (202) 628 0433

Consulate of Pakistan: 12 East 65th Street, New York, NY 10021, ✆ (212) 879 5800

Consulate of Turkmenistan: 2207 Massachusetts Avenue NW, Washington, DC 20008, ✆ (202) 737 4800

Embassy of Pakistan: 2315 Massachusetts Avenue NW, Washington, DC 20008, ✆ (202) 939 6200

Embassy of the People's Republic of China: 2300 Connecticut Avenue NW, Washington, DC 20008, ✆ (202) 328 250

Kazakh Embassy: 3421 Massachusetts Avenue NW, Washington, DC 20007, ✆ (202) 333 4507

Russian Consulate: 9 East 91st Street, New York, NY 010128, ✆ (212) 348 0926

Russian Consulate: 2790 Green Street, San Francisco, CA 94123, ✆ (415) 202 9800

Russian Embassy: 1825 Phelps Place NW, Washington, DC 20008, ✆ (202) 939 8905

Uzbek Embassy: 1511 K Street NW, Washington, DC 20005, ✆ (202) 638 4266

Australia

Russian Embassy: 78 Canberra Avenue, Griffith, Canberra ACT 2603, ✆ (6) 295 9033

Embassy of the People's Republic of China: 247 Federal Highway, Watson, Canberra ACT 2602, ✆ (6) 273 4780

Embassy of Pakistan: 59 Franklin Street, PO Box 198, Manuka, Canberra ACT 2603, ✆ (6) 290 1676

In Central Asia

Details of foreign embassies in former Soviet Central Asia are given in the sections on republican capitals.

The United States has embassies in each capital, though the one in Dushanbe is open only when security allows. US embassies can provide financial assistance in emergencies to

United States citizens only. The UK and Germany have embassies in Tashkent and Almaty; Germany, France and Italy have them in Tashkent.

There are Chinese embassies in Bishkek and Almaty, and while both issue visas on production of an invitation, it is simpler to get a visa before leaving home. There are no foreign embassies or consulates in Ürümqi or Kashgar. In Ürümqi Kazakh visas are available from the Kazak Airways office but only with a Kazakh invitation or an onward air ticket.

The Embassy of Pakistan in Tashkent can issue Pakistan visas to foreigners, and there is a Kazak Embassy in Islamabad at 10 Embassy Road, open 9am–12 noon and 4–6pm. In general, visas are more available in Islamabad.

Entertainment

High culture is on tickover. Every former Soviet capital has its opera house, its philharmonia and its Russian theatre. In Tashkent, in season (September to May), you really can see *Aida* one night and *Figaro* the next for about $2. Most of these institutions, however, are mothballed, being de-Russified, or both.

Turkic folk music, by contrast, is a growth industry. In Bishkek solo balladeers perform the *Manas*, the epic oral history of the Kyrgyz people, to full houses in the main concert hall. In Tashkent enquire at the Palace of People's Friendship.

Young bloods tend to prefer Western rock and videos, to the extent that the *videoza* (video saloon) has almost superseded the cinema. Jean-Claude Van Damme's kick-boxing movies, dubbed by a single male voice, are hits in all the former Soviet republics.

Spectator Sports

The best spectator sport in Central Asia is probably the annual summer polo tournament between Gilgit and Chitral on Shandur top in northern Pakistan. It takes place early in July.

Polo's equivalent in the Tian Shan is *ulak-tartysh*, in which frenzied riders tear apart a dead goat. Kyrgyz and Uighur mountain-dwellers also wrestle and play kiss-chase (*kiss-ku* or *kesh-kumai*) on horseback. Occasional exhibition tournaments are reportedly held on public holidays and Sunday afternoons at the hippodromes in Bishkek and Almaty, but otherwise these sports have no pitches, stadia or calendar. The natural venue is a flattish piece of Alp. The natural moment is a wedding or a birth.

Festivals and Public Holidays

In the former Soviet states the high points of the Muslim calendar are gradually replacing those of the Communist one. **Ramadan**, a month of daytime fasting which starts on 22 January in 1996 and moves backward about eleven days a year, is far from universally observed here, though it is in Pakistan. More popular, and now an official three-day holiday, is **Kurban Bairam**, exactly four weeks after the end of Ramadan. This is the feast of sacrifice, commemorating Abraham's agreement in principle to sacrifice his son. Traditionally a lamb is slaughtered, but most families or collective farms find a bumper *plov* more affordable.

Navroos ('new days') is a two-day festival of renewal falling around 20 March. It was officially reinstated for Soviet Muslims in 1989, along with the **Russian Orthodox New Year** (31 Dec–1 Jan) and **Christmas** (7 January) for Soviet Christians.

The Ismailis of Badakhshan and northern Pakistan have two extra feasts: the anniversary of the accession of the current Imam (11 July) and that of his birthday (13 December). These are not public holidays and tend to be celebrated discreetly for fear of offending non-Ismaili Muslims.

Secular festivals include the **Tashkent Film Festival** for Third World films, held in the spring or autumn of even-numbered years, and the annual **Gilgit Festival** at the beginning of November, which includes a week-long polo tournament and commemorates the Gilgit rising against the Maharajah of Kashmir in 1947. Each August the **Voice of Asia Song Festival** is held in the mountains just outside Almaty and attracts competitors from the CIS and Europe.

The major secular public holidays, on which banks and post offices are closed, are:

1 January: New Year's Day (CIS and China)

21 March: Navroos (New Year)

23 March: Pakistan Day
(when, in 1940, India's Muslims first demanded an independent state)

1 May: International Labour Day

9 May: Victory Day

18 May: Constitution Day (Turkmenistan)

14 August: Independence Day (Pakistan)

31 August: Independence Day (Kyrgyzstan)

1 September: Independence Day (Uzbekistan)

6 September: Defence of Pakistan Day
(commemorating 1965 India-Pakistan war)

9 September: Independence Day (Tajikistan)

1 October: China's National Day
(celebrating foundation of People's Republic in 1949)

6 October: Republic Day (Kazakhstan)

27 October: Independence Day (Kazakhstan)

16 December: Republic Day (Kazakhstan)

Food and Drink

Eating Out and Local Specialities

Do not expect too much. The heavy hand of the Soviet cabbage-chopper still haunts many a hotel kitchen, and shortages of all but the most basic foodstuffs have reduced most menus to a choice of two starters and two main courses. At its hotels in Tashkent, Samarkand and Bukhara, Intourist gives its clients what it thinks they want. The result is perfectly adequate, but neither adventurous nor very Asian. This section concentrates on the alternatives.

The best food in Central Asia is, inevitably, home made. Accept any invitations to sample it, bearing in mind the sacrifices most families are already making just to keep their children fed. A small gift is often appropriate.

Meanwhile, acquire a taste for *shashlyk* and *lepeshka*. *Shashlyk*, skewered chunks of mutton barbecued over charcoal, are better known in the West and in Xinjiang as kebabs. *Lepeshka* (pronounced 'lipioshka') is round, unleavened bread. Between them they sustain everyone who ever feels a pang of hunger on a Central Asian street corner. Don't avoid the fat deliberately left on the meat or the raw onion draped over it. Both are integral to the pungent, juicy, irresistible *shashlyk* experience—the humblest but also the most reliably satisfying meal from Khiva to Kashgar. *Shashlyk* grills are always outdoors even if there is covered seating nearby. Downwind, you can smell them several blocks away. You will always find them at bazaars and often in parks—and where there is *shashlyk* there is usually *chai* (tea). People usually order four or six skewers per person at a time.

Central Asia's other staple dish is *plov*: scraps of mutton and shredded yellow turnip in a mountain of rice. Traditionally prepared in a giant, blackened, wok-like pan over a fire, it can be a perfunctory roadside snack or the centrepiece of a banquet at the festival of Kurban Bairam. In Central Asian homes everyone eats it from the same plate. In an *ash-khana*, which is to food what a *chai-khana* is to tea, you get a bowlful.

Regional specialities tend to follow the mutton-plus-carbohydrate pattern: in Turkmenistan and Uzbekistan the meat is often minced, boiled with rice and stuffed in peppers or cabbage leaves. In Kyrgyz, Kazakh and Uighur dishes like *laghman* and *beshbermak*, the bulk consists of long, thick noodles. These may be garnished with a spicy meat sauce or swimming in greasy stock. A specifically Uighur variant, popular in Kashgar's bazaars and round Lake Issyk-Kul in Kyrgyzstan (where Uighurs are called Tungans) has a dollop of jellied potato starch on the noodles instead of meat. On special occasions in the high Tian Shan, a sheep and a potato patch, with a few spring onions, are turned into a cross between a stir-fry and a stew. Otherwise, yurt-dwellers live off milk, *koumis*, butter, yoghurt (*airan*) and tough old *lepeshka* brought up from the valleys at the beginning of the summer.

Fish is scarce, despite the hundreds of reservoirs created at great cost to the environment in Uzbekistan precisely to provide Uzbeks with fish. It is sometimes sold ready-fried in Bukhara's bazaar. Even in towns round Lake Issyk-Kul the only kind of fish is dried.

Snacks. In most bazaars either side of the Tian Shan you can keep hunger at bay with *manty* (boiled noodle sacks of meat and vegetables) or a kind of samosa called a *samsa*. Much less appetizing are deep-fried flat dough cakes, oozing oil, called *chiburekki*. Dry biscuits sold in polythene bags at most bus and railway stations and bazaars make a good standby for long journeys.

Fresh fruit. Apricots, grapes, pomegranates, cherries, plums and, dwarfing them all, melons. In late summer and autumn the bazaars groan with them and trucks trundle all the way to Moscow to sell them. Somehow space is found to grow them between the cotton plantations of the southern republics. Further north, Almaty is famous for, and named after, its apples. Central Asians are proud of their fruit, and foreigners, especially vegetarians, will be thankful for it. Fresh fruit is not generally served in restaurants; buy it in bazaars or wherever you see it.

Restaurants

Korean restaurants are the best in former Soviet Central Asia but exist only in Tashkent, Bishkek and Almaty.

Russian food still dominates in many hotel restaurants—hence the hearty, meaty soups like *bortsch* and *lapsha* often offered as starters. *Bouillon* is a generic term for lighter soups. Standard Russian main courses are beef stroganoff, *bishteks* (like a hamburgers) and *kotlyet* (usually unspecified ground meat, covered in breadcrumbs).

Ordering. The waiter or waitress will usually simply say what there is rather than hand out menus. *Piervy* means starter (literally, 'first'). *Vtaroi* means main course ('second'). If you do not understand, but fancy something someone else is eating, point to it. Alternatively, ask what the waiter/waitress recommends (*see* **Language**, pp.370–2). Service is usually quicker than nightmare stories of Soviet restaurants let you dare hope.

Breakfast (zavtrak). In hotels this is a light, quick meal: tea, drinking yoghurt (*kefir* or *airan*) and *bliny* or *blinchiki* (fried pancakes filled with cottage cheese). Intourist sometimes provides bread and jam. If a hotel's restaurant does not open early enough, it may have a buffet which does. You can find a pot of tea and something to eat in most bazaars from dawn. Those who need sucrose in the morning will be frustrated by the general sugar shortage. Ask for honey (*myod*) or buy some in a bazaar.

Lunch (obyed) is the main meal of the day. Consuming it can take up the first half of the afternoon; digesting it can take the second. **Dinner** (uzhen) is a scaled-down version of lunch.

Music. From 8pm and sometimes earlier, expect deafening live music in most restaurants. Except for fans of crass synthesized cover versions of Turkish and Russian pop hits, this is the most off-putting aspect of eating out in former Soviet Central Asia.

Xinjiang. Most stomachs crossing from Kyrgyzstan or Kazakhstan into Chinese Central Asia will sniff the air and dance for joy. Shortages are things of the past here; menus are booklets and nothing is 'off'. Restaurateurs are used to Western whims, and economic reform has made it worth catering to them. The result is bewildering choice, from authentic Chinese food to *steak au poivre* at the Ürümqi Holiday Inn and *kashburgers* in Kashgar.

Prices. The restaurant categories in this book correspond to a meal for one, as specified in the text.

expensive	over US$15
moderate	US$10–15
inexpensive	less than US$10
cheap	less than US$5—generally snacks available at market stalls

Tap water in Intourist hotels is usually drinkable. If in doubt, and anywhere else, sterilize it with tablets. Floor ladies in most hotels will provide tea or hot water (*tipitok*) with which to make your own. It may help to offer a few rubles. Thermoses of hot drinking water are standard in Chinese hotel rooms. **Fizzy mineral water** is unevenly available in the former Soviet republics. It comes in unlabelled clear glass vodka bottles and usually tastes more of minerals than water. The still version is found in the more expensive stores that stock imported goods. The best of the bunch is 'Neviot' from the Jordan Valley.

To cool off and slake your thirst, follow the local custom and drink hot **tea**. This cools you down far more effectively than a cold drink, by making you sweat. It has the additional advantage, in a land of shortages, of being available everywhere. Green tea (*zelyoni chai*) is served in *chai-khanas* and Asian homes; brown Indian tea (*Indiski chai*) is served in most Russian homes and some restaurants. Green tea is the more refreshing, and is generally drunk without sugar, though people often nibble raisins or suck sweets as separate sweeteners. When sugar is available, Russians add it automatically and liberally. Tea is also ubiquitous in Xinjiang and northern Pakistan. It is said to have been introduced to Pakistan by the British in the 19th century to secure a market there. Their method was to serve it free at railway stations for ten years and then start charging for it once the habit had stuck. In the Northern Areas it is drunk sweet and milky.

Coffee is an expensive delicacy in the former Soviet republics. Some Intourist hotels have coffee shops, and imported Brazilian coffee powder is sold in larger bazaars and some private shops—but is beyond the reach of most housekeeping budgets. The only place in Central Asia for a genuine *espresso* is Ürümqi's Holiday Inn.

Fruit from the southern republics is abundant in season, but **fruit juice** is not. The nearest thing to it is *kompot*, the diluted juice of black and red berries. Usually homemade, it is neverthless worth asking for in restaurants. Iranian fruit drinks make their way across the border into Turkmenistan. Turkish cherry juice is in evidence, too.

Alcohol is banned in Pakistan except for non-Muslim foreigners in certain hotels in Rawalpindi and Islamabad. There is no such taboo in former Soviet Central Asia, where beer, vodka, brandy (*cenyak*) and sparkling wine (*shampanski*) are available in many restaurants. Be aware also of *spirrt*, also known as '96%' (*dyevyanosto shest pra tsent*). This is neat alcohol, preferred by some Russians to vodka because it drowns twice as many sorrows for the same volume. Local wine used to be hard to find, despite the large-scale grape cultivation in the Fergana valley and the Turpan oasis in Xinjiang. Today it is less so. There is a Samarkand vintage more akin to port, and another sweet red call Kogor. The white is drier and lighter (Stalovoye and Bayan-Shireh) and the champagne sweet. Imported options tend to be rough Armenian or Georgian port, or Spanish red from the European wine lake. *Koumis* is fermented mare's milk; mildly alcoholic, very sour and a source of intense national pride in both Kyrgyzstan and Kazakhstan. It is the world's most refreshing drink, you are told. It will drive away all aches, pains and altitude sicknesses. Refusing to try it may cause offence, though at first it can be hard to keep down.

A bad tour guide can bring new deathliness even to a mausoleum. A good one can bring it alive. The best learned their English at university and their patter with Intourist but in many cases now work freelance too. Inez Abalova knows everything there is to know about Samarkand and much that is merely rumoured about it. Phone her at home on 29 02 13. In Bukhara you *may* be lucky with a guide hired at the Hotel Bukhoro, but according to several glowing reports you would do better asking for Noila at the Ark. Don't consider going to Mary in Turkmenistan without Tania Lunina.

Even if you read Russian captions it is well worth joining an Intourist group to visit Tashkent's museums. Enquire at the Hotel Uzbekistan on Prospekt Navoi.

Health

Immunization

No inoculations are required for former Soviet Central Asia, but there is a check for cholera immunization on the train from China to Kazakhstan. Both Pakistan and China occasionally check for immunization against cholera and yellow fever from travellers arriving from areas infected with these diseases, but usually do not bother Westerners. In addition, it is advisable to be in date for polio (i.e. last immunized less than 10 years ago), tetanus (10 years) and typhoid (3 years in most cases).

Hepatitis A is fairly widespread, especially in China. The new, more effective, and longer lasting injections called Havrix, which have replaced the old gamma globulin ones, are recommended. Three shots are required, the first two four weeks apart with a later booster.

Outbreaks of diphtheria are increasing throughout the CIS. Most visitors from Europe and North America will have been immunized against this as children. A low-dose booster is the most they will need, but anyway avoid close contact with people in crowded places. This includes sharing bottles and glasses. Those not immunized as children should have a full course of diphtheria vaccine.

Rabies is endemic in Central Asia. Exposure to this and hepatitis B (transmitted through sex or contact with contaminated blood) varies according to where you're going (cities or the countryside) and what you'll be doing there. There is a vaccine available called Engerix B which can prevent further complications should you need hospital treatment. The pattern of injections is similar to those for hepititis. Discuss with your doctor whether immunization is worthwhile, but plan well in advance.

Between May and September there is a risk of malaria in southwestern Tajikistan, near the Afghan border. Obtain chloroquine tablets ('Nivaquine' or 'Avloclor') before leaving home, and take them as prescribed before, during and after visiting the area. Keep malaria-carrying mosquitoes at bay with insect repellent, mosquito netting, air conditioning or smoke coils. Also take from home Halfan or Fansidar for self-treatment if you develop a fever of 38°C or higher a week or more after arriving; this could be malaria. Follow dosage instructions precisely.

There is also a risk of cholera in this area, brought over the border by returning refugees. Be scrupulous about food and water hygiene and boil all drinking water or purify it, ideally with an iodine resin purifier. For queries call:

USA: International Traveler's Hotline, ✆ (404) 332 4559, Mon–Fri 8am–4.30pm (EST). Or, via the Internet, Centre for Disease Control, http://www.cdc.gov.

UK: MASTA, ✆ (0891) 224 100, 24-hour travel health line which provides detailed printed information sent by first class post.

AIDS

Chinese and Uzbek health officials may ask incoming visitors if they are HIV positive and, with those arriving for long stays (students, diplomats, etc.), may require proof that they are not. HIV negative certificates are rumoured as prerequisite for some ticket purchases and visa applications. So far they have not been demanded in practice, and rules that an existing certificate is invalid if more than a month old have not been observed. However, it would be wise to bring your own sterilized needles and syringes.

Stomach Upsets

Mild attacks of diarrhoea are likely if not inevitable in the former Soviet states. Food poisoning and intestinal infections are rare, though the risk is probably highest in northern Pakistan. Diarrhoea dehydrates. Concentrate on rehydrating with plenty of purified, boiled or bottled water, rather than blocking up your system with tablets. Eat sparingly for a day or two, restricting your diet to simple, dry, reliably clean food: bread and biscuits.

Altitude Sickness

Trekking, climbing or even just sitting in a truck above 3000m, you will feel the altitude. Lack of oxygen can cause headaches, dizziness, nausea and sleeplessness. The most dangerous effect of altitude sickness is a pulmonary or cerebral oedema, which can strike even fit climbers without warning and prove fatal within minutes. The way to minimize the effects of altitude is to acclimatize by gaining height slowly, preferably under your own steam. The way to reverse them is to lose height. Taking painkillers to deal with altitude-induced headaches can suppress other symptoms which only reappear, worse, later on. If trekking and suffering from the altitude, stop or go down. Drink plenty of water. Don't smoke or drink alcohol and **don't gain more height until fully recovered**.

Hospitals

Don't take chances with Central Asian hospitals unless absolutely necessary. Take out travel insurance which covers you for emergency repatriation.

Hunting and Fishing

> *...there, like a statue, stood a beautiful old ram on an overhanging ledge of rock... My first bullet had shattered his hind-quarters to pieces, and he had probably been bleeding so hard that he had no more strength to move.*

The Russians have always been avid hunters. This one was Prince Demidoff, face to face with the biggest prize of his four-month trip to the Altai in 1901.

The Altai, the Tian Shan and the Pamirs were and remain some of the world's choicest mountain hunting grounds. Difficulty of access before the Russian Revolution and restricted access thereafter have preserved the animal populations; those of Xinjiang and the Himalayas, however, have been eroded not only by hunting but by tourism as well. Now Kyrgyzstan and Tajikistan support between them what are probably the world's largest populations of snow leopard and wild, curly-horned Marco Polo sheep. The former are still extremely rare and strictly protected. The latter are listed as an endangered species, but are still hunted by quota.

For two of the world's hardest-pressed economies, hunting is a valuable source of hard currency: an export licence for one Marco Polo head costs about $18,000. Since before the end of the Soviet Union, Western hunters, mostly from Germany and the USA (including on one occasion former US defence secretary Dick Cheney), have been paying up to $40,000 each to be helicoptered to high-altitude bases for three weeks' or a month's Marco Polo hunting. Other hunted species include ibex and, in the Hissar range near Dushanbe, wild boar.

Twenty-pound trout are said to rule the rivers north of the Gilgit–Chitral road in Pakistan. The season is from April to September and permits (from the Fisheries Department in either town) are required.

The Tajik firm **Badakhshan** (c/o Intourist, Hotel Tajikistan, Ulitsa Shotemur 22, Dushanbe 734001, CIS, ✆ 274973) specializes in the high Pamirs.

The **Xinjiang Nature Travel Service** (XNTS, 10 Guangming Road, Ürümqi, Xinjiang, China, ✆ 77174) is a Chinese state hard currency earner offering hunting in the Chinese Tian Shan and fishing trips to the western and eastern Altai mountains.

Laundry

The Hotel Uzbekistan in Tashkent, the Hotel Tajikistan in Dushanbe and the Ürümqi Holiday Inn have laundry services. So does Sasha's Bed and Breakfast in Bukhara. Otherwise do it yourself in your hotel bathroom (your own plug often helps) or negotiate with your floor lady. There are no laundromats in Central Asia.

Lavatories

In the CIS all restaurants and most bus and railway stations have them. If you have to pay they will be moderately clean. If you don't they will be foul. The grandest are beneath Tashkent's Zerafshan restaurant. Ж is for *zhenski*, meaning 'women'. M is for *muzhskoy*, meaning 'men'.

Most public lavatories are the Turkish type; you stand or squat. Those in hotel rooms are the more familiar kind, and are usually clean and odour-free. Loo paper is hard to find, even in hotels. Bring your own and buy it whenever you see it.

Maps

Spies and pilots will be content with nothing less than the CIA's Tactical Pilotage Charts, produced from American military satellite imagery. They cover every inch of Central Asia, as of the globe, in minute detail—though some place names will now be out of date. Scale: 1:500,000. Price: £7.50 a sheet from Stanfords, 12–14 Long Acre, London WC2E 9LP, ✆ (071) 836 1327.

A parallel series of Operational Navigational Charts from the same source on a 1:1,000,000 scale is also available from Stanfords at the same price per sheet.

The best single-sheet map covering the former Soviet republics is Hildebrand's of the CIS (pre-1991 editions: UdSSR). Generally available from Stamfords, the Hildebrand series is published by Karto Grafik, Schonberger Weg 15–17, 6000 Frankfurt/Main 90, Germany, £8.50.

East View Publications, Inc., 3020 Harbour Lane North, Suite 110, Minneapolis, MN 55447, USA, ✆ (612) 550 0961, 🖷 (612) 559 2931, E-mail: eastview@eastview.com, pinpoints what maps are required and sells them from their large collection.

In the carefully controlled world of Soviet publishing, showing Soviet citizens how to get around their own country was not a priority. Soviet maps were either deliberately vague or of ludicrously restricted areas. A large-scale map exists of the Transcaspian railway, presented as parallel strips covering the railway itself and a few hundred metres of territory on each side, so as to avoid showing the Iranian border. (If coming through Moscow you could ask for this at Atlas, a specialist map shop at Ulitsa Kuznetsky Most 20). Topographical maps for trekking in the Tian Shan are available in Bishkek (ask Dostuk Trekking, ✆ 42 74 71) and at the Hotel Chimbulak above Almaty, but they show only the recommended routes, with cartoons of jolly backpackers where the other mountains should be.

A basic but nonetheless useful map of Uzbekistan, designed for long-distance lorry drivers, is available for a dollar or so from a kiosk in front of the Registan in Samarkand.

Media

The former Soviet republics still get their international news, soap operas and game shows in Russian from Moscow. Watching the news on Channel 1 is a good way of practising Russian, and you will get very used to the two bars of 'Moscow Nights' which introduce Radio Moscow's hourly news. Local editions of *Pravda* are still printed in all the capitals.

Since the start of *glasnost* Moscow's media has been ahead of Central Asia's in terms of objectivity and digestibility. Local television, especially in Uzbekistan and Turkmenistan, is a throwback to Soviet times, with reverent coverage of presidential speeches and po-faced 'newsreaders' delivering the Party line.

For English-language news bring a short-wave radio. The BBC's World Service and Voice of America can usually be picked up on their South Asian or Middle Eastern frequencies, depending on the time of day. Try 15.310, 15.575, 15.070, 12.095, 7.135 and 14.100 mHz. Reception is better on balconies than in rooms, on the 10th floor than the 1st and on mountainsides than in valleys. Guest rooms in the Hotel Dostuk in Almaty receive CNN for a few hours a day and the Ürümqi Holiday Inn gets BBC World Service TV.

China Daily, the Chinese government's English-language propaganda sheet, goes on sale in Ürümqi a few days after being printed in Beijing. *Time* and *Newsweek* can usually be found in Gilgit, along with Pakistan's English-language newspapers.

Money

The Russian ruble is no longer accepted in Central Asia, except in some remote provinces of Tajikistan. All the republics now issue their own currency. For Kazakhstan this is the tenge, for Turkmenistan the manat and for Tajikistan the Tajik ruble. Uzbekistan's currency, the sum, is, for the unsuspecting, easlily confused with the Kyrgyz som.

Until 1989 inflation had been minimal, but it took off with the phased relaxation of price controls by Russia's President Yeltsin. It has continued post independence, as Central Asia no longer benefits from Moscow's handouts and moves towards a market economy. But inflation is a new phenomenon to ex-Soviet citizens and has left all but the most streetwise angry and bewildered as well as poor. A majority in Central Asia regard it as the inseparable twin of *democratsia*, that alien fad, and blame the whole loathesome mess on Gorbachev.

Initially tourists took a different view, benefitting from ruble devalutaion that outpaced inflation. The end of Intourist's monopoly ensured that Westerners could take advantage of what amounted to falling ruble prices. For a time, travel in Central Asia, avoiding aeroplanes and hard currency hotels, cost around $5 a day.

Today travel hasn't backtracked to pre-1991 ($130 a day), but it is not cheap. As satellite TV beams pictures of Western affluence into people's homes, and more expense accounts than backpackers grace the streets, many Central Asians deduce, quite simply, that Western equals rich. Be prepared for prices that defy imagination—and explanation. Some you can haggle down, others you cannot. Internal travel is expensive for no other reason than the high cost of fuel. This said, it is still possible to travel cheaply by bus, buy food from bazaars that tempt even the most resolute, and use the growing bed and breakfast accommodation. Expect moderate rather than consistently high overall costs, but budget for the unexpected.

Because of inflation, prices in this book are given not in local currency but as a rough US dollar equivalent.

Chinese currency is the Renminbi yuan, available from most branches of the Bank of China, and from hotel exchange counters run by the bank. The commission and exchange rate are identical everywhere and cash or cheques in any hard currency accepted. Credit card withdrawals are possible from larger branches of the bank. The

Foreign Exchange Certificate, or FEC, was a parallel currency reserved for foreigners but now defunct. Officially, 1 FEC was worth 1 yuan, but black-market moneychangers offered more yuan for your FEC, because with FEC they could buy hard currency. You may still see references to it. Chinese inflation is variable, anywhere between 10 and 24% in recent months. It's well worth having some yuan for snacks and shopping.

Pakistan's currency is the rupee, increasingly the victim of inflation, and buyable at slightly variable rates from banks and *bureaux de change*.

Travellers' cheques are accepted as payment and changed into local currency only in major Intourist hotels. American Express cheques in US dollars are the most widely recognized. A **credit card** is well worth carrying. You can use it to pay for some hotel rooms rooms and services (including international telephone calls, but not air tickets). Credit card cash withdrawals are possible at the Bank of China in Ürümqi and Kashgar (FEC only), and at the Bank of America in Islamabad for Visa cards and American Express in Islamabad and Rawalpindi for American Express cards.

Unless you intend spending most of your nights *chez* Intourist, there is no alternative but to bring most of your money in US dollars **cash**, preferably in $20 bills and smaller, including plenty of $5 and $1 bills. No one has change. In countries anxious for hard currency the fussiness over dollar bills comes as a surprise. Take only post-1990 dollar bills and preferably those that are not ink-stained or worn. Official institutions are the only willing recipients of pre-1990 versions and it's not worth the risk. Avoid keeping it all in one stash, so as not to show how much you've got when fumbling for money and to minimize the chances of losing it all in a robbery. Never leave cash in a hotel room.

Changing Money

People will constantly sidle up and ask you, '*Dollar yest?*' ('Do you have dollars?'), but the financial argument for changing money with them depends from state to state. In some states, notably Kazakhstan and Kyrgystan, the currency has remained relatively stable; rates offered by private moneychangers are unlikely to be higher than the bank's or Intourist's, and may be lower. You also risk being short-changed. On the other hand, you can earn invaluable goodwill by changing in private with someone you trust—a hotel floor lady, for example—and this is no longer a terrible offence: when the market rate became the only real exchange rate, the phrase 'black market' ceased to mean much. By contrast, inflation in Turkmenistan makes a mockery of the official rate, and the gulf between official and unofficial in Uzbekistan fluctuates. Tajikistan's currency is a victim of the instability that afflicts the country as a whole. Immediate devaluation followed the Tajik rouble's introduction in May 1995. After an initial 50 to the dollar, there were 300 four months later.

When changing privately, it's best to do so literally in private—in a hotel room or host's living room, for example. Have ready the amount you want to change rather than peel-ing two notes off a tempting bundle; don't hand them over until you've counted your currency. You are still required to fill out currency declarations on entering and leaving the

CIS, but receipts from *bureaux de change* are seldom inspected. If necessary, an otherwise unexplained discrepancy between your entry and your exit figure can be accounted for with the word 'taxi'.

Mosques and Madrasas

All but a handful of Soviet Central Asia's 24,000 mosques were closed by the Bolsheviks in the 1920s and 30s. In 1991 it was reported that they were reopening in Uzbekistan at the rate of 10 a day. In use or not, it is usually possible for non-Muslims to enter a mosque providing that they are modestly dressed and ask politely, and that formal prayers are not in progress. (This applies equally in Pakistan as in former Soviet Central Asia.) Ask before taking pictures, and, of course, take off your shoes (but not your socks).

The working madrasas (Islamic seminaries) in Bukhara, Tashkent and Kokand do not normally admit non-Muslim visitors.

Ismaili Muslims do not have mosques as such. Their prayer-houses, recognizable in Hunza by their green doors, are closed to visitors.

Museums

Soviet curators were a meticulous but predictably unimaginative bunch. Every town of any size in Central Asia, or with any significance in the history of the class struggle, had its museum. The standard format used to be one third natural history and folk art (stuffed animals, models of ancient settlements, traditional jewellery); one third pre-revolutionary history (ceramic fragments, portraits of anti-feudal agitators); and the final third devoted to the Great October Socialist Revolution and the achievements of the Soviet era.

Today these museums remain, but with a changed perspective. As each multi-ethnic state seeks to carve out a new identity, museums do their part by replacing the Soviet past with a 'national' one (in Uzbekistan this is focused on Timur), and displays on all things pertaining to the traditional way of life.

In most capitals each subject has its own museum, including, in Tashkent and Bishkek, Lenin museums (now reorganized). Other politically inspired curatorial developments include displays on the Nevada-Semipalatinsk anti-nuclear testing movement in Almaty and Semipalatinsk, and the conversion of the Museum of the 26 Baku Commissars in Turkmenbashy into a general history museum.

The most dazzling exhibits in Central Asia are the Bukharan royal robes in Tashkent's art museum. The most poignant museum is in Nukus, where the shrinking of the Aral Sea is charted. The most European is Dostoyevksy's house in Semipalatinsk. The least visited is probably the museum of desert studies at Repetek in the middle of the Kara-Kum.

All museums charge a small amount in local currency for entry. A guide speaking a Western language, not necessarily English, is often on hand to accompany you for a further modest payment, sometimes whether you like it or not. (*See also* 'Guides' above).

Opening Hours

There are no standard opening hours in the former Soviet republics—for offices or commercial premises. However, every last restaurant, café, shop, ticket office and museum has its own opening hours clearly displayed outside. First opening and last closing times are usually given first (using the 24-hour clock) followed by details of breaks.

Aeroflot offices and most cafés are open by 8am, and museums by 10am. Eateries tend to close briefly mid-morning and mid-afternoon. Cafés and museums close around 6pm, though museums usually stop letting people in at least an hour before closing time. Restaurants generally stay open at least until 10pm.

Most museums are open at weekends and closed for one day during the week, though there is no rule about which day.

Packing

Be prepared for extremes of temperature, bright sun, Muslim sensibilities and certain niggling shortages.

Clothes. Loose, lightweight, pale-coloured trousers and long-sleeved shirts are better in intense heat than shorts and T-shirts. They reduce water loss and sunburn, and in any case shorts were virtually unknown outside sports grounds in former Soviet Central Asia. But as the hem level has crept up in cities such as Almaty, so has the appearance of shorts. The difference is that shorts, if not rare as before, always mark out a foreigner. Short skirts, by contrast, tend to be worn not by foreigners but by the younger Russian population. Sensitivity is required in some areas. Don't model such garb in mosques, or in certain areas. The more Islamic Fergana Valley is one, and Turkmenistan, increasingly, another. As you gain altitude or travel north, or as summer changes to autumn, keep warm by adding several thin layers, which are more useful and less bulky than one thick one. For trekking or winter travel, though, at least one thick woollen layer or 'fleece' is vital, plus a weatherproof outer one, preferably of a breathable material like Goretex.

Toiletries. Pack sunglasses, sunblock, an emergency loo-roll, all the film and paperbacks you may need, a basic first aid kit and a bath plug. Soap is widely available, Tampax not. Other toiletries you can't do without should be brought from home.

If trekking, further essentials include a sleeping bag, a tent, a camping stove (preferably a petrol-burning primus) and a decent pair of boots; you *might* be able to buy these in Gilgit, but there is no chance anywhere else in Central Asia. For small gifts to take with you to offer in exchange for hospitality, *see* 'Social Niceties', p.44.

Photography

Central Asians love having their picture taken—so long as they have time to compose themselves and do up their middle button. They can be embarassed or angry if taken by surprise. Unless you have a 'round-the-corner' lens, 'authentic' shots of people will be hard to come by—you could easily end up with an album full of solemn faces that have pleaded for a portrait.

Early morning and evening are the best times for photography. Bright sunlight in the middle of the day and in the mountains can turn a stupendous view into a study in white, so beware of over-exposure. If in doubt stop down the aperture, shorten the exposure, or use a negative density filter. A polarizing filter will deepen glaring skies, and above the snowline a UV filter is essential.

Kodak or Fuji colour print film is increasingly available in the main cities—Almaty, Tashkent and those frequented by tourists, like Samarkand—but nowhere else in the former Soviet states. The only other film available is Orwo (East German) and Russian black and white, which is hard to get processed professionally in the West. **It's best to bring most of the film you'll need from home.** Agfa, Kodak and Fuji print film is widely available in Gilgit; Kodak and Fuji, plus local brands, can be found in almost every city in China. The slide variety takes more perseverence to locate but it is available in Ürümqi.

It's not advisable to photograph military installations, border fences or, on the Karakoram Highway, bridges.

Security at CIS, Chinese and Pakistan airports claim that their X-rays will not fog film, but it is advisable to carry it with you and have it inspected by hand.

Police

There are two forces: the *militsia* (military police) in cream-coloured tops, and the GAI (*Gosudarstvennaya Avtomobilnaya Inspectsia*, State Traffic Police), pronounced to rhyme with 'high'. The GAI wear grey and have checkpoints at all city limits and at regular intervals along all highways. If driving your own vehicle you may be pulled over by them several times in a day. It's nothing personal. First shake hands and say hello, then show them all your papers. Such encounters are usually either short and friendly or long and friendly.

The two forces are, collectively, the *politsia*. In all but major cities they tend to share headquarters. The *militsia* are generally considered corrupt to a man, the public face of organized crime. Whatever the truth of this, a policeman's lot is not an unhappy one. It consists principally of storing up and calling in favours to soften the trauma of everyday life, and no one would seriously expect it to consist of anything else. None of this should affect a foreigner, though the occasion might arise, as with anyone you meet, when a small gift becomes appropriate.

Never offer a policeman a bribe. It would be an unpardonable affront to his professional integrity, the only thing that might get you into serious trouble.

Post

Sending letters home is cheap and reliable, though in Turkmenistan the ghosts of the KGB still apparently read them on the way. They take two to three weeks to reach Europe or America, and less if posted from Tashkent or Almaty.

Every town and city has its post office (*pochta*), usually open at least from 8am to 6pm. So do major Intourist hotels, though these can close in the middle of the day when tourists are expected to be on excursions, and often at weekends.

Proffer your envelopes or postcards, preferably with the country of destination in Cyrillic as the *first* line of the address. The rest will be done for you. Postage will cost a few US cents in local currency.

With enough stamps on, even a letter posted in the remotest rural post box (these are blue) will eventually reach its destination. The local practice is to write your own address below the recipient's, and envelopes bought *in situ* have designated spaces for each. You can use envelopes brought from home, which are likely to stick down better.

Postcards used to be hard to find and ,when you did, they were usually as much a relic as the buildings they showed. Increasingly these collectable characters are metamorphosing. In the course of 1995 new glossy versions appeared in the main hotels. These, and post offices, are still the best places to find postcards—of any vintage.

Letters to the CIS from abroad may, in principle, be addressed in English. In practice it helps to use Cyrillic and to write the country first, then the city, the street, and so on.

Poste restante. In 1914 Stephen Graham collected 'thirty or forty copies of *The Times*, saved up for me, with letters, at the post office of Semipalatinsk'. Times have changed. Letters marked 'To await collection' and addressed to you, c/o Intourist at Tashkent's Hotel Uzbekistan or Almaty's Hotel Otrar, stand the best chance of being saved, but don't count on it.

Shopping

Bazaaring, actually. Shops in the former Soviet republics have an alluring weirdness for Westerners, being the lopsided public face of a recently retired command economy, but unless you're looking for volleyball nets, Bakelite slide projectors and very low quality exercise books, they are unlikely to contain anything you actually want.

Supermarkets are springing up in the main cities, selling imported foreign goods often from Turkey and Iran. They're a useful source particularly of non-perishable items. Some have Western-style checkout tills and many, in traditional Soviet fashion, prefer to conceal their identity from the outside.

Bazaars are different. Every town has one and all are worth a snoop. They mainly sell food, but most include a truly exotic array of rolled-down cloth sacks of **herbs and spices**. In tourist towns bazaars are now attuned to tourists. In Samarkand, glass phials of **saffron** will be thrust at you. Here and in Bukhara and Ashkhabad you can buy by the metre the gaudy printed **silk** of which Uzbek and Turkmen women are so fond. Souvenir shops in certain madrasas in both cities have limited selections of 'Bukhara' **carpets**, but by far the best place for these is the main bazaar at Ashgabat, where the city meets the desert. Real Bukharas are woven in Turkmenistan and bear Turkmen designs.

Even at this bazaar, where you cut out most middlemen, expect to pay upwards of $150 for a small handmade carpet.

Bukhara itself was once known for silverware, but most items sold by the stalls near the Magok-i-Attari mosque nowadays are indifferent reproductions.

Stock up on rubies, emeralds, amethysts and lapis lazuli in Gilgit and Hunza, northern Pakistan. They are hewn from the local mountains or just picked up off their continually shaking surfaces. Flawed and uncut, but genuine, rubies come amazingly cheap individually—down to less than $1 a stone—while strings of cut stones start at around $100. Garnets are sometimes passed off as rubies. They are wine-red; rubies are pinker.

But shoppers beware: taking your bazaar bargains home is not always easy. Rigorous baggage checks at the airports can mean that your holiday photos become your only memory of your shopping expeditions. Officials are hard on items that they consider to have some antique or historical value. Turning up at the airport determined to bluff your way through is unlikely to work. If you are taking a carpet home, for example, you must spare the time to get the necessary export certificate or 'permission' first. In Uzbekistan and Turkmenistan go to the Ministry of Tourism and Culture. For paintings and crafts purchased in Almaty, try the State Art Museum and the Central Museum. In all cases a small fee will be charged. Bring some colour photos in case required and don't leave it to the day of departure.

Skiing

Some of the finest downhill skiing in the CIS is at Chimbulak, above Almaty in the Tian Shan. As in Utah, the snow is fine and dry after its long desert crossing, making it powdery when fresh and fast when compressed.

There are several small ski bases above Bishkek, where you will get shorter runs but shorter lift queues as well, and the same kind of snow. For summer skiing, try the glacier at the head of the Ala-Archa valley.

Dostuk Trekking in Bishkek offers heliskiing in the Kyrghyz Ala-Too and above Lake Issyk-Kul, for what they claim is half the going rate per hour in Canada.

In November, when Samarkand is at last tolerably cool, the Altai are already under a metre or two of snow and the Russian cross-country ski team will be gliding round the *loipes* in the forests above Rakhmanovski.

Where there is skiing there are usually comic, ankle-breaking Soviet skis and boots for hire. Costs are minimal by comparison with western Europe but still expensive for most locals. Queues are not a problem.

Social Niceties

When invited to a Central Asian home, accept. Central Asians don't want to *appear* hospitable; they *are* hospitable, and declining may offend. Besides, you will probably be fed better than in almost any restaurant, and will learn a little of 'real' Central Asian life. You may be offered a parting gift, in which case it is polite to offer something in return.

Anything obviously Western will be treasured. Postcards and coins don't take up much space. Mars Bars, Snickers and instant coffee are just as exotic, being beyond most inflation-hit housekeeping budgets, and can be bought locally in Tashkent and Almaty.

If you are invited to stay, in Russian households you are traditionally a guest for three days, during which time you are one of the family, with your share of the chores. In Central Asian ones, a male visitor's place is at the front of the room as guest of honour. Women may get away with a little domesticity.

Women should bare a minimum of flesh in Pakistan, and should expect a somewhat schizoid treatment from less educated Pakistani and Central Asian men: politeness and even genuine charm on an individual level, combined with a half-baked notion, inspired by the seamy side of Hollywood, that all Western women are 'hot'. **Men** should avoid wearing shorts, except for sports.

Telephones

Phoning home is possible but generally either slow and cheap or slow and expensive. All towns have a telephone office, often in the same building as the post office or nearby, for intercity (*mezhdugorodni*) and international (*mezhdunarodni*) calls. This is the cheap option. Write the country (preferably in Cyrillic) and the number on a piece of paper and present it to the woman who summons people to the numbered booths when their call comes through. This is usually the woman at the far end of the longest queue. Then wait till you hear 'London', for example, and head for the specified booth. If you did not catch the number, look at the woman and she will raise that number of fingers.

Your chances of getting through are not necessarily greater in larger towns. The smaller the town, the more fuss will be made over a foreigner far from home. The exception is Tashkent, whose Urgent International Call Booth charges twice the normal rate but gets you straight through almost every time. You get a similar service when booking a call from a room in Dushanbe's Hotel Tajikistan or Almaty's Hotel Otrar.

The expensive option is to pay in hard currency at Tashkent's Hotel Uzbekistan (with no guarantee of getting through) or Almaty's Hotel Dostuk, which has international direct dialling by satellite for residents only, or by credit card using the AT&T satellite phone in the Hotel Bukhoro in Bukhara, which works when the hotel keeps up its payments to AT&T. Another expensive option is to call from one of the business centres that have sprung up in all the main hotels. Some will accept credit cards.

For local calls use a hotel, restaurant, shop, office or private phone—most payphones have been out of action since inflation rendered coins worthless.

Time

The 24-hour clock is used in general conversation as well as in all printed matter in both Xinjiang and former Soviet Central Asia. Western Kazakhstan, Turkmenistan and all of Uzbekistan except Tashkent and the Fergana valley are two hours ahead of Moscow time and five ahead of GMT. Eastern Kazakhstan, Kyrgyzstan, Tashkent, the Fergana Valley and Tajikistan are three hours ahead of Moscow time and six ahead of GMT. Air and train timetables in the former Soviet republics still use Moscow time.

Xinjiang runs on Beijing time (8 hours ahead of GMT) but is the equivalent of two time zones west of Beijing, so most offices open at 10am rather than 8am and close at 7pm rather than 5pm. Many Uighurs operate in unofficial local time, two hours behind Beijing time.

All of Pakistan is five hours ahead of GMT.

Tourist Information

In the CIS

Intourist's service bureaux are the closest thing to a chain of tourist offices in the CIS, but they are still much more used to groups than individuals, and much more willing to sell excursions than give free gobbets of useful information. The bureaux in Tashkent's Hotel Uzbekistan and Dushanbe's Hotel Tajikistan are exceptions. Staff here are knowledgeable and obliging and speak good English.

New, private travel companies are generally more flexible, friendly and eager to help. Details are given in city **Tourist Information** sections.

In Xinjiang

The **China International Travel Service (CITS)** is the state tourist office network. Like Intourist, it prefers to sell excursions than give information. Its Kashgar personnel are nevertheless helpful. In Ürümqi take your queries to the private operators in the Hongshan Hotel (*see* pp.350–2).The head office is in Beijing: 103, Fuxingmennei Avenue, Beijing 100800, China, ℗ (10) 601 1122, ℗ (10) 601 2013.

In Pakistan

The **Pakistan Tourism Development Corporation (PTDC)** understands about independent travel. The tourist offices in its hotels in Besham, Gilgit and Aliabad (Hunza) are excellent sources of up-to-date information on the Karakoram Highway and the Northern Areas. PTDC accommodation and jeep hire, though, is expensive by local standards.

PTDC Head Office: House No. 2, Street 61, F7/4, PO Box 1465, Islamabad 44000, ℗ (9251) 818601 (has a small library).

PTDC Tourist Information Centre: Flashman's Hotel, The Mall, Rawalpindi, ℗ (9251) 518480.

In the UK

Intourist: 219 Marsh Wall, Isle of Dogs, London E14 9FJ, ℗ (071) 538 8600, ℗ (071) 538 5967 (phone, fax or write first).

China National Tourist Office: 4 Glentworth Street, London NW1 5PG, ℗ (0171) 935 9427.

China Travel Service Information Centre: 124 Euston Road, London NW1 2AL,
  ✆ (0171) 388 8838.

PTDC: 35 Lowndes Square, London SW1X 9JN (in consulate building),
  ✆ (0171) 235 2044.

In Holland

Khan Travels, Albert Cuypstraat 44, 1072 CV Amsterdam, ✆ (020) 662 5255.

In Canada

Bestway Tours, Suite 202–2678, West Broadway, Vancouver, ✆ (604) 264 7378.

In the USA

Intourist: Suite 868, 630 5th Avenue, New York, NY 10111, ✆ (212) 757 3884.

China National Tourism Administration: Suite 6413, 534 5th Avenue, Empire State Building, New York, NY1018, ✆ (212) 760 9700 (information)/ 760 8218 (business).

PTDC: Suite 506, 303 5th Avenue, New York, NY 10016, ✆ (212) 889 5478.

other

World Tourism Organisation (WTO): Capitán Haya 42, 28020 Madrid, Spain, ✆ (341) 571 0628, ✆ (341) 571 3733. Their Silk Road Project, launched in Tashkent and Samarkand in 1994, aims to promote tourism along the ancient trading routes in Asia and the Middle East. Contact the **Ministry of Tourism and Sport:** Kazakhstan ✆ (3272) 67 39 86; Kyrgyzstan ✆ (3312) 22 64 91; Turkmenistan ✆ (3632) 41 02 10; Uzbekistan ✆ (3712) 33 84 31.

Trekking

As the trek to Everest base camp comes to resemble the path up Scafell Pike from Wasdale Head on a bank holiday, most valleys in the Tian Shan and Pamirs remain unseen by Western eyes since before the Russian Revolution, or, in many cases, ever.

The scope for unguided trekking in these ranges is restricted mainly by a shortage of reliable maps (*see* 'Maps', p.37). If unsupported as well, you would need to be totally self-reliant, since it would be foolish, not to say unethical, to depend on local people for food; in the eastern Pamirs you could walk for days if not weeks without seeing a soul.

Nevertheless, the best way to see Central Asia's mountains is, inevitably, on foot. Every town at the foot of the mountains is a possible trekking base, but the best-known starting points for recognized treks are Medeo and Chimbulak in Kazakhstan and Cholpan-Ata and Kara-Kol in Kyrgyzstan.

Before trekking in Xinjiang or Pakistan, check at a Public Security Bureau or PTDC office that you don't need a permit. *See* the sections on these places for more details.

Steppes East, OTT Expeditions, Exodus and several local operators offer supported treks in former Soviet Central Asia. *See* 'Specialist Holidays', pp.8–9, and under individual towns for addresses.

The very best trekking guide to the region is Frith Maier's *Trekking in Russia and Central Asia: A Traveler's Guide* (Cordee, 1994). The detailed itineraries include:

Lyanglif to Kan: 16 to 19 days into the Pamir Alai and east to the Fergana mountains. The start of the trail is a 3-day drive from Samarkand, and the end a day from Kokand. This trek requires mountaineering skills, and equipment such as crampons and ice axes for glaciers and steep snow.

Artuch to Iskanderkul Lake: A moderate 5- to 6-day trek, 6500–9800ft, from villages between Samarkand and Dushanbe.

Margazor Lake to Iskanderkul Lake: An easier, though slightly longer, trek in the same area.

Alyam Pass Loop: A moderate 4- to 6-day trek within easy reach of Tashkent, starting from the Chingan ski base.

Chimbulak to Mutnoi River: An easy 3- to 4-day hike through the Talgar Valley and over the Turistov Pass.

Lower Kul-Sai Lake to Lake Issyk-Kul: An easy 3- to 4-day hike from the lowest of three small mountain lakes in the Zailiisky Alatau, 7 hours' drive southeast of Almaty, across the Sarybulak Pass.

Ak-Sai Glacier and **Ala Archa Valley** are both easy overnight treks starting from the Ala Archa lodge, a 1½-hour drive from Bishkek.

Alamedin East Pass: Slightly more difficult than the treks above, this is a leisurely 4- to 6-day round-trip in the same area, via the Tyuk-Tyor Glacier and climbing to 13,000ft.

Ala Archa Valley to Alamedin Valley: A strenuous 3- to 4-day trek; hiring a local guide is advised, as the route is difficult to find.

Maida Adyr Base Camp to Engilchek Base Camp: In the central Tian Shan area know locally as the Muztag or 'Ice Mountains', this challenging trek takes 4 to 6 days and requires experience of glacier walking. Maida Adyr is 45mins by helicopter from Karakol.

Where to Stay

Hotels

A clean room, a high ceiling, a hot shower and a balcony with a view of the Tian Shan is about as good as accommodation gets in former Soviet Central Asia. That could be Almaty's Hotel Otrar, Bishkek's Hotel Ala-Too or the Hotel Medeo in Almaty. Intourist hotels traditionally charged the most but have now been overtaken by the new five-star private hotels that cater for businessmen.

For the foreigner, ex-Soviet hotels fall into two categories: those that demand hard currency and those that accept local currency. The former include all Intourist hotels and work out on average ten times more expensive than the latter, allowing for their doubling and sometimes tripling of prices for foreigners.

Rooms are uniformly dull. Dollar rooms and pricier ruble ones will be clean, with *en suite* shower or bath and hot water at certain times of day at least. The most basic rooms, in small-town Kyrgyzstan for example, share lavatories and washing facilities with the rest of the corridor. If the room itself is shared it probably won't have a lock, but you may be able to have it to yourself by paying for all the beds.

There is no sense of 'you get what you pay for'. Prices do not necessarily reflect what's on offer and can, in many cases, be open to negotiation (Intourist and five-star hotels excluded). For this reason, while every attempt has been made to ascertain the correct price, those quoted in this book should be used as a guide only. Unless travelling with Intourist or on a Russian tourist visa, there is no need to book hotels ahead.

The best value and most interesting accommodation in Central Asia is bed and breakfast. The number of houses where this is available is growing, particularly in Samarkand and Bukhara, and it's well worth taking advantage of.

Beds along the Karakoram Highway cost from under US$1 in rupees for a bed in a dorm geared for trekkers in Hunza, to $70 for a comfortable double ahight the Gilgit Serena Hotel.

Chinese hotels are no more inspiring than ex-Soviet ones. Strictly speaking, foreigners are only allowed in those displaying an 'authorized tour unit' plaque. Prices range from $2 in local currency for a bed in shared room in Kashgar, to $25 for a twin with bath in Ürümqi's Overseas Chinese Hotel, to $100 plus at the Holiday Inn.

Accommodation in this book is listed under three price categories, which are intended as guidelines and nothing more: prices may vary in high and low season, and rates vary within some hotels, such as when some rooms have a pretty view and others do not.

Price ranges for one person, in either private or shared accommodation:

expensive	over US$30
moderate	US$17–30
inexpensive	less than US$17

Travellers using Moscow as the entry point to the CIS and starting on a budget could try the Hotel Molodezhaya at Dimmitryevskoe 27, © 210 4556, close to the Timirayevskaya Metro. The best deal is found not at the main reception, where rooms cost $35–60, but on the 20th floor, where a double is $15–20 negotiable. If this floor is full they'll direct you to another, still value for money in the Moscow price range. The well-known Traveller's Guest House, run by an American and Russian partner, is at Ulitsa Bolshoya Pereslavskaya 50, © 971 4059. Rooms range between $15 for a dorm, $30 for a single and $35 for a double. Take the metro to Prospekt Mira, then take the third turning right, heading north, and at the T junction turn left. The TGH is good for information and an easy place to buy tickets. Their visa support letter works well ($25). Ask about discounts on the trains from Moscow through Central Asia.

Turbazas

An alternative to hotels in many CIS tourist towns is the *turbaza* ('tourist base'). Here you pay a small amount in local currency for basic bungalow accommodation, three meals a day whether you eat them or not, and hour upon hour of amplified Radio Moscow. Places with *turbazas* include Bukhara, Osh, Sary-Chelek, Arslanbob, Dzhalalabad, Dzhety-Oguz and Rakhmanovski, the last three being based around curative springs. These days some have been claimed by private companies and refurbished, or else, due to the reduction in the number of 'Soviet' tourists, closed.

Camping

The only designated campsites in former Soviet Central Asia are the permanent base camps from which its high peaks are climbed. There is nothing to stop you pitching a tent elsewhere in the mountains, though. It is not difficult to find convenient and comfortable sites. However, beware those marked with 'camping' or water tap signs—they're reserved for truck drivers and itinerant labourers, not foreign tourists—and, near to villages and other settlements, check you won't be trampled by livestock being driven up to high pastures in the morning. Bring all your own equipment.

The same applies in Pakistan, though here many hotels in Hunza and Gilgit offer tent space and the use of toilets and washing facilities for a fraction of the price of a room.

In Xinjiang, check at a Public Security Bureau before camping in the mountains, in case you need a permit. You don't need one to stay by the Heavenly Lake near Ürümqi.

History and Culture

FORTRESS AT HISSAR, NEAR DUSHANBE

Central Asia has an all-star past. Alexander the Great and Tamerlane strutted back and forth across it, building and destroying in roughly equal measure. Genghis Khan concentrated on destruction, but left an impression just as lasting. In the19th century the daredevils of London society shadowed their Russian rivals over the Pamirs, then told their boys' own stories in *The Times*. But in truth, personalities are a mere garnish on Central Asian history. Pitched battles are rare. The real story is of long drawn-out migrations, the hunger which caused them and the shock waves they produced; of the endless contest between nomads and settled 'civilization' for control of strategic oases in an otherwise hostile part of the world.

Beginnings

The first hominid to venture into the void between China and the Caspian Sea was Neanderthal Man, anything up to 800,000 years ago. He may not have stayed long: planet earth was going through phases of extreme heat and cold, and Central Asia, then as now, intensified them by its distance from the oceans.

By 100,000 BC the last great ice age had set in. Neanderthal Man's successors, *homo sapiens*, adapted well to life on the edge of the ice sheets. They lived in caves, in isolated groups, leaving flint leather scrapers in the hills north of Tashkent, and eerie rock carvings in the Shakhty grotto, way up in the eastern Pamirs.

Then, around 10,000 BC, the ice age ended and the great heat began. It turned the vast swathe of lowland between the Caspian and the Tian Shan into desert. On the cooler grasslands north of here lived the Altaic nomads, from whom the Huns, Turks and Mongols were descended. But the desert was virtually unexplored for another 8000 years.

Ancient History: 1500–334 BC

The first known migration to the oases that became Bukhara, Merv and Samarkand was by the Aryans. They came from the west, a pale-skinned Iranian branch of the Indo-European family. Some continued over the Hindu Kush and invaded northern India around 1500 BC. Others settled the Fergana valley, where their descendents, the Scythians, were the first mounted archers of recorded history. They made rich gold jewellery as well as bows of bone and tendon and arrowheads of bronze and iron. They were a people to be reckoned with. Cyrus the Great, Persia's first Achaemenid emperor and self-styled King of the World, duly reckoned with them. Using their own cavalry tactics against them, he defeated the Scythians in a series of campaigns between 545 and 540 BC, and organized the survivors into the three satrapies of outer Iran (Turan). One of these, based on the river Zerafshan, was Sogdiana. The Sogdians would later become famous as Silk Route traders, wood carvers and carpet makers. But in their finest hour they were rebels.

Alexander the Great: 334–323 BC

Destiny took Alexander to India (his geography teacher Aristotle believed that from the summits of the Hindu Kush you could see to the end of the world), but chance took him to Turan. He crossed the Hellespont aged 22 in 334 BC, swept through Asia Minor, burned the Persian capital Persepolis and pursued its last Achaemenid ruler Darius III north towards modern Tehran. He envisaged a final, glorious pitched battle with the Persians, but when he caught up with the royal caravan he found Darius murdered by his own subjects. Immediately, deftly, to the amazement of his troops, he switched roles, proclaiming himself Darius's heir and avenger.

Alexander then chased Darius's murderers to Sogdiana. Approaching from the south, he crossed the Hindu Kush in 15 days of terrible suffering in the spring of 329 BC. Bessus, the traitors' ringleader, was caught and sent to be tried by the Persians, who spared his life but cut off his nose and ears. Alexander took ancient Samarkand and continued to the site of modern Khŭjand on the Syr Darya. There he was proudly laying plans for Alexandria Eschate—Alexandria-the-furthest—when news arrived of trouble in the rear.

Spitamen, a Persian regicide still at large, had incited the Sogdians to rebellion and beseiged Samarkand. When Alexander despatched 2000 mercenaries to deal with him, Spitamen butchered them. Alexander raced back to crush the rebellion himself—but its leader had escaped down the Oxus to Khorezm. For Alexander it was immensely frustrating. For Soviet historians it was 'one of the earliest people's liberation movements in the history of Central Asia.' It fizzled out only when Spitamen's own commanders killed him and presented his head to Alexander.

He made sure of the Sogdians' loyalty by marrying one of their princesses, then recrossed the Hindu Kush and descended into the Punjab in 327 BC. Most tribes along the way surrendered without a fight. Those that didn't fled before him to Aornos, a mountain on the west bank of the Indus signposted from the Karakoram Highway as Pir Sar. It was his easternmost conquest.

Seleucids and Parthians: 313 BC–AD 224

Alexander died in Babylon in 323 BC. He had founded at least eight Alexandrias in Central Asia, settled them with his Macedonian veterans and presided at mass weddings between them and Persian women. He had decapitated regimes which resisted him, installing his generals as their new rulers.

In 312 BC one of them, Seleucus Nicator, founded the Seleucid dynasty, which survived until the mid-1st century BC. He ruled a great swathe of land stretching from Turkey to Afghanistan. But the difficulty of holding his far-flung dominions together from his capital at Antioch in Syria led him to cede the Punjab to the Mauryan emperor Chandragupta in exchange for 500 war elephants. His successors experienced the same difficulties, and in 247 BC northern Persia was lost to a tribe of horsemen called the Parni. They made Nisa in present-day Turkmenistan their capital and, known to history as the Parthians, became a superpower to rival Rome.

The Birth of the Silk Route: 138 BC–AD 484

In 138 BC a Chinese general called Chang Ch'ien set out from the imperial court at Chang'an on a horse-buying mission. For centuries, the Hsiung-Nu nomads of the Mongolian steppe had bedevilled imperial China's northern frontier. Now the forward-thinking Han emperor Wu-ti aimed to put them in their place with horses which, legend had it, could run so fast they sweated blood. When Chang Ch'ien reached Fergana he learned that its Heavenly Horses bled because of a skin parasite rather than exertion. But he also learned that Sogdian merchants would pay a fine price for silk.

Though the Chinese had been making silk for more than 2000 years, export had always been forbidden. Now, hearing of this promising foreign market, Wu-ti lifted the ban. The Silk Route was conceived—but the Hsiung-Nu still threatened much of it. In 52 BC the Chinese finally contained them with a treaty, leaving only the lands between Kashgar and Parthia outside a stable empire. The gap was plugged a century later by the Kushans, whose mountainous empire was based on Taxila and Peshawar in present-day Pakistan, and lasted 150 years.

Caravans could at last plod unmolested from the Jade Gate to imperial Rome. West went silk, spices and jade, arms, mirrors and laquerware. From Rome came glass, coral, textiles, pottery and gold and silver coin. Goods took months if not years to make the journey, changing hands at least once along the way.

The Silk Route was not a single road but a vast system carrying all trade between the European and Chinese ends of Asia. Its main branches skirted north and south of the Tarim basin, meeting at Dunhuang at one end and Kashgar at the other. From Kashgar southbound traffic crossed the Karakorams; westbound the Tian Shan. Once in Sogdiana, caravans could follow the Amu Darya and Syr Darya rivers to the Aral Sea, continuing north of the Caspian into southern Russia—but most kept south, crossing the Kizyl-Kum and Kara-Kum deserts to Persia and enriching Samarkand, Bukhara and Merv on the way.

Early in the 3rd century the Romans finally dealt their Parthian rivals the *coup de grâce*, only to find them replaced by a resurgent Persia under the Sassanians. The dynasty's founder Ardashir (AD 224–41) styled himself heir to the great Achaemenids. He centralized taxes, revived Zoroastrianism, purged the Persian aristocracy through his high priest Mazdak, and presented Rome with a new, more formidable threat in the east.

Huns and Turks: 484–651

The Sassanians hung onto much of Central Asia until the Arab invasions in the 7th century—despite the return of mounted nomads in the 5th. Huns formed the first wave. Also called the Hephthalites after a succession of kings called Hephthal, they captured the

Sassanians' eastern empire in 484. Their migrations frightened the Chinese at one end of Eurasia and the Romans at the other. So they should have done. The Huns' world view was bounded only by the steppe: everything under its limitless sky was theirs to conquer. They got as far south as Sialkot in the Punjab and raided India from there for 50 years before vanishing from history, taken from behind by the Turks.

This next nomadic race from an apparently limitless supply was descended from the mythical union of a she-wolf and a youth in the Altai mountains. The Turks drove the Huns out of Sogdiana after defeating them at the first battle of Talas around 560. Their khan, finding himself straddling the Silk Route, showed a fine instinct for business by sending an envoy to the Byzantine emperor to propose that all trade between them should bypass Persia. But loss of trade was soon to be the least of Persia's worries.

The Coming of Islam: 651–992

The Arabs conquered first and worried about converting people later. Within 20 years of the prophet Mohammed's death in Mecca in 632 they had overrun the Near East and the Sassanian empire. The last Sassanian ruler, Yazdigerd III, was pursued to Merv and killed there in 651.

Then, on the line of the Amu Darya, the armies of Islam paused awhile, waiting perhaps for their Napoleon. He came in 705 in the person of Qutaiba ibn-Abbas, viceroy of Khorassan (then the easternmost province of the Umayyad Islamic empire based on Baghdad).

In 712 Qutaiba accepted an invitation to help crush a rebellion in Khorezmia—and conquered the province in the process. He returned up the Amu Darya and took Samarkand, Bukhara, Tashkent and Fergana. But then he got above himself. Trying to stir up a revolt against Baghdad, he was assassinated by more loyal followers of the caliph in 715. After that the Turks and Sogdians combined to take advantage of the Arabs' disarray, and expelled them from Fergana.

It was only a temporary setback. When a Chinese army took Fergana and, in 751, seemed about to conquer all Central Asia, the Arabs thrashed it comprehensively at Talas. Thus did Islam prevail in Transoxiana, and with it the Arabic script and non-representational art—which, as prescribed in the Koran, depicts no living thing.

Baghdad's authority did not last so long. The Arab viceroys in Merv ruled Transoxiana by proxy, extracting tribute but leaving everyday decisions to governors appointed from local aristocracies. Such an arrangement suited ambitious governors. In the mid-9th century four of them, who happened to be brothers and controlled between them Samarkand, Fergana, Tashkent and Herat, declared themselves hereditary rulers. These were the Samanids, first and greatest promoters of Bukhara as a centre of Islamic learning. Their 10th-century mausoleum, with its intricately faceted brickwork, still stands in Bukhara's Samani park, the oldest intact building in Central Asia.

Karakhanids and Seljuks: 992 – c. 1150

In 992 the Karakhanid Turks dislodged the Samanids from Bukhara, just as their forebears had dislodged the Sassanians. But this time the invaders aspired to settled civilization. The Karakhanids continued the building of Bukhara, adopted Islam and took it over the Tian Shan to Kashgar while their rival Mahmud of Ghazni (971–1030) converted northern India.

Yet another Turkic dynasty soon usurped them. Half-way through the 11th century the Seljuks—long since established on the lower Syr Darya—set out to conquer the world. They defeated Mahmud's son Masud in 1041, reduced the Karakhanids to the status of vassals, removed the Abbasids from power in Baghdad and even imprisoned the Byzantine emperor Romanos IV after defeating him at Manzikert in 1071. Their great viceroy Sultan Sanjar shifted the centre of the Islamic world eastwards from Baghdad to his capital at Merv. By the mid-12th century the Merv oasis was the biggest and richest in Asia—and was coveted by a whole new breed of conqueror.

The Mongols: c. 1150 – c. 1370

First came a vanguard: a Mongol race from the Far East called the Kara-Khitai. They pushed the Seljuks out of Afghanistan and Transoxiana in the early 1150s and, unlike the Turks, did not convert to Islam. They tried to impose a Chinese-style administration, but failed conspicuously in the Amu Darya delta where the Khorezmshahs of Urgench kept Muslim and Turkish traditions alive. In the early 13th century the Khorezmshahs even enjoyed brief leadership of the Islamic world.

By this time another strange act of procreation had taken place deep in the Altai mountains. A deer and a wolf begat a boy named Temujin, who became Khan of all the Mongol tribesmen and head of a mighty army. This was Genghis Khan. Under him, in historian J. M. Roberts' words, the Mongols 'blew up like a hurrricane to terrify half a dozen civilizations, slaughtered and destroyed on a scale the twentieth century alone has emulated... By the time of his death in 1227 Genghis Khan had become the greatest conqueror the world had ever known.'

No one knows quite what drove him, but in 12 years of campaigning he took Beijing (the only nomad emperor ever to do so), conquered India, the Near East and southern Russia. Like all Mongol armies, his used inelegant but sturdy steppe horses and derived their battle tactics from hunting. They never engaged until they were virtually certain of victory, and usually achieved it by feigning retreat with a small force to lure the enemy into the giant jaws of the main army.

Mongol soldiers could live for days in the saddle, consuming only mare's milk and plundered meat. They were, according to one Persian account, a bestial bunch:

'Their stench was more horrible than their colour. Their heads were set on their bodies as if they had no necks, and their cheeks resembled leather bottles full of wrinkles and knots. Their noses extended from cheekbone to cheekbone. Their nostrils resembled rotting graves... Their chests, in colour half-black, half-white, were covered with lice which looked like sesame growing on bad soil. Their bodies, indeed, were covered with these insects, and their skins were as rough-grained as shagreen leather, fit only to be converted into shoes.'

Genghis Khan was uniquely ruthless with beseiged cities. If their people resisted, they were massacred, and their dwellings razed. This is what happened to Samarkand, Bukhara and Urgench in 1220, and to Merv the following year. Scarcely a building remains in Central Asia from all its pre-Mongolian civilizations.

The Mongols' business was destruction but their legacy was 150 years of stunned peace—*pax Mongolica*. On Genghis Khan's death in 1227 Asia was carved up between his sons. The northern steppe, land of the Golden and White Hordes, went to the eldest son, Dzhuchi. His younger brother Chaghatai got the territory northeast of Samarkand as far as Mongolia, which was divided between the third and youngest sons, Ögödei and Toloi. Communications across their empire by pony relay were not bettered until the Russians strung a telegraph line along the Trans-Siberian railway. And it was said that a young girl carrying a pot of gold could walk unmolested from one end of the Mongol empire to the other.

Tamerlane and the Timurids: *c.* 1370–1500

In 1336, in the town of Kesh near Samarkand, a son was born to a minor tribal chieftain. The son's name was Timur, but an arrow wound to his right thigh caused him to be known in English literature as Timur-the-lame, or Tamerlane. He started his career as a highwayman, but in his late twenties formed the larger ambition of becoming a second Genghis Khan.

By 1370 Tamerlane had taken control of Transoxiana and made Samarkand his capital. In 1372 he sacked Urgench, which since the Mongols' destruction of Merv had been handling most of Central Asia's trade and enriching itself at Samarkand's expense. In 1382, on an expedition to Herat, he built towers with the skulls of those who resisted him and forced the local ruler to commit suicide. Over the next 15 years he conquered Persia and Baghdad and mounted expeditions into Anatolia and over the Caucasus. In 1398 Tamerlane set out for India.

He took 100,000 prisoners on the way to Delhi, and then put them to death to free his hands for the coming seige. He killed 100,000 more inside the city for resisting him, and on the way home, in fulfillment of a holy vow, he skinned alive any surviving Hindus. It is said that not a bird moved in Delhi for two months after Tamerlane's departure.

In Samarkand Tamerlane built innumerable palaces, but preferred to relax in silk tents on the banks of the Zerafshan with his followers encamped and festive on the plain nearby. In 1403, at a feast, the Spanish envoy Ruy Gonzalez de Clavijo watched corrupt officials being hung up by their feet to die.

Tamerlane himself died in 1405 shortly after setting out to invade China. Within a few years of his death his empire fell in on itself. His fourth son Shahrukh ruled Persia from Herat until 1447, and Shahrukh's son Ulug Bek ruled Samarkand until he was assassinated by his own son in 1449 for questioning the existence of Allah. The last Timurid, Babur, tried to resurrect Tamerlane's empire in the first years of the 16th century, but is better known as the founder of the Mughal dynasty in Delhi, which he took in 1526 having been driven from his homeland by the Uzbeks.

The Khanates: 1500–1717

The modern Uzbeks' ancestors were Mongols. Named after Khan Uzbek (1282–1342), who converted the Golden Horde to Islam, they began to move south from present day Kazakhstan in the 15th century. Under Mohammed Sheibani, they crossed the Syr Darya in 1500. One branch of the Sheibanid dynasty founded the Khanate of Khiva, which lasted until 1920. Another ruled Transoxiana from Bukhara until the death of the great Abdullah Khan in 1598.

In his 40-year reign Abdullah commissioned some of the city's finest mosques and madrasas, and extended the khanate east to Kashgar and north to Tashkent. The 'pillar of Islam' had not known such fame and power since the Samanids—nor has it since.

From the turn of the century Bukhara was ruled by the inept Astrakhanid dynasty, which failed to reverse a steady decline in the city's trading fortunes. The northern caravan route had not recovered from Tamerlane's devastation; the Portuguese had discovered sea routes to Asia via Africa; and the secrets of silk-making had long since reached the West. The Silk Route was all but dead. Those caravans that still trekked across the Kara-Kum were at the mercy of Turkmen raiders. Those that went north down the Amu Darya had to pass through the Khanate of Khiva, now a notorious slave market. The Fergana valley broke from Bukhara in the early 18th century when what seems to have been a dormant branch of the Sheibanids founded the Khanate of Kokand.

Bukhara, Khiva and Kokand were cruelly ruled. They had inflated senses of their importance in the wider world, and they squabbled constantly. While Europe underwent 200 years of intellectual and industrial revolution, they demonstrated what Curzon called 'the magnificent immobility of the East'. It was only a matter of time before an altogether more modern power would swallow them up.

Enter the Russians: 1717–1868

The first czar to toy with Central Asia was Peter the Great (r. 1672–1725). Determined to modernize Russia but lacking the funds to do it, Peter was lured by reports of gold on the Oxus and immeasurable wealth beyond the Pamirs in India. He despatched a task force to help the Khan of Khiva subdue raiders in the Khorezmian oasis. It reached Khiva in the summer of 1717—only to be butchered once inside the city walls.

The Russians were never very good at desert raids. Much more successful was their steady advance across the steppe, which started around 1730 with the capture of a line of forts along the Irtysh and continued for 120 years. A vague notion that Russia's expansion into Central Asia was the equivalent of America's 'Manifest Destiny' to expand into the Wild West was fuelled by a potent mixture of motives: the never-ending search for a defensible southern frontier; the fact that the khanates would not sign and honour treaties; the lure of trade; and the perceived threat of British expansion from India. Above all, there was Russia's sense of cultural superiority, cut down to size by Engels in an 1851 letter to Marx:

'For all its baseness and dirt, Russian domination is a civilizing element in Central Asia.'

Thus the Fourth Orenburg Line Battalion found itself charging through Tashkent's Kamalan Gate at daybreak on 15 June 1865. The fighting lasted barely a day and a half; the Russians had accurate intelligence of the city's defences, probably from two rich Tashkent merchants who resented being part of the Khanate of Kokand, as Tashkent then was.

In 1867 General Konstantin Kaufmann, Anglophobe and veteran Caucasian empire-builder, became the first Governor-General of Russian Turkestan. In April 1868 he set out for Samarkand and Bukhara with 3500 men. His troops were outnumbered by the emir's, but better equipped. Samarkand fell with hardly a struggle. The rest of the Emirate of Bukhara became a protectorate of the czar's, and the Khanate of Kokand was effectively annexed with a harsh commercial treaty.

Of all the khanates, Khiva held out longest, tormenting Russian Orthodox souls with its trade in Russian slaves. It fell eventually to a three-pronged attack by General Kaufmann, complete with German artillery, in 1873.

Meanwhile, Britain's client the Maharajah of Kashmir had finally clubbed the bandits of his northwest frontier into submission in 1863. The two greatest empires of the 19th century suddenly found themselves with a disputed frontier on the roof of the world.

The Great Game: 1868–1895

Death or glory, escape from stiff society, unparalleled adventure—Central Asia offered all this to the young, the brave and the lunatic of the British and Russian empires of the 19th century. Rudyard Kipling called their contest the Great Game and immortalized it in *Kim*. The Russians called it the Tournament of Shadows.

Fear and ignorance fuelled it more than did appetite for territory. Fear on both sides that the other coveted their colonies; ignorance about what lay between them. So the Great Game consisted of two main kinds of expedition: the gift-laden wooing trip to turn a distant emir, khan, or prince into an ally, and the survey. But sycophants and surveyors alike were usually, first and foremost, spies.

Up to 1868 St Petersburg insisted that her 'forward' moves in Central Asia were defensive. British scaremongers ridiculed these claims. British governments, in the end, accepted them. Likewise the Russians protested angrily at the British invasion of Afghanistan in 1839 but did not go to war over it.

Kaufmann's conquests raised the stakes. The possibility of a Russian invasion of India now had to be taken seriously. The most likely route was through Afghanistan, which the British invaded for the second time in 1878. In July 1880 they installed a friendly new emir in Kabul and withdrew, hopeful that—for the time being at least—their northwest frontier was secure.

The Russians' next move took the two countries to the brink of war. They had founded Krasnovodsk (now Turkmenbashy) as a military base on the east shore of the Caspian in 1869. From here, in 1880, General Skobelev and two special divisions started building the Transcaspian railway in 1880. Skobelev's aims were to secure a natural southern frontier on the Kopet Dagh mountains, and to take Merv. On the way there he besieged and slaughtered the massed forces of the Tekke tribe at Geok-Tepe. A Russian governor was installed at Merv in 1884 and the following year he occupied the town of Pandjeh on the northern border of Afghanistan.

This was the sovereign territory of Britain's Afghan ally, and the superpowers faced a 19th-century Cuban missile crisis. Troops were mobilized. Queen Victoria wrote to the czar begging him to back down. At the eleventh hour, Russian troops withdrew... and the Great Game's playing field shifted eastward.

The Russians had not invaded British India through Afghanistan, but might they not do so over the Pamirs? In 1883 the British 'surveyor' William McNair had found their passes smooth and wide—no obstacle for an acclimatized invasion force. So the British signed a treaty with the Kafirs of northern Chitral and set up an agency at Gilgit. From here they invaded the remote kingdom of Hunza in 1893, nipping in the bud an all-too-cosy relationship between its Mir and a Russian spy called Gromchevsky. A bothersome slice of no man's land still lay between the empires—the so-called Pamir Gap but an 1895 boundary commission solved the problem by giving it to Afghanistan.

The superpowers at last knew where they stood. They went on spying on each other and vying for influence in western China from their consulates in Kashgar, but the mutual fear and ignorance had gone. The sabre-rattling died down.

Colonial Interlude: 1895–1917

Like the British in their Indian cantonments, the Russians kept aloof from those they colonized. At Bukhara, Samarkand and Tashkent they built separate Russian towns beside the old ones, with churches, football pitches, schools, clubs, racing tracks and tree-lined boulevards arranged in grids. Two million Russian farmers, artisans and tradesmen emigrated to Central Asia between the middle of the 19th century and 1917. Local populations were forced to submit to Russian government and Russian-dominated trade, while richer Sart families (as the Russians called the Uzbeks) engaged Russian tutors.

In 1897 a Sufi brotherhood in Andizhan launched a holy war against the colonists. It provoked bloody reprisals and a campaign of Russification for the local Muslim elite. A more serious threat to czarist rule came in 1916; a decree drafting Muslims into non-combatant units on the Eastern Front sparked an uprising that spread quickly from Dzhizak to Fergana and the Kyrgyz highlands, where farmers and herdsmen had steadily lost land to the Russians. After decades of pent-up resentment thousands of Muslims risked—and lost—everything. Ringleaders faced the firing squad. Whole villages were burned to the ground. Kyrgyz rebels fled to China, and the Russian troops returned to their barracks. Real change would come not from the edge of the empire but from its hub.

Revolution and Civil War: 1917–1921

Moscow's first revolution in 1917, the social democratic one, won popular support in Central Asia since it encouraged criticism of czarist repression and seemed to promise self-determination. That promise wasn't kept. Instead, the provisional government in Tashkent excluded Muslims from government, lost their support and left the Bolsheviks to sieze power in November.

The secret police instituted a reign of terror in Tashkent after a botched coup there in January 1918. The following month the 'Kokand autonomy', led by a local religious leader named Irgash, came to an end in a massacre by the Red Army. The British agent F. M. Bailey, lurking in Tashkent in a wardrobe-full of disguises, tried to prepare the ground for a British expeditionary force, which he believed could easily have unseated the Bolsheviks. But it never came.

Meanwhile, 40,000 battle-hardened Austrian and Hungarian prisoners of war in Tashkent sided with the Reds. Socialist ideas had found some sympathy among the indigenous majority, too. From 1920, Central Asian Muslims were joining the Communist Party *en masse*, hoping for some say in their future government. This gave the Soviet general Frunze a breathing space in which to march on Khiva and Bukhara, oust their last dynastic rulers and install what Moscow thought would be puppet socialist governments.

But the Bolsheviks' troubles were not over. The desert cities were hungry. Irrigation systems were in disrepair. The Red Army, far from helping, was requisitioning all the food. The new regimes in Khiva and Bukhara swung away from Communism and towards pan-Turkic nationalism, which now had a standard bearer in the egomaniacal—but undoubtedly courageous—Enver Pasha, self-styled 'Commander-in-Chief of all Muslim troops, son-in-law of the Caliph, and representative of the Prophet'.

Enver had been hired by Lenin himself, 'to pacify Central Asia'. But he was ambitious. He saw a chance to build a Turkish empire stretching from the Caucasus to the Tian Shan. In November 1921 he swapped sides. Briefly, at the head of his army of Basmachis, he united Turkish oppostition to the Bolsheviks, but was trapped and killed by them in the western Pamirs six months later.

The Soviet Era: 1921–1991

Following Enver Pasha's death, Central Asia's communist parties were purged of anyone suspected of pan-Turkic leanings. In 1924 a Soviet Border Commission carved up their homeland. Brand new borders were drawn to give the region's main ethnic groups the national homelands which, according to Soviet propaganda, they had always sought. In fact it was a simple policy of divide and rule.

Soviet Uzbekistan got the Bukharan lands between the Amu Darya and Syr Darya (including the Pamirs, which did not become Tajikistan until 1929), plus the floor of the Fergana valley and a few awkward enclaves in the mountains around it. The mountains themselves, north of the Alai range, became Soviet Kyrgyzstan in 1926. The Kara-Kum desert and part of the Amu Darya delta became Soviet Turkmenistan. Kazakhstan was part of the Russian Federation until 1936.

These invented republics were ruled and homogenized as a bloc. The Cyrillic alphabet replaced the Arabic. Russian became compulsory in schools. All but 400 of Central Asia's 26,000 mosques were closed, and Party officials began recruiting groups of *Allahsizlar* ('Godless people').

Central Asia's role in Stalin's planned economy was overwhelmingly agricultural. Collectivization began in earnest with the first Five Year Plan in 1928. It was an unprecedented trauma. Kyrgyz and Kazakh herdsmen slaughtered their sheep by the million rather than hand them over to collective farms. More than 800,000 peasant farmers in Kazakhstan alone were done away with. The Kyrgyz, Kazakh and Uzbek leaderships were purged again in the 1930s for 'obstructing collectivization', among other crimes.

After World War II the politburo tried to turn northern Kazakhstan into a bread basket with its massively publicized Virgin Lands campaign. In practice the steppe choked on the fertilizer, and wheat harvests were an embarrassment, as US spy satellites confirmed. But other uses had already been found for the steppe, including a missile test range, cosmodrome and nuclear test site.

The southern republics were given over to cotton. Traditional mixed farming in Uzbekistan, western Tajikistan and the oases of Turkmenistan was sacrificed in a headlong rush for Soviet self-sufficiency in 'white gold'. Vast new irrigation systems were built, including the 1100-km Kara-Kum Canal through southern Turkmenistan. The Amu Darya and Syr Darya rivers were bled almost dry, the Aral Sea shrank by nearly half and the economies of these three republics were left lop-sided and dependent on barter with Moscow.

Glimmers of dissent began emerging from Central Asia towards the end of the Soviet era—but more against Russia than the regime. Uzbekistan's leading Communist, Sharaf Rashidov, was officially condemned but unofficially applauded on his death in 1983 for having swindled Moscow out of millions of rubles of cotton revenues. When his Kazakh counterpart, Dinmukhammed Kunaev, was replaced in 1986 by a Russian, students in Almaty took advantage of *glasnost* to protest on the streets. Nevada-Semipalatinsk, an anti-nuclear testing campaign, used the same tactic in 1989 and was ultimately successful; testing at Semipalatinsk stopped the following year.

In June and July 1990, 200 people died in inter-ethnic fighting in Osh, Kyrgyzstan's second city. Journalists predicted further strife and perhaps even a war like the one then in progress in the Caucasus—no one predicted five new independent countries within 18 months.

Independence: 1991

In the last months of the Soviet Union the Baltic republics set the pace while the Asian ones, somewhat reluctantly, followed it. The Baltics had known independence before. The Central Asian republics had not. Some made declarations of sovereignty as early as 1990, but none expected the Soviet collapse and none, in truth, was ready for it.

They stepped, blinking, onto the international stage with a deep-rooted suspicion of democracy that has left former Communists in power almost everywhere, and with an ignorance of market economics that has astonished even veterans of Western know-how projects in Eastern Europe.

Washington's state department feared these countries might be overtaken by Iranian-style Islamic fundamentalism. So did the normally unflappable *Economist* magazine. 'The ground is prepared for an Islamic upsurge which is likely to shake the crumbling pillars of secular authority in Central Asia,' it declared in September 1991. American embassies appeared promptly in hotel suites in all their capitals, and the then Secretary of State James Baker glad-handed the entire region in February 1992.

Except in Persian-speaking Tajikistan, though, such fears proved unfounded, and not a little insulting to the new regimes. Their Turkic languages, their mainstream Sunni Islam, and a widespread desire to continue drinking and dressing like Europeans, orient the Central Asian states towards Istanbul and Ankara rather than Tehran. Meanwhile Pakistan, keen to secure its share of trade and influence in the region, has undertaken with Uzbekistan and Afghanistan to build a new Tashkent–Karachi highway.

Kazakhstan and Kyrgyzstan have dived into the kind of economic reforms of which they hope the West approves—and indeed, Western oil giants are striding onto the Kazakh steppe while the IMF props up a new Kyrgyz currency. Uzbekistan and Turkmenistan seem in no particular hurry to dismantle their police states but at the same time see the necessity of encouraging foreign investment.

Tajikistan is the victim of a simmering civil war which has drawn in the Afghan *mujahedin* on the side of Islamic rebel forces, and is kept from boiling over only by the dominant presence of Russian troops along the Afghan border. Boris Yeltsin's government claims that these troops are playing a peacekeeping role which, in a better-known part of the world, would be performed by the UN. They are also there to protect Kyrgyzstan's Russian minority from nationalist factions demanding that Russians 'go home'.

Russians and Ukrainians, some of them the descendants of 19th-century settlers, are already returning from all Central Asian republics in numbers their homelands are hard-pressed to support. But the impression this has created for many Muscovites of Central Asia as a second war-torn Azerbaijan is inaccurate. Compared with the Caucasian fringe of the former Soviet empire, the Central Asian one is making a calmer transition to independence than many dared hope. Except in western Tajikistan, visitors should not be deterred by the political situation. Wherever they go, they can be sure of witnessing history in the making.

Topics

ARAL SEA

Beside a river in a quiet valley near the Afghan border, hard to get to since the bridge at Nurek was bombed in the Tajik civil war, there is an unmarked grave. A handful of academics in Dushanbe know who lies here, near Abiderya in the oblast of Kulyab—but few locals do. Even if you told them they might not be interested; the Tajiks are a Persian race, and this is the final resting place of a Turk. What's more, his fame was erased from Soviet history after he nearly toppled the Bolsheviks in Central Asia.

Enver Pasha was the embodiment of uncontrollable ambition. Born of lowly parents in Turkey in 1882, he joined the army, rose swiftly through its ranks, led the Young Turks in their manoeuverings against the crumbling Ottoman regime, and on the eve of World War I was Turkish Minister of War. He was, writes Peter Hopkirk, 'small and dapper, and of mercurial temperament... as agile as a panther and said to be the finest fencer in the Turkish empire.'

When that empire was defeated in the war, Enver's career took a downward turn. He was arrested, degraded, smuggled out of Turkey in a German warship, and condemned to death *in absentia*. A humbler man would have kept to the shadows, thankful to be alive. Enver flew to Moscow and offered Lenin British India in return for Bolshevik help in building a new Turkish empire stretching from Istanbul to Turkestan. Lenin did not agree these terms precisely, but dispatched his unlikely new ally to Bukhara anyway, to urge some troublesome Central Asian freedom fighters, whom the Soviets called *basmakhi*, to give up their struggle. Enver reached Bukhara on 8 November 1921, and remained a Soviet ally for one day. The next, he joined the rebels and proclaimed himself their leader.

Until now the *basmakhi* had failed to score a palpable hit. Most of their leaders were Sufi mystics engaged in holy war, but none had emerged as uncontested C-in-C. Good Muslim men and true had not been flocking to their banners because the *basmakhi* themselves were, by training, bandits. But now every anti-Soviet Muslim—and since the Red Army's pounding of Bukhara in September 1920 they had grown steadily in number—could look to Enver as a figurehead.

In February 1922 he took Dushanbe. From here he controlled present-day Tajikistan and could launch raids into Soviet Bukhara using arms supplied by King Amanullah of Afghanistan. Lenin suddenly had a fight on his hands for Central Asia. Unfortunately for Enver, he also had the necessary troops; with the Civil War coming to an end, they could be released from other fronts.

The Georgian general Ordzhonikidze was assigned to liquidate the treacherous Turk, who went into hiding in the mountains east of Dushanbe. Soviet secret agents fanned out in disguise to track him down. He was traced to Abiderya in late July, and an entire Red division was summoned to complete the job. Sources differ on the manner of his death, but they agree that it was noble. Whether fighting to the last or taken from behind while praying, Enver Pasha died holding the Koran.

His successor committed suicide in the Pyandzh. Though some *basmakhi* cells held out until the early 1930s, their heyday passed with Enver. Under him they had fought a brief but genuine war of liberation. And he had not just been their leader. He had been the first pan-Turkic megalomaniac since Tamerlane.

Everybody loves a winner, which is probably why Tamerlane, not Enver, is having streets and restaurants named after him in post-Soviet Central Asia. But you never know. That unmarked grave beside a river near the Afghan border may yet receive a headstone.

Glasnost and the Godfathers

Spare a little sympathy for the pimp in the Hotel Uzbekistan, for the muscle-bound youth idling away his evenings in the Zerafshan restaurant, for the street-corner soft porn trader. He has been bought. Some unseen ruble billionaire is doing him the favour of not kidnapping his son or burning down his kiosk. He may be better fed and dressed than most Central Asians, but in the underworld he's the lowest of the low.

The governments of former Soviet Central Asia deny they have a problem with organized crime. They would; many of their personnel are believed to be involved. Prostitution, robbery and racketeering are merely the base of a pyramid. Its apex was exposed in the mid-1980s: a nest of gangsters, Party bosses and senior policemen up to their epaulettes in bribery, extortion and awesome swindling at the highest level.

The man who made it all possible was Sharaf Rashidov, for 24 years General Secretary of the Uzbek Communist Party. He presided over massive and routine over-reporting of the Uzbek cotton crop, partly to reach unreachable targets, mainly to line the pockets of everyone involved. An estimated billion tonnes in all was paid for by the central Soviet government but never grown. Some of the revenues oiled the very mechanism by which they were generated, bribing the necessary officials in Moscow. The rest went to Rashidov's inner circle, whom he liked to reward for their loyalty by giving them collective farms, rural districts and in a few cases entire oblasts to run as personal fiefdoms.

One of his most notorious henchmen was Akhmadzhan Adylov, lord of the Gurumsarai cotton combine in the Fergana valley, which he ruled from a granite podium beneath his favourite tree. He retained his own security force to patrol his own borders. He dispensed his own justice, imprisoning and allegedly torturing its victims in an underground gaol. He kept a harem, bred race-horses, claimed to be descended from Tamerlane and had a direct line to his friend the Party General Secretary.

The party came to an abrupt end in 1983. Rashidov died in office and was posthumously disgraced. Thousands who had worked under him were arrested and tried, including the Minister of Internal Affairs (who committed suicide) and Adylov. Such public figures were easily arraigned. More difficult to prove were their suspected links with faceless mafiosi. Moscow-based journalists had taken advantage of *glasnost* to reveal a world of systematic blackmailing, of embezzlers in the bureaucracy, and of tit-for-tat contract killings by rival gangs. But then, as now, no one would testify against them.

There was another problem. Gangs were shown to be active in the other Central Asian republics too, but the whole Pandora's Box became known as 'the Uzbek affair', angering many Uzbeks, who saw it as a pretext being used by Russia to put Russians back in charge of their country.

Fears that this indignation might obstruct a proper clean-up have proved well-founded; since the break-up of the Soviet Union, Rashidov has been rehabilitated as an Uzbek national hero who stood up to Moscow. (Visit his birthplace in Dzhizak; the house with the plaque on Ulitsa Sharafa Rashidova.) And everyone in Tashkent knows that gangs still control most of its 'non-labour' economy.

Moscow has grown wise to inflated production reports (*pripiski*)—but is hungrier than ever for narcotics, which can travel there from anywhere in former Soviet Central Asia without a single customs check.

Tourists, here as anywhere, are vulnerable to petty crime. Thankfully they are unlikely to encounter the organized variety. However, anyone who doubts that heroin poppies are being cultivated as a cash crop should walk for a day up from Madovra village above Pendzhikent in north-west Tajikistan, to Lake Dushakha under Pik Chimtarga. Pick a few heads from the delicate flowers neatly planted on a grassy shelf above the lake. Boil them up, lie down—and begin to sip.

The Islamic Renaissance

Central Asia is a cradle of Islam that squads of Soviet propagandists tried to convert to atheism. Not surprisingly, the aftermath is confused. Islam is now encouraged, but Islamic parties are outlawed. Every Central Asian proudly calls himself *musulmanin*, but few have any but the briefest acquaintance with Muslim theology.

Stories are legion of restaurant parties raising their vodka glasses to the local mosque, but no one has displayed his new-found, skin-deep faith with less shame than the Uzbek President, Islam Karimov. In October 1992 he closed a press conference on the occasion of a state visit to Tashkent by Burhanuddin Rabbani, president of Afghanistan, with the words, 'we must end now because the time for prayer is approaching'. Rabbani, as a leader of the *mujahedin*, played a big part in driving the Soviet army from Afghanistan. Karimov is a life-long Communist who was in power when the Soviet invasion of Afghanistan was launched from Tashkent in 1979.

In Stalin's early years, and later under Khrushchev, mosques were shut down by the thousand, their clergy was purged and Communism tried to offer an alternative to Islam with universities of atheism and a purpose-written genre of anti-Muslim literature.

Between these blitzes, to keep Central Asia on his side in World War II, Stalin had given 'official Islam' a place in Communist society. The Mufti of Tashkent was given an office and a printing press. Here and in Bukhara, madrasas were reopened to provide the few remaining city mosques with clergy. Thus Muslims could say their prayers on Fridays—

but the Mufti knew his place in the Communist hierarchy. On Moscow's orders, he even issued a *fatwa* banning pilgrimage to the Throne of Suleiman in Osh.

The real work of keeping Islam alive was done by Sufis—mystic missionaries of the same Nakshbandi sect, based in Bukhara, that had stirred up the Andizhan revolt against the czarists in 1897 and provided the *basmakhi* movement with many of its leaders five years later. Sufi activity was secret, informal and most significant in rural areas where all mosques had been closed down. Sufi 'adepts' wear the long woollen robes after which their order is named (*suf* being an Arabic word for wool), and usually tie a silk scarf round their waists. You can see them taking tea beside the pool at Lyab-i-Khauz in old Bukhara.

Central Asia's current Islamic revival predates independence. By 1989 the state was sanctioning the reopening of mosques in the Fergana valley in hopes of defusing growing anti-Communist unrest. With the Soviet collapse, successor regimes—and the Americans—feared rampant fundamentalism, hence the outlawing of the Islamic Renaissance Party everywhere except Tajikistan, and the swift appearance of a US embassy in the capital of every republic.

In general, such fears have proved unfounded. Most Central Asian Muslims, including most Tajiks, are Sunnis. Unlike the Shi'ites of Iran and the Ismailis of Badakhshan, they have no religious leaders who claim direct descent from the Prophet Mohammed. Their *imams* merely teach theology and lead them in prayer. The pillars of their creed are nothing more nor less than the five pillars of Islam.

Even these are being remembered slowly and patchily. Mosques tend to be full at midday on Fridays, but few pray five times a day and the *muezzins* prefer not to waste their breath; visitors who know Cairo or Damascus, Istanbul or Marrakesh, will find even Bukhara strangely quiet. The month-long fast of Ramadan is observed by a minority only. The giving of alms to the poor (*namaz*) is not yet widespread, and few can afford the *hadj*, the pilgrimage to Mecca. The easiest pillar to observe is the simple repetition of 'There is no god but Allah, and Mohammed is his prophet,' and this is catching on.

Central Asians will no doubt find their own middle ground between traditional Islamic life and the western mores that most find tempting. In the meantime, their leaders study Turkish and Pakistani ways of keeping religion and politics apart; they are unanimous in rejecting an Iranian-style merger, to the relief of Washington's State Department.

As old mosques are reopened and new ones built, Russian Orthodox congregations survive in colonial-era churches in Dushanbe, Tashkent and Almaty, and many towns have synagogues as well. Some Muslims would like to see them closed, but their governments have pledged to protect religious freedom. Many Jews are not convinced; Dushanbe's synagogue had 20,000 members in 1989, since when half have emigrated. More would follow, says their rabbi, if they could afford the new direct flight from Tashkent to Tel-Aviv.

No disrespect to the four Turkmen women who toiled for three and a half years to produce the world's biggest carpet, still hanging in suburban Ashgabat—but it's a travesty.

It is red, and perfectly symmetrical. So are some of the world's most precious carpets, the classic Tekke Turkmen rugs known misleadingly as Bukharas. But whereas they make exquisite virtues of symmetry and colour, the Ashgabat monstrosity repeats its basic motif so often as to be plain dull, and its red is so deep you almost drown in it.

This slide to Soviet excess began in 1881. The Russian conquest that year of the Tekke, the largest and most warlike Turkmen tribe, marked the beginning of the end of the nomadic culture that for thousands of years had fostered carpet-making as brilliant decorative art. It also, ironically, brought Turkmen carpets for the first time to a wide European audience and an international market. (They were never woven in Bukhara, but most were sold there; hence the misnomer.)

The Turkmens did not invent knotted carpets, but their ancestors may have done. One of the oldest in existence, now in the Hermitage in St Petersburg, was found near Pazyryk in the Altai mountains, where it had been preserved in ice since the 5th century BC. It may have been acquired by Altaic nomads from Persia, but it is also possible that they wove it themselves: curved carpet-making knives have been found in women's graves in former Soviet Central Asia dating from 1400 BC.

What is certain is that when the Turks, and in the 14th century the Turkmens themselves, migrated south across the steppe, they came in tents furnished almost exclusively with carpets. The largest formed the floor. Smaller ones called *ensi*, often with prayer niches in their patterns, served as prayer mats and door flaps. Others weren't carpets at all; called *chuval* or *torba*, they were folded in two and sewn into storage bags hung from the tent frames.

The hallmark of Turkmen weaving appears only on full-size carpets. This is the *göl*. It's basically octagonal, looks a little like an eye, and the significance of its symbolism is the subject of long and learned debate—though it probably has none. It has been called an elephant's

WEAVING THE
TURKMEN DESIGN,
ALSO KNOWN AS
'THE BUKHARA PATTERN'

foot and likened to yurts, flowers and even birds. In the end it's just the *göl*—abstract, austere and mesmerizing.

Traditionally, Turkmen women and girls combed, spun and wove wool from the sheep they travelled with. Shearing and dying it were male jobs. Blue dye, for the lines which join the *göls*, came from India in cakes of indigo. Red came from the root of the widely-cultivated *rubia tinctorum*, fermented in vats of camel urine. So much for raw materials. The skill came in memorizing a complex pattern of up to 4000 knots per 100 square cm, none of which could be undone once cut—a mental feat that has been compared to learning the entire score of a Mozart symphony by heart.

If you stumble on a genuine antique it will be small; five rows of 11 *göls* was the maximum in the first half of the 19th century, when size was still determined by the width of weaving frame that could conveniently be carried on a camel and set up, pegged horizontally to the ground, inside a tent. There will be narrow borders only; three stripes at most round the central 'field'. And—a tiny but deliberate irregularity—there may be a triangular amulet woven into a corner as spiritual protection for those sitting on or round the carpet. Such a carpet could well be a museum piece, so check with a curator before trying to export it.

You can still buy genuine Turkmen rugs and *ensis* in the bazaar at Ashgabat, and the weaving is still done by hand. But most of it happens in carpet factories, not tents, and on steel rather than wooden frames. Bar some unsettling inter-war carpet portraits of Lenin and Stalin, traditional designs still prevail, but they have been codified for mass production, so a girl can be a carpet weaver even if she never learned the *göl* on her mother's knee. The Turkmens love their carpets, though they are now reduced to spreading them and hanging them in boxy two-room flats. Never was architecture so honoured, nor so undeservingly.

The Shrinking Sea

The history of mankind knows no other example where, before the eyes of a single generation of people, an entire sea disappears from the face of the earth.

P. Khabibulaev, President, Uzbek Academy of Sciences

The Aral Sea, the largest body of water between the Caspian and the Pacific, has shrunk by more than half its surface area and by more than two thirds of its volume since 1960. If current levels of water consumption in the Aral basin continue, it will have disappeared altogether by 2020.

Its largest port, Muynak, is now 100km from the shore, haunted by skeletons of fishing boats rusting on dunes on the edge of town. Its waters once supported 24 species of fish but now support none. Its 60,000 fishermen are unemployed, though until the end of the Soviet Union some still worked in the local cannery, canning fish from the Baltic and the

Soviet Far East. The former sea bed is now a salt desert swept by the prevailing north-westerly wind, which dumps between 40 and 150 million tonnes of sand and salt on the precious fertile land of the Amu Darya delta each year.

The destruction of the Aral is one of the world's major environmental disasters. It was avoidable; it was even predicted by those responsible for it. It is easily explained. The Aral has shrunk because the two rivers which fed it, the Amu Darya and the Syr Darya, have been bled to death by cotton irrigation schemes. Stalin decided in the 1920s that the Soviet Union should become self-sufficient in cotton, and that Central Asia should grow it. Cotton was king, the new white gold. Time-honoured traditions of mixed agriculture were thrown out and the oblasts of eastern Uzbekistan and western Tajikistan were forced into a breakneck race to meet the cotton targets of the Five Year Plans. The result: in 1927 the USSR imported 41 per cent of its cotton. In 1933 it imported 2.6 per cent.

Up to this point, the Aral Sea was unaffected, self-sufficiency having been achieved at the expense of other crops. But self-sufficiency was not enough. With exports in mind, the central planners demanded ever higher output. Exisiting irrigation systems in the Fergana valley and the Amu Darya delta were enlarged. In the 1950s and 60s the Kara-Kum canal, which uses 15 per cent of the Amu Darya's flow, was built to bring southern Turk-menistan into the cotton belt, and the level of the Aral Sea began to fall.

Much of the water was and is lost through evaporation and seepage; irrigation channels are unlined and open to the thirsty Central Asian sun, which anyway vaporizes 60 cubic km of the Aral Sea each year. (The sea has no outflow; this was how its level was natu-rally maintained.) Nothing was done to reduce this waste. On the contrary, through the 1960s and 70s it increased exponentially as hundreds of reservoirs were built, mainly in Uzbekistan, for municipal water supply, electricity, fish and recreation.

Meanwhile, Central Asia's soaring cotton production, over the long term, was spectac-ular: between 1913 and 1963, in Uzbekistan alone, acreage sown to cotton quadrupled to 4.1 million acres, and the yield doubled. The sacrifice of the Aral Sea seemed a reasonable trade-off.

Not for long. Scientists had predicted that the sea-bed would form a hard, stable crust. In fact it stayed as sand, and the people of Muynak now get sandstorms and respiratory dis-eases instead of sea breezes. Worse still, water taken from the rivers for the cotton fields is poisoned by pesticides and chemical fertilizers. Some of it evaporates, falling eventually as poisoned rain. Some is channelled into sterile reservoirs (like Lake Sarykamish, west of Dashkhovuz), which grow as the Aral shrinks. Some flows back into the rivers, poisoning them and what remains of the Aral Sea. The rest trickles down to the water table, poi-soning it and causing it to rise. In the cotton-producing areas, stomach and liver cancer rates are markedly higher than average, and much land that was naturally fertile before being turned over to cotton is now barren.

A plan to divert water from the Ob and Irtysh rivers over the steppe from Siberia in a 1600-km canal to refill the Aral was dropped for good, after 20 years of politburo wrangling, in 1986. This, like the problem the plan was meant to solve, was interpreted in Central Asia as a victory for Russian nationalism.

The Soviet collapse has left a solution to the Aral crisis further than ever from view. It now affects three independent countries which cannot agree on what to do and, even if they could, would not be able to fund a rescue programme. Turkmenistan depends for its very existence on the Kara-Kum canal. Uzbekistan cannot afford to reduce its cotton cultivation significantly. All the former Soviet Central Asian states need ever more water for their fast-growing populations.

In Nukus, the largest town in the Amu Darya delta and capital of the autonomous region of Karakalpakstan, a tiny band of activists campaigns for the mute and disappearing Aral. Their leader is a melon-shaped wind-power engineer who invents things in his spare time. He admits that, on present reckonings, he has about as much chance of saving the Aral Sea as he does of pioneering man-powered 'floppy' flight—his other cherished ambition.

Yurts

They look like a cross between a mountain and a mushroom. They are soft and cuddly, being made of felt and having no sharp edges. They protect their owner from the sun in summer and the snow in winter. Their design has not changed for millennia, and they are still used on the lonely pastures of the Tian Shan and the steppe. Yurts, said the escaped World War I POW—and occasional yurt-dweller—Gustav Krist, are 'unquestionably one of the greatest inventions Asia has brough forth.'

The yurt is a round felt tent on a wooden frame, preferred by Kyrgyz and Kazakh nomads to the European-style canvas tent for the most practical of reasons; it lasts longer and excludes the elements more completely. In both countries it is also something of a national symbol.

A yurt takes 25 days to make and lasts 25 years. Its vertical wall (*kerege*) forms a drum roughly eight metres across and as high as a stooping herdsman. Made of painted wooden slats lashed diagonally into a lattice, it contains not a single nail. More slats (*uuk*) slope up to a cartwheel-sized birch hoop (*tunduk*) which serves as both chimney and skylight. Thick white felts clad the outside of expensive yurts (which in Soviet times used to cost as much as a Lada); grey ones are used for cheaper models.

The inside of a yurt is a riot of colour. Here the owner displays his true wealth, and his womenfolk their decorative skills. Facing in from behind the *kerege* are patterned reed mats called *chij*. The more sumptuous yurts have felt rugs (*shyrdak*) to line their roofs, and all are held together with tough strips of woven wool called *boo*, which come in several widths. The narrowest of these attach the *uuk* to the *tunduk*. The next-widest tie together the slats of the *kerege*; the next hold down the outside felts; the widest and most gorgeously-patterned describe great arcs across the inside of the roof for no other purpose than to dazzle.

The key to warmth and comfort is the floor. The bottom layer is *chij*—reed matting. On this, in winter, functional grey felts are laid to create a layer of insulation up to several centimetres thick. On top lie yet more felts; either *shyrdak* rugs, whose patterns are sewn on, or *ala-kijiz*, in which the designs are rolled out with the felt itself. The Kyrgyz always sleep on felt. They maintain, according to Krist, 'that neither the giant spider nor the scorpion will venture to set foot on it'.

There are certain constants about the inside of a yurt. Rugs and quilts used for sleeping are folded and stacked at the back every morning. Men sit and hang their riding tackle on the left; women sit and store their work-in-progress on the right. Guests of honour sit between them, protected from the draughty doorway by the fire. This is where a foreigner caught loitering near a yurt encampment is sure to be installed and put to shame by Kyrgyz hospitality.

Yurts survive as the main form of summer shelter round Lake Son-Kul and along the roads from Kara-Kol to Inylchek and Bishkek to Toktogul. In museums they look faintly ludicrous. In their element they make you wonder why you ever needed bricks and mortar.

Turkmenistan Туркменистан

Most of Turkmenistan looks only marginally more suited to human habitation than the moon. Still, 3.5 million people live in this southernmost, hottest, dryest and harshest of the former Soviet republics. Their lifeline is the world's longest irrigation canal, which stretches 1100km west from the Amu Darya river across the Kara-Kum desert, continuing to the Caspian coast by piped extension. Turkmenistan provides an austere introduction to Central Asia, leavened by a hot underground swimming pool at Bacharden and the ruins of the 12th-century Seljuk capital at Merv; by Turkmen 'Bukhara' rugs in Ashgabat's bazaar and, if you get the timing right, by a desert in dazzling bloom. But timing is critical. In winter, snow comes down almost to Ashgabat, the low-rise, low-interest capital at the foot of the Kopet Dagh mountains which form the Iranian border. In summer, on a car roof in the desert, you can fry an egg in two minutes and a chicken breast in five. The time to go is in spring, when the desert flowers, or autumn, when melons reach the markets. Just don't try it in summer.

One startling year-round sight is the giant, shaggy hat worn by old men of the dominant Turkmen tribe, the Tekke. Their ancestors were famous for horse-breeding and carpet-making, and notorious for slave-raids on desert caravans. Descended from the so-called Black Sheep and White Sheep Tartars of the Altai, they did not invade what was to become their homeland until the late 14th century. This thirsty part of the world was hardly rich or populous, and only twice had it dominated Central Asia: under the Parthians from the 2nd century BC to the 3rd AD, and under the Seljuks in the 12th. Otherwise, the Kara-Kum and its oases remained an almost empty annexe of neighbouring powers, crossed only

N

200 km
100 miles

UZBEKISTAN

Nukus

Kunya Urgench
Lake
Sarykamish

Dashkhovuz

Khiva

Amu Darya

MENISTAN

Bukhara

Chardzhou

Repetek

Transcaspian Railway

Amu Darya

Kara-Kum Desert

Geok-
Tepe

ASHGABAT

Anau

Firyuza

Tedzhen

Mary

Bairam Ali

Kara-Kum Canal

Dagh

IRAN

Sarakhs

Murgab

Meshed

AFGHANISTAN

by Silk Route caravans—a traffic interrupted in 1221 when the Mongols destroyed Merv. When the Turkmens arrived a century later, they had to compete with aggressive rivals for control of the oases. Hemmed in by hostile neighbours—Persians, Khivans and Sheibanid Bukharans— the Turkmens eventually had no choice but to seek protection from Russia. In 1791 they made a supposed 'oath of allegiance' to the czar, but the Tekke were only really brought to heel by massive Russian force at Geok-Tepe in 1881.

The Soviets did not take control of Ashgabat until 1920, and only then because the British decided that Turkmenistan was not worth fighting for. The landmark events of the Soviet decades were the 1948 earthquake that flattened Ashgabat, the arrival of the Kara-Kum Canal on its outskirts in 1962, and the discovery of prodigious natural gas reserves at Shatlik ('Joy'), near Mary, which may yet make Turkmenistan rich. Since independence, Turkmenistan has made few appearances in western newspapers. One was when President Saparmurad Niyazov gave John Major a horse on the occasion of his visit to London in March 1993. But this low profile does not reflect the interest Turkmenistan has attracted from other nations. Turkey, Iran and Saudi Arabia vie for attention through mosque building and business interests. Russia is anxious about the direction of pipelines. The Europeans provide technical know-how and watch and wait.

In one important respect, the 20th century changed little. The Tekke never lost sight of their nomadic past, and clans, not cities, have remained the key to power. Since independence, the Tekke have consolidated their stranglehold on power in Ashgabat and don't bother to pay even lip-service to a 'transition to democracy'. Styling himself Turkmenbashy, President Niyazov has created six free economic zones to attract foreign investment, and his Ten Year Development Plan has pledged a new Mercedes to every Turkmen family. But no attempt has been made to dismantle his one-party state. The press remains censored. The leaders of the opposition movement *Agzybirlik* were put under house arrest during James Baker's visit in 1992 and a small protest in August 1995 was quickly and quietly squashed.

Turkmenistan sits rather aloof from the other republics, having chosen not to affiliate itself to any regional grouping. Relations with neighbouring Uzbekistan are influenced as much by the Amu Darya's precious water supply as by the considerations of high politics. And Turkmenistan was the first Central Asian state to join the Nato-sponsored 'Partnership for Peace'.

Meanwhile the Yomud tribe dominates the north and west, from Turkmenbashy and Nebit Dag to Tashauz, and the Ersary hold the southeastern oases on the Murgab river near Afghanistan.

All Turkmen share an 'immense superiority complex', says Alexandre Bennigsen. He probably exaggerates, but at the festival of Bayram in early June, Turkmen women bring the streets of Ashgabat to life simply by walking down them, tall and supremely elegant in full-length irridescent silk.

Krasnovodsk [now Turkmenbashy] *is one of the hottest, most desert and miserable places in the world. The mountains are dead; there is no water in them. Rain scarcely ever falls, and the earth is only sand and salt.*

Stephen Graham, *Through Russian Central Asia,* 1916

Fresh water has become more abundant since Graham's visit thanks to the Kara-Kum Canal, but there is still something strangely lunar about this quiet, lonely town, which calls itself the 'gateway to Central Asia', stuck on the end of a railway by a stagnant sea. Turkmenbashy, formerly Krasnovodsk, was founded as a Russian garrison in 1869 by General Skobelev, and named after the cliffs that rise behind its fine natural harbour and hide the desert from incoming boats. Compared to the Black Sea resorts and the spas of the northern Caucasus, this cannot have been a popular military posting. But it was an important one, for it was (and is) the western terminus of the Transcaspian railway, built by the Russian army in the 1870s and 1880s to consolidate their hold on the region. In 1918 the railway became the focus of a bizarre sideshow of the Russian Civil War, when Turkmen counter-revolutionaries were briefly helped by British troops from northern Iran.

The Transcaspian remained a military railway, only opening to foreigners after the collapse of the Soviet Union, and Turkmenbashy preserved the atmosphere of a garrison town. During World War II it became a place of exile for the first president of independent Lithuania, banished here by Stalin in 1942, and a few thousand Japanese POWs. Nowadays it is indeed a gateway to Central Asia, for Azerbaijanis seeking to do business with their Turkic brothers across the Caspian, for oil from Baku, and for a very few foreign tourists.

Getting to and from Turkmenbashy

by air

There's one flight a week to Moscow and two a day to Ashgabat with a possiblity of a third on Sundays. Regular flights also go to Dashkhovuz and Mineralniye Vody in Russia. At present there is no regular flight to Baku (Azerbaijan).

by sea

Ocean-going ferries with cabins and car-decks arrive from Baku in theory every day. Three rust-streaked stalwarts work the route; the *Azerbaijan*, the *Turkmenistan* and the *Kyrgyzia*, each with the word 'Soviet' painted out. If one breaks down the frequency falls to three crossings a week at best. And often the ferries will depart only when full; you might arrive in good time to find yourself in for a very long wait. The crossing takes 14 hours and costs a few dollars for a cabin. (For the Baku end, *see* p.7.)

The station is a cheap 5-minute taxi ride from the port. Trains leave for Ashgabat twice a day and take 12 hours. Their closed compartments can turn into ovens in daytime in summer. Travelling at night is cooler and the view that you miss is unrivalled only for bleakness.

A Stroll Around Town

Turkmenbashy has two **museums**, both west of the station down Ulitsa Rilova, beyond a huge hoarding celebrating the doubtful 'fact' that 68 different nationalities cohabit in this town of 60,000. The **museum of history and natural history** in the old Russian fort has a better-than-average collection of stuffed animals, including a bearded eagle of which there are thought to be only 15 pairs left in the country, Turkmen jewellery and costume, and a black yurt, known locally as a Kara-Oi ('black house'). There is also a painting of the 1714 meeting between Peter the Great and a Turkmen ambassador, at which Russia was apparently granted a gold-mining concession in return for protecting the western Turkmen tribes. Soviet historians were keen to play up any hint that Central Asians actually invited Russian—even czarist Russian—help.

The **26 Baku Commissars' museum**, a block towards the sea from here, commemorates a batch of prominent Bolsheviks abducted from Baku and killed in the desert in 1918. A British agent, Captain Reginald Teague-Jones, was active in Transcaspia at the time, trying to prevent the Central Asian cotton crop reaching the Eastern Front. Accused by Moscow of murdering the commissars, he became a target for the Cheka and disappeared without trace. His extraordinary story was only told after his death in 1988, in his posthumously-published autobiography *The Spy Who Disappeared*. Meanwhile the 26 Baku Commissars became a major Soviet cult. Their museum has been turned into a non-ideological history museum. Peter Hopkirk's book *Setting the East Ablaze*, which rubbished the Soviet version of how the commissars died, was already, in 1992, a prized exhibit in a glass cabinet beneath a Soviet painting of Reginald Teague-Jones giving orders to a firing squad.

Turkmenbashy (℡ 43222–)   ***Where to Stay and Eating Out***

The station **Turkmenbashy** hotel restaurant may be sickeningly pink but serves good, workmanlike *plov* and *laghman*.; it has lost its monopoly since the arrival of the **Awaza Hotel**, ℡ 1 76 05. This small waterfront hotel, 25 minutes out of town to the west, built by a Turkish company, has 15 to 20 rooms. It has had problems with its water supply but its facilities include a sauna and a reasonable restaurant with indifferent service. Take a taxi from the airport and be prepared to pay for your room in dollars ($100).

There are monuments to the 26 Baku Commissars all over the former Soviet Union, now in varying stages of neglect and dismantlement, but their holiest shrine is where they died, three hours east of Turkmenbashy by train, then 26km south into the desert from Nebit Dag, along a specially built road.

The train also stops at Bacharden, 98km before Ashgabat. This place is famous for its hot springs. You can walk into a cave at the foot of the Kopet Dagh mountains, down 60 metres' worth of steps, and swim in sulphurous water at 35°C, which invigorates even more than it smells. Intourist charges to bring you here from Ashgabat, so you might as well get out of the train.

At Geok-Tepe, 40km before Ashgabat, a Russian force under General Lomakin was routed by the Tekke in 1879. The Great Game was then at its height. Britain was watching Russia's every move in Asia, and the czar was humiliated.

The following year a new expedition led by General Skobelev, a ruthless veteran of the recent Russo-Turkish war, set out to crush the Tekke once and for all. Skobelev had 11,000 men, 100 cannons and a personal message from the czar:

MAGTUMGULY
MONUMENT,
ASHGABAT

'Under no circumstances may the fixed plan be departed from, nor the least backward step be taken, for this would be for Europe and Asia a sign of our weakness, would inspire still greater boldness on the part of our adversaries, and might cost Russia infinitely more than the whole expedition.'

After nearly a month of bloody preliminary engagements, Skobelev's sappers, using a tonne of gunpowder, blasted a breach in the ramparts of the Geok-Tepe fortress. The Tekke's last stronghold was stormed on 24 January 1881. Skobelev reported 14,500 enemy losses, but observers put the figure closer to 20,000. Indistinct mounds of earth are all that remain of the fortress today.

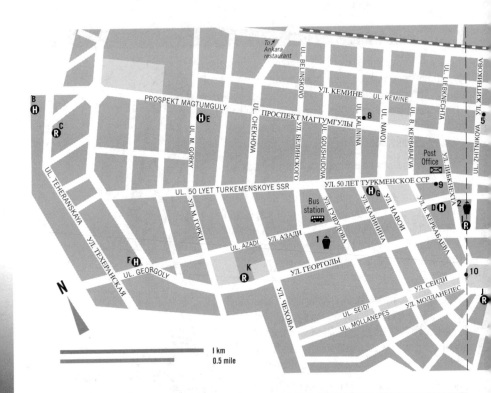

Ashgabat (Ашгабат)

Some think Ashgabat the hardest Central Asian capital to fall in love with and the easiest to pity. The undisputedly good things about it are the Sunday market, probably the best place in the world to buy 'Bukhara' rugs, and the virtual absence of Soviet high-rise blocks of flats because of earthquake danger. But Ashgabat has little to show for its history, which is anyway short. There may be little of architectural interest except to students of small-scale Socialist realism in reinforced concrete, but what there is has been given a face-lift; repainted last Independence Day on Niyazov's order.

North of the city there is a desert of fearsome reputation. South of it there is a range of rugged mountains with barbed wire border fences to prevent you going near them. And off the road leading back into Ashgabat, is the president's new 'pink passion palace'.

A few years ago you would have found yourself gravitating gratefully towards the colour and light of the Benetton shop (for which Ashgabat was unique in Central Asia) on Ulitsa Azadi (formerly Ulitsa Engelsa). Today, thanks to the economic benefits of huge natural gas reserves, or at least the belief in their potential to make Turkmenistan another Kuwait, the number of interested parties is on the increase and so are the hotels and restaurants. But seeing is believing, if not comprehending: cruise along 'the strip', Ash-

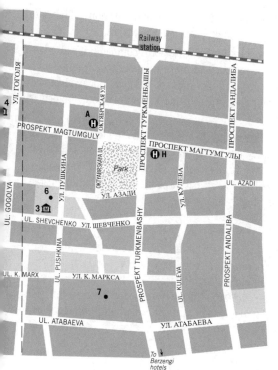

KEY

1 Tikinsky bazaar
  Тикинский Базар
2 Russian bazaar
  Русский Базар
3 History Museum
  Музей Истории
4 Fine Art Museum
  Музей Изобразительных Искусств
5 Magtumguly Monument
  Памятник Магтумгулы
6 Lenin statue
  Памятник Ленину
7 Presidential Palace
  Ресиденция Президента
8 Iran stores
  Магазины Иран
9 Opera and Ballet Theatre
  Театр Оперы и Балета
10 Free Shop

HOTELS & RESTAURANTS

A Hotel Ashgabat
  Гостиница Ашхабад
B Hotel Yubileynaya
  Гостиница Юбилейная
C Restaurant Aini
  Ресторан Аини
D Grand Turkmen
  Гостиница Большой
  Туркмен
E Ak Altyn
  Ак Алтын
F Turist
  Турист

G Daikhan
  Даихан
H Oktyabrskaya
  Октябрская
I Florida
  Флорида
J Destan
  Дестан
K Dipservis
  Дипсэрвис

gabat's tourist attraction. In the upmarket Berzengi suburb this line of twenty-odd palatial hotels, largely unoccupied, is at its most stunning when illuminated at night.

Ashgabat was founded as a Russian garrison town three days after the killing of 20,000 Turkmens at nearby Geok-Tepe in 1881, and was hit by earthquakes in 1893, 1895 and 1929 before the Big One. The 1948 disaster measured 9 on the Richter scale, killed 110,000 and levelled almost the entire city. The new capital of Turkmenistan, population 400,000, is quiet, clean and well-shaded.

Getting to and from Ashgabat

The Iranian border post on the Meshed road is open for those with visas. An agreement in principle to build a Meshed–Ashgabat railway was signed in 1989 and should be completed in May 1996. It will link Europe to Asia by rail; from the Continent to Iran via Istanbul and the Caspian.

by air

At least one of the two daily flights from Moscow (3 hours) comes via Turkmenbashy. Ticket cost is $300 and can be paid for with a credit card. There are five daily flights to Mary and Dashkhovuz and daily ones to Tashkent (90 minutes). Baku flights (2 hours) leave on Thursdays and Saturdays, flights to Samarkand on Thursdays. To fly to Bishkek, change at Chardzhou.

The airport is modern and new, a joint project with a UK company. It's also surprisingly close to the city centre. A taxi, and there are many waiting for you, should cost no more than a few dollars. Offer the fare in manat (local currency) for better value. There's a helpful information desk, where some English is spoken, on the departures level.

To buy tickets foreigners have to go to the old airport. Go to the left-hand side of the modern, one-storey building where a sign says 'international booking office' (*open daily 9am–8pm with breaks from 11.45 to 12 noon, 2 to 3pm and 5 to 6pm*). The Aeroflot office in the Hotel Ashgabat has gone and the Turkmenistan Airways office on Prospekt Magtumguly does not serve foreigners.

by rail

Trains arrive twice a day from Turkmenbashy, and go once a day to and from Dashkhovuz and Chardzhou. There are no trains to Moscow. For Tashkent and Dushanbe, change at Chardzhou which is strategically the more important station. Ashgabat station is central; to reach it from Hotel Ashgabat turn left and walk one block on Prospekt Magtumguly then turn left again onto Prospekt Turkmenbashy (formerly Lenina) and walk two blocks into the city.

by bus

Turkmenistan's buses operate mostly within the republic. There are no regular long-distance services that cross into Uzbekistan. Closer to home, four go daily to Mary (350 manat for the state-run option; 800 for the private). Chardzou buses are intermittent and, strangely, there are no scheduled state buses that make the trip across the desert to Dashkhovuz. They do, however, come from Dashkhovuz and there is the occasional bus to Kunya Urgench from Ashgabat. The bus station is on Ulitsas Azadi (formerly Engelsa) and Gushudova (formerly Shaumyana), opposite the Tikinsky bazaar. You can also find here a number of private buses, which cost more and only go when full, but are worth checking out.

Getting Around

Between and beside the parallel streets, Magtumguly and Georgoly, are the majority of hotels, museums and parks. Trolleybuses 1 and 2 go along Magtumguly. Bus 10 deals with Georgoly and Shevchenko.

Tourist Information

Intourist's office is on the third floor of the Hotel Ashgabat, 74 Magtumguly, © 39 00 26. Its deputy chairman is helpful; if in need of an English-speaking guide, you should ask for Rodik.

Iran Air: Prospekt Magtumguly 73, ✆ 51 06 41/42, flies to Tehran once weekly, on Sundays.

PIA: Prospekt Magtumguly 73, ✆ 51 08 98/51 18 38. PIA's weekly international flights all go via Karachi.

Turkish Airways: Prospekt Magtumguly 71, ✆ 51 16 66/51 06 66. Four flights per week go from Ashgabat to Istanbul with international connections.

Locations are in a state of flux as more permanent accommodation is found.

Afghanistan: Hotel Kolkhozchi, Ulitsa Azadi 13, ✆ 25 70 87/25 74 35

China: Ulitsa Razina 2, ✆ 47 36 83/47 46 76

Germany: Ak Altyn Hotel, Prospekt Magtumguly, ✆ 24 49 11/51 21 44, ✉ 51 09 23

Iran: Ulitsa Teheranskaya, opposite Hotel Yubileynaya, ✆ 24 97 07/24 14 42

Kyrgyzstan: Prospekt Turkmenbashy 1, ✆ 46 88 04

Pakistan: Ulitsa Kemine 92, ✆ 51 23 88/ 51 23 17, ✉ 51 23 04

Russia: Prospekt Turkmenbashy 11, ✆ 25 39 57/29 15 05, ✉ 29 84 66

Tajikistan: Prospekt Turkmenbashy 13, ✆ 25 13 74/29 61 59

Turkey: Ulitsa Shevchenko 9, ✆ 25 55 95/25 41 18, ✉ 51 08 94/25 55 95

UK: ABC Business Centre, Berzengi, ✆ 52 01 12

USA: Ulitsa Pushkina 9, ✆ 35 00 45, 51 13 06, ✉ 51 13 05, 25 53 79

Uzbekistan: Hotel Yubileynaya, Ulitsa Teheranskaya, ✆ 24 47 71

In the Centre of Ashgabat

The **History Museum** (**Музей Истории**/*Muzey istorii*), Ulitsa Shevchenko 1 (*open 10–5.45; closed Tues*), contains stone fragments sharpened by man 200,000 years ago, and 17 of a cache of 40 priceless 2nd- and 1st-century BC carved ivory horns (*rhytons*) from Nisa. Used by the Parthians as water vessels in Zoroastrian rituals, their decoration betrays the cultural impact of the Greek invasion two centuries earlier; the sculpted figures at their pointed ends are centaurs, winged horses, lions and griffins, while the engraved scenes at the wide ends are based on the cult of Dionysius. The exhibits are interesting, not only to ancient history enthusiasts, and well-presented. Ask for Tatiana as your guide and then visit Old Nisa.

All paths in the park behind the museum lead to an unusual **statue of Lenin** whose pedestal is clad in a ceramic version of a Turkmen rug. This statue seems destined to stay—and for that reason is quite a rarity in these independent republics. Soviet icons meet Turkmen decorative art again in the **Fine Art Museum (Музей Изобразительных Искусств**/*Muzey izobrazitelnykh iskusstv*), Prospekt Magtumguly 84 (*open 10–6; closed Tues*). Sinister 1930s carpet portraits of Lenin and Stalin were billed in 1992 as a temporary exhibition, but remain amid the jewellery and paintings of Russians challenged by Turkmen warriors. Next to the art museum in a tree-lined square is the Magtumguly monument. The world's biggest Turkmen carpet still hangs in the **Carpet Museum (Музей Коврей**/*Muzey Kovrey*), Ulitsa Georgoly 5, opposite the Florida restaurant. *Open daily except Mon, 10–6pm; closed 1–2pm; adm. 2500 manat.* If you come at ten, noon, two or four, a guided tour of the museum is included in your ticket price. The carpet is 80m long, 10 wide, took four women three and a half years to make and is displayed folded in two.

CARPET BAZAAR
ASHGABAT

Neither of the two central bazaars (the 'Russian' one on Ulitsas Azadi and Zhitnikova and the Tikinsky bazaar five blocks west) compares with those of Uzbekistan for bustle or exoticism. But the sprawling **Sunday market**, held beyond the **Kara-Kum Canal** on the edge of the desert at Tolychka, more than compensates. Camels, sheep, cattle, motorbikes, and half-tracks which fell off the back of an army base are sold outside a large walled enclosure. Inside is a riot of colour and haggling which cannot have changed much since the Russians arrived in 1881. Buses leave from the town centre two blocks east of the Hotel Ashgabat. Turkmen women in acres of silk sell acres more, old men in suffocating hats sell suffocating hats (and resent having their picture taken), and younger men, more alert because the stakes are higher, sell **carpets**. There are antique as well as new ones. All represent hundreds of hours of work at the very least—work done exclusively by women. The selection is far wider and the prices far lower than anywhere else in Central Asia. Most carpets sold to tourists in Bukhara, Samarkand and Tashkent come from here. Serious carpet-buyers should not waste time elswhere. And be prepared to get permission to take the carpet home. Bags are more stringently checked at Ashgabat airport than any other in Central Asia. Another weekend event well worth investigating is the **horse racing** at the Hippodrome. Here the famed Akhal Teke horses race with riders as young as eight years old. Entrance is free and while there's no official gambling, a crowd of boys lurk near the commentary box offering odds for small bets. The **Circus** next to the Ak Altyn Hotel is host to the occassional show, mostly on holidays. At Ulitsa Azadi 9, the **Opera and Ballet Theatre** (**Театр оперы и балета**/ *teatr opery i balyeta*) provides a cultural evening for 20 cents and the **gallery** next door shows works by local artists (*open Mon–Fri 10am–8pm*).

Around Ashgabat

Old Nisa

Slightly above Ashgabat, nearer the mountains and 15km to the west are the ruins of **Old Nisa**, seat of the Parthian kings from the late 3rd century BC to the early 3rd century AD. At the height of its power Nisa was capital of an empire stretching west as far as Iraq and Syria. Having wrested Transoxiana from the Seleucids, the Parthians also ruled Persia, on which, in a gesture of magnificent *hauteur*, Nisa's back is turned. Old Nisa was the citadel, comprising royal palaces, temples and tombs, though the single excavated level of clay-walled rooms and passages will mean little to non-specialists. Even less has been excavated of New Nisa, a nearby town which survived until the Middle Ages—though its defensive wall is known to have been ten metres thick at the base. But the site is rather grand, looking out over the desert from a natural veranda backed by green mountains. A 90-minute Intourist excursion for one person with car, driver and guide is $12. The entrance fee is $3. Or you can offer a taxi driver $5–10.

Anau

For the same price Intourist goes to **Anau**, 12km east of Ashgabat, where the ruins of a 15th-century Timurid mosque, mausoleum and *chai-khana* are merely the youngest traces of a very ancient settlement; Anau was inhabited from the late Stone Age (4th millenium BC) and when first studied in 1904–5 was thought to be the site of the world's oldest farming culture—a theory later disproved. The 1948 earthquake left little standing.

The Firyuza Gorge

The closest you can get to the Kopet Dagh mountains without an Iranian visa is the Firyuza Gorge, a former royal hunting preserve which snakes through the foothills not far west of Nisa. Come here to cool off. Buses marked Firyuza go from the bus station on Ulitsas Azadi and Gushudova. An Intourist trip here can be arranged. As you come back into Ashgabat, ask your driver to take the road from which you can see the new presidential palace, known as the 'pink passion palace'. The **hot springs** and cave at the foot of the Kopet Dagh are at **Bacharden**, 98km away from Ashgabat.

Intourist also offers trips to one of Ashgabat's nine carpet factories ($5), and a three-hour excursion into the desert via the Kara-Kum Canal ($12). These are probably the best prices for Intourist trips in the whole of Central Asia. **Volodia Bahaz** works for an excellent private company that organizes international and local tours. Call him for information on Ashgabat offers: ✆ 25 70 91.

expensive

Those on expense accounts will enjoy the two multi-facilitied 'western' hotels: **Ak Altyn**, on Prospekt Magtumguly close to the Circus building, ℗ 51 21 81, ✐ 51 21 77/79, offers rooms starting at $150 for a single room, $180 a double, and includes a health club, two swimming pools—in summer the outdoor one is open to non-residents (*adm $8*)—and a business centre.

The more central **Grand Turkmen**, Ulitsa Georgoly 7, ℗ 51 20 50, ✐ 51 20 48, has rooms for $120 a single, $140 a double. Up the illuminated stairs by the fountain is the souvenir shop (*open 11am–9pm daily except Sun; dollars only accepted*). Medical help is available from the doctor at the Ak Altyn and recommended, if necessary, rather than a trip to the hospital. To sample the splendours of Berzengi, book a stay at the Italian-owned **Independent Hotel**, ℗ 52 00 02, ✐ 52 00 01; here, a single costs $120, a suite $200.

Closer to the centre at Prospekt Magtumguly 74, the **Hotel Ashgabat**, ℗ 35 70 65, is rather emptier than it used to be. Rooms cost $53 for a single and $86 a double, reduced by $3 and $6 respectively after the first night. There's a currency exchange till in the lobby.

At the west end of Magtumguly and Ulitsa Teheranskaya, the **Hotel Yubileynaya** will take foreigners for a few nights only and not at all while government guests are staying. If you don't manage to book in here, it's no great loss. If you do, pay in manat (the equivalent of $60 single and $100 double).

moderate

For air-conditioning and a room with a bathroom, the state-run **Turist**, Ulitsa Georgoly 60a, ℗ 24 41 19, will charge $20. From here buses 10 and 6 go to the city centre and the Russian market, where you can change to number 22 or 18 for the airport. The **Daikhan**, on the corner of Ulitsas Azari and Navoi, ℗ 25 30 78, and close to the Russian market and Carpet Museum, is a recently renovated and more affordable alternative to the nearby Grand Turkmen. For reservations, call ℗ 25 56 72; a single costs $25, a double $50.

inexpensive

The hotel with the greatest range in price and type of room, and that takes foreigners, is the **Oktyabrskaya**, Prospekt Magtumguly 67, on the corner of Turkmenbashy, ℗ 25 65 28. All rooms are air-conditioned, payable in dollars, manats or rubles and go from $5 per person in a room for six to $15 a single, $25 a double. From here, you can take bus 18 to the airport.

For rock-bottom budgets and steady nerves, Ulitsa Gushudova 106 (former Shaumyana), about 1.5km south of Tikinsky bazaar, charges $5 per night including a hot bath and cooking facilities. This address is also home to a **psychiatric institution** (for harmless patients) which rents out bed space in dormitories for pocket money. This is legal and guests do not share accommodation with the patients.

Ashgabat (© 3622–)   *Eating Out*

expensive

At the top of the price scale are the restaurants at the **Grand Turkmen** and the **Ak Altyn**. The European–Turkish menu of the latter is generally acknowledged as the best in town and costs $30–40 dollars a head.

The **Independent**'s restaurant comes a close second in quality but, being in Berzengi, the hotel is not as central.

moderate–inexpensive

The various restaurants in Ashgabat offer meals at more affordable prices than the hotels. The **Turkish Patisserie** is an incongruous venue grafted on to the Ashgabat landscape, facing the park at the corner of Ulitsas Georgoly and Navoi. It's not empty despite its prices: a gâteau costs $15 and a coke over $2. The **Aini**, 13 Teheranskaya, © 24 32 58, is definitely worth a try; the staff are much friendlier than at the Yubileynaya opposite, dinner costs, on average, $10 per person and reservations are essential.

Probably the best value is the **Ankara**, Ulitsa Gagarina 11, © 24 97 98. Here you will pay $2–4 for the 'Turkish kebab' menu; pizza and salads with beer is around $1. Try the circular **Destan** too, Ulitsa K. Marxa (*shashlyk* $1–2); it's sunk beside the largest library in Central Asia and surmounted by an aerodynamic-looking metal sculpture. *Open 12–12.* Both the Lebanese **Dipservis** restaurant, Ulitsa Georgoly 48, © 24 34 32 ($4–6), and the **Florida** restaurant/bar/casino, diagonally opposite the Grand Turkmen on Georgoly, are just slightly more expensive. The menu at the Florida restaurant ranges from a $6 salad to a portion of king-size prawns for $40. Those bemoaning the scarcity of cheese can try the $7 'cheese platter'. *Open 12 noon–12.30am.* Beyond the fruit machines is the bar, which provides beer and a sandwich for $5 during happy hour and even fish and chips; come here to meet the ex-pat community. Payment in the bar and restaurant is with hard currency only. The casino is open until 5–6am. In 1996 the owner plans to open a so-called 'British Pub' with draft beer. Next door, the same management run a fast food café with bright yellow tables, where young Turkmen children hover hopefully, mesmerized by plastic pictures of oozing burgers. All these novelties are way beyond their pocket (coffee under 50 cents, a basic burger around $1 and a pizza in the region of $2). The place is busy and with all the trappings of fast food including, so far, enthusiastic service. *Open 8–10pm.*

For a budget lunch, head for the **chai-khana** behind the Ministry of Agriculture, on the corner of Ulitsa Shevchenko and Prospekt Turkmenbashy; enter through the black gates at the side. There are various other *chai-khanas* in the parks.

Provisions

It's worth bringing some supplies with you. In Ashgabat you'll find certain provisions, bread and mineral water in particular, harder to track down than in the other republics. Purchase cheap drinks from the kiosks at the Russian market but go to the Tikinsky bazaar, opposite the bus station, for fresh produce. The two Iran stores, one on Magtumguly (close to the junction with Navoi) and the other on Navoi (between Azadi and Marpro), are easily spotted at night because of their neon lights. Here you can stock up on imported goods from mineral water and biscuits to cosmetics and wedding dresses. *Open daily 9.30–6.30; closed 1.30–3.* The Free Shop, opposite the intersection of Seidi and Kerbabaeva, has a similar range; more western goods at virtually western prices. Bread queues are probably the best way of spotting the cunningly concealed bakeries; there's one opposite the Hotel Ashgabat, to the right of the parade of shops that includes the Turkish Airways office.

Nightlife

Take your own vodka to the **pitseria** in the park diagonally opposite the Hotel Ashgabat, and dance. Or go grooving at the Florida and Grand Turkmen **discos**.

Sarakhs (Capaxc)

Patches of thick woodland around Tedzhen, three hours east of Ashgabat by bus, hint at how the oases of the southern Kara-Kum must once have been; but here and at Mary cotton plantations and concrete irrigation canals have virtually taken over.

Don't break your journey in Tedzhen unless you want to visit **Sarakhs**, 90km south on the upper Tedzhen river. A kilometre from its twin of the same name over the Iranian border, Sarakhs flourished as a Silk Route oasis until the Mongols destroyed all of it bar the 11th-century **Abul Fazl mausoleum**, now restored.

The Arabs brought wealth and prominence to Sarakhs in the 8th century by establishing a southern branch of the Silk Route which passed through it on its way from Nishapur and central Persia to Merv. Al-Fadl ben Sahl, a famous vizier of the Abbasid Caliph of Baghdad al-Ma'mun, was born here and, in 819, was murdered here in his bath. Exactly eleven centuries later Colonel F. M. Bailey nearly perished at Sarakhs in a border skirmish with Red Guards only yards from the safety of British-controlled Iran after his epic flight across the desert from Bukhara.

The mausoleum of Abul Fazl, a Sufi mystic who died in 1023, was built by the architect also responsible for the Sultan Sanjar mausoleum in Merv, and stands 3km south of modern Sarakhs beside an unexcavated mound which was the shahristan or citadel. It is a holy place. Ask the mullah under the nearby awning before going inside. Muslims touch the cenotaph three times, wipe their faces, walk out backwards and require silence. The tomb itself is 8m under the floor.

About 10km further south, near a reservoir used for swimming, the ruined portico of the **Ahmed al-Khadin mausoleum** (also 11th-century) must be the loneliest, southernmost Silk Route site in the CIS. Four buses a day come here from Tedzhen and one goes each morning at 8am to Merv.

Where to Stay

There is a charming one-storey colonial-era hotel 100m from the bus station across Ulitsa Magtumguly. If you are stranded for the night in Tedzhen there is a hotel a block from the bus station. Rooms are air-conditioned but communal basins are the only washing facilities. The lavatories are outside and nauseating.

Mary (Мары)

Scattered over hundreds of acres of desert a short drive east of Mary there is a desolate collection of walls and ramparts and one huge, partly ruined mausoleum. This is what remains of old Merv, the 'pearl of the East', second city of Islam after Baghdad between the 8th and 13th centuries—and site of the most horrific slaughter in all the Mongols' bloody rampaging through Eurasia.

New Merv has a rather shorter history. Founded by the Russians in 1884, it changed its name to Mary in 1937 and has grown since then into Turkmenistan's second biggest industrial city. Outside the bazaar it is charmless and in summer it is staggeringly hot, but it has a museum and the nearest hotel to the ruins.

History

Until the coming of the Kara-Kum Canal, Merv was at the mercy of the Murgab River, shadowing it as it shifted its course over the desert sands before disappearing under them. Current excavations suggest that the first settled Murgab oasis was a Bronze Age one, founded in the 15th century BC 130km out into the desert from Mary.

Then the legends begin. Some say Merv was founded in the 7th century BC by the Persian prophet Zarathustra, others that this is where Scheherezade spun the stories of the *Thousand and One Nights*.

In fact the oldest relics found at the main site near Bairam Ali date from the 6th century BC and Merv proper, originally called Margiana, is thought to have been founded 300 years later by the Seleucid king Antiochus I (r. 280–261 BC).

From Outpost to Capital

Merv was never a mere staging post for caravans and nomads. It always belonged to settled empires and its most ancient ties are with Iran to the southwest rather than with Transoxiana or the Turkmen tribes. For five centuries, from the decline of the Seleucids in the 2nd century BC until the rise of the Iranian Sassanids in the mid-3rd century AD, Merv was part of the Parthian empire. Then it became a northeastern outpost of the Sassanian one and enjoyed an era of religious tolerance with Buddhists, Zoroastrians and Nestorian Christians cohabiting peacefully.

That era ended with the Arab invasion of 651. The last Sassanid emperor, Yazdigerd III, fled to Merv but was hunted down and killed, causing the city to be nicknamed *Khudah-dushman*—'inimical to kings'. To ensure that Islam took hold, 50,000 Arab families from Basra and Kufa were settled in the oasis. Despite endemic guinea worm, Merv grew into the eastern capital of the Islamic Abbasid empire.

As Baghdad's power waned Merv's waxed. In 1037 she switched her allegiance from the Caliphs to the Seljuk Turks and became the adopted capital of their great viceroy Sultan Sanjar, who shifted the city westwards and gave it new defences and a giant mausoleum in his own memory. The Seljuk empire stretched from the Aral to the Mediterranean and controlled most of the western Silk Route. By the end of the 12th century Merv had never been richer nor more populous; the oasis as a whole supported more than a million people. And yet Armageddon was nigh.

The Mongols

Genghis Khan's youngest son Toloi arrived at the head of an army in January 1221, and spent six days preparing to besiege the city with terrifying catapults and battering rams. This was merely a phase of psychological tenderizing—and it worked. On the seventh day, just as Toloi gave the order to attack, Merv's governor surrendered on the understanding that his people would be spared. As they evacuated the city they were slain. Each Mongol soldier had orders to behead between 300 and 400 inhabitants. From half a million to a million of them died in the initial massacre. Then the buildings were destroyed, and Toloi's army plundered the wreckage and withdrew. Just when the survivors thought it safe to return, the Mongols trapped them in their ruined city and butchered them too.

'As I gazed across the barren brown plain of the Turkmen', Geoffrey Moorhouse wrote in 1990, 'it seemed to me that pictures of Hiroshima after the atom bomb did not more clearly illustrate what happens when a place is razed to the ground.'

Rebuilding and Neglect

Merv was rebuilt piecemeal over the next five centuries, south of the ruins of the Seljuk city, by Timurids, Persians and Turkmens. Their efforts were in turn laid waste by Masum Khan of Bukhara in 1785. He assassinated the local Turkmen chieftain, Bairam Ali Khan, then broke the main dam on the Murgab River 30km upstream from the city. When 'Bukhara' Burnes passed through in 1832, he found Merv in a state of complete neglect.

Its capture by the Russians in 1884 prompted an outbreak of 'mervousness' in far-off Whitehall; for Russian armies the way now lay open to Herat, and onwards—wailed Russophobes—to the Khyber. In fact all the Russians did was station a small garrison here and re-build the irrigation system. They found Merv an unhealthy place to live.

In the Soviet era that reputation was supressed. Bairam Ali, 25km from Mary, became a mecca for sufferers of kidney ailments who were told that by sweating buckets and eating local melons to replace lost fluids they would be cured. Meanwhile Mary's industrial future was assured when a drilling team struck gas, an estimated 600 billion cubic metres of it, under the desert at nearby Shatlik in 1968.

Getting to and from Mary

by air

The Aeroflot office is at the junction of Ulitsas Kievskaya and Internatsionalnaya, two blocks south of the hotel. There are five flights a day into Mary from Ashgabat ($55) and at least one to Tashkent.

by rail

Moscow–Ashgabat and Tashkent–Turkmenbashy trains do not pass through daily as they used to. For connections to the other republics, change at Chardzou. Moscow bound travellers go either to Urgench or Chardzou and change. It's now easier to get to other parts of the CIS from Uzbekistan than from Turkmenistan.

by bus

Buses go west to Tedzhen almost hourly (2 hours); twice a day to Ashgabat (6 hours); east to Chardzhou three times (4 hours); and once a day to Sarakhs, 160km to the southwest. Take the timetable as a guide not gospel. Departures depend on the bus arriving from the opposite direction, which leads to delays, especially later in the day. Tickets are sold on the bus just before departure.

As an alternative to the state bus, opt for the private service. These wait in the bus park, towards the station entrance and away from the state ticket office. State buses charge foreigners up to $4 for the Ashgabat run. Commercial ones charge more and, while having a basic timetable, still only depart when full. But be an hour early to ensure a seat.

To get to the ruins take a local bus to Bairam Ali and hire a taxi there, or hire one in Mary, or let Tania Lunina hire one for you (*see below*). Old Merv is too spread out to visit on foot.

Tourist Information

There is a new Intourist office is in town not at the hotel, but it's not often open. The best bet is to go to the **Hotel Sanjor**, where the director has formed his own tourist organisation. Ask at reception for the Merv Tour. Or contact **Tania Lunina**, an excellent, Intourist-approved English-speaking guide, at the hotel, © 5 76 44 or at home © 3 94 22. Her tour of the ruins at Bairam Ali costs $40 for an individual or group and is well worth it—without a good guide the ruins mean little.

Boat trips on the Kara-Kum canal are still possible but only two boats are in operation. Arrange them through Tania, and at least two days in advance.

Old Merv

Old Merv is confusing because it kept moving. There are 130 sq km of ruins north of Bairam Ali, still only partially excavated and understood. It is said (by Edgar Knobloch) that there were five different walled cities here dating from five different eras, and that the oldest was named Iskander Kala after Alexander the Great. But Alexander never came through Merv and anyway **Erk Kala**, on the northeast side of the site, probably pre-dates him by 200 years. A giant circular clay rampart is all that remains of what the German expert Klaus Pander believes was a 6th-century BC fortress. It forms part of the north side of **Giaur Kala**, the Seleucid city founded in the 3rd century BC as Margiana. The name 'Giaur Kala' came later and means 'Castle of the Infidels'. Only the four-sided outer wall survives, 20m high and 2km long.

The city had been moving gradually west since the 8th century, so the third Merv is situated next to Giaur Kala on its west side. **Sultan Kala** is much bigger than its predecessor, and potato-shaped. Its outer wall was built by the Seljuks in the 11th century. By the time of the Mongol invasion it enclosed a city world-famous for its mosques, madrasas, mansions and a 150,000-volume library.

Sultan Sanjar Mausoleum (мавзолей Султана Санджара)

Gaunt and huge in the middle of Sultan Kala is the Sultan Sanjar mausoleum, completed in 1140 as Moscow was being born. Its outer dome, 38 metres high and originally clad in blue tiles, was said to be visible a day's march away. A second, inner dome appears to be supported by a lattice of brick ribs but these are probably only decorative. The squinches which make the transition from cubic base to dome are elegantly hidden on the inside by four corner galleries and on the outside by an arched arcade (restored).

Muhammad Bini Atciz Az Seracksin, the architect of this and Sarakhs's Abul Fazl mausoleum, signed the base of the dome on its east side, modestly plastered over his signature, and was identified to the world only when the plaster fell off in an earthquake. The structure itself is earthquake-proof, with foundations 6m deep; it moves but doesn't fall.

Sultan Sanjar himself lies 4m below the cenotaph in the middle of the chamber, protected from rising saline groundwater by a deep seal of water-resistant reed ash mortar and an elaborate ventilation system with one shaft which comes to the surface next to the cenotaph and was long thought to be a well, and eight more round the outside of the mausoleum.

Kys Kala

Sultan Sanjar was known for his parties. Kys Kala, an unusual windowless castle outside the city wall and southwest of the mausoleum, was nicknamed 'the house of maidens' tears' when the sultan started using it for intimate gatherings in which all the guests were men and all the women were slaves. By then, Kys Kala was already 600 years old. Built in the 6th century by a Sassanian governor for his eldest daughter, its walls consist of half-columns possibly designed to deflect missiles. They were pockmarked but not destroyed by Arab siege catapults in 651.

Mohammed Ibn Said Mausoleum

North of here, partly hidden by holy saxaul trees, the Mohammed Ibn Said mausoleum is named after the founder of the Shi'ite sect, even if it is not his real resting place. Ibn Said, a fifth-generation descendant of the Prophet, died in the 8th century, but the mausoleum dates from the early 12th and until the 16th was thought by Sunni Muslims to be a shrine to their *imam* Mohammed Ibn Hannab. The cupola was rebuilt in 1936 but the yellow bricks in the north wall and the sea-shell decoration in the *mihrab* in the east wall are original. Outside the mausoleum are remains of an even older caravanserai and kitchen. These housed and fed pilgrims during the spring festival of *khudajuli*, when wishes that had been

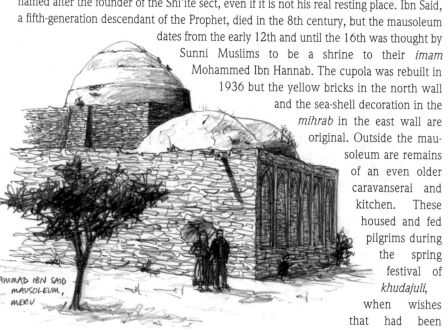

AHMAD IBN SAID MAUSOLEUM, MERV

made the previous year by tying strips of white cloth to the saxaul trees were supposed to come true.

Two centuries after the Mongol invasion, Merv rose again as **Abdullah Khan Kala**, built by Tamerlane's son Shahrukh, to which the Turkmens added **Bairam Ali Khan Kala** at the end of the 15th century. Their remains are south of Sultan Kala on the outskirts of modern Bairam Ali.

A Stroll Around Town

Mary's **bazaar** is ten minutes' walk east of the Hotel Sanjar off Ulitsa Poltaratskovo. In season it has grapes, cherries, succulent scarlet plums and mountains of melons.

The **museum** (*open Tues–Fri 9–5 and sometimes Sat*) is across the road in a colonial-era caravanserai next to a **park** whose eastern edge is the canalized Murgab River. Call Tania (*see* 'Tourist Information', p.94) if you would like it opened.

A small entrance fee equivalent to $1 is charged in manat and inside there are various displays on Turkmen culture—rugs, dresses and stunning jewellery. A recent addition, open in 1996, are the new rooms with archaeological finds from Old Merv and Bronze Merv (15th century BC).

The **Sunday market** at **Bairam Ali** is worth a stop *en route* to Old Merv. Nestled beside the old city walls, this is largely a livestock market and includes the occasional camel.

Mary (© 37022–)   ***Where to Stay and Eating Out***

The **Hotel Sanjar**, © 5 76 44, is 200m from the bus and railway stations. It has rooms with showers and air-conditioning from about $12 to 15. There are only a few single rooms. Ask for second- or third-floor accommodation. Of the two restaurants, the downstairs one is flyblown and basic; upstairs there is music and liquor but not much chance of being served.

The best place is the new **private chai-khana** opposite the hotel. Look for its small cupola and you will find excellent, fresh shashlyk. There are more cafés and *chai-khanas* near the bazaar.

To Chardzhou

The 220km across the Kara-Kum from Merv to the Amu Darya were some of the thirstiest on the Silk Route; thinly covered with saxaul bushes but ill-supplied with wells. For horses and camels it was rough going—'rather like a stormy sea, the waves of which had been frozen solid,' wrote F. M. Bailey after his 1919 winter crossing.

At Repetek, 100km from Chardzhou, there is a desert research station founded in 1912 with a small **natural history museum** containing stuffed desert rats and foxes, scorpions in jars and snakes in formaldehyde. Ask for Ahmed if it's closed. Trains going to and from Ashgabat stop here, or you can come from Chardzhou with Intourist.

Chardzhou (Чарджоу)

Midway between Ashgabat and Tashkent on the Amu Darya, Chardzhou is a dismal place. Never has a great river failed so completely to bring charm or cheerfulness to its major port.

Despite the river the land is almost completely flat, so there are no views except of shabby Soviet apartment buildings. Despite the river this is desert; a crossing point, not an oasis, without the natural shade of Mary or Tedzhen to see it through the searing summers.

Getting to and from Chardzhou

By air: Frequent flights to Ashgabat.

By boat: There used to be a steamer service to Khiva, but downstream of Chardzhou the Amu Darya is no longer deep enough for anything but speedboats and flat-bottomed gravel barges.

By rail: Situated at the junction of the Transcaspian and the former Moscow–Dushanbe railway lines, Chardzhou has excellent railway connections in all directions, including daily trains from Moscow and Tashkent.

By bus: Chardzhou is on Turkmenistan's main trunk road, the M 37, and buses go from here to Dashkhovuz and Mary.

Tourist Information

Intourist is at Ulitsa Malaya Bukharskaya 15.

At the **Hotel Amu Darya,** opposite the railway station at Ulitsa Lenina 5, © 2 58 22, reservations are essential but accommodation is cheap and payable in manat.

Uzbekistan Узбекистан

LYAB-I-KHAUZ,
BUKHARA

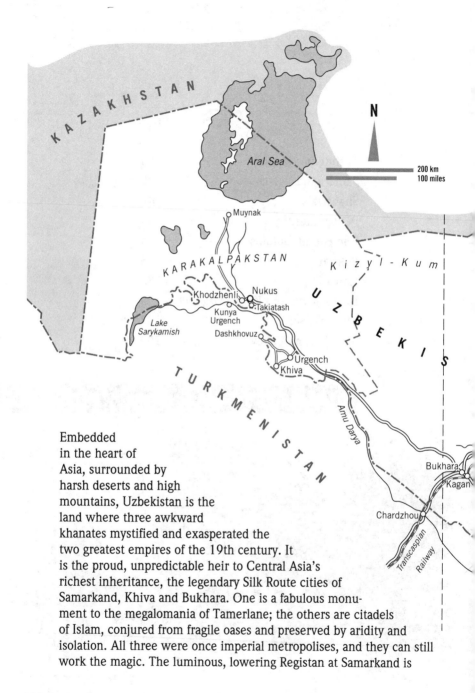

Embedded
in the heart of
Asia, surrounded by
harsh deserts and high
mountains, Uzbekistan is the
land where three awkward
khanates mystified and exasperated the
two greatest empires of the 19th century. It
is the proud, unpredictable heir to Central Asia's
richest inheritance, the legendary Silk Route cities of
Samarkand, Khiva and Bukhara. One is a fabulous monument to the megalomania of Tamerlane; the others are citadels
of Islam, conjured from fragile oases and preserved by aridity and
isolation. All three were once imperial metropolises, and they can still
work the magic. The luminous, lowering Registan at Samarkand is

nothing less than awesome. And if Bukhara's Kalyan minaret stops you in your tracks, be assured it did the same to Genghis Khan.

But Uzbekistan does more than take you back in time. Every street corner and *chai-khana* bears witness to one of this century's most fascinating cultural collisions. This is the country where Lenin and the Prophet had their high noon, and Lenin lost his nerve; where Uzbeks have always preferred skull caps and silk sashes to cheap grey European suits; soft, unleavened *lepeshka* to brick-shaped Russian loaves; mutton *shashlyk* to beef stroganoff and green tea to brown. Despite a cotton cash-crop fetish in the corridors of power, the bazaars groan with melons, grapes and pomegranates, and private tobacco crops hang

Uzbekistan

101

out to dry along the roads of the Fergana valley. Modern Uzbekistan may be a 20th-century Soviet invention with an awkward name and an extraordinary shape, but it is without doubt the heart of Central Asia. Remove it, and the region would implode. Uzbekistan is the only country in the region which borders on all the others. It is also the most populous, with 20 million people, the most ethnically diverse, with 120 different nationalities and—in desert terms—the richest, since it has all the big oases.

The people and wealth of the nation are concentrated at its southeast end, near the grand junction of the Tian Shan and Pamir mountain systems. Closest to China, the Fergana valley is an Uzbek peninsula hemmed in by Kyrgyz highlands, and an agro-industrial powerhouse.

Further west, Samarkand and Bukhara soak up most of the Zerafshan River, which runs out of the western Pamirs into the Kizyl-Kum desert. These rival provinces pivot about the capital, Tashkent, rebuilt as a showcase of Soviet development after a catastrophic earthquake in 1966. The rest of Uzbekistan is desert. In satellite pictures the only green smudge in the featureless brown of the Kizyl-Kum is the delta of the Amu Darya river, 1000km northwest of Tashkent. The delta and the salt-caked littoral of the shrinking Aral Sea are actually part of Karakalpakstan, an 'autonomous republic' within Uzbekistan whose extreme northwestern tip is a mere 300km from Russia.

The independent Uzbekistan that has emerged from the wreckage of the Soviet Union is a confused place. Nowhere is Russian domination of the recent past so resented, yet nowhere is there such nostalgia for the stability that went with membership of the Soviet Union. President Islam Karimov is a thinly-disguised Brezhnevite, and there are many who applaud him for it. The Uzbek Communist Party, renamed the Popular Democratic Party, still runs the country; the KGB, now the National Security Committee, is still fully operational; the press is censored and the democratic opposition, *Birlik*, is banned. In common with Turkmenistan and Kazakhstan, a referendum has confirmed the president in office until the next century. Economic reform is cautious. Fom 1994, the auctioning of small shops and service enterprises was given the go-ahead. Loans necessary to set up private business are, however, not easy to come by. And the actual privatization of land, according to Karimov, would exhaust the country's dangerously limited water supply.

Pulled every which way by contradictory trends, Uzbekistan is still trying to forge a new, post-Soviet identity. While a sleek new business class fills the hotel car parks in Tashkent with BMWs, the mullahs of the Fergana Valley call for Islamic rule. MTV, CNN and the Playboy channel are beamed into private apartments while waiting lists lengthen for madrasas re-opened after 70 years. The Uzbek government, meanwhile, lags behind those of Kazakhstan and Kyrgyzstan in opening up the country to badly needed foreign investors, but has formed a free customs union with these two republics.

The stakes are high. If Uzbekistan finds a path to real democracy and a niche in world markets, there is hope for its neighbours. If not, tourism may be the least of the casualties. Meanwhile, Uzbekistan's extraordinary past, and the way that it keeps resurfacing in the present, make it the most engrossing of the independent Central Asian republics.

Tashkent (Ташкент)

The capital of Uzbekistan is the biggest, most modern, most cosmopolitan city in Central Asia. People have been living here, where the western tip of the Tian Shan pans out into the Kizyl-Kum desert, for two thousand years—though there is not much to show for this history.

In April 1966, Tashkent was shaken by a major earthquake. Another quake struck in May, and in the two years that followed a further 800 earth tremors left the city virtually levelled. The big ones hit the city from directly underneath, paradoxically saving some buildings by making them bounce rather than topple sideways. The rebuilding of the city by architects and 30,000 'volunteers' (labour gangs) from all over the Soviet Union passed quickly into official legend: 'The whole country helped to build a new Tashkent. Now it is considered by right one of the most beautiful cities...'

It is not beautiful. You would not visit Tashkent for its modern public buildings any more than you would Seattle, with which it is twinned. But these buildings are at least arresting and different from each other. Better still, they are surrounded by abundant space and trees, and 'micro-climate' fountains through which cooling breezes blow on 45-degree days in August. This is the centre of Tashkent and its people are proud of it.

The city's most glamorous role was as hub of Soviet cold war espionage in Asia. Now, more prosaically, it is Central Asia's conference centre. Its main hotels were built for delegates from Asia, Africa and South America, come to witness Uzbekistan's transformation from feudal backwater to socialist paradise, bypassing the intervening capitalist stage in one bold leap of planned economics and ideology. They can still be frustratingly block-booked by Turkish businessmen.

For unlabelled visitors this is also the Central Asian city which most generously rewards curiosity and stamina. It has museums and restaurants unheard of by Intourist. There are suburbs big enough to have their own bazaars and ambience. There is opera for a dollar, horse racing on Sundays, exquisite autumn foliage, and an intoxicating whiff of *chutzpah* on the streets; a strong sense that with or without the mafia, with or without the dead hand of Karimov's government, this city, perhaps alone among those of ex-Soviet Central Asia, has the momentum to ride out hard times and capitalize on new ones. In the years since Independence it has done just that.

History

There has been a settlement at the Tashkent oasis on the Chirchik River since the 1st century AD, though it was called Chach or Shash or Dzhadzh until the 8th. It was called Binkent (cousin of nearby Chimkent) in the 8th and 9th centuries, and Tashkent, meaning 'stone village', from the 11th. By then it had passed from Samanid to Karakhanid control, and early in the 13th century it was taken by Mohammed Ala'-al-din, Shah of Khorezm, who, fearing it might become a rival centre of power, destroyed it in 1214. Genghis Khan, Tamerlane and Bukhara's khans and emirs ruled Tashkent from their more famous oases from the 13th century until 1809, when it became part of the Khanate of Kokand.

From the beginning of their advance south of the Syr Darya in the mid-19th century, the Russians regarded Tashkent as the strategic key to Central Asia. They probably over-rated its importance—but it was rich, populous (70,000) and because of its position at the end of the line of garrison towns the Russians had built along the edge of the Tian Shan, it was already trading heavily with Russia.

Early in 1865 word reached St Petersburg that Emir Muzaffar al-Din of Bukhara had plans to re-take Tashkent from Kokand. Prince Gorchakov, the Russian Foreign Minister, urged restraint on General Cherniaev, his commander in the field; Tashkent should be encouraged to break from Kokand by itself and then offered Russian protection from its neighbours. To take it by force would jeopardize relations with a suspicious British India. But Cherniaev believed the town was within his grasp and wanted to make a present of it to the czar. When orders came not to attack he deliberately left them unopened.

With 1300 men and 12 cannon against a defending force of 30,000 he moved up to the city walls on the night of 14 June. Gun carriage wheels were wrapped in felt for maximum stealth. Scaling ladders were in position by 2.30 am on the 15th. When they struck at dawn, first with a decoy attack, the Russians' surprise was complete. Fierce fighting continued all day and part of the next, but the city elders gave in on the 17th when they saw that the alternative was to see Tashkent reduced to ash and rubble.

The czar applauded Cherniaev's bold coup, implicitly endorsing a new forward phase in Central Asian policy. Tashkent was annexed and branches of major Russian trading houses were established there within the year. The Russian aim for the rest of the century was to shift the regional balance of power away from Bukhara to Tashkent by convincing its people of the benefits of Russian rule and commerce.

This aim was not convincingly achieved. Part of Russian imperial policy was to ignore Islam, so that most of Tashkent's Muslims felt increasingly ignored themselves. The situation was not helped by the total separation of Russian and 'old' Tashkent. The former existed for the army; in its early years, in Curzon's view, 'the refuge of damaged reputations and shattered fortunes, whose only hope of recovery lay in the chances afforded on the battlefield..' The latter was an overcrowded and insanitary maze of dried mud streets. When cholera took hold of it in 1892 the Muslim leaders forbade examination of Muslim women by Russian doctors and resisted burial of the dead in a new cemetery outside the city. Their followers roughed up the city commander and ransacked his headquarters, and were arrested—but not executed; a rare implicit admission of Russian tactlessness.

Still the breach between Russians and Muslims went on widening. In 1906 Muslims from throughout the Governorate General of Turkestan met in Tashkent to demand of the authorities full religious freedom and a Muslim Ecclesiastical Administration in Tashkent. Neither was granted. After revolution in Moscow and humiliating defeat by Japan in the Far East the year before, the Russians felt this was no time for concessions.

But the longer they delayed reform, the more sudden and drastic it would have to be. Thus, when the revolution of February 1917 led to the establishment of a Provisional Government, it had the support of most of Tashkent's Muslims, hungry for representation and full religious rights. Once again, they got neither. The Muslims withdrew their support and the Bolsheviks seized power.

Bolsheviks and *Bourjoui*

Keeping it proved a murderous business: in January 1918 a former Bolshevik commissar called Ossipov switched sides and seized power for a day in the name of the counter-revolution. But he got prematurely drunk to celebrate his victory, and the Bolshevik secret police, the NKVD, rounded up and shot 4000 suspected traitors.

'I heard many harrowing stories,' wrote British agent F. M. Bailey. 'It was sufficient to wear a collar to be classed as *bourjoui* and arrested. One engineer who had come from Bukhara for the Christmas holidays of his daughter was among those arrested and shot.'

In September that year direct links were restored between Tashkent and Moscow and a 'Turkic Commission' under Generals Frunze and Kuibyshev was despatched at once to Tashkent to begin the numbing processes of purging its élite, re-educating its people and industrializing its environs. A giant cotton-picking machine factory called Tashselmash, which remains the biggest industrial complex in Central Asia, was built on the outskirts of town, and a cascade of hydro-electric stations was constructed on the Chirchik River to power it. During the first two Five Year Plans (1928–38) forced migration increased Tashkent's population by 200,000 to half a million; an industrial proletariat was created from a city of artisans and tradesmen. Sovietization touched everything. Uzbek singers in the Tashkent Opera were re-trained because their traditional 'plaintive' tone was 'a carry-over from feudal times', not appropriate for 'the optimistic new socialist world'.

All of which makes Fitzroy Maclean's observations of 1930s Tashkent very heartening: 'It also has a tremendous reputation for wickedness... A queue had only to form outside a bread shop for a free fight to begin which generally ended in the shop being taken by storm and in any member of the Militia who was unwise enough to intervene being left seated in the mud, trying to collect his wits.'

World War II caused much of European Russia's engineering industry to be evacuated to Tashkent. Without this boost—not part of Stalin's original plan for his cotton capital—the city's industrial output would not have increased 23-fold between 1941 and 1974. Meanwhile, 1966's earthquake left 300,000 homeless and created a 20-year re-housing job.

Tashkent became capital of the Uzbek SSR in 1930 and of independent Uzbekistan in 1991. After 60 years as the Soviet model for a developing city, it is like a duck just out of boarding school in the global village pond; fully grown but naive, anxious to preserve its dignity above water, while paddling furiously below the surface to catch up with its worldly rivals, Islamabad, Istanbul and Delhi.

Getting to and from Tashkent

It would be hard to visit Central Asia and miss out Tashkent even if you wanted to. It has the region's only major international airport and its busiest domestic one, is served by buses from Almaty and the Afghan border, and forms the junction of the three great Central Asian railways; the Transcaspian, the Orenburg–Tashkent line and the TurkSib. For international flights *see* **Travel**, pp.2–5; for tour operators, *see* 'Tourist Information', pp.109–12.

by air

Kerosene allowing, there are Aeroflot/Uzbekistan Airways flights to Tashkent from Moscow (two wide-bodied jets daily), Samarkand (three flights a day, $51), Bukhara (at least three, $61), Urgench/Khiva (five, $76), Nukus (three), Bishkek (two, $93), Ashgabat (three, $92), plus daily flights from Almaty, Termez, Andizhan, Kokand and Fergana ($50), and less frequent services from virtually everywhere in the CIS. Flights between Ashgabat and Tashkent suffer first during any political dispute; they have been suspended since late 1995. Instead, you can use the train or, if it makes logistical sense, fly to Urgench and bus/train over the border to Dashkhovuz. From there it is a forty-minute flight to Ashgabat (*but see* 'Entry Formalities', p.14) .There is no air service between Samarkand, Bukhara and Urgench. This means that the Tashkent–Khiva–Bukhara–Samarkand– Tashkent round trip is no longer possible. Be prepared also for the occasional domestic flight cancellation. Fuel is increasingly expensive and if a flight has too few passengers you'll be told to come back later for the next one.Leaving Tashkent, air tickets to all CIS destinations are sold at the Hotel Uzbekistan Service Bureau, ☏ 33 35 59 (there is up to $20 surcharge but they offer last-minute seats and take credit cards). The best place for tickets is the Uzbek Airways city office opposite the Hotel Rossiya on Ulitsa Kunaeva, former Sapyornaya ☏ 56 38 37. English is spoken here at desks 22 (where you order your ticket), 21 and 23 (where you pay) and 28 (information). There are no surcharges and no credit cards are accepted. The airport bus is number 67, which passes Hotels Uzbekistan and Rossiya.

There are Aeroflot and Uzbek Airways ticket offices on the second floor of the international airport terminal and Transaero on the third floor. Foreigners must show their passports when buying flight tickets. Your details are written on your ticket; it's therefore not possible for a local friend to buy a ticket for you at the lower price that nationals pay. The special price for foreigners is paid in dollars.

Tashkent airport has a mixed reputation; either you'll glide effortlessly through or you'll wish you'd stayed at home. But if you follow the 'rules' there should be no problem. Independent travellers leaving Tashkent on domestic flights should arrive at least one and a half hours before departure, and must go first to the right-hand end of the departures hall and register with Intourist in the room to the left of the VIP lounge. Be prepared to wait; when no one appears, you can enquire at the small office inside the registration area. After registration, foreigners are escorted through the international departures—don't be alarmed—and ultimately to the usual bus. Tourist groups, more simply, proceed as instructed by their tour operator.

by rail

Trains to Moscow run daily; the most comfortable, no.5, runs four times a week, does the journey slightly faster than the usual 3 days and costs $98. Trains to Siberia (daily), Kazakhstan (even days of the month) and Turkmenistan (daily via Chardzou), and through trains from the Fergana valley (daily) all use the main *vokzal* at the east end of the red metro line, Ⓜ Sobir Rakhimov. When there is no direct train to Almaty, take one of the daily Siberia trains. There is one train a day that stops at Samarkand, Bukhara and Urgench, and a Bishkek service via Chimkent (journey time is 15 hours).

For train information and advance ticket sales, walk out of the station to the road straight ahead. On the right-hand side is a long building; the information booth is through the main entrance on the right. To buy your ticket, go out of the main doors and turn left to come to the side of the building where, up a few steps, you'll find the foreigners' booking office (*open Mon–Sun, 9–5; closed 12–1pm*). While you wait in the queue, notice the entwined stems on the traditionally painted walls. Day-of-travel and through ('transit') tickets are sold at the main station. There's a new ticket office for foreigners, next to the OVIR Immigration Department. Walk to the right-hand side of the Locomotive Hotel and turn left onto the station platform; the office is on the right. Through tickets go on sale two hours before departure. Fill in time, for a few cents, at the nearby Railway Museum.

by bus

There is at least one bus to and from Samarkand every hour, 5am–5.30pm; the 5-hour journey costs $5. Five buses daily make the 8-hour journey to Bukhara for $10–11. One bus daily makes the 12-hour journey to Termez for $11–12. Buses to Chimkent depart every 25 minutes, 6am–6.30pm, making the 2-hour trip for $2–3. Buses also go to Turkestan, Dzhambul, Bishkek (5 overnight buses taking

10 hours, $11–13) and Almaty (5 buses, 16 hours, $15–17) from the *avtovokzal* on the western edge of the city. Passengers usually alight at the nearby metro station on the end of the blue line, Ⓜ Sobir Rakhimov. Buses for the Fergana valley, including Andizhan (2 buses daily make the 9-hour journey for $7–8), Namangan (2 buses, 7 hours, $7) and Fergana (4 buses, 8 hours, $7–8), can be suspended when there is unrest in Tajikistan because many routes go through Khŭjand. This does not mean you have to go by air; it takes all-out civil war to stop the trains. Tashkent bus station requires foreigners to register with OVIR before they can buy a ticket. Take your registration document and present it at the ticket counter. OVIR's office is at the left-hand end of the first floor, inside the main building. If you are going from Tashkent by bus to anywhere further than Samarkand or Chimkent, it's worth getting your ticket the day before from the special ticket office, which closes at 5pm, also upstairs.

Getting Around

Tashkent has Central Asia's only **metro**, with two lines and a third under construction. It is shallow, clean, fast, cool, and, like Moscow's metro, built without regard to cost because prestige is priceless. Giant fans change the air in the tunnels and stations eight times an hour and the entire system sits on rubber cushions to make it earthquake-proof. The two lines follow Tashkent's two main axes: east –west between the train and long-distance bus stations, and from the northeast through the city centre to Chilanzar. The most spookily stunning of the lavish themed stations is *Kosmonavtov* (**Космонавтов**), a blue-black monument to the cult of the cosmonaut, with ovoid ceramic portraits of Gagarin and his comrades in their spacesuits. Let the first train go without you and gaze.

Above ground there are trams, trolleybuses, buses, *marshrutnoe* (fixed-route) taxis and ordinary taxis. The first three and the metro cost well under twenty cents a ride. For taxi rides within the city centre, expect to pay $1–2 in local currency. From the airport or long distance bus station to the centre the asking rate is $3–4. From the Hotel Uzbekistan, unless you are rich, walk round the corner and hail a taxi rather than accept an offer from a shark on the forecourt.

Tourist Information

Tourist information is at the Hotel Uzbekistan's **Intourist Service Bureau**, ✆ 33 27 73, on the first floor (or second according to local navigation). The women here are helpful, speak fluent English and all wear leather jackets. There are still Intourist city maps available but the best map is produced, in English, by the **Katran** company. A few details have changed since the map was published— an occupational hazard for any printed matter on Central Asia—but it remains the clearest street guide. Check the newspaper stand and souvenir shops in the Uzbekistan and India hotels for a copy. These are also the best sources for the new-look, glossy postcards.

БЕРУНИЙ
BERUNIY

ТИНЧЛИК
TINCHLIK

ЧОРСУ
CHORSU

ГАФУР ГУЛОМ
GAFUR GULOM

ХАЛКЛАР ДУСТЛИГИ
KHALKLAR DUSTLIGI

ЁШЛИК
YOSHLIK

ХАМЗА
KHAMZA

УЛУГБЕК
ULUGBEK

ЧИЛОНЗОР (CHILANZAR)*
HILONZOR (CHILANZAR)*

БИР РАХИМОВ
BIR RAKHIMOV

ЮНУСАБАД
YUNUSABAD

ПУШКИН
PUSHKIN

МАКЦИМ ГОРКЬИЙ
MAXIM GORKY

ХАМИД ОЛИМЖОН
KHAMID OLIMJON

МАРКАЗИЙ ХИЁБОН/АМИР ТИМУР
MARKAZIY KHIYOBON / AMIR TIMUR

МУСТАКИЛЛИК МАЙДОНИ
MUSTAKILLIK MAYDONI

АЛИШЕР НАВОИ / ПАХТАКОР
ALISHER NAVOI / PAKHTAKOR

УЗБЕКИСТОН
UZBEKISTON
(UZBEKISTAN)*

КОСМОНАВТОВ
KOSMONAVTOV

ОЙБЕК
OYBEK

ТОШКЕНТ
TOSHKENT (TASHKENT)*

МАШИНАСОЗЛАР
MASHINASOZLAR

ВОКЗАЛ ЖАНУБИ
VOKZAL ZHANUBI

ЧКАЛОВ
CHKALOV

— Chilanzar line
— Uzbekistan line
— Berumi line under construction
*words in parentheses are more familiar English versions of the local (Uzbek) spellings

The main **post office** is at Ulitsa A. Tukay 2, near the Alaysky bazaar. From the Hotel Uzbekistan walk a block east up Mehtar Ambar, turn left and walk another block. To make international phone calls from here you have to book a day ahead. You can also go to the **Urgent International Call Booth** in the main telecom building at Prospekt Navoi 28 (*open 8–noon, 1–6; closed Sun*).

Ignore the queues and book your call at the telex desk; calls to Europe cost $4 for 3 minutes. Alternatively, and at greater cost, try the **business centre**s attached to the Uzbekistan and India Hotels. These facilities can be paid for with credit cards. At the India Hotel, you can buy an international phone card for use in the lobby phone near the service bureau.

E-mail services are available and more reliable than the phone sytem. Silknet at PERDCA ($25 joining fee), Ulitsa Furkata 1, Ⓜ Khalklar Dustligi, and Relcom at Ulitsa Buyuk Ipak Yoli 42 (follow Mehtar Ambar), Ⓜ Pushkin. A company called Kamalak, ✆ 35 22 32/44 20 28, at the TV Tower and the main post office can provide **Cable TV**.

Intourist has been revamped as a national company called, **Uzbektourism**, ✆ 33 54 14, 🖹 32 79 48. Their main office, tucked between the Hotel Uzbekistan and the new India Hotel (*open Mon–Fri 9–5pm*), offers information on Tashkent and other parts of Uzbekistan. A number of **private tour companies** have appeared in Tashkent. For any travel queries, the best place to start is **Sam Buh**, ✆/🖹 63 75 85, who offer tours (or just drivers) throughout Uzbekistan, including Samarkand–Bukhara–Khiva and trips to Chimgan in the mountains with stays in

KEY

1 Bakhor Concert Hall
Бахорский Консертный Зал

2 Conservatoire
Консерватория

3 Alisher Navoi Opera House
Театр Оперы и Балета имени А. Навои

4 Palace of People's Friendship
Дворец Дружбы Народов

5 Uzbek State Museum of Art
Музей Искусства Узбекистана

6 Exhibition Hall of Painters' Union
Выставочный Зал Союза Художников

7 Decorative and Applied Art Museum
Музей Декоративных и Прикладных Искусств

8 Former Exhibition of Economic Achievements (VDNKh)
ВДНХ

9 Aybek Museum of the History of the Peoples of Uzbekistan
Музей Истории Народов Узбекистана имени Айбека

10 Mukhtara Ashrafi Museum
Музей Мухтара Ашрафи

11 Navoi Literary Museum
Музей Литературы имени А. Навои

12 Earthquake memorial
Памятник Землетрясению

13 Former Lenin monument
Памятник В.И. Ленину

14 Timur monument
Памятник Тимур

15 Navoi monument
Памятник А. Навои

16 Tomb of the Unknown Soldier
Могила Неизвестного Солдата

17 Abdul Khasim madrasa
Медресе Абдул Хазим

18 Barak-Khan madrasa
Медресе Барак-Хан

19 Kukeltash madrasa
Медресе Кукельташ

20 Telashayakh mosque and Kafali-Shash mausoleum
Мечеть Телашаях Мавзолей Кафали-Шаш

21 German church
Немецкая Церковь

22 Russian church
Российская Церковь

23 Alaysky bazaar
Алайский Базар

24 Old bazaar
Старый Базар

25 Elixir baths
Бани Эликсир

26 Boating pond
Пруд

27 TV Tower
Телевизионная Башня

28 National Bank for Foreign and Economic Activity
Банк Иностранной и Экономической Деятельности

UL. ZARKAINAR / УЛ. ЗАРКАЙНАР

УЛ. ШАСТРИ

УЛ. ФУРКАТА

UL. SHASTRI

UL. FURKATA

PROSPEKT KHALKLAR DUSTLIGI

Chilanzar

N

1 km
0.5 mile

HOTELS and RESTAURANTS

A Hotel Uzbekistan
Гостиница Узбекистан

B Hotel Tashkent
Гостиница Ташкент

C Hotel Chorsu
Гостиница Чорсу

D Hotel Rossiya
Гостиница Россия

E Hotel Yoshlyk
Гостиница Ёшлик

F Hotel Leningrad
Гостиница Ленинград

G Hotel Lokomotif
Гостиница Локомотиф

H Hotel Dostlik
Гостиница Достлик

I Teon Business Club
Ресторан Теон

J Istanbul Restaurant
Ресторан Истанбул

K Zerafshan Restaurant
Ресторан Зерафшан

L Blue Dome Café
Кафе Синяя Купола

M Arirang
Ариранг

N Richman
Ричман

O Café Oleg
Кафе Олег

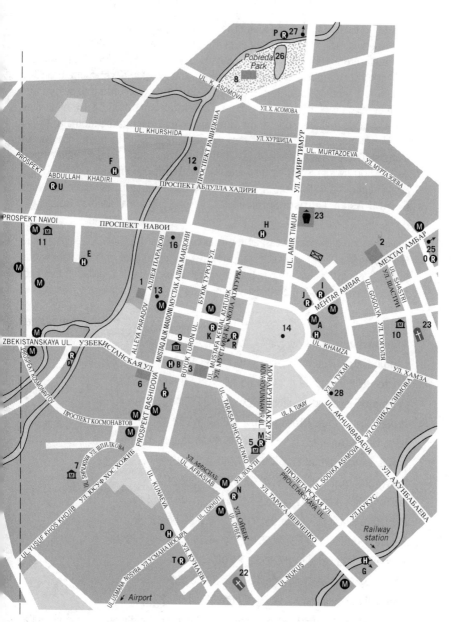

P Boguy Shamoy
   Богуы Шамой
Q Alazzi Café
   Кафе Алаззи
R American Food
   Американ Фуд
S Nasiba's Café
   Кафе Насиба
T Shashlyk
   Шашлык

U Black Dragon
   Чёрный Дракон

Tashkent

bed-and-breakfast accommodation. Their round trips to Khŭjand, Tajikistan ($80) and reservation service for flights from there to Dushanbe are often used by businessmen. From **Uzintour** at Ulitsa Buyuk Ipak Yoli 115, ✆ 68 67 31, you can collect a list of itineraries which range from the Tashkent–Khiva circuit ($367 group) to a mountain hunting trip ($481). Prices vary according to season and exclude inter-city transport and airfares. **Uzbektourism**, ✆ 33 54 14, offers similar itineraries including one to the Chatkal National park in the moutains ($194 per person per day in a group of ten). Apart from tours of Tashkent, **Tashkent Tourist Travel Agency**, ✆ 44 12 94, can take you to the Fergana Valley (for 7 days, $800 by air, $700 by bus) and Iran. **Adventure Travels**, Ulitsa Tarasa Shevchenko 44, ✆ 33 10 55, offers trips to the mountains, deserts and rivers. **Central Asian Tourism Service** has a Tashkent office at Mehtar Ambar 66, room 34, ✆ 33 14 15.

Travellers cheques can be cashed for local currency at the Hotel Uzbekistan and the India Hotel. Cash advances (apparently unlimited, paid in US dollars and at only a 5% commission) are possible from the National Bank for Foreign and Economic Activity, Ulitsa Akhunbabaeva 23, ✆ 33 60 70.

Embassies

Afghanistan: Ulitsa Gogolya 73, ✆ 33 91 71/33 91 89

China: Ulitsa Gogolya 79, ✆ 33 80 88/33 13 96

France: Ulitsa Lokhuti 42, ✆ 33 53 82/33 53 84

Germany: Prospekt Rashidova, ✆ 34 47 25/34 62 59/34 45 30

India: Ulitsa Aleksey Tolstovo 3, ✆ 33 82 67/33 83 57

Iran: Ulitsa Timiryazova 16/18, ✆ 35 07 77/34 45 07/34 65 53

Israel: Ulitsa Lokhuti 16a, ✆ 56 57 59/56 78 23

Italy: Ulitsa Amir Timur 95, ✆ 35 42 72/35 20 09

Japan: Ulitsa Sodika Azimova 51/2, ✆ 32 37 46/33 44 15

Pakistan: Ulitsa Chilanzar 25, ✆ 77 10 03/77 66 87

Russia: Ulitsa Nukus 83, ✆ 55 29 48/55 79 54

Turkey: Ulitsa Gogolya 87, ✆ 33 21 04

UK: Ulitsa Murtazoeva 6, ✆ 34 56 52/34 76 58*

USA: Ulitsa Chilanzar 82, ✆ 77 69 86/77 14 07/77 10 81

*In late 1996 the **British Embassy** is moving from the diplomatic compound at Ulitsa Murtazoeva to Ulitsa Gogolya 67. Until then, the visa section of the Embassy only is located at Prospekt Rashidova 15, ✆ 34 29 49 (*open Mon–Fri, 8–11am*).

Air India: Airport, International Terminal, ℰ 54 16 21

Ariana (Afghanistan): Airport, International Terminal, ℰ 55 50 01

Iran Air: Airport, 3rd Floor, Room 11, ℰ 50 44 44/59 13 74

Lufthansa: Airport, Room 307, ℰ 54 85 69/55 34 20

Pakistan International Airways: Prospekt Khalklar Dustligi 4, for reservations, call ℰ 45 19 56/45 91 92; and at the airport, ℰ 54 92 15/☎ 45 39 42 (*closed Sun*).

Transaero: Airport, International Departure Lounge, ℰ 55 15 05/59 16 59, flies CIS and international routes via Mosow.

Turkish Airways: Airport, ℰ 54 82 81, and Ulitsa Mustafa Kemal Ataturk 24 , ℰ 56 15 63/56 46 54

Downtown Tashkent

To begin to get the feel of Tashkent walk east up Mehtar Ambar from the Hotel Uzbekistan around lunchtime. Minor mafiosi, half hidden by fountains, are probably enter-taining prostitutes on the terrace of the hotel restaurant. The doorman at the former Teon Business Club across the road is nodding the Armani-suited brigade through his stuccoed porch and turning tourists away. Further on, Hare Krishna followers compete with Koran sellers and are gawped at like zoo exotica, while music students try to haul you off the street into a concert at the conservatoire. But keep going as far as the Elixir Baths because there, guarding both the entrance and the black Lada with the tinted windows, splendid in ochre baggies and billowing silk shirt, is 200 pounds of 100 per cent pure gangster.

This is the cultural melée of Central Asian street-life, updated for the 1990s and laced with big city pizazz. You can find it only in Tashkent. Adding to this is a growing interna-tional business community and more hotels and restaurants. But while this makes life more palatable for foreigners, it has not so far detracted from the essential Tashkent. There are fine museums here and and an old quarter much less beautiful than Bukhara's or Khiva's but much more lived-in.

The Old Town

Across Prospekt Navoi from the 22-storey Hotel Chorsu, Ⓜ Chorsu, the **Kukeldash madrasa** (медресе Кукельташ)(1560) was originally an Islamic seminary. Having served as a Soviet local government building, it is now being restored. The tiled facade over the entrance arch, with its repeated sun motif, is a virtual copy of Ulug Bek madrasa in Samarkand (1420).This may be as much as you will get to see of the madrasa. Foreigners are not generally able to venture further. But through the arch is a large domed courtyard and behind that the ruined 15th-century **Kukeldash Djuma mosque** (Мечеть Кукельташ Джыма—Friday mosque). The **Old bazaar** sprawls north and east of the madrasa and is not really old any more. A huge modern dome keeps the sun off about three acres of fruit, vegetables and meat. There is take-away salad in turgid tubular plastic bags, sheep's gut by the metre and the usual abundance of nuts, dried fruit, fresh herbs, unlabelled spices and hallucinogens. Outside in the unlicensed bit crowds fight for Chinese-made shiny black shoes and craftsmen make cradles and stencil motifs. Meanwhile the exhausted, the idle and the garrulous retire to cafés and *chai-khanas* for green tea. To get to the **Barak-Khan madrasa, (медресе Барак-Хан)** headquarters of the (Sunni) mufti of ex-Soviet Central Asia and Kazakhstan, either set off up the un-named streets of un-numbered mud houses north of the bazaar and ask directions frequently, or return to Prospekt Navoi, pass the Kukeldash madrasa, turn left up Ulitsa Zarkainar and follow it for about a mile to No.103. Barak-Khan is usually closed to visitors but is worth a look for the intricate hotch-potch of mosaic and Arabic calligraphy on its late 16th-century brick façade. The intricately carved doors look old but were in fact made in 1980 by a Samarkand craftsman. Specialists may be allowed in by prior arrangement with Intourist or the mufti's office (✆ 40 01 96). Across the street is the working **Telashayakh mosque (мечеть Телашаях)**, part of which houses the important religious library of the 16th-century **Kaffali-Shash mausoleum (мавзолей Кафали-Шал)**, and the Imam al-Buchari Islamic Institute, where aspiring mullahs come after seven years at Bukhara's Mir-i-Arab madrasa for four years of Arabic language, literature and history. The complex is closed to non-Muslims but adorned at weekends by wedding motorcades using it as background for the camcorder. The narrow streets behind the Barak-Khan madrasa are formed by the windowless outside walls of private homes and courtyards. Built only of mud and wood, they withstood seismic and in many cases communistic levelling. When doors stand ajar by all means peep in at these apricot- and mulberry-shaded oases of defiant luxury, though it may be wise to ask not whence the wherewithal. And be ready for evasive action when a wedding motorcade squeezes past through the maze of pot-holed streets. Two silver cupolas belong to the 17th-century **Abdul-Khasim madrasa (медресе Абдул-Хасим)**, situated 1.5km south of Kukeldash behind the enormous Palace of Peoples' Friendship, which serves as a concert hall for Uzbek music (*see* p.124). Named after the man who built it in 1895 and who paid for the education of its thirty students each year, the madrasa was used by the homeless after the terrible earthquake of 1966.

Today's 250 students share with a small museum and a host of Uzbek craftsmen. Around the courtyard are tiny workshops where traditional jewellery in silver, coral and bronze, Koran-stands from single blocks of wood and painstakingly detailed miniatures can be bought for hard currency. The closest metro is Ⓜ Khalklar Dustligi, where the old Soviet emblems remain on the walls (attempts to remove them caused too much damage). During World War II, the Uzbek Shomahmudov adopted many orphans of various USSR nationalities and the monument in front of the People's Palace is in his honour. The statue under the blue cupola in the park in front of the madrasa is of **Alisher Navoi**, founder of Uzbek literature, whose 550th birthday was celebrated in 1992. Couples parade from the nearby Navros wedding registration office to have their picture taken under the statue's dome, then spend the evening at the Olympia Night Club.

Main Attractions
Aybek Museum of the History of the Peoples of Uzbekistan
(Музей истории народов Узбекистана имени Айбека/ *Muzey istorii narodov Uzbekistana imeni Aybeka*)

Open Tues–Sun, 10–6; $3 entrance fee for foreigners; Ⓜ *Mustakillik*

Three blocks down Ulitsa Buyuk Turon, opposite the Hotel Tashkent, the Aybek Museum has incorporated the old Lenin Museum to make a big, general museum of Uzbek history. Having grown from the Tashkent Public Museum founded in 1876, the Aybek is the oldest museum in Central Asia and has good displays on archaeology in the Termez region. What is most interesting about the former State museums of Central Asia is how they present their history post independence. The guide book refers to the work done to determine the 'conformities and features of the Peoples of Uzbekistan'. With Karimov 'presiding' over not only the entrance foyer, the museum is divided into Ancient, Medieval and Modern History (including post-independence sections). Its most important possessions are an immaculate alabaster Buddha brought to Surkhandarya by Chinese missionaries in the 1st or 2nd century, and the 8th-century Osman Koran. This giant book once belonged to Osman I, founder of the Ottoman dynasty, but was taken from Turkey to Samarkand by Tamerlane, to St Petersburg by the Russians in 1869, and back to Uzbekistan after the 1917 revolution. In the museum you see a copy; the original is kept in the Telashayakh mosque. Worth the investment is the museum guide book; it's only a few dollars and written in English, Russian and Uzbek.

Alisher Navoi Opera and Ballet Theatre
(Театр оперы и балета имени А. Навои/ *Teatr opery i baleta imeni A. Navoi*)

Ⓜ *Mustakillik*

Diagonally opposite the Aybek Museum, dignified by its own plaza, this 1500-seater is Tashkent's principle monument to Stalinism. Designed by the man responsible for Lenin's mausoleum and the Lubianka, it evokes, according to American critic Arthur Sprague, 'the image of a small-town "First National Bank" decked out in the frivolities of Hollywood's Moorish "East".' The neo-classical façade is topped off with

ALISHER NAVOI OPERA & BALLET THEATRE, TASHKENT

Muslim-style stalactites; mosaics incorporate Leninist slogans where Muslims would have quoted from the Koran. The point, Sprague believed, was to persuade the unwary that Muslim civilization was not disappearing, merely changing. 'Thus, with rather frightening simplicity, Central Asian tradition became an ideological weapon against itself in the continuing attempt to convert local people to atheism and socialism.' Inside you can still see what must be the world's cheapest professional opera (*see* pp.123–4).

Uzbek State Museum of Art

(**Государственный музей искусства**/ *Gasudarstvyenny muzey iskusstva*)

> *Open Wed–Sun 10–5, ticket office closes 4pm; Mon 10–2; closed Tues. It is well worth joining an Intourist group or attaching yourself to one once there. Entrance fee is less than $1 and includes the current temporary exhibition;* **Ⓜ** *Amir Timur and take Tram 28, bus 7.*

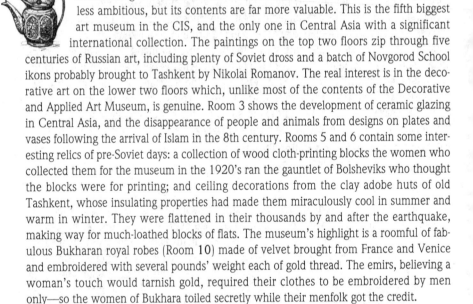

The building to the south of the Navoi Theatre, on Ulitsa Tarasa Shevchenko, is less ambitious, but its contents are far more valuable. This is the fifth biggest art museum in the CIS, and the only one in Central Asia with a significant international collection. The paintings on the top two floors zip through five centuries of Russian art, including plenty of Soviet dross and a batch of Novgorod School ikons probably brought to Tashkent by Nikolai Romanov. The real interest is in the decorative art on the lower two floors which, unlike most of the contents of the Decorative and Applied Art Museum, is genuine. Room 3 shows the development of ceramic glazing in Central Asia, and the disappearance of people and animals from designs on plates and vases following the arrival of Islam in the 8th century. Rooms 5 and 6 contain some interesting relics of pre-Soviet days: a collection of wood cloth-printing blocks the women who collected them for the museum in the 1920's ran the gauntlet of Bolsheviks who thought the blocks were for printing; and ceiling decorations from the clay adobe huts of old Tashkent, whose insulating properties had made them miraculously cool in summer and warm in winter. They were flattened in their thousands by and after the earthquake, making way for much-loathed blocks of flats. The museum's highlight is a roomful of fabulous Bukharan royal robes (Room 10) made of velvet brought from France and Venice and embroidered with several pounds' weight each of gold thread. The emirs, believing a woman's touch would tarnish gold, required their clothes to be embroidered by men only—so the women of Bukhara toiled secretly while their menfolk got the credit.

Museum of Decorative and Applied Art

(**Музей прикладного искусства**/ *Muzey prikladnovo iskusstva*)

> *Open daily 10–5. Adm less than 50 cents, and still under $1 with guide (Russian, French and English available). If you require an English-speaking guide, ask for Mira and come before 12 noon;* **Ⓜ** *Kosmonavtov*

The museum is at 15 Ulitsa Shpilkova, in the Hotel Rossiya area. The best thing about the museum is the building, former residence of A. A. Polovtsev, a diplomat and admirer of

Islamic art from the court of the last czar. He had the house built in 1907 in authentic Uzbek style with mosque-like verandas under slim wooden columns round three sides of a courtyard. The interior and main veranda were decorated by master craftsmen from Bukhara, Khiva and Samarkand, complete with a *mihrab* in the main reception room to point Polovtsev to Mecca, and an Arabic inscription over the door to the smoking room: 'The world is a great room with two doors: one entrance, one exit.' It's worth a visit just for this; a welcome haven from the city bustle.

The rest of the museum contains wall hangings and reproduction antique jewellery designed to protect rooms and people from evil spirits, and some Soviet-era furniture and porcelain. Look out for the printed silk space rocket next to the more traditional crow's wing and peacock feather motifs. There is also a dried courgette *chilim* for smoking cannabis and opium.

A Stroll Around Tashkent

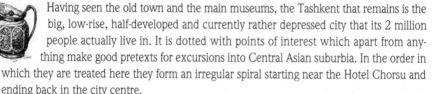

Having seen the old town and the main museums, the Tashkent that remains is the big, low-rise, half-developed and currently rather depressed city that its 2 million people actually live in. It is dotted with points of interest which apart from anything make good pretexts for excursions into Central Asian suburbia. In the order in which they are treated here they form an irregular spiral starting near the Hotel Chorsu and ending back in the city centre.

The **Navoi Literary Museum** (**Музей литературы имени А. Навои**/*Muzey literatury imeni A. Navoi*; *open Mon–Fri, 10–5 pm, Sat until 2pm; closed Sun*) on the south side of Prospekt Navoi towards its west end, contains manuscripts by the 15th-century poet Alisher Navoi and other Uzbek writers. Navoi is credited with founding the Uzbek literary language, but he actually wrote his epic poems, most of them idolizing his land and its women, in Persian. His pioneering achievement was to break from the Arabic language and script.

In the late summer and autumn, a huge **melon market** is piled up next to the Navoi Museum. This is a melon extravaganza; every kind is available, and also honey if you've brought your own pot. Three tram stops east, Prospekt Rashidova crosses Prospekt Navoi. The **Earthquake memorial**, much visited by wedding-day couples presumably hoping the earth will move for them too, is by the former Museum of People's Friendship of the USSR on the second block north on Rashidova. Continue north for the sad pavilion of the ex-Exhibition of Economic Achievements of the Uzbek Soviet Socialist Republic in **Park Pobiedy** (Victory Park, also served via Ulitsa Amir Timur by buses 9, 51, 60, 67, 72 (express) and 91, and trams 2, 3, 28 and 16). A huge shed full of cotton-picking machines (or equivalent) was mandatory for all Soviet republican capitals. They are now either shut or used for trade fairs. There is boating on the pond in Victory Park.

A little further north and very obvious on Amir Timur, the **TV Tower** (*closed Mon*) looms 375m over Tashkent. It has two revolving restaurants 100m up, red décor for

'European' food, blue for Uzbek. Local people are justly proud of the view, which is mostly of trees. Eating is not compulsory but a ticket is, from below and to the right of the base. The **Alaysky bazaar**, the second largest in Tashkent, occupies an entire block two thirds of the way back down Ulitsa Amir Timur, behind a Berlin-style wall on the left. In season most of it is given over to melons. From the far side of the bazaar Ulitsa Shastri curves round behind the city centre and becomes Ulitsa Sodika Azimova. Mukhtar Ashrafi, one of the first Soviet-trained Uzbek composer/conductors, lived and worked from 1969 to 1975 at Ulitsa Sodika Azimova 15, which is now the **Mukhtara Ashrafi Museum** (*open Mon–Fri, 10–1and 2–5, Sat 10–3; closed Sun*).

More poignant and much more frequented is the **Russian church** near the **Gospitalny bazaar** on Ulitsa Oybek, formerly Kafanova, though its address is Ulitsa Poltaratskovo 91. On Sundays it is filled with incense and candle smoke and the mournful chanting of old Russian women with bandaged ankles. Trams return to the centre up Ulitsa Kunaeva (Sapyornaya). This feeds into Prospekt Rashidova which between Uzbekistanskaya Ulitsa and Prospekt Navoi is called Mustak Alik Maidoni, ceremonial centre of Uzbekistan and closed to ordinary traffic. This used to be Lenin Square, but Lenin has disappeared from his pedestal of dark red marble, replaced for the time being by a globe. The **Tomb of the Unknown Soldier** is at the north end; at the south end the **Exhibition Hall of the Painters' Union** houses a permanent exhibition of contemporary (Soviet) Uzbek art and also a special Silk Route display (*closed Sun*).

One of the principle houses [of Tashkent],' wrote Lord Curzon in 1889, 'is inhabited by a Grand Duke, a first cousin of the Czar, who is said to be a very *mauvais sujet*.' Meet Nikolai Konstantinovich Romanov, suspected kleptomaniac and pervert, thrown out of St Petersburg to prevent him embarrassing the czar and alleged to have married and badly beaten the daughter of an Orenburg policeman on his way to Tashkent. 'The exile of this degenerate scion of royalty is understood to be lifelong,' finished Curzon, who did not deign to visit him.

Years later, the British masterspy F. M. Bailey met the grand duke's widow and learned that 'he had been exiled... on account of an escapade in which the crown jewels figured... His large house, full of beautiful pictures and furniture and *objets d'art* had been nationalized and was a museum to show the people how the *bourjoui* lived in the bad old days.'

N. K. Romanov seems to have been fond of Tashkent, and is remembered fondly by its curators and museum guides.The core of the Uzbek State Art Museum's pre-revolutionary Russian collection is thought to have been stolen by him from the Hermitage. Romanov's absurdly ornate residence, in a quiet garden on Buyuk Turon Ulitsa (formerly Ulitsa Lenina) can be viewed only from the outside. Today a different kind of nationalization has turned the building over to government use. Some of the contents of this former **Museum of Antique and Jeweller's Art** can be seen in the Aybek Museum of the History of the Peoples of Uzbekistan. Overlooked by the Hotel Uzbekistan, Karl Marx, the man without whom there would have been no Lenin Square or Soviet art has been replaced by today's hero, **Amir Timur**. Opposite the Hotel Uzbekistan, across the small park, is the pedestrianized area known locally as **Broadway**. Between colonnades and against a billboard featuring government wisdom about the market economy, local painters gather and display their works. Kodak film is widely available from the kiosks that line the road. As is *shashlyk* and ice-cream from the numerous cafés. This is a good place for a snack and to contemplate the carnival atmosphere in close proximity to the old KGB. Their office is further along by the Zerefshan Restaurant.

Shopping

Only buy carpets in Tashkent if you are not going to Ashgabat, Samarkand or Bukhara. There are some in the Afghan **gift shop** on the 2nd floor of the Hotel Uzbekistan, in the courtyard of the Museum of Decorative and Applied Art and in the Aybek History Museum, for hard currency only. Jewellery, Koran-holders and miniature laquered boxes are made and sold, also for hard currency only, at the Abdul-Khasim madrasa near ⓜ *Khalklar Dustligi*. You can sometimes buy paintings at the Exhibition Hall of the Painters' Union on Ulitsa Buyuk Turon and along Broadway, close to the Hotel Uzbekistan. The **Khamar** shop is part of the Painters' Union building, faces Prospekt Rashidova, and has a wide, if expensive, selection of paintings, pottery and textiles (*open Mon–Fri, 9–6*). Paintings at more reasonable prices can be found on Broadway, at the Hotel Uzbekistan end. Anyone interested in art and architecture books should browse in the **kiosks** of the pedestrian subway close to the Hotel Tashkent, where there's a variety of second-hand books and maps in Russian. Or look in the **bookshop** in the shopping centre close to ⓜ Khamid Olimjon. Should you need a car or motorbike, wait for a Sunday morning and go to the hippodrome on the edge of town on the road to Samarkand (*see* p.20 for details). All this can be captured on film, which, if supplies are short, can be purchased at the department store diagonally across from the Hotel Tashkent. Established brand names and in-store processing are available.

Several supermarkets sell western non-perishable items, which are more easily recognizable than the shop exteriors. Check out **Tesco**, ⓜ Khalklar Dustligi, Uzbekistanskaya Ulitsa; **Mir**, a Turkish-run supermarket and fast-food place on Ulitsa Mustafa Kemal Ataturk; the German **Ardus** opposite Alayksy bazaar on Ulitsa Amir Timur; a Dutch supermarket behind the same bazaar; **Al-Aksa** on the corner of Ulitsa Kunaeva and Buyuk Turon; and **Ital Foods**, with Italian products, near the American Embassy on the corner of Ulitsa Ivan Franco and Al-Khorazmy. The best place to stock up on alcohol, juice or junk food is a wholesale market on the right-hand side of Ulitsa Usmana Nosyra.

Tashkent (✆ 3712–)　　　　　　　　　　　　　　　　　　　**Where to Stay**

expensive

Competition has changed things at the **Hotel Uzbekistan**, Ulitsa Khamza 45, ✆ 33 13 49/89 11 15. Prices have gone down, but still don't represent value for money (single $75, double $106). The bargain room, $55, is the one near the security lady's desk.

Rooms, though small, are clean and have a shower but no bath; sometimes the temperatures for hot water and air-conditioning get confused (this might change after refurbishment, due to be completed by January 1997). Rooms may be paid for in dollars or by Visa/Mastercard. The hotel has its own tourist office, or 'service bureau', plus the Intourist office on the 4th floor (now called the commerical office), and a business centre that is open 24 hours a day. In the lobby are various hard currency souvenir shops, city maps, coffee and the Uzbek Airways office (*open daily 8.30–8*). Uzbek, European or Korean food is available in the two good restaurants, often frequented by ex-pats, and there is dancing in the basement nightclub. International calls can be made from the business centre ($9 Europe, $15 USA), but are even more expensive than at the **Urgent International Call Booth**. If calling abroad from your room, you must pay the floor lady in local currency. The hotel remains Tashkent's major landmark, standing like a giant angle iron looming over a metro station at the nexus of three traffic arteries.

The Hotel Uzbekistan's rival is a hotel without a name, situated almost behind it. Known variously as the **Tata**, Indian or pink hotel. Built by the Indian Taj company and run by Uzbektourism, with sister hotels in Samarkand and Bukhara, it is billed as 'western'. Certainly its foyer lacks the gloomy austerity typical of most Soviet-built hotels: marble, fountains and deep carpets set the tone. The Bombay Restaurant serves European food and another dining-room, on the first floor, Uzbek food. All facilities such as the sauna, gym and business centre are open to non-residents. Carpets and paintings can be bought in the gallery-cum-shop at the rear of the ground floor, maps and postcards from the counter nearby. Close to this is the service centre for city tours. Pay for your room with Visa, travellers cheques or hard currency; single, $90, double $110.

The three-sided, 22-storey **Hotel Chorsu**, blending imperfectly with the old town at the west end of Prospekt Navoi, has no air-conditioning but does offer breezy rooms on the upper floors and relatively helpful staff. Bus 11 comes here from the airport and trolley bus 20 from the train station. For an extra $3 guests are entitled to breakfast (single $40, double $50) and as part of a group of at least ten, a city tour with an English guide provided by the tourist office on the first floor. Try the excursion bureau at ⓜ Pakhtakor. Trolleybus 8 goes along Prospekt Navoi to the Hotel Uzbekistan.

moderate

Situated opposite the opera house on Uzbekistanskaya Ulitsa is the very large, very solid **Hotel Tashkent**, ✆ 56 43 75, ✉ 89 11 30 (single $30, double $50). Built in 1958, it retains a Soviet air in keeping with the architecture and offers BBC World Service TV but no air-conditioning. Reservations are generally required but persistence is known to pay off too. International phone calls can be made from the third-floor business centre which also doubles as the hotel tourist

HOTEL CHORSU,
TASHKENT

service bureau (city tours: $12 per individual or $3 per person in a tour group). Next door is the restaurant with a terrace and décor that combines tradional Uzbek design with the Communist message.

Slightly further out of town (follow Mehtar Ambar), at Ulitsa Buyuk Ipak Yoli 115, is the **Sayohat Hotel**, ✆ 68 67 72, Ⓜ Maxim Gorky. Rooms are paid for in dollars and prices vary according to visa type and season: tourist visa holders pay $17/$22 for a single, $45–60/$55–80 for double.

Other hotels include the **Turon** (formerly the Leningrad) north of Prospekt Navoi on the corner of Ulitsa Yusupova and Prospekt Abdulla Khadiri. The yellow curtains in the foyer and the silver ceiling are a cheerful contrast to the drab concrete exterior. Pay per bed in dollars, singles $25 and doubles $20.

inexpensive

Compared with any of these, the **Hotel Rossiya**, Ulitsa Kunaeva 2, Ⓜ Kosmonavtov, ✆ 56 28 74 ($16 single, $22–40 double), is an unbelievable bargain. The rooms may not be completely cockroach-free but all have a bathroom and hot water. Reception staff usually start by saying they're full and demand a marriage certificate if you request a double, but they seem to be amused by foreigners. Tell them where you come from or ask to see the manager for foreigners' accommodation (in the office on the right-hand side of the reception desk). Don't leave valuables in your room. Express bus 67 comes here from the airport; trams 9 and 24 from the railway station; trams 7 and 28 from the long-distance bus station. Payment is in local currency.

Hotel Yoshlyk, south of Prospekt Navoi, Ⓜ Pakhtakor, ☎ 41 44 10, is under renovation; a joint venture with a German company. At the **Hotel Dostlik** the rooms aren't the cleanest, hot water is an extra (around $4 inclusive) and a foreigner may be refused a room here; likewise at the **Hotel Locomotif** by the train station.

Tashkent (☎ 3712–)　　　　　　　　　　　　　　　　　　　　　　**Eating Out**

expensive–moderate

Hard-currency restaurants abound. One of the best in Tashkent is **The Black Dragon**, on Prospekt Abdulla Khadiri, which offers Chinese cuisine at $20 a head, including a service tax of 20%. The **Arirang**, Ulitsa Lokhuti 22 (close to the Uzbek State Museum of Art, down a narrow alley between the bus stop and the kiosk), offer outstanding service in quiet, clean and light surroundings. The Korean menu averages $20–40 and, if you go regularly enough, you will get a 10% discount. If you fancy karaoke and Korean, try the **Seoul**, Ulitsa Usmana Nosyra 65. Three courses and the floorshow (8.30–9.30pm) cost $30. Pay in either local or hard currency. At the same price but payable in local currency only, the **Richman** at Ulitsa Lokhuti 16a, Ⓜ Oybek, tucked between the ACCELS office and an Uzbek government institute, offers pale blue white-fringed drapes in its European Hall or bamboo décor in its Asian option. There's classical piano music in the afternoon and the obligatory floor show in the evening. Ex-pats favour the **Café Oleg** on Mehtar Ambar, Ⓜ Khamid Olimjon, where ornamental lamps soften the busy location and there's a Russian menu served with imported Carlsberg ($15–20).

Reliable if not gourmet Uzbek and Russian food is served on the ground floor of the **Hotel Uzbekistan**, in the **TV Tower**'s revolving restaurants (express bus 72 to the Park Pobiedy stop) and in the main (first-floor) dining-room of the **Zerafshan** restaurant. The aircraft hangar-sized Zerafshan is managed by Armenians and protected by one mafia organization from two others; restaurant prices reflect this. Apart from the main dining-room, the building houses a multi-level café complex. Come here for loud music, coloured lights, ice-cream and the latest Russian soap opera on TV. At ground level is the **Labarynth** and downstairs the most sumptuous lavatories in Central Asia. Live music starts at 8 pm. Across the road from the Hotel Uzbekistan there's caviar, belly-dancing and overcharging for the mixed menu at the **Istanbul** ($15–20). A small shop inside sells imported beer and chocolates. The former Teon Business Club, now renamed the **Asr**, equidistant from the Uzbekistan and the Tata on Mehtar Ambar, is one of the first privatized restaurants in Uzbekistan. It serves Russian, Uzbek and Italian food to classical music from 5–8pm and then the cabaret begins. *Closed Sun; open Mon–Sat, 12–12.* Both these restaurants attract the foreign and business communities.

For reasonably priced **Turkish** food in clean surroundings, go to the corner of Ulitsas Oybek and Chekhov, just behind the Fiat car dealer, to this unsignposted restaurant; a substantial meal shouldn't be more than $5. Try the Manchurian chicken ($2) at the **Islamabad**, on the left-hand side of Amir Timur, past Ulitsa Khurshid. An unexpected venue for a cheap lunch ($2) is the canteen of the **Indonesian Embassy** in the diplomatic compound at Ulitsa Murtazoeva 6, first floor, through the third entrance on the left (*open Mon–Thurs from 1pm*).

Tashkent's parks are not short of the odd pit-stop. Among the more salubrious are the **Boguy Shamoy**, close to the TV Tower in the Park Pobiedy, where credit cards are accepted (*open 11am–midnight daily; cheaper before 5pm*), and cafés like the **Blue Dome** between Prospekt Rashidova and Ulitsa Buyuk Turon. Pay the cashier by the entrance, take the ticket and place your order with the chefs at the turquoise tiled chimneys for a cheap meal of reasonable *shashlyk, samsa* and *plov.* To combine a walk in the park with views of the river, try the **Anhor**, close to the presidential house, or cross over the bridge from Prospekt Rashidova, near the intersection with Uzbekistanskaya, to **Alazzi** and its *shashlyk* production line. Fast food has arrived in Tashkent: the **Hot dog** (*closed Sun*) is next to the Asr on Mehtar Ambar; **American Food** is at Mustafa Kemal Ataturk 22 (burgers $1); conveniently placed next door is the **Diet Bar**. Close to the Alaysky bazaar and between the Ⓜ Pakhtakor and street is the famed **White Crocodile**.

To fill up very cheaply walk down Ulitsa Karla Marxa past the Zerafshan and choose from half a dozen dispensaries of *shashlyk, plov* and bulk-fried chick peas. Try the café underneath the **Exhibition Hall of the Painters' Union** for good coffee. If the prices at the Café Oleg shock, there's ice-cream, pop and *shashlyk* snacks at the **Semurg** and **Ildam** cafés close to Ⓜ Khamid Olimjon on Mehtar Ambar; cheap chicken and pizzas at **Nasiba's** close to the Alisher Navoi Wedding Park and *shashlyk* on the roof of the Hotel Tashkent. But the best and **freshest shashlyk** comes from the narrow alleyways of the old town bazaar and close to the Hotel Rossiya.

Entertainment and Nightlife

If you need nightlife, take advantage of Tashkent. Nowhere else in Central Asia can you see *Aida* at six, proceed to an orgy of Turkish food and belly-dancing and still find a bar open at two in the morning.

Theatres, concert halls and the **Alisher Navoi Opera and Ballet Theatre** (on Prospekt Rashidova and Uzbekistanskaya Ulitsa) only function from September to April. There are about a dozen operas in rep at a time, including western classics and Soviet operas with Central Asian themes. They alternate nightly with the ballet; performances are listed outside the building. Tickets cost the equivalent of $1–2 from the box office, $6 from the Hotel Uzbekistan. Performances start at 6pm and play defiantly, competing with excitable school children who are given free tickets. Splash out on the glossy programme which is in English. The cheaper is in Russian only. Classical concerts at the **Bakhor Concert Hall** (in the yellow building near the former Lenin monument on Alleya Paradov), and the more popular Uzbek folk concerts at the **Palace of People's Friendship** (Дворец дружбы народов/*Dvoryets druzhby narodov*), **Ⓜ** *Khalklar Dustligi*, also start at 6 pm. Tickets are obtainable from the venues only, except for Intourist outings from the Hotel Uzbekistan to see the Bakhor

UZBEK FOLK GROUP 'BAKHOR'

dance ensemble. There are occasional organ recitals at the Conservatoire of Music at Mehtar Ambar 31.

Lower-brow entertainment is mostly at restaurants. There is a very sober nightly song-and-dance show in the gigantic Zerafshan Restaurant on Ulitsa Karla Marxa, and a marginally raunchier one in the Hotel Chorsu's main dining-room. There is belly-dancing downstairs at the Istanbul Restaurant opposite the Hotel Uzbekistan. According to a poster in the airport, a chorus line performs at the 'Music Hall' in Park Pobiedy, Ulitsa Amir Timur 107, ✆ 34 40 88.

To Samarkand

The four-lane highway from Tashkent to Samarkand is straight, fast and mostly very dull. Just beyond Chinaz, 64km from Tashkent, it crosses the Syr Darya river. This drains the northern Pamirs, the western Tian Shan and the Fergana valley, but, like the Amu Darya, is mostly diverted into irrigation canals before it reaches the Aral Sea 1000km away.

After another 100km of non-stop cotton plantation you reach the turn-off to **Dzhizak** (Джизак), birthplace of Sharaf Rashidov (leader of Soviet Uzbekistan, 1959–83) and of his post-Soviet re-habilitation (*see* p.62). A giant portrait of the man covers a factory wall at the town's eastern entrance. The street where he was born, near *kolkhoz Moskva* (Moscow collective farm), is named after him. The house, Ulitsa Rashidova 35, is no different from the others in the street, and is not open to the public.

Abdullah Khan of Bukhara staged a tremendous massacre near Dzhizak in 1571, and an anti-Russian rising was ruthlessly crushed here in 1916. The area was an important power-base for Rashidov. Dzhizak itself is contemporary small-town Uzbekistan without the medieval frills, and none too uplifting. There are plenty of Tashkent–Dzhizak buses and onward ones to Samarkand. Beyond the town the Dzhizak River, the old road and most buses enter a defile between the Nuratan hills to the west and the foothills of the Turkestan range to the east. The new road goes over the hills.

Samarkand (Самарканд)

Everything I have heard about the beauty of Samarkand is true— except that it is even more beautiful than I could have imagined.

Alexander the Great, 329 BC

...crumbling sun-baked bricks, decorated with glazed tiles of deep blue and vivid turquoise that sparkle in the sun... a walled stairway with, on either side, a row of small mosques of the most exquisite beauty... wainscoted with alabaster and adorned with jasper... glimpses of courtyards and gardens... and in the open bazaars great heaps of fruit...

Fitzroy Maclean, *Eastern Approaches*, 1949

It's still there, still inspiring sentences of great earnestness and wonder from every writer who beholds it. But besides being Central Asia's premier tourist attraction, Samarkand is Uzbekistan's second city, with a population of 600,000, a major university, five other institutes of higher education, 15 'vocational colleges', a cannery producing 200 million jars of fruit and vegetables a year and a porcelain factory producing 22 million items of porcelain a year. All of which affects the general feel of the place quite as much as its ancient monuments do.

If Samarkand's industrial backwardness ended with Soviet power, so did its isolation. It is said that only two Europeans got here in the 400 years to 1850. Nowadays Aeroflot flies in tens of thousands of them each year and the people of Samarkand are more used to foreigners than are any other Central Asians. Watch your wallet. This is what the police mean when they call their city 'Bombay number two'.

Yet the Soviet impact on Samarkand was by no means all malign. No one had bothered to restore its great Timurid monuments until Lenin, in 1918, issued a decree that 'treasures of art and ancient culture' should be preserved, restored and put on show for the edification of the masses. Teams of scientists from Leningrad descended on Samarkand, rediscovered ancient glazing and gilding techniques and substantially rebuilt the three madrasas of the Registan. Purists called it sacrilege. Tourists voted with their chequebooks, and their expectations, raised by centuries of literary hype, are very seldom unfulfilled.

'Patterns that were only tentative in Bukhara had reached their full flourish here,' wrote Geoffrey Moorhouse in 1990. 'Colours which had mingled blithely there achieved even more spectacular harmonies now... For all the sumptuous inlay of its semi-precious stones, the Taj Mahal in Agra was made to seem virginal beside the Registan in Samarkand.'

So the Registan is beautiful. Also, very importantly, it is big. The ruins of the Bibi Khanym mosque are big too. Indeed, they are so big that seen from a distance in silhouette with their apparently permanent adjuncts of tower-crane and scaffolding they are easily mistaken for a half-built high-rise office block. Bibi Khanym and the Registan are the grand old men of Samarkand, and sheer size is what enables them to hold their own, defiantly and dramatically, against the big, loud, functional Soviet city that now surrounds them.

History

Samarkand is an oasis, but not the kind where human life stops beyond an outer ring of palm trees. Set on the edge of the Kizyl-Kum desert within sight of two mountain ranges, it is watered by the river that runs between them, the Zerafshan.

For at least 10,000 years and possibly as many as 40,000, *homo sapiens* has found this an amenable spot. If Silk Route trade made it rich in historic times, nature was the provider in prehistoric ones: mountain streams running off the northern slopes of the Zerafshan range supported trees which grew nuts and berries which in turn supported wild fowl and other animals. Everything that Palaeolithic man could wish for was here, and his (or rather her, for they were women's) jaw and thigh-bones were discovered in a former children's park in Samarkand in 1937.

Neolithic man was altogether more settled and sophisticated, hunting gazelles and wild bulls with bows and arrows, but also breeding sheep and goats on wide terraces above the Sazagan river south-west of modern Samarkand. Fine stone arrow-heads and other items dating from between 6000 and 4000 BC were discovered at four sites along the river between 1966 and 1972. The oldest evidence of urban settlement on the territory of Samarkand is a collection of jewellery from a Bronze-Age burial ground beside the River Siab, which still runs grubbily along the eastern edge of the Afrasiab site. The remains of an outer city wall here have been dated around 1500 BC, but Samarkand proper is generally accepted to be 2500 years old, and Afrasiab was its first name.

Afrasiab may have been the first Sogdian king, Sogdiana being the land between the Oxus (Amu Darya) and Jaxartes (Syr Darya) rivers, or he may have existed only in an epic poem called 'Shakhname', as king of what became the northern Persian satrapy of Turan. Alternatively the word may not refer to a person at all and be derived instead from the Tajik word *parsiab*, meaning 'over the Siab (black river)'. Either way, Afrasiab the place is a short walk east of the centre of modern Samarkand. In its heyday it covered 800 hectares. The modern site covers 300 hectares, 96 per cent of which have not been touched by builders or archaeologists since they were trampled and torched by Genghis Khan's horsemen in 1220.

By the 4th century BC Afrasiab was the major urban centre of Sogdiana, famous for its size and general magnificence. Marauders were for the most part kept at bay by a city wall 14km long and, in one surviving section, 13m high. But in 329 BC the city faced the greatest marauder of his and possibly of all time. Alexander the Great crossed the Hindu Kush in the spring of that year and took Samarkand without a struggle. But Spitamen, the local Sogdian ruler, led a spirited rebellion that delayed the Greek conquest by 18 frustrating months, and ended only with Spitamen's assassination by his own followers.

Having finally taken the city Alexander became arrogant. On the feast of Dionysus he made sacrifices to Castor and Pollux, and claimed to be descended, like them, from Zeus. Some courtiers took this as a cue for flattery and likened him to Hercules, but his old friend Cleitus decided to cut him down to size. Emboldened by drink, he told Alexander he was not the equal of his own father Philip, let alone of Hercules. Alexander ran him through with a spear—and was filled with remorse for the remaining five years of his life.

Samarkand and the Silk Route

With the arrival of the first Chinese in the mid 2nd century BC, Samarkand entered an era of invasion-proof prosperity and semi-mythic international status. It was to last more than a thousand years and it began because the Chinese found that silk, which they alone knew how to make, was worth more than its weight in gold in the empires of the West.

Samarkand was at the very centre of the Silk Route system. The only Chinese caravans which did not pass through it were those heading straight for Russia from the passes of the Tian Shan—and Russia was but a minor client until Kiev rose to power and prosperity in the 9th century.

Considering the volume of through traffic, remarkably little is known about life in ancient Samarkand. Archaeologists are hampered by the wind; before Tamerlane the city was built mostly of mud, so that over the centuries buildings simply dried up and blew away. And Asian caravanners do not seem to have kept diaries. So we have an account by Arrian, Alexander's chronicler, and then nothing until 1200 years later when the Arabian traveller Abulkasim ibn-Khakal was much taken by Samarkand's canals. Marco Polo's *Travels* kept alive the legend of Samarkand for Europeans, even if he never actually went there. Thereafter Europeans arrived at the rate of about one every hundred years until the 1860s. In the end the rarity of writings about Samarkand is eloquent confirmation of its extreme isolation; until 1868 it was still, in Geoffrey Moorhouse's words, 'a great deal more remote from the rest of civilization than the moon is today.'

At least we know that when those first Chinese arrived, Samarkand was part of the (Persian) Achaemenid empire, and that, like the rest of Transoxiana, it passed to Kushans, Hephthalites and Turks before the coming of the Arabs. From bowls and fire-proof altars in Afrasiab's museum it also seems that the potting wheel arrived on the scene in the 1st century AD and that the prevailing religion was Zoroastrianism.

The secrets of silk-making reached the West in the 6th century and the flow of Chinese silk through Samarkand gradually diminished as Italy, Spain and southern France began making their own. But Samarkand was to remain a crossroads of international trade in other commodities until sea routes were established between Europe and the Orient in the 16th century.

The Prophet and the Camel-Saddle

Islam failed to snuff out Samarkand's Zoroastrianism at the first attempt. The armies of the Prophet crossed the Amu Darya in 654 but Samarkand, like Bukhara, defied them for half a century. Soviet historians stopped just short of claiming the city was already a secular people's republic: 'the population refused to accept foreign oppression and the city became a centre of the liberation struggle against the caliphate,' says Y. N. Aleskerov. But the liberation struggle foundered on semantics. In 712 Qutaiba ibn-Muslim, governor of the province of Khorassan which was then part of the Islamic Umayyad empire, arrived with his soldiers at the gates of Samarkand. Its defenders tried to snub him. 'We have found it written,' they shouted from the battlements, 'that our city can only be captured by a man named Camel-Saddle.' Unfortunately, in Arabic 'Qutaiba' means precisely that, camel saddle, so in rode Qutaiba (on a horse).

Samarkand's first mosque was built in the western corner of what is now the Afrasiab site. The city was absorbed into Khorassan (based on Merv) and, in the late 9th century, into the Samanid empire based on Bukhara. Islam, and its pervasive influence on art and architecture, was here to stay.

Meanwhile, for all her neighbour's political pretensions, Samarkand remained the largest, richest city in Transoxiana. When Abulkasim ibn-Khakal visited Samarkand in the mid-10th century he climbed the citadel and saw 'one of the most beautiful views that man has ever gazed upon: the fresh greenness of the trees, the glittering castles... All of this is reflected in the canals running with water and the artificial ponds... Samarkand is a city with large market places, blocks of dwellings, bath-houses, caravanserai... The running water flows through canals that are partially made out of lead... With few exceptions there is not a single street or house where there is no running water, and very few houses do not have gardens.'

Even a new era of nomadic invasions, starting with that of the Karakhanid Turks in the late 10th century, failed at first to destroy this irrigated idyll or the commerce which financed it. Over the next 200 years control of Samarkand alternated between Muslim Turks—the Seljuks, and later the Khorezmshahs from the Amu Darya delta—and another tribe of pagan nomads, the Kara-Khitai. Then came a terror of a different order.

The Mongols

When Genghis Khan sacked Samarkand in 1220 he slit its jugular first, damming up the canals which supplied it from the River Zerafshan. He also 'slit open the wombs of pregnant women and killed the foetuses,' according to a 13th-century historian called Ibn-ak-Asir. 'The flames of the massacre spread far and wide, and evil covered everything like a cloud driven by the wind.'

The aftermath may not have matched the initial apocalypse. Some sources say Samarkand surrendered without a fight, that most of its people were spared in return and that fewer buildings were razed than at Bukhara. But according to Ak-Asir's account Genghis Khan was utterly ruthless. He waited outside the city to be joined by his sons Chaghatai and Ögödei, (fresh from the destruction of Otrar), then drove its inhabitants out, butchered the garrison and levelled the buildings. Less than a quarter of the city's population of 400,000 survived, and it stayed at around 100,000 afterwards because that was all the wrecked irrigation system could support.

Samarkand bounced back. In 1333 the great Arab traveller Ibn-Battuta was able to describe it as 'one of the largest and most perfectly beautiful cities in the world.' No wonder Tamerlane, born three years later to a minor tribal chieftain, chose it as his capital.

The Timurids

The history of Samarkand during Tamerlane's campaigning years (1372–1402) is a reflection of the history of the world. He rampaged to Delhi and Baghdad and to the gates of Moscow and Constantinople, sending back to Samarkand Asia's finest craftsmen and most precious treasures. He named its districts after far-flung cities, and fearful emissaries sought him there from Beijing, Madrid and most points in between.

Like Alexander the Great and Genghis Khan he wanted to rule the world. 'As there is one God in Heaven there must be one king on earth,' he explained early in his career. 'The entire world is not worth more than one king.' But his fighting was also driven by economics: trade along the classic Silk Route through Samarkand, Merv and northern Persia had fallen sharply since Genghis Khan's destruction of its oases. Urgench, to the north, was now thriving at Samarkand's expense, and was Tamerlane's first victim. Later, in his longest campaign (1391–95), he conquered the lands with which Urgench had traded; those of the Golden Horde on the Volga and in southern Russia. His aim was always to bring trade back to Samarkand, which was now not just an entrepôt but a famed manufacturer of velvet and paper.

The best description of Samarkand before the Russian conquest is by Ruy Gonzalez de Clavijo, ambassador extraordinary from the court of Henry III of Castile. In 1403 he began an epic journey from Spain to Samarkand in the wake of Tamerlane's victorious army, which by capturing Ankara had given Western Europe a breathing space from Ottoman expansionism. But Europe was still more alarmed by Tamerlane himself. Henry wanted a treaty.

Clavijo did not get him one, but he got a fluke glimpse of Samarkand and its builder in their finest hour. Throughout the envoy's sojourn the emperor was to be found among his wives and subjects feasting on wine, mutton, horse-flesh and fruit in a succession of palatial silk tents. In one of them Clavijo saw 'a flat emerald, four palms long, on a golden table. In front of this table there was a golden tree made to resemble an oak, with the trunk as big as a man's leg. The fruit of this tree consisted of rubies, emeralds, turquoises, sapphires and wonderfully large pearls. On this tree there were many birds made of enamelled gold of various colours...

'The city itself,' he continued, 'is rather larger than Seville, but lying outside are great numbers of houses which form extensive suburbs. The township is surrounded by orchards and vineyards and between them pass streets with open squares. These are all densely populated and all kinds of goods are on sale with bread-stuffs and meat. Among these orchards outside Samarkand are found the most noble and beautiful houses and here Timur has his many palaces and pleasure grounds...'

It was 1404. Two massive construction projects, the Bibi Khanym mosque and Tamerlane's own mausoleum, Gur Emir, were in progress in the city centre. On a whim he ordered the construction of a grand bazaar in 20 days—or else his engineers would pay with their lives. A thousand men were imprisoned in the citadel making arms and armour for his planned invasion of China.

The following year, shortly after setting out, he died. The empire quickly shrunk, but as it did, Samarkand enjoyed half a century of peace and prosperity under Tamerlane's grandson Ulug Bek (r. 1407–49). To him we owe the Ulug Bek madrasa and the remains of an observatory—the most intriguing relic of medieval Samarkand.

Ulug Bek was murdered by his son in 1449 for perceived heresy. Tamerlane's great-great-great-grandson Babur was hounded out of the city in 1512 by the Uzbek Turks, having taken possession of it at the turn of the century aged 14. He was the last of the Timurid dynasty–and the first of another, the Mughal, at Delhi.

The Forgotten Market Town

From the end of the 15th century Samarkand suffered 400 years of near-terminal decline. Ming China had closed her borders in 1426 to keep out foreign influence. The Ottomans had imposed prohibitive tolls and tariffs on Anatolian sections of the old Silk Route and Europeans were discovering seaborne alternatives. Samarkand's trade all but dried up, and grass began to grow through the cracks in her azure domes. Under the Sheibanid, Mangit and Astrakhanid dynasties it was, in the German historian Klaus Pander's words 'just another unknown market town' in the Khanate of Bukhara. Samarkand was neither a bastion of resistance to Russian conquest in the 1860s nor a major centre of revolutionary or counter-revolutionary activity in the first two decades of the 20th century.

The railway arrived in 1888 but tourists were slow in following. Stephen Graham of *The Times* wrote in 1916: 'There stand among the deserts of Turkestan and beside the irrigated cotton fields of a new civilisation, the remains and ruins of a mediaeval glory, the mosques and tombs and palaces of the days of Timour and of his loved wife, Bibi Khanum. The Russians are not touched by archaeology, and have no interest in pagans, even splendid pagans... So Tamerlane is little thought of.'

Soviet and Post-Soviet Samarkand

Despite being ethnically half-Tajik, Samarkand became the first capital of Soviet Uzbekistan. The Uzbek Soviet Socialist Republic was proclaimed in the Registan in 1924 . Tashkent became capital in 1930, once its anti-Soviet rowdies had been dealt with, but the Sovietization of Samarkand continued. Factories were built to give it a proletariat and the surrounding plain was irrigated to give Moscow cotton, which students have to spend each October picking. An opera house and the headquarters of the regional Soviet were built on the hill opposite the Registan, site of Tamerlane's Blue Palace.

In 1992, the year after the collapse of the Soviet Union, tourism in Samarkand fell by 75 per cent because ex-Soviet citizens could no longer afford to come and Westerners were frightened by the fighting in nearby Tajikistan. But the new Foreign Minister of Afghanistan came. In an emotional visit he claimed credit on behalf of the *mujahedin* for toppling the Soviet regime, and welcomed ancient Samarkand's return to the Islamic brotherhood of Central Asia.

Getting to and from Samarkand

It is now quite easy to get from Samarkand via Moscow to London in a day, but going the other way the time change works against you (and it would be hard to imagine a heavier dose of culture shock). For international flights to Moscow and Tashkent, *see* pp.2–4.

by air

Aeroflot/Uzbekistan Airways offers one direct flight a week from Moscow to Samarkand and one to St Petersburg.Within Central Asia there are at least two flights a day to and from Tashkent ($51), but no connections to Bukhara and Urgench or Khiva. This means that the Samarkand–Bukhara–Khiva–Tashkent round trip is not at present possible by air. There is one flight to Ashgabat weekly, leaving at 6am on Wednesdays. The airport is north of the centre next to the long-distance bus station.

Air tickets are available from the Uzbek Airways office on Ulitsa Gagarina (take bus 10 from the Hotel Samarkand) and must be paid for in hard currency.

by rail

A pristine new railway station opened in 1993 next to the old, chaotic one near the junction of Ulitsas Gagarina and Titova northwest of the centre. Its landmark is Samarkand's answer to Big Ben. In front, at basement level, is further evidence of the new entreprenurial spirit; numerous small shops and more under construction nearby. Local buses and *marshrutnoe* arrive and depart from the car park to the left. Inside, eight fan pillars support a mosaic ceiling of turquoise tiles and 'gold' chandeliers. The grey marble floor came courtesy of the local Zerafshan mountains. Buying a ticket here is no mundane experience.

Despite the grandiose building Samarkand is not a train terminus nor even an important railway junction Through trains to or from Tashkent, Dushanbe, Chardzou, Bukhara and Moscow often stop here in the middle of the night: the Moscow–Tashkent train stops here on alternate days; the Nukus–Tashkent service once daily and the Almaty version once a week. There are plans for a direct Samarkand–Moscow train from the summer of 1996. At present, tickets for the Moscow–Dushanbe through train can be purchased only two hours in advance of departure. Foreigners must pay for tickets in local currency.

by bus

This is the easiest way to travel between Samarkand, Bukhara and Tashkent. Ten buses a day travel to Tashkent, between 6.30am and 3.15pm, taking 6–7 hours; ten go to Karshi from 6.50am to 5pm. Bukhara buses leave roughly every two hours from 7.15am until mid-afternoon, taking 5–6 hours. There's one a day to Chimkent, Dzambul and Termez via Zeravshan. The daily Dushanbe bus departs at 6pm (taking 16 hours) There are no buses to Pendzhikent or Chardzou.

Two buses leave each afternoon for the 14-hour run across the Kizyl-Kum desert to Urgench—you could be in Khiva for a late breakfast—and two buses a day go the long way (taking 4 hours) to Shahrisabz. There are daily services to and from Andizhan, Kokand, Namangan and Fergana, all of which except the Kokand service (departs 1pm) leave late afternoon for their 11–12-hour journey. In the opposite direction, there's one Nukus bus daily. In theory a special visa stamp is no longer necessary but it is worth checking before departure. Ticket counters at the bus station are open 6am–5pm.

Getting Around

Bus 10 is Samarkand's Piccadilly Line. It goes from the bus station to the railway station via the airport, bazaar, hotels Samarkand, Zerafshan, Leningrad and Turist, and the Uzbek Airways office. Trolleybus 5 goes from the railway station to the bazaar.

On cool days the major tourist sites are within walking distance of each other. Two streets link them up: Registanskaya Ulitsa, from near the Gur Emir mausoleum to the Registan; and the pedestrianized Tashkentskaya Ulitsa, from behind the Registan to Bibi Khanym mosque and the bazaar. The Shah-i-Zinda complex is a short walk south of the bazaar and Ulug Bek's observatory is 20 minutes up the Tashkent road, which starts opposite the bazaar by the Khasret Khyzr mosque and goes through Afrasiab.

In summer walking is exhausting. Bus 10 and *marshrutnoe* taxis 17, 18, 19 and 23 go from the Hotel Samarkand to the bazaar. Taxi 17 continues to Afrasiab and the observatory. For the most efficient use of time hire a taxi by the hour. Offer about $5 in local currency per hour.

The helpful English-speaking **Intourist Service Bureau** is at the Hotel Samarkand, ✆ 35 88 12/35 71 52. Their main business is selling **excursions** which are worthwhile only with a good guide. When information-gathering ask for Mutabar, who has 25 years of experience, and try to get Muso as a guide . Both speak excellent English.

A guide from **Intourist** and a 3-hour city tour for three costs $25 ($43 for a group of nine), excluding site entrance fees. You can book daytrips to Shahrisabz and Pendzhikent, Tajikistan.

According to the Embassy in Tashkent, a visa is not necessary for the latter; if you are told to the contrary in Samarkand, Intourist or another company can arrange for one for you, ($15 approximately). Prices for tours vary according to vehicle used and whether or not dinner is provided. Roughly, a car with driver to Pendzikent will cost $72, and to Shahrisabz $90. A guide is extra at $32 and $50 respectively. Excursions usually start at 9am at the hotel. Before attaching yourself to an existing group ask it and the guide if they mind and establish what you will pay to whom.

A travel company called **Asia Travel**, ✆ 35 86 76, has offices on the Hotel Samarkand's second floor. They offer city tours and can organize camel trips into the Kizyl-Kum, sleeping in yurts.

Among the private travel companies, try **Esprit de Tamerlane**, ✆ 35 41 53, ✉ 31 06 41, Ulitsa Umarova 7/1 (French and Russian spoken), run by former a foreign language institute teacher, Abduvakhid Eshankulov, who can arrange your entire trip. **Orient Star**'s French-speaking deputy director, Shohista Saidaminova, ✆ 33 00 28, ✉ 31 14 23, is an experienced and reliable organizer of tours of the city. Alternatively, try the joint **Swiss-Uzbek** company located in the business centre at Kuk-Sarai Ploshchad 1, ✆ 35 35 02, ✉ 311023, who can sort out Tajik visas if required.

There are also a number of independent guides that have established themselves in the last few years, many ex-Intourist. Try **Sabira Alieva**, ✆ 35 72 91, Ulitsa Rudaki 255. Or **Elena Urikh**, ✆ 24 48 46 (for Russian speakers) or ✆ 29 49 60 (for English speakers). Also **Inez Abalova**, ✆ 29 02 13, or **Valentina Belova**, ✆ 29 14 65, an English teacher from the Foreign Language Institute. Anyone particularly interested in archaeology should call **Ludmilla Lapkina**, an archaeological researcher, ✆ 21 37 72. **Yuri Fyodorov**, ✆ 21 59 95, will arrange trips to the mountains for $15–20 (groups of 3 or 4), if you need a complete change of scene.

A word of warning. Tourism in Samarkand is recognised as good business. Consequently foreigners are charged for each monument they visit and extra for cameras.

Samarkand

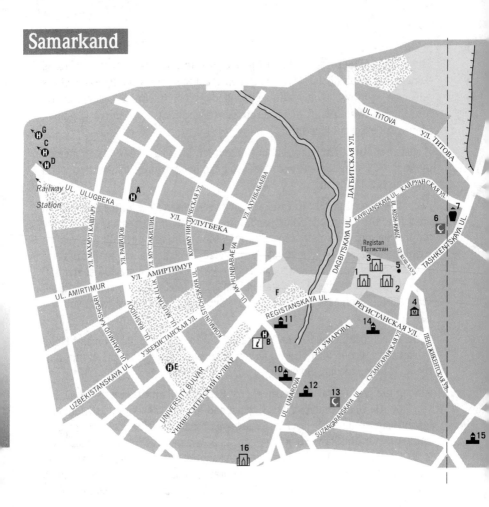

Ticket prices should be in the region of $1 in cym. Ask for your ticket as you enter; occasionally prices err on the creative side.

The **post office** in the Hotel Samarkand (*open Mon–Fri, 9–6*) is still the easiest place to get airmail stamps and envelopes. To the right of the exchange desk in the reception area, it is possible to make **international phone calls**, paid for in hard currency.

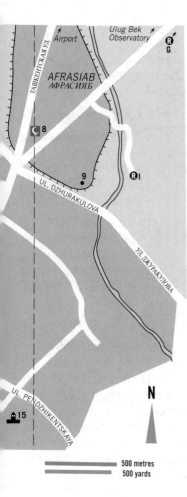

KEY

1 Ulug Bek madrasa
Медресе Улугбека

2 Shir Dor madrasa
Медресе Шир-Дор

3 Tillya Kari madrasa
Медресе Тилля-Кари

4 Museum of History, Culture and Art
Музей Истории, Культуры и Искусства

5 Chorsu
Чорсу

6 Bibi Khanym mosque
Мечеть Биби-Ханым

7 Bazaar
Базар

8 Khasret Khyzr mosque
Мечеть Хасрет-Хызр

9 Shah-i-Zinda
Шах-и-Зинда

10 Gur Emir mausoleum
Мавзолей Гур-Эмир

11 Rukhabad mausoleum
Мавзолей Рухабад

12 Ak-Saray mausoleum
Мавзолей Ак-Сарай

13 Khodja Nisbatdor mosque
Мечеть Ходжа-Нисбатдор

14 Khodja Abdi Darun mausoleum
Мавзолей Ходжа-Абди-Дарун

15 Khodja Abdi Birin mausoleum
Мавзолей Ходжа-Абди-Бирин

16 Khodja Akrar madrasa
Медресе Ходжа-Акрар

HOTELS & RESTAURANTS

A Hotel Registan
Гостиница Регистан

B Hotel Samarkand
Гостиница Самарканд

C Hotel Sayor
Гостиница Саёр

D Hotel Tourist
Гостиница Турист

E Hotel Zerafshan
Гостиница Зерафшан

F Tata Hotel
Гостиница Тата

G Bagishamal Hotel
Гостиница Багишамал

H Vatan Hotel
Гостиница Ватан

I Chai-khana Siab
Чай-хана Сиаб

J Donald Duck Café

Maps including the new street names are apparently only available in Uzbek. The best place to go for orientation for English speakers is the reception area of the Hotel Samarkand. On the wall facing the entrance is a large map.

American Express travellers cheques can be cashed into US dollars at the Bank of Uzbekistan, Ulitsa Firdarsi 7, © 33 57 50 (*open Mon–Fri, 9–6*), at a commission of three per cent.

The Registan (Регистан)

> *Suddenly we caught a glimpse of painted minarets trembling in the blue astringent light and the great Madonna blue domes of mosques and tombs shouldering the full weight of the sky among bright green trees and gardens.*

Laurens van der Post, *Journey Into Russia*, 1964

It is worth coming all this way for the Registan, the most spectacular architectural ensemble in Central Asia and the centre of Samarkand since the Mongol invasion. When you see the three great madrasas for the first time, rising petrol blue through the petrol fumes, it's hard not to feel you have arrived somewhere significant. Today the monuments are open daily.

Registan (pronounced with a hard 'g') means 'place of sand'—it was strewn on the ground to soak up the blood from the public executions that were held here until early this century. This is where Tamerlane stuck his victims' heads on spikes, and where people gathered to hear royal proclamations, heralded by blasts on enormous copper pipes called *dzharchis*. But first and foremost this was a market; a riot of stalls and stallholders' shacks until Tamerlane had them flattened for his grand bazaar in 1404.

Ulug Bek Madrasa (медресе Улугбека)

Caravanserais for itinerant traders formed part of the square even after the construction of the Ulug Bek madrasa (1417–20) on its west side. Commissioned by and named after Tamerlane's astronomer son, who probably lectured here, this ancient seminary is appropriately decorated with a mosaic of stars over its enormous *pishtak* or portico. Every other square inch of its exterior is covered in mosaic too, using virtually every motif permitted in Islamic art: floral ones sculpted into faience tiles around the niches and doorways, spirals up the pillars on the edges of the portico, bands of Kufic calligraphy round the inside of the *iwans* (the high vaulted arches in the middle of each wing), and geometric patterns known as *girikhs*—some of them amazingly reminiscent of computer graphics—on the minarets and the façade. The minarets were never used by *muezzins*; they were said instead to hold up the sky. The northern one is famous for its inward lean, attributed variously to architectural genius, the weight of the sky, earthquake damage and optical illusion. Soviet engineers tried, by rotating it 180 degrees, but failed to straighten it. The main door leads to a courtyard bounded by a mosque at the far end and two storeys of lecture halls and students' cells on the sides, but it's closed to visitors.

Sher Dor Madrasa (медресе Шир-Дор)

Two centuries were to pass before anyone found the energy to continue building round the Registan on the grand scale set by Ulug Bek. By the time the Sheibanid khan Yalang-tush Bahador took up the challenge, wind-blown sand and the detritus of endless markets had caused street level to rise three metres. This is why the Sher Dor, or 'lion-bearing' madrasa (built 1619–35) seems higher than the Ulug Bek madrasa which it faces and of

REGISTAN SQUARE, SAMARKAND

which it is a near-copy. (It could not be a perfect copy because, as the Koran says, 'nothing is perfect except Allah.') The lions in question—said to be the ones in the Persian emblem— are striped, which makes them look more like tigers. You will find them chasing baby deer across the space above the principal arch, breaking the Islamic rule so rigidly adhered to in the older building: to depict no living thing. The twin suns rising over their backs are even given human faces. The Sher Dor has ribbed cupolas either side of the pishtak which the Ulug Bek madrasa lacks—possibly, again, to break any blasphemous symmetry—but overall, in the opinion of the Czech specialist Edgar Knobloch, this madrasa has 'cruder craftsmanship, larger patterns, over-accentuated lines, exalted floral ornaments and less harmony in colour,' than the original. You can go inside, however. The cells round the courtyard produced an oversupply of student accommodation and were never full until the madrasa became a Russian hotel in colonial times. Some are now hard-currency gift shops, one of whose owners is called Sergei and can let you onto the roof for an unusual view of the Registan. For a historical view of Samarkand, take a look at the small black-and-white photo exhibition in the right-hand corner of the courtyard, near the entrance.

Tilla Kari Madrasa (медресе Тилля-Кари)

A caravanserai was pulled down on the north side of the square to make way for its biggest, newest, most extravagant building, the Tilla Kari madrasa (built 1646–59). Its 120m-long facade is unusual in incorporating the outward-facing arched balconies of students' cells. What sets it apart, though, is the mosque on the west side of the courtyard. 'Tilla Kari' means 'gilded', and though there is gilding on the madrasa's upper façade, it is nothing compared with the 1000 sq m of gold leaf used in the restoration of the 'Golden Mosque' in 1979. It left Geoffrey Moorhouse open-mouthed:

'Here was a richness of colour greater than I had ever seen anywhere before, a splendour of red beyond the opulence of rubies and a royal blue of such intensity that it would have hurt the eyes if it had been unrelieved. It was made perfect not only by the alliance with red, but by flashes of orange and dull gleamings of gold which punctuated it...'

The Soviet view was that the use of gold was decadent, a lazy way of surpassing the splendour achieved by superior craftsmanship in the Ulug Bek madrasa. But the craftsmanship in the Golden Mosque is not bad. Beneath the huge turquoise dome, for example, the ceiling appears domed; actually it is flat, and the *trompe l'œil* effect is achieved by an extraordinarily intricate pattern of plant stems in gold leaf, which get smaller and smaller towards the centre. The mosque was built along with the madrasa but was always a separate institution, built to succeed Bibi Khanym—which had already collapsed—as the city's main place of worship. Women were allowed in on Fridays. Now, just 14 years after being restored, all its decoration is threatened by rising groundwater resulting from cotton irrigation. The papier mâché onto which much of the red and blue is painted is going soggy and peeling off, and restoration funds no longer flow from a Moscow which is now part of a foreign country and is anyway destitute. In 1994 cracks caused by an earthquake added a further challenge. As if in defiance, this part of the mosque is used to display Uzbek wall hangings, made according to traditions passed from mother to daughter through the generations, and a museum showing Uzbek art from the 9th to the 20th century. Amoung the exhibits are also black-and-white photos of Soviet restoration work on Ulug Bek madrasa.

For now, the substance of what Curzon called 'the noblest public square in the world' remains intact, and it may still be true that 'no European spectacle indeed can adequately be compared with it, in our inability to point to an open space in any western city that is commanded on three of its four sides by Gothic cathedrals of the finest order.' Today there are rows of plastic seats for the weary tourist; and for $3 you can gaze with the aid of a **son et lumière**. **Concerts** are given in the courtyards of the madrasa.

Museum of History, Culture and Art (музей истории, культуры и искусства / *muzey istorii, kultury i iskusstva*)

Closed Wednesdays.

The museum on the southeast corner of Registan Square has a copy of the Afrasiab frieze (*see* p.143) and material on ancient sites near Termez which are still hard to get to. The room on Samarkand's role in the Bolshevik revolution has been replaced with one depicting aspects of Uzbek culture from carpets to yurts. There's a fine selection of anti-capitalist posters and beautiful Korans from various countries.

Bibi Khanym Mosque (мечеть Биби-Ханым)

From the museum it's a short walk behind the Sher Dor madrasa, past the **Chorsu** (a 19th-century vaulted market which now sells ice-cream and secondhand furniture) and down Tashkentskaya Ulitsa to one of the largest mosques ever built.

According to legend this was the brainchild of Tamerlane's Chinese chief wife Bibi Khanym, who meant to surprise him with a colossal monument on his return from his

1398–99 Indian campaign. Instead he was surprised by a love-bite on her neck, left there by the mosque's philandering Persian architect. Tamerlane sent a platoon to seize the adulterer dead or alive, but he fled up one of the soaring minarets he had just built, leapt off the top and flew home to Persia.

The reality was scarcely less prosaic. The mosque was Tamerlane's own idea and was to be grander than anything he had seen on his travels. It was built between 1399 and 1404 by 500 labourers and 95 elephants brought back from India, and 200 architects, artists, master craftsmen and masons from the rest of the empire. As it neared completion, Ruy Gonzalez de Clavijo witnessed the infirm emperor throwing coins and meat to the workmen from his litter to goad them on, 'as one should cast bones to dogs in a pit'.

An observer wrote of the finished mosque: 'Its dome would have been unique had it not been for the heavens, and unique would have been its portal had it not been for the Milky Way.' The portal was nearly 30m high and the dome even higher. Decorated with majolica mosaics, carved marble and painted and gilded papier mâché, they stood at the west end of a marble-paved, colonnaded courtyard larger than a football pitch (130m by 102m), with a minaret at each corner. The main gates opposite the mosque were made of seven different metals and were flanked by ceramic columns 50m high. Two minor mosques looked inward from the north and south towards a giant marble Koran-holder in which rested the Osman Koran, said to be the second Koran in history, whose script was so big the *imams* could read it from balconies along the colonnade. The Koran-holder is still there and crawling under it is said to make barren women fertile. The Koran itself was brought to Samarkand from Damascus by Tamerlane and sent to the Hermitage in St Petersburg by General Kaufmann in 1875; then to the Uzbek Academy of Sciences in Tashkent in 1919. The Muslim authorities in Tashkent finally recovered it in 1989.

The Bibi Khanym complex had been completed in an almighty rush and started crumbling even before Tamerlane's death the following year. A 17th-century earthquake destroyed more than half of it and another in 1897 left cracks in the main dome, already hit by a Russian shell in 1868. Lay-people had stopped praying here for fear of falling masonry. Now the clergy left too, and the courtyard became a cotton market. The walls had long served as a brick quarry for other building projects and the great gates had been melted down by an avaricious emir of Bukhara.

Original plans for the site were discovered in Leningrad in 1974, and five years later reconstruction began. Much brickwork has been strengthened and the courtyard walls and minor domes have been re-built, but the money has run out and the main mosque's scaffolding and crane are now permanent features of the Samarkand skyline. There is a chance of funds from UNESCO, but not if the mosque is closed to non-Muslims as some local Muslims want.

Despite everything, enough remains of Bibi Khanym to imagine its former scale and splendour, and somehow the rusty building apparatus lends the place a gritty realism the Registan lacks. The queen herself, who was habitually attended by up to 300 ladies-in-waiting when alive, may be buried across Tashkentskaya Ulitsa under the brown-domed **Bibi Khanym mausoleum**, still unrestored and closed to the public. Nothing remains of a madrasa to which it was attached nor of the nearby city gates which stood at the bottom of Tashkentskaya Ulitsa where the 'Golden Road' entered Samarkand from Tashkent.

But the **bazaar**, pressed up against the east wall of the Bibi Khanym complex, is alive, teeming and unbothered as ever by western talk of 'free' and other sorts of markets. It is still called the *kolkhoznaya* bazaar, but collectivization never really affected what was sold here or by whom or how much for. Chinese goods are making a comeback after 400 years, but more in the line of tracksuit tops than silk and lacquer-ware. For tourists who troop in after seeing Bibi Khanym there are glass phials of saffron and painted *lepeshka* (round loaves) which are said to keep for two years. Traditionally, the last thing an Uzbek son does before leaving home on a long journey is take a bite from a fresh loaf baked by his mother. She hangs it in a safe place and, when he returns, sprinkles it with water, puts it in the oven and invites his friends round to help him finish it. The bazaar has an annexe across Tashkentskaya Ulitsa selling mainly onions and live chickens.

Opposite the bazaar, on an ancient site in the corner of Afrasiab, the **Khazret Khyzr** mosque (1850) is unusual for its separate asymmetrical portico. The elaborate designs on the mosque's wooden ceiling are being repainted with a Swiss grant and is basically closed to foreigners.

Shah-i-Zinda Ensemble (ансамбль Шах-и-Зинда)

One of the most breathtaking stunts in all mythology took place a five-minute walk from the bazaar down Ulitsa Dzhurakulova around the time of the Arab invasion. A cousin of the prophet Mohammed named Qasim ibn-Abbas, believed to have visited Samarkand in 676 AD while converting Sogdiana to Islam, was at prayer in a shady spot on the edge of old Afrasiab when a band of zealous fire-worshippers stole up and beheaded him. Not one to be distracted by trifles, Qasim first finished his prayer. Then he picked up his head, tucked it under his arm and jumped down a nearby well where he has lived ever since, ready at a moment's notice to return to the defence of Islam. In another version he escaped the infidels by walking into a cliff which opened miraculously for him.

Qasim (or Kussam) is the 'Living King' from whom the Shah-i-Zinda royal necropolis takes its name. The position of his well is unknown but his mausoleum, a place of pilgrimage, is one of a street of tombs with what is reckoned to be the finest glazed decoration in Central Asia.

A memorial complex already existed here in the 12th century, but the Mongols destroyed everything except Qasim's shrine, of which Ibn Battuta wrote in 1333:

'The inhabitants of Samarkand come out to visit it every Sunday and Thursday night. The Tartars also come to visit it, pay vows to it and bring cows, sheep, dirhams and dinars. All this is used for the benefit of visitors and the servants of the hospital and the blessed tomb.'

Nowadays you enter Shah-i-Zinda through a portal commissioned by Ulug Bek and built 1434–35. Carpets are sold in the modest **Davlat Kush-Begi madrasa** (1813) on the right. On the left is a working mosque with an enclosed 19th-century winter section and an open summer one built in 1910.

Straight ahead the 'Stairway to Heaven' leads past what was thought to be the **tomb of Kazi Zade Rumi** (built 1420–35), Ulug Bek's teacher and a renowned Turkish astronomer—but the only bones found here are of a 30 to 35 year-old woman with Mongol features who may have been Tamerlane's nurse. Pilgrims count the steps on the stairway with great care. If they count wrong they have to climb them all again, once for each step in the staircase, or risk not going to heaven. There are 36 steps.

First on the right at the top is the **Emir Hussein mausoleum** (1376). Hussein, also known as Tuglu-tekin, seems to have been the son of a Turk named Kara Kutluk, to have died a martyr 600 years before his tomb was built, and to have been claimed by Tamerlane as an ancestor. The **Emir Zade mausoleum** (1386) is opposite.

The next pair of tombs, also from Tamerlane's time, commemorate three of the women in his life and are the best preserved and most dazzling in the complex. On the right, the **Shirin Bika Aka mausoleum** (1385) has an unusual 16-sided drum as the base for its cupola, designed by an architect specially imported from Khorezm. The interior decoration shows Chinese influence, with mosaic landscapes including shrubs, streams, clouds, and trees with birds. Shirin is thought to have been one of Tamerlane's nieces.

One of his wives and one of her daughters are buried opposite under the **Shadi Mulk Aka mausoleum** (1372). Its façade is an unrivalled *tour de force*; nowhere else in the world of ceramic art, it has been argued, have so many decorative techniques been brought together which such skill and refinement. Long faience panels sculpted with stylized flowers, calligraphy and pure, abstract designs are bordered by bands of mosaic and terracotta. Every shade of blue and every visual motif available to the craftsmen, probably from Azerbaijan, is on show here in apparently endless combinations, and in near-perfect condition after 600 years.

The octagonal structure next to the Shirin Bika Aka mausoleum may be a mausoleum itself, though no bones have been found under it. Or it may have been a minaret. No one knows. Neither is much known about the next three mausolea on the left of the 'street'. The last and biggest of them, next to the arch at the end, is thought to be the tomb of Emir Burunduk, one of Tamerlane's generals. All three are dated about 1380.

Through the arch, the first mausoleum on the left, completed in 1404, is that of **Tuman Aka**, yet another wife of Tamerlane's. The colour violet makes a rare appearance in its exterior decoration. The interior, reached through a fine carved wood door, is also unusual, in this case because it has been left white and completely unadorned except for tiny painted landscapes under the cupola. The **Khodja Akhmad mausoleum** is the second oldest in the complex and forms its north end. Excavations beneath it have revealed a crypt containing fragments of marble tombstones painted gold and blue. Dating from the mid-14th century, this and the adjoining **Shah Arab mausoleum** (c.1360) may have been built by the same man, a local master named Fakhri Ali.

Opposite the Tuman Aka mausoleum stands the 600 year-old 'Door of Paradise'. Once encrusted with gold, silver and ivory, it is now plain wood. It leads to the oldest part of Shah-i-Zinda; the **Kussam ibn-Abbas mausoleum** and its adjoining mosque. This is where the Living King lives. The inside of the 15th-century mosque, reached via an entrance hall, used to be completely covered in tiles; panels of locally-made ones surrounded Persian imports. To the left of the door leading from mosque to tomb there is a wooden frieze carved with words from the Koran—but also, in the *mihrab* or niche in the western wall, there is a smudge of soot claimed as evidence of continuing fire-worship. Some of the mausoleum's foundations date from the 10th century, but the grave itself is 11th, which means the Prophet's cousin had to spend at least 300 years headless down his well.

The Ulug Bek Observatory (Обсерватория Улуг Бека)

Museum open 9 am–6 pm daily.

After so much death and religion it's a relief to get clear of the city centre and inhale some secularity on the hill from which Ulug Bek studied the heavens. The remains of his observatory are 20 minutes' walk north of the bazaar up the Tashkent road. Alternatively, take *marshrutnoe* taxi 17 from the Hotel Samarkand or the bazaar.

The Conquest of the Stars

The grandson of Tamerlane, Ulug Bek was less interested in conquering the earth than the stars. His was the best-equipped observatory in the medieval world; a magnet for leading scientists and a centre of progressive, often heretical thought. 'Where knowledge starts religion ends,' was the motto of his teacher, Kazi Zade Rumi, and Ulug Bek's quest for enlightenment led him to sponsor debates on such topics as the existence of God. This did not go down too well with Muslim orthodoxy, and among those who found his beliefs hard to stomach was his own son, who assassinated him on 29 October 1449. Shortly afterwards, religious fanatics tore down the observatory.

Ulug Bek's astronomical observations, which put him on a par with Copernicus or Kepler, did not become known in the West until 1648, when a copy of his *Catalogue of Stars* was discovered in Oxford's Bodleian Library. He had plotted the position of the moon, the planets, the sun and 1018 other stars with amazing precision, and calculated the length of the year to within 58 seconds (or even less; the earth span slower then than it does now). These were some of the greatest achievements of the 'non-optical' (pre-telescope) era of astronomy.

Having fallen victim to one orthodoxy, Ulug Bek was a ready-made hero for another. The Soviets made him the object of a minor cult and officially designated his murder as 'tragic'.

What nobody knew was where, or quite how, Ulug Bek had worked. Then in 1908, after years spent studying ancient manuscripts, a Russian primary school teacher, amateur archaeologist and former army officer called Vladimir Viatkin unearthed the lower portion of a giant sextant on Kukhak Hill beside the road to Tashkent. It was one of the major finds of the 20th century.

The original sextant was a perfect arc of marble-clad brick, 63m long with a radius of 40 m, calibrated in degrees and minutes, decorated with the signs of the zodiac and aligned with one of the earth's meridians. Observations and measurements were made with an astrolabe mounted on metal rails either side of the sextant. What survives, complete with calibrations and fragments of rail, is the lower section of the arc, set in a deep rock trench to minimize disturbances from earth tremors. The arc originally continued upwards above the trench inside a round, three-storeyed observatory at least 30m high. Traces of its foundations are all that remain. The top two floors were arcades used as solar and lunar calendars. Ulug Bek probably used the ground floor as a summer residence. There is a small **museum** on Uzbek astronomy and the opening of Tamerlane's tomb (*see* **Gur Emir** below). The astronomy section includes an old engraving of great astronomers in which Ulug Bek sits alongside Copernicus and Galileo dressed as a Cossack, whose garb was the most eastern-looking the engraver could envisage. The modest grave near the entrance to the sextant is Viatkin's; he was buried here in accordance with his will.

Shrine to Chupan-Ata (мазар Чупан-Ата)

Not far beyond the observatory on the Tashkent road there is an unusual shrine to **Chupan-Ata**, mythical patron of shepherds. With a cupola on a high, slender drum, decorated with a kufic inscription in coloured tiles, it looks like a mausoleum, but no one is buried here. It was built around 1440 expressly as a place of pilgrimage in what was then a park laid out around one of Tamerlane's many palaces, none of which survive.

Afrasiab Museum (музей Афрасиаб)

Open daily 9 am–6 pm except Thursday. Winter closing time is 5pm.

 The Afrasiab museum is at the entrance to the site, half way back to the bazaar on the right-hand side of the Tashkent road. Its most important possession by far, occupying the entire central hall, is a 6th-century stucco frieze of a caravan of gifts for the ruler. Found during excavations of the palace of Afrasiab in the 1920s and 30s, this is one of the finest examples of Sogdian art anywhere. The principal gift is a princess on a white elephant from Surkhandarya, followed by three ladies on horseback, two male torch-bearers on a camel and four sacred white geese. On the central wall are Chinese silk traders, long-haired Turks, mountain-dwellers from the Tian Shan and Koreans identifiable by pig-tails on the tops of their heads. All the human figures had their eyes scraped off in the 8th century because they offended the Arabs; a copy in the history museum near the Registan fills in some of the gaps. The museum also contains 4th-century BC Greek coins brought by Alexander the Great, and a 2nd-century AD Zoroastrian altar. There is also a hall of fame of Russian archaeologists, although they are less than universally revered by Uzbeks for sending Samarkand's treasures to the Hermitage.

To reach the excavated part of Afrasiab turn left out of the museum and follow the north edge of the site to its highest part, the citadel, from which there is a sheer drop to the river Siab and a fine view of Timurid Samarkand to the south-west. The mud bricks of the massive outer walls are revealed in only a few places but the palace excavations at the far end go down two floors. Beyond, the ground slopes down to the airport road littered with fragments of ancient-looking pottery.

Gur Emir (Гур Эмир)

Tamerlane died in February 1405 on his way to China with an invasion force of 200,000 men. His body was perfumed with rose-water, musk and camphor, placed in a coffin decorated with pearls and despatched—in the dead of night to avoid unsettling his troops—back to Samarkand 400 miles away. He was buried in the mausoleum he had built for his grandson Mohammed Sultan, who had died fighting in Turkey in 1403. It became known as Gur Emir—the Ruler's Tomb—and nowadays it stands among quiet, un-Sovietized backstreets not far along Ulitsa Akhunbabaeva from the Hotel Samarkand.

The first version of Gur Emir, completed in 1404, was not grand enough for Tamerlane. He had its famous ribbed canteloupe dome, and the drum on which it stood, rebuilt on the scale of the Bibi Khanym mosque in two weeks flat. The outer dome is now 32m high and the inner 18m, with a complex system of supporting struts between them. Round the drum beneath the outer dome runs a kufic inscription 10 m high: 'There is no God but Allah and Mohammed is his prophet.' Under this, in an octagonal hall, lie six cenotaphs of white marble and one of jade. The marble ones commemorate, among others, Mohammed Sultan the grandson; Shahrukh, Timur's youngest son and heir, who ruled the rapidly shrinking Timurid empire from Herat in modern Afghanistan; Ulug Bek, who ruled Samarkand as Shah Rukh's viceroy; and Mir Said Berekh, sage, descendent of the Prophet and Tamerlane's spiritual mentor.

The seventh cenotaph is Tamerlane's. As he lay dying he had whispered, 'Only a stone, and my name upon it,' but he got what was then the biggest slab of jade in the world. Some say it was sent from the mountains of Chinese Turkestan by a Mongolian princess; others that Ulug Bek brought it from there himself in 1411. The Persian invader Nadir Shah tried to carry it away in 1740 but it broke in two so he left it alone. Cemented back together, it normally appears black in the low light that filters through the four fretted arches round the hall. Only direct sunlight through the east door in the early morning brings out its true green.

No expense was spared on the hall itself. Its walls are covered with hexagonal green alabaster tiles up to a band of once-gilded marble at head height. Higher up, bands of calligraphy frame clusters of stalactites and blue and gold geometric panels. Laid end on end, the gilding on the underside of the dome would stretch for 3km. Below the cenotaphs, 3m down in a crypt lie the real graves and tombstones. These are generally closed to the public but 25 cents buys a quick look. There are two more Timurid tombs nearby: The grandiose but uninspiring **Rukhabad mausoleum** (closed to the public), built for Sheikh

Burhanuddin Sagharji in the 1380s on what is now Registanskaya Ulitsa near the Tabbasum Restaurant; and the modest-sized **Ak-Saray mausoleum** built in the 1470s for the last of the Timurids a short distance southeast of Gur Emir on Ulitsas Akhunbabaeva and Umarova.

Tamerlane's Ghost

Tamerlane took a while to settle in his tomb, according to Hans Schiltberger, a German who had served at his court: 'After he was buried the priests that served the temple heard Timur howl every night for a year. Finally, they went to his son and begged that he set free the prisoners taken by his father in other countries, especially those craftsmen he had brought to his capital to work. He let them go, and as soon as they were free Timur did not howl any more.'

Now that he lay at peace he was not to be disturbed. Legend had it that, engraved on the underside of his tombstone, was the epitaph, 'If I am roused from my grave the earth will tremble'. He was not roused for five and a half centuries. Then a distinguished Russian anthropologist, Mikhail Gerasimov, obtained permission to exhume the body. In order not to offend local sensibilities Gerasimov entered the crypt in secret, on the night of 22 June 1941. He opened the coffin around 3am— and within minutes an assistant burst in with the news that Kiev and Minsk were being bombed and that Hitler's armies had invaded Russia. Gerasimov's examination, which confirmed that Tamerlane had indeed been lame from a wound to his right leg, took nearly two years. Within days of the skeleton being reinterred, the Germans surrendered after losing nearly a million men at Stalingrad.

Samarkand's central area also has a **Russian** quarter, built at the end of the 19th century, with attractive Russian merchant houses, now converted into shops. Not surprisingly, it's here that most of the street names have changed. Close by is the city's second department store and, at the end of the pedestrianized area, is Gorky park, complete with *shashlyk* and entertainment venues. Emerging from here onto Prospekt Rashidova walk past the Hotel Zerafshan, and on the right-hand side you'll find the Russian Orthodox Cathedral. Used as army barracks during the Soviet years, it is now being restored.

South Samarkand

To see how Samarkand's 19th-century mosques were decorated, take a taxi to the working **Khodja Nisbatdor mosque** on Ulitsa Yutuk, which leads off Suzangaranskaya Ulitsa south of the Registan. The team which restored the striking patterns in primary colours on the wooden ceiling and *mihrab* is now working on the **Khazret Khyzr mosque** near the bazaar. The resident holy man seems happy to let non-Muslims inside.

The most attractive working Muslim centre in Samarkand is in the middle of a cemetery on the southeastern edge of the city, reached via Ulitsa Sadreddin Aini. **Khodja Abdi Darun** consists of a 12th-century mausoleum, to which a dome and portico were added in the 15th century, and a 19th-century mosque and madrasa, all set round a deep and tempting *khauz*. Spectacular shade is cast by four giant and very ancient Chinor trees round the pool. Nearby and largely ruined is the **Ishrat Khana mausoleum** (1464), which became the family crypt for minor female Timurids. Its turquoise dome collapsed in 1903 but the portico survives. The main hall was cross-shaped, leaving room for spiral staircases in each corner.

Some maps locate the 17th-century **Khodja Abdi Birin** mausoleum next to the similarly-named Khodja Abdi Darun. (The names refer to the city walls: *birin* means without, *darun* within). In fact it is some distance away in the Silski *rayon* (district), reached via the road out to the Kuibyshev *kolhoz* (collective farm). Willing and amused old men on a dais outside will open the mausoleum to show off its plain white interior. The adjacent mosque is being restored with local money for local use.

Getting to the **Khodja Akrar madrasa** is easier and definitely worthwhile (minibus 31 from the Hotel Samarkand and buses 9 and 20 from the bazaar). Sheikh Khodja Akrar came to Samarkand from Tashkent in the 14th century and founded this madrasa, which was rebuilt in 1638 by the energetic Bukharan dervish Nadir Divanbegi after whom it is also sometimes named. Restored in 1982, it is, like the madrasas of the Registan, completely covered in mosaic. Unlike them, its focus is its courtyard. There are modest *iwans* on each side rather than one gigantic one, and smaller arches for each classroom and dormitory, all of which are in use. This is Samarkand's only working madrasa, with 100 students on a four-year course, half of them boarding. They pay modest fees to the mullah which are topped up by the state. In the corner to the right of the entrance there are photographs of the restoration. You may have to pay to look at them.

Samarkand (℡ 3662–)   **Where to Stay**

expensive–moderate

The best—and best-placed—hotel in Samarkand is the **Hotel Samarkand** at the west end of Registanskaya Ulitsa, ℡ 35 88 12/35 71 52. Prices vary according to season. From April to November, a double room, breakfast included, will cost $70, or $55 for one person (out of season rates are $50 and $40). There are no single rooms but all are air-conditioned, clean and comfortable with phones and hot water in the showers instead of baths. Baths are only in the $100 *lyux* room. The restaurant, Intourist Service Bureau, post office, all night coffee shop and Afghan carpet shop are on the ground floor. There is a hard-currency bar in the basement and in the lobby, and a gallery displaying Uzbek and Tajik painters' work is open daily. Rooms can be paid for in dollars, and with American Express or Visa cards, as long as they are not within one month of their expiry date. Occasionally staff can be awkward about reservations made by Uzbek tourist offices elsewhere in Uzbekistan and declare that your booking is not valid without a fax from the reserving office. Save an hour of aggravation by obtaining a copy of the fax before arriving. Bus 10 and minibuses 18, 23 and 31 link the hotel with the airport, bus station and railway station. Minibus 45 goes to the Afrasiab museum.

Samarkand now has its own **Tata** hotel, one of the chain built by the Indian Taj company. Located down the hill from the Hotel Samarkand on Registanskaya, the three-storey honeycomb with swimming pool is completed but empty; furniture will be provided by an Uzbek company. Another joint venture is the **Swiss-Uzbek Business Centre**, on Ploshchad Kuk Sarai. This building metamorphosed from the headquarters for the regional Communist Party in the 1980s to a 1990s hotel/office complex.

The **Hotel Zerafshan**, Ulitsa Rashidova 65, ☎ 33 18 14, used to be the city's official number two. After the Samarkand it is closest to the Registan and from outside it looks solid, even handsome. Renovated in 1995, the new rooms have imported oriental furniture, air-conditioning, fridge and telephone ($30). Some are being converted into single rooms ($25). Hot water operates on a schedule of sorts; aim to wash 7–8am and 8–9pm.

The multi-storey, 535-bed **Hotel Turist** stands sentinel at Ulitsa Gagarina 85, ☎ 24 07 04. This is the only 15 storey building in the city and the hotel water system suffers accordingly. Rooms are clean and reasonably spacious, with phones and hot showers and the reception staff smile, but there's no air-conditioning or TV ($25 single, $20 double). Buses 10 and 3 serve both hotels.

Hotel Vatan (formerly Hotel Saikal), on University Bulvar, close to the Alisher Navoi monument and the library, ☎ 33 72 12, owned by the army but allowed to take foreigners, is quiet, safe and within walking distance of the Registan. The exterior is low key with a wrought iron entrance porch. Rooms are comfortable, clean, reasonably priced ($20 and $30) and decorated in gilded ganche; all, especially the bathrooms, reflecting the better conditions traditionally enjoyed by the military. For transport into town cross over the boulevard and choose between trolley buses 1 or 2, buses 10 or 14 and *marshrutnoe* 45, 32 or 23.

inexpensive

Hotel Registan on Ulitsa Ulugbek, ☎ 33 52 25 is the cheapest in town and 10 minutes walk from the Registan. The receptionist is friendly and pleased with the renovations, which have amalgamated two hotels. Rooms in the older part are basic but clean, have communal shower facilities and a small balcony if street-facing ($4 per person). Those in the newer part will have bathrooms and telephones ($8). Ultimately 360 rooms will be available and, since there are only four storeys, there should be no problems with the water supply.

Samarkand's first private hotel the **Sayor**, ☎ 21 49 16, ✉ 31 10 82, is almost opposite the department store Tsum, at Ulitsa Ulugbek 148. Some rooms have air-conditioning, others a fan. There is no-holds-barred belly-dancing in the better-than-adequate restaurant every evening except Mondays; the music shakes the whole building. Across the roundabout the now privately-owned **Hotel Bagishamal**, Ulitsa Mirsharapova 17, ✆ 26 26 88, is in the last throes of renovation, its reception areas attractively decorated in traditional Uzbek style with intricately carved doors, and when reopened it will take foreigners. Russian and German are spoken and rooms paid for in local currency ($6 single, double with bathroom $10). Transport to the Registan is easy from here and takes about 20 minutes: take trolley buses 1 and 3 and *marshrutnoe* 45,18 and 17; the only buses to avoid are 6 and 7, and if catching 21 or 66 get off when the bus turns right before the Registan. Bus 21 goes to the airport and the bus station; bus 27 and trolleybus 1 to the railway station. All buses stop outside Tsum.

Bed and breakfast accommodation is becoming more widespread in Samarkand. The best for location and the copious amounts of food is **Emma's**, apartment 7, Ulitsa Akhunbabaeva 78, ✆ 33 54 47 ($15). **Zarina's**, ✆ 35 41 53, ✉ 31 06 41, offers a range of accommodation, from flats virtually opposite the Registan to rooms in the oldest part of Samarkand close to the Ulug Bek Observatory ($20–25). Airport and bus station pick-ups can be requested but make independent arrangements for a city guide.

Zoya and **Viktor Buligyova**, Ulitsa Gagarina 230, ✆ 37 40 64, make you feel one of the family and **Yuri Fyodorov**, ✆ 21 59 95, rents out two apartments, and can also provide bed and breakfast.

The real moneyspinner is the **Turbaza**, Dagbitskaya Ulitsa 33. Twenty minutes' walk from the Registan, it offers clean double rooms without bath or shower, easily forgone for 50 US cents per night.

Samarkand (✆ 3662–) **Eating Out**

Samarkand has the best Uzbek restaurant in Uzbekistan, the **Chai-khana Siab**. Get a taxi to take the first right turning off the Tashkent road after the Afrasiab museum. Where this road forks there is an eatery that turns *laghman*, *plov* and *shashlyk* into formative culinary experiences, preceded if you like by cream cheese and spring onions, served in a garden by the river from 11am to 1pm.

The best **hotel restaurants** are at the Samarkand (with Uzbek dancing; and on request the waiter will arrange such delicacies as sheep's head) and the Sayor (with belly-dancing). The Zerafshan hotel restaurant serves inexpensive Russian, Uzbek and European food and is open from 7am to 2am the next day.

Much favoured by local Russians is the *chai-khana* with carved doors to the left of the Zerafshan. There's *shashlyk* and snack kiosks to the left of the Bagishamal hotel and excellent soup and laghman from the row of *chai-khanas* at the bus station. For anyone needing an early morning caffeine fix, a small '**coffee** shop' sells an addictive substance under that name along with sweet cakes from 7am. But the best place to watch the world go by while you eat is the **chai-khana** at the Registan end of Tashkentskaya Ulitsa, where *plov* and *shashlyk* of doubtful nutritional value are cooked with great panache from dawn to dusk by men in white coats.

Donald Duck often stands on the pavement off Amir Timur, 5 minutes' walk from the hotel Uzbekistan; check out the café nearby for good chicken and sausages at $2–5 a head. Or you can try dinner at a **private house**: call **Oksana Falyeva**, ✆ 34 47 06, or the **Swiss-Uzbek Tourism Company**, ✆ 35 35 02.

Shahrisabz (Шахрисабз)

Tamerlane was born in 1336 over the Zerafshan mountains from Samarkand in the village of Kesh. He did not forget it. He built his biggest palace here, plus mausolea for himself and his favourite son, and re-named the place Shahrisabz ('Green City'). At the end of the 16th century most of Shahrisabz was destroyed by Bukhara's Abdullah Khan in a fit of anger at having mistaken it for Samarkand. But enough survives to make a trip worthwhile, and the drive over the 2000-m Tashtakaracha pass gives a wonderful if tantalizing glimpse of Central Asian mountains.

Getting to and from Shahrisabz

One full-size bus takes the 4-hour low route each day from Samarkand's long-distance bus stati*f*on and very occasional small ones go over the mountains from the unofficial local station in Samarkand's Suzangaranskaya Ulitsa. Shahrisabz's official bus station is at the south end of Ulitsa Ipak Yoli, former Sholkoviput but Samarkand buses use Kitab's station, 10km north of here and linked to Shahrisabz by frequent local buses. From Shahrisabz two buses go daily to Samarkand at 8 and 10 am and taxis from the Urgut bus stop. Expect to pay around $5 for a taxi.

For Intourist day-trips from Samarkand, *see* p.133.

Getting Around

The mountain road from Samarkand becomes Ulitsa Ipak Yoli, Shahrisabz's main street, and everything worth seeing is on or just off it. The Ak-Saray palace at one end is just 20 minutes' walk from Kok Gumbaz at the other. Every passing bus and *marshrutnoe* taxi links them and everything in between.

Tourist Information

English is spoken and town plans are sold at the Hotel Shahrisabz, ✆ 3 38 61, Ulitsa Ipak Yoli 26. Bus pick-ups from Samarkand to Shahrisabz and the mountains can be arranged, upon request, by the hotel owner. The private company **Adventure Tourism** has moved from the hotel to Ipak Yoli 49 and is run by

Nariman Umarov, ✆ 4 18 52 (home), ✆ 4 11 57 (office). He offers treks to the cave where Timur was born and a dinosaur footprint hunt. Costs range from $20- to $100 and include camping in the mountains. Umarov also provides accommodation at $36 for a double room ($18 for one person).

Timurid Shahrisabz

Ak-Saray Palace (Ак-Сарай)

Tamerlane's vast residence covered an area the size of an olympic stadium, took a quarter of a century (1380–1405) to build, and was still not finished when he died. The Spanish envoy Ruy Gonzalez de Clavijo got the best look at it of any European, as he did of so much that Tamerlane built. He judged the main courtyard to be 300 paces wide, and beyond it he entered 'a great reception hall... where the walls are panelled with gold and blue tiles, and the ceiling is entirely of gold work'. In the smaller rooms and private apartments 'all was so marvellously wrought that even the craftsmen of Paris... would hold that which is done here to be of very fine workmanship.'

Only part of the main entrance arch still stands, but this is awesome enough. Before the arch itself collapsed it was nearly 50m high and spanned 22m, dwarfing even that of Bibi Khanym in Samarkand. Its sides are 38m high and covered in acres—it seems—of magnificent tilework. Some gold leaf still clings to the glaze out of sight and robbers' reach and at the top of the right-hand pillar (looking south). The black-rimmed diamond-shaped tiles beside the blue and green corner spirals were a signature of imported Azerbaijani craftsmen.

Horizontal Arabic inscriptions near the bottom of each side of the arch were supposed to read, 'The Sultan is a shadow of Allah', but on the right hand side the craftsman started too big and only managed to fit in, 'The Sultan is a shadow,' for which he was severely punished. It is also said that the architect was thrown off the job for apparent idleness. In fact, when he hung a chain from the top of a half-built section of the arch and then waited a year, he had subsidence in mind. The chain sank imperceptibly towards the ground. When it stopped the architect declared it was safe to go on building, and was reinstated.

The great courtyard, paved in white stone, stretched south from this arch across the modern car park to the four-storey palace proper where there is now a war memorial. Some guides say the palace had a swimming pool on its roof, fed by an aqueduct from the Tashtakaracha pass. The aqueduct bit may be true. The pool, according to Clavijo, was at ground level in the middle of the courtyard.

Mosques and Mausolea

Ulitsa Ipak Yoli skirts Ak-Saray and the car-park, turns south and heads for a 17th-century **Chorsu** (domed market). On the way it passes the **Khodja Mirkhamida mosque** (1914) on the right (now a *chai-khana*) and, set back on the same side a little further on, a 16th-century **bath-house** which was in use until 1983.

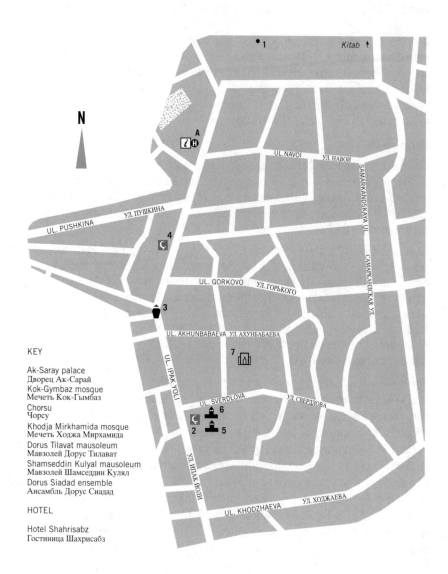

N

KEY

1   Ak-Saray palace
     Дворец Ак-Сарай

2   Kok-Gymbaz mosque
     Мечеть Кок-Гымбаз

3   Chorsu
     Чорсу

4   Khodja Mirkhamida mosque
     Мечеть Ходжа Мирхамида

5   Dorus Tilavat mausoleum
     Мавзолей Дорус Тилават

6   Shamseddin Kulyal mausoleum
     Мавзолей Шамседдин Кулял

7   Dorus Siadad ensemble
     Ансамбль Дорус Сиадад

HOTEL

A   Hotel Shahrisabz
     Гостиница Шахрисабз

One bus-stop or 10 minutes' walk further south, at the junction of Ulitsa Ipak Yoli and Ulitsa Sverdlova, you come to the **Kok-Gumbaz mosque** (1435–6), named after its blue dome and built by Tamerlane's grandson Ulug Bek to sanctify the two mausolea behind. **Dorus Tilavat**, on the right, was finished in 1438 and intended for one of Ulug Bek's sons, though none is buried here. Of the four tombstones, the one on the right has a hollow worn out of if by hands hoping it was a cure for smallpox. The original floor of the older **Shamseddin Kulyal mausoleum** next door was two metres lower than the present one. Hence the apparently low arches and dome and the name sometimes used for both: *Gumbasi Saidon* (*gumbasi*=dome; *saidon*='descended from Mohammed'). Shamseddin was Tamerlane's father's spiritual mentor. The pair of them were supposed to be buried here. They may or may not be.

Dorus Siadad

One block east and another north is Shahrisabz's most mysterious site, the Dorus Siadad, or 'Seat of Power and Might'. Here Tamerlane built a giant mausoleum on the pattern of one he had already commissioned in memory of Khodja Ahmed Yasavi in Turkestan (*see* p.277). But this one was for himself and his favourite son Jehangir, after whose death at the age of 23 he is said never to have smiled.

Abdullah Khan tore down most of it, but the local clergy persuaded him to spare **Jehangir's tomb** by claiming it stood next to that of an 8th-century Persian holy man called Khazreti Imam. The tomb formed the southwest corner of the mausoleum; the tiled three-quarter pillar nearest the street was part of its entrance arch. The incongruous conical dome, 27m high, was of Khorezmian design, like the one over Chashma Ayub in Bukhara. Inside, the squinches supporting it are of bare brick (ornamental stalactites may have fallen off), giving a rare view of the complex geometry involved when a circular load is transferred to the walls of a square chamber.

The mullahs' fabricated story about Khazreti Imam being buried here passed into local lore. When a **mosque** was built next to the tomb in the 18th century it was named after him. Meanwhile the very modest **crypt** Tamerlane had built for himself in the southeast corner of the mausoleum after feeling a premonition of death while campaigning in Persia, had been buried and lost. It was rediscovered on the eve of World War II when a girl playing in her yard fell through the ground into the grave, which Tamerlane had ordered to be kept open to receive him at any time. To get here return to the street and turn left twice. You come to a green door in the middle of the road to which only Intourist guides, in principle, have keys. Behind it a few steps lead down to a small, humid, windowless room containing a stone casket and the remains of two bodies, neither of them Tamerlane's—he ended up in Gur Emir in Samarkand. The inscription over the lower entrance was one of his favourites: 'Wise men act with lofty intentions while fools merely wait with lofty intentions.'

Intourist's **Hotel Shahrisabz**, Ulitsa Ipak Yoli 26, © 3 38 61, is cool and clean. Rooms have phones and bathrooms with half-length baths. The only way to get to and from the airport is by taxi. The hotel restaurant is predictable but well-meaning. The hard-currency bar is a rip-off. Good snacks and buns are sold near the bus station and opposite the Chorsu, a **café** with plentiful *laghman* and *chibureki* served under willow trees. Along the main road, by the bazaar, is a private restaurant called the **Oybek**, offering good mutton stew and onions for $1.

Pendzhikent (Пенджикент)

Although Pendzhikent is in Tajikistan, it is usually visited from Samarkand, which is three times closer than Dushanbe and linked to it by ancient history. Pendzhikent is also gateway to the Fan Mountains, the highest of the western Zerafshan range and their permanent snow is usually visible from Samarkand.

Founded in the 5th century as a principality of the Sogdian empire based on Afrasiab 75km to the west, old Pendzhikent was built out of reach of floods on a loess terrace above the Zerafshan River, and was known as Bunjikath. Most people find the ruins less inspiring than the setting, but for specialists this is the most revealing of all Sogdian sites because no one built on it after the Arabs destroyed it.

Its existence remained unknown for centuries until in the summer of 1933, a Tajik shepherd wandering near Mount Mug, east of Pendzhikent, stumbled on an 8th-century Sogdian manuscript, which brought the archaeologists running. They found 90 more manuscripts and the remains of a castle to which the last prince of Bunjikath, called Divastich, fled when the Arabs arrived. They pursued him, crucified him and destroyed the castle, but the manuscripts described the city he had left and painted a picture of a sophisticated, cosmopolitan and tolerant society. Indians and Chinese lived at peace with Sogdians. Buddhists meditated. Zoroastrians worshipped fire. And all the while caravans laboured over the passes behind towards Afghanistan or even Kashgar. This Silk Route variant was in use for freight until the construction of the mountain road over the Anzob Pass to Dushanbe after World War II. It still makes a great trek.

Getting to and from Pendzhikent

While Tajikistan remains unstable, the best way is probably with an Intourist group from the Hotel Samarkand (*see* p.133). Even for an organized trip you will need a Tajik visa. If arriving in Pendzhikent by bus, change at the station to a local bus to Koshtepa and get off where the road forks for the first time once out of town. Take the left fork and walk about 500m to the map.

The Ancient City

Excavation at the **Bunjikath** site began in 1946, and is far larger than Afrasiab. But the most interesting item for tourists is the 20th-century map on a post beside the road which tries to make sense of the lumpy expanse behind. As you face the map the ruins of the Shahristan, which comprised two Zoroastrian temples and the wealthiest families' heavily frescoed houses, are at 11 o'clock. The citadel was beyond it and to the left. On the rising ground behind you there was a necropolis of family burial vaults to which bones and hearts were transferred in separate casks, the bodies having been exposed on hillsides for scavengers and the elements to deal with the flesh; Zoroastrians didn't bury meat.

The **Rudaki Museum (музей Рудаки)** in Ulitsa Rudaki in the modern town contains reproductions of frescoes found in Bunjikath. One, behind some columns in the largest room, depicts a Sogdian mourning by tearing his hair out and cutting his face so it bleeds. In another, at the right hand end of a line of five, a Chinese ambassador is presenting his credentials. The original frescoes are in the Hermitage. The museum also contains sections of ceramic pipe which brought water to Bunjikath from the mountains. Rudaki, the 9th-century founder of Tajik literature, is buried about 30km into the mountains in the village of Pandzhrud.

The Fan Mountains (Фанские Горы)

From the central knot of the Pamirs two long, parallel ranges head in a straight westerly tangent for Samarkand. Both are spectacular by European standards, with countless peaks over 5000m. Both are almost unknown outside the CIS but popular among climbers and walkers inside it. Neither was spoilt by Soviet industry, and neither has yet been spoilt by western trekkers.

The road to Pendzhikent climbs beside the Zerafshan River between the two ranges; the Turkestan to the north and the Zerafshan to the south. Before it turns south and over the Anzob Pass (3373m) to Dushanbe, innumerable tracks lead off it towards the foothill villages and high pastures of the Fan Mountains, the highest and most beautiful in the Zerafshan range. In normal times any of these could be the start of an epic adventure. But given present politics, which have brought AK-47s to the smallest mountain villages, stick with the professionals.

Getting to the Fan Mountains

Steppes East, Castle Eaton, Cricklade, Wiltshire SN6 6JU, ✆ (01285) 81 02 67, organizes summer and autumn treks of varying difficulty in the Fan Mountains, usually combined with tours of Samarkand and/or Bukhara. Their Moscow partner, Travel Russia, Per. Trubnikovsky 21/22, 121069 Moscow, ✆ 290 3439, ✉ 290 8783, is worth contacting direct if you're already in the CIS. You sleep in tents in achingly beautiful campsites. Everything is cooked and carried for you. The guides speak fluent English and are encyclopaedic on the area's history, biology and narcography. This is not roughing it—it's unforgettable.

Maps

Large-scale (1:100,000) maps of the Fan Mountains exist. Try the climbing shop near the Cathedral of St Martin the Confessor a block from Taganskaya Ploshchad on your way through Moscow, or, in extremis, Travel Russia.

Bukhara (Бухара)

Bukhara was once 'the Noble', 'the most interesting city in the world', according to Curzon, generous as ever with superlatives. The holiest city in Central Asia, it had 360 mosques and 80 madrasas, from which the sun shone upwards while on ordinary cities it shone down.

Now it is a medium-sized city (population 250,000) in the middle of the Kizyl-Kum desert, with Central Asia's only inhabited intact historic core. To paint a rosier picture might lead to disappointment. Where Samarkand is bright blue Bukhara is an exhausted shade of khaki; where Bukhara was holy, Islam is now having to be re-learned; where its famous domed bazaars once teemed with people from every corner of Asia and smelt of their wares, nowadays there are only carpets and reproduction silverware for tourists.

Still, historic monuments are strewn more densely here than in Samarkand and they illustrate 1000 years of history, not just two centuries of intensive building by outrageous exhibitionists. And among them, down mud-walled streets, walk people who live and work here. They outnumber the tourists, unlike the inhabitants of old Khiva. They take tea by the sacred pool at Lyab-i-Khauz and wash in the 16th-century public baths exactly as they have for centuries.

They have also dug a huge hole in the middle of the old town which will take the foundations of an international three-star hotel for Muslim visitors to the Mir-i-Arab madrasa, Central Asia's biggest Islamic seminary. The fabric of the city has always waxed and waned with Islam; the Bolsheviks deliberately let it shrink and decay in the 1920s as a way of stamping out religion.

Whatever happens to Bukhara next, its major monuments will still be there for us to gawp at. The mausoleum of the Samanids is not about to crumble after a thousand years. And the great Kalyan minaret, which stopped Genghis Khan in his tracks 700 years before Bolshevism was invented, may reasonably be scanning the next millennial horizon with a certain worldly *ennui*.

History

The best estimate of Bukhara's age is about 20m, the depth of the archaeological remains under some of its fortifications. Years are more problematical. Textbooks say the city is

Bukhara

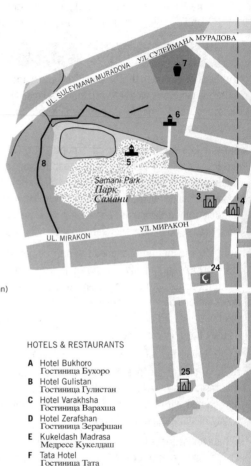

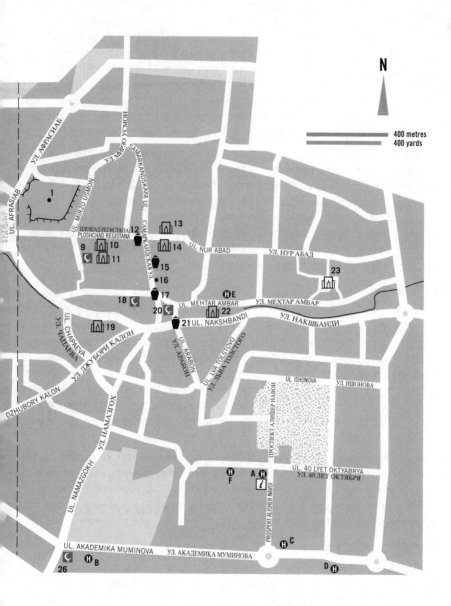

N

400 metres
400 yards

УЛ. АФРАСИАБ
UL. AFRASIAB

1

UL. MIRZO USMON
УЛ. МИРЗО УСМОН

SAMARKANDSKAYA UL.
САМАРКАНДСКАЯ УЛ.

ПЛОЩАД РЕГИСТАНА
PLOSHCHAD REGISTANA

9 10
11 12 13

14 UL. NUR ABAD УЛ. НУР АБАД

15

16 23

17

18 UL. MEHTAR AMBAR E

19 20 УЛ. МЕХТАР АМБАР

21 UL. NAKSHBANDI 22 УЛ. НАКШБАНДИ

UL. CHAPEVA
УЛ. ЧАПАЕВА

УЛ. ДЖУБОРИ КАЛОН

UL. ARABON
УЛ. АРАБОН

UL. LVA TOLSTOVO
УЛ. ЛЬВА ТОЛСТОГО

DZHUBORY KALON

UL. ISHONOVA УЛ. ИШОНОВА

UL. NAMAZGOKH
УЛ. НАМАЗГОХ

PROSPEKT ALISHER NAVOI
ПРОСПЕКТ АЛИШЕР НАВОЙ

UL. 40 LYET OKTYABRYA
УЛ. 40 ЛЕТ ОКТЯБРЯ

F A
i C

UL. AKADEMIKA MUMINOVA УЛ. АКАДЕМИКА МУМИНОВА
26 B D

2000 years old; Bokhariots themselves say 3000. There was certainly something for Alexander to conquer in 329 BC: 'He overcame a lion in single combat, extorting from the Spartan envoy the exclamation, "Well done Alexander, nobly hast thou won the prize of kingship from the king of the woods!"' (Curzon). There was human settlement too, but probably nothing as big as a city. The name Bukhara dates from the 1st century AD and may come from *vihara*, Sanskrit for monastery, or *bukhar*, a Farsi word for 'source of knowledge'. Either way, Bukhara would clearly like to be known as a place of prayer and learning from the very beginning. Like the rest of Sogdiana, it fell successively within the Achaemenid, Greek, Seleucid, Parthian, Kushan and Sassanian empires before the Arabs arrived. It was capital city for none of them, although the Hephthalite capital was only 40km away at Paikend.

By 712 it was a wealthy trading centre, but then three years of resistance led by a princess with expensive taste in slippers failed to deter Qutaiba ibn-Abbas and his army, and Bukhara's 700 richest families left town rather than submit to Arab rule. Soviet history, as ever, puts a different gloss on things: the invasion prompted in the 770s the first of several 'large scale anti-feudal risings' that came to nothing. The authority of the Caliph of Baghdad prevailed. Islam gradually eclipsed the competition: Buddhism, Zoroastrianism and various fringe cults. And when Bukhara broke from the Caliphate under Ismail Samani in 873, it was as capital of Central Asia's first independent Muslim state.

The Samanids

The 10th century was Bukhara's heyday. With a population of 300,000 it was bigger than it is today, and its empire covered all of modern Uzbekistan and Tajikistan and much of Iran and Afghanistan. Students came to its 250 madrasas from the distant emirates of coastal Arabia and even from Moorish Spain. Its 45,000-volume royal library rivalled the largest in Baghdad and the medical encyclopedia written there by Hussain ibn Abdullah ibn-Sina, known in the West as Avicenna, made Bukhara the intellectual capital of the East. Avicenna's book was a core medical text worldwide, and remained so until the 19th century. He was also a poet, mathematician, philosopher, musician and for several years grand vizier at the court.

Not much is known about the Samanids themselves. Why did they choose Bukhara as their capital? What role did Islam play in holding their empire together? The Karakhanids overran it in 999 and destroyed the answers. All that remains of Samanid Bukhara is the emperors' mausoleum, ignored by the Karakhanids, buried by 200 years of dust and thereby saved from Genghis Khan.

Genghis Khan and Tamerlane

When he reached Bukhara, according to Curzon's account, the Great Khan rode into the Kalyan mosque, and, 'being told that it was the House of God, dismounted, ascended the pulpit, and flinging the Koran on the ground, cried out: "The hay is cut; give your horses fodder"—a permission which his savage horde quickly interpreted as authority for a wholesale massacre.'

He was humbler in front of the Kalyan minaret, staring at it with 'a finger to his mouth in a curious token of amazement', and sparing it while the rest of the city was razed. Within a few days the blooming oasis was transformed into a lifeless desert.

The holy city went through an unholy 300 years after Genghis Khan's visit; maybe he had shaken its faith in God. Ibn Battuta wrote in the mid-14th century that 'all but a few of its mosques, academies and bazaars are now lying in ruins. Its inhabitants are looked down upon because of their reputation for fanaticism, falsehood and denial of truth. There is not one of its inhabitants today who possesses any theological learning or makes any attempt to acquire it.'

Bukhara smelt bad too, and was known for its water-borne plagues. Tamerlane didn't have much to do with it. His grandson Ulug Bek built a prototype here in 1417 for his more famous madrasa in Samarkand's Registan. But the water stayed dirty. Anthony Jenkinson, a dour representative of the London Muscovy Company, described it in 1559 as 'most unwholesome, for it breedeth sometimes in men that drinke thereof... a worm... which commonly lieth in the legge betwixt the flesh and the skinne, and is pluck out about the ancle with great art and cunning, the Surgeons being much practised therein, and if she break in plucking out, the partie dieth, and every day she commeth out about an inche, which is rolled up, and so worketh till shee be all out.'

The Khanate

Bukhara did not re-emerge from Samarkand's shadow until Abdullah Khan, descended from Genghis Khan's grandson Sheiban, rebuilt most of it in the second half of the 16th century. He also formed the Sheibanid empire by conquering Balkh, Fergana, Tashkent, Khorasan and Khorezm.

During the 17th century the empire shrank back to its core between the Amu Darya and Syr Darya rivers and became known as the Khanate of Bukhara. Abdullah Khan's less competent Sheibanid successors wasted their limited energies bickering with other khanates until Nadir Shah invaded from Persia and founded the Astrakhanid dynasty in 1740. In 1784 the merely unimaginative Astrakhanids were replaced by the positively backward-looking Mangits, who called themselves emirs instead of khans and ruled till 1920. Their founder, Emir Maasum, was, according to Curzon, 'a bigoted devotee, wearing the dress and imitating the life of a dervish'. He was also, by contemporary standards at any rate, a pervert. If the writings of a German doctor who penetrated Bukhara in disguise in 1820 are to be believed, the emir retained, in addition to his harem, 'forty or fifty degraded beings', with whom he indulged in 'all the horrors and abominations of Sodom and Gomorrah'.

Maasum's son Nasrullah received in 1832 the audacious, polyglot British officer Alexander Burnes, whose *Travels Into Bukhara* contains the most colourful and intelligent description available of the city in the early 19th century. Its population of 150,000 was half that of pre-Mongol times, and three quarters of it was of slave extraction, mostly descended from Persian slaves captured and sold at Bukhara's infamous slave market by Turkmen nomads. There were also Russian slaves:

'A red beard, grey eyes, and fair skin, will now and then arrest the notice of a stranger, and his attention will have been fixed on a poor Russian, who has lost his country and his liberty, and drags out a miserable life of slavery.'

Not everyone was oppressed. Hindus, Jews and European merchants lived and traded unmolested in return for observing certain ground rules. Only Muslims might ride horses within the city. Whosoever failed to look away as the emir's harem passed risked 'a blow on the head'. Anyone out at night without a lamp would be assumed by the emir's police to be a burglar. And the sabbath (Friday) was strict: 'If a person is caught flying pigeons on a Friday he is sent forth with the dead bird round his neck, seated on a camel.'

Students were numerous—Burnes reported 366 madrasas each with from 10 to 80 students—and privileged; each had a right to a yearly maintenance grant from their madrasa, and to a share of the state's income. They were not all young: Burnes found 'many of them grave and demure old men, with more hypocrisy, but by no means less vice, than the youths in other quarters of the world.'

Women blackened their teeth and were absolutely not to be looked at except by their husbands, who were entitled to shoot peeping Toms.

The city centre, finally, contained 'many ponderous and massy buildings, colleges, mosques and lofty minarets,' while 'the common houses are built of sun-dried bricks on a framework of wood, and are all flat-roofed'—as they are today.

Age did not mellow Nasrullah. Ten years after Burnes' visit he gained worldwide notoriety by throwing two less diplomatic British officers, Colonel Stoddart and Captain Conolly, into his bug pit and then beheading them, slighted that Queen Victoria had not pleaded in person for their lives. It was one of the most gruesome and, thanks to an eccentric clergyman, highly publicized episodes in the Central Asian war of nerves between Britain and Russia which Kipling called the Great Game.

Bukhara had huge symbolic importance for Central Asian Muslims and for British Russophobes who thought its annexation by St Petersburg would be a prelude to a Russian invasion of India. So Russia trod carefully. When Bukhara's clergy declared a holy war against her in 1868, General Kaufmann had his pretext for attacking Samarkand to protect Tashkent. He didn't meddle with Bukhara but he did take control of her water supply. The holy war petered out, the frustrated clergy led a revolt against the emir, and the Russians stepped in to crush it for him. Without ever attacking the city they reduced it to vassal status in a treaty of 1873.

Colonial Bukhara

Russian, or 'New' Bukhara was even more separate from the old city than were the Russian cantonments at Tashkent and Samarkand. Born when the railway came from Krasnovodsk (now Turkmenbashy) in 1888, it was centered on the station ten miles south of Bukhara proper at Kagan. The now disused Russian church is still there.

There followed a delicate 30-year-long, four-cornered power struggle. In the Ark and the gaudy summer palace resided the last emir, Alim Khan, hanging onto the trappings of power. Outside the city strutted the Russian garrison and political agent, wanting stability and trade and prepared to support the emir as long as he delivered it. In the mosques and madrasas the mullahs swore death to the infidel and cursed the emir for his dubious loyalty. On street corners and in smoke-filled rooms angry young men whispered a dangerous new jargon about reforms and rights and pan-Turkic brotherhood.

In 1910 a general massacre of Shi'ite Muslims by Sunnis ended the city's traditional interdenominational harmony and was blamed on the reformers, who went underground. The Russian premier Stolypin threatened outright annexation of Bukhara. To forestall it the emir promised financial and educational reform but entrusted it to the clergy, who smothered it. In the years leading up to the Russian Revolution of 1917 the once-liberal underground, funded by a merchant millionaire called Mirza Muhitdin Mansur-oghli, grew more frustrated and extreme. But it was not the works of Marx and Lenin they were reading. Mansur-oghli paid for them to go to university in Istanbul and get high on the anti-Russian, pan-Turkic teachings of Mustapha Kemal.

The Russian Revolution

When revolutionaries took over St Petersburg and Moscow in 1917, the Emir of Bukhara was nearly dizzied by the political weathervane. At first, goaded by a murky Russian agent with the un-Russian name of Miller, who had himself switched quickly from the czarists to the communists, he offered his own package of reforms. But when he saw that Bukhara was not at the top of revolutionary Moscow's agenda he withdrew it. His people seethed. A communist among them, Khodja-oghli (Khojaev), told the Bolsheviks in Tashkent that Bukhara's proletariat was ready to revolt. He was wrong. When the Bolsheviks came the emir had them slaughtered at the station, and Bukhara became unofficial centre of the Central Asian counter-revolution.

Early in 1920 the emir forbade trade with Russia or Soviet Turkestan. It was a self-imposed blockade. By July three quarters of the khanate's livestock was dead and its people were running out of water. The Istanbul-trained Young Bukharans were at odds with the new and mainly Russian Bukhara Communist Party—but a marriage of convenience looked imminent.

In August the Red Army bombarded the city and in September, while the emir was away trying to assemble an army, it took possession. Moscow still feared provoking an Islamic uprising, so home-grown revolutionaries were allowed to found the Bukharan People's Republic, nominally independent of the Soviet Union. But the BPR proved awkwardly receptive to overtures from Istanbul, and when the Bolsheviks had a breathing space from their European struggle, they purged Bukhara's communists. On 19 September 1924 the Bukhara Communist Party voted unanimously at its fifth congress to abolish the BPR and found a Soviet Republic in its place.

Soviet Bukhara

As a stronghold of Muslim culture, Bukhara presented the evangelically atheistic Bolsheviks with a tricky choice: to raze it and start again, or to let it decay. They chose the latter. In the 20 years following the revolution its population fell by half. Fitzroy Maclean wrote after his visit in 1938: 'With the exception of a highly incongruous Pedagogic Institute which has made a somewhat half-hearted appearance within its walls, the dying city of Bukhara has remained purely Eastern. The only changes are those which have been wrought by neglect, decay and demolition.'

The purging of anti-Soviet elements had continued steadily, culminating in 1938 with the execution after a show trial of Bukhara's most famous communist son, the same Khojaev who had invited the Bolsheviks to lead an insurrection in 1918 and who subsequently became Soviet Uzbekistan's first president.

The Soviets did Bukhara the favour of draining and filling in most of its famous pools (there had been 100 when Burnes paid his visit). The diseases they harboured—'Bukhara Boil', 'Sartian Sickness', Guinea worm—disappeared, but so did most of the city's soul. An alternative water supply arrived in 1968 in the form of the 180-km Amu-Bukharski Canal from the river Amu Darya. Water was suddenly ten times more abundant and President Sharaf Rashidov took the credit while the Aral Sea took the strain.

Meanwhile Bukhara was industrialized. Processing plants were built on its outskirts for cotton, silk, wool, meat and milk. The city was honoured with the Soviet Union's biggest Karakul 'factory', in which Karakul lambs are killed before or shortly after birth for their tightly-curled coats which are said to be warmer and softer even than those of Astrakhan lambs. There is also a guano factory staffed by pigeons.

Getting to and from Bukhara

By air: There are three direct flights to and from Tashkent each day (40 minutes) and one a week in the winter, two in the summer, to Moscow. *Marshrutnoe* taxi go from the airport to Hotels Bukhoro (Intourist) and Varakhsha.

By rail: Every evening at 17.35 Moscow time a special train with *lyux* 2-berth compartments leaves Kagan station, 15km south of Bukhara, for Samarkand (6 hours) and Tashkent (12 hours). Buses and *marshrutnoe* from Kagan station terminate at Lyab-i-Khauz.

By bus: There are five buses a day to Tashkent (10 hours); six to Samarkand (6 hours). A bus goes daily to Urgench (9–10 hours), Andizhan and Namangan, each leaving in the afternoon. The daily Samarkand–Nukus express passes Bukhara around 6pm going north; midnight going south. It stops on the main road east of town, not at the bus station. Taxi drivers know where.

Bus 7 goes from the bus station to the Hotel Bukhoro.

All Bukhara's major sites are within walking distance of each other and of the hotels, which are clustered 10–15 minutes' walk south of the centre. Not to see the old town on foot is to miss out on the best in Central Asian time travel. Bus 10 goes to the airport. Buses 6, 7, 9 and 13 go to the bus station. All stop on Ulitsa Ulyanova two blocks east of the Hotel Bukhoro.

Tourist Information

The **Intourist Service Bureau** is at the Hotel Bukhoro, ✆ 3 51 83/3 01 24 (*open daily 8–12 noon, 12.30–8pm*). Their deadening 3-hour city tour includes the Kalyan mosque and minaret, the Ulug Bek and Abdulaziz Khan madrasas, the Magok-i-Attari mosque and Lyab-i-Khauz—but usually not the Ark or Samanid mausoleum. Prices vary according to type of transport and size of group. For the individual sightseer, $54 includes a guide, car and driver. A 2-hour trip to the unmissable Bakhautdin complex outside Bukhara is also $54. For the same service at a fraction of the price, take an ordinary taxi and hire one of the guides from the hotel ($3-4 hourly rate). Intourist accepts credit cards but not travellers' cheques for excursions.

The Hotel Bukhoro has a **post office** and **international satellite credit card phone** which taps loud and clear into the AT&T network as long as Intourist keeps up its payments on the dish. Collect calls aren't possible.

The best place for tourist information and street maps is the new centre at the art gallery on Ulitsa Nakshbandi, ✆ 4 22 46 (*open daily 9–5*), formerly the Lenin Museum. Staffed by English-, German- and French-speaking student volunteers, it provides E-mail, fax and money-changing facilities.

Since independence a number of ex-Intourist guides have set up their own tourism businesses. The best are **Salom**, ✆ 3 72 77/(3712) 56 87 22 and **Bukhara Visit**, ✆/@ 6 46 00/6 00 85, E-mail: visit@bl.silk.glas.apc.org. Raisa at Salom will arrange tours and meetings with local specialists including craft workshops, lunches and self-catering apartments. Mila at Bukhara Visit offers visa support, transport and accommodation as well as tours throughout Uzbekistan.

For a guided tour of Bukhara itself, try **Noila** (ask for her at the Ark, ✆ 4 13 78) and **Zinat Ashurova** (also at the Ark, ✆ 4 14 04), ✆ 2 20 37. Expect to pay $3–4 per hour. And consider buying a **Super Saver ticket**. Bukhara, like Samarkand, charges for entrance to each monument so this initial outlay of around $10 could well save you money. Ask at the Ark; Noila will explain.

Travellers' cheques (in US dollars only) can be cashed at the **Bank of Bukhara**, Ulitsa Muhammed Ikbol 3, 3rd floor, room 16, ✆ 3 67 13, 3 71 08.

The Shakhristan (Шахристан)

The Ark (Apx)

Open Thurs–Mon, 9–4.30, Tues, 9– 2.30, closed Weds.

The snootiest neighbourhood of a Central Asian city was traditionally its northwestern corner. In Bukhara, this is where you find the rulers' 2000-year-old fortress, the Ark. The Registan outside its main gate used to contain a mosque, the royal arsenal and a huge open-air bazaar, but is empty nowadays. The rest of the quarter, inhabited by aristocrats and artisans until the death of class society in the 1920s, was known as the Shakhristan, or city proper.

Bukhara's first citadel was built before the dawn of recorded time by one Siyavush ibn-Keikavus, who ran away from home and won the hand of the daughter of Afrasiab (of ancient Samarkand fame), together with all his father-in-law's property. Siyavush intended the citadel as a memorial to himself and it became one when Afrasiab had him killed for alleged slander. He was buried under the east gates, which the city's fire-worshippers revered ever after and to which, once a year, a sacrificial cockerel was brought.

Whoever really built the first citadel, the Arabs destroyed it in the 8th century. The Samanids and Karakhanids built on the rubble in the 10th and 11th centuries, and the Mongols turned their work into more rubble in the 13th. By the 16th century the Sheibanids were building on an artificial hill 800 m round and some 20 m above the Registan. The Ark became a city within a city, housing in the 18th century the police

THE ARK, BUKHARA

department, prison, mint, treasury, armoury, its own mosques and a population of 3000, as well as the royal apartments, reception rooms and stables. Most of the buildings had wooden frames, and in 1920 they were destroyed by a fire which the last emir, Alim Khan, may have started himself as he fled the Bolsheviks.

The Gatehouse

The great 18th-century gatehouse survives, however, flanked by twin turrets and (restored) toothed walls of baked brick. The ramp to the entrance arch continues beyond it as a dark tunnel, curving up through the ages past 12 niches, on the left, in which prisoners sat in shackles. In one of these a lamp used to be lit in memory of Siyavush. They were guarded by soldiers in more niches opposite, one of which is now ticket office for a Museum in the emirs' greeting hall (*salomkhana*) which has carpets, embroidery, jewellery, pottery and photographs from the reign of Alim Khan. Everyone but the emir had to dismount and walk up the ramp.

The Friday Mosque

At the top of it on the left stands the large 17th-century Djuma (Friday) mosque, which the emirs used on the Muslim Sabbath. The pillars are of *karagachi*, a rare sycamore-like wood. The central carved wood *iwan* was added by Alim Khan at the turn of the century.

The Audience Chamber and Music Pavilion

A stone passage leads south from the mosque to the roofless 17th-century *korunishkhana* or audience chamber. The emir sat on a marble throne—made in 1669—in a deep niche on the far side, which his vassals approached crawling on all fours. They had to face the emir at all times, and therefore walked backwards when leaving the chamber, turning round only when hidden by the low wall across the entrance. The wooden pillars on the north side are from a colonnade which originally shaded three sides of the chamber. Having walked backwards out of the chamber, proceed up the steps on your left to the museum which illustrates Bukhara's ancient and modern history.

The only other extant royal preserve is the *nagorakhana* (music pavilion) directly above the gatehouse, where the emir's orchestra played *makoms* by which people in the Registan below could tell the time of day. The royal family gathered here to watch public festivities and executions.

The Zindan (Зиндан)

> Open Thurs–Mon 9–4.30, Tues 9–2.30, closed Weds. Winter closing time is tourist determined.

The emirs earned their real notoriety down a sidestreet to the left of the gatehouse, in the **Zindan,** or city gaol. Minor miscreants lived in its less noxious cells and were allowed out in their chains on Fridays, the Muslim sabbath, to beg for food on which they lived for the week. But particular unfavourites of the emir shared the bottom of a 6-m-deep underground brick cylinder with rats, scorpions, lice, cockroaches and sheep ticks. The Sia

Chat (Black Well) or Bug Pit admitted no light except through a small opening high above the prisoners' heads. It was 'truly the inspiration of an evil mind'.

The most famous victims of the Bug Pit, those depicted by the curators' dummies, were British. In the winter of 1839 Lieutenant-Colonel Charles Stoddart arrived in Bukhara to forge an alliance with Emir Nasrullah on behalf of Whitehall and Calcutta before the Russians did. But he rode where he should have walked, walked where he should have crawled and presented a letter not from Queen Victoria but from the Governor General of India. Nasrullah did not like him. Stoddart spent six months in the Bug Pit, then faced the executioner's knife if he did not convert to Islam. He converted, and got clean clothes, clean quarters, freedom of the city and circumcision into the bargain. More than two years later a fellow Briton, Captain Arthur Conolly of the Bengal Light Infantry, arrived to rescue Stoddart. But soon afterwards the East India Company's army was routed in Afghanistan and Nasrullah, out of a mixture of spite and glee, threw both his British captives back in the Bug Pit. On 17 June 1842 Conolly was offered mercy if he too converted to Islam. He refused to do so and both men were executed in front of the Ark, where one British expert believes their bodies still lie.

Their fate was not known in London for certain until an ageing and eccentric Church of England missionary called Reverend Joseph Wolff entered Bukhara 'in full canonicals' in 1845 and recovered the increasingly desperate journal Conolly had kept during his last months in the Bug Pit. Wolff avoided the same fate by making the emir laugh. He refused to accept Islam but prostrated himself, stroked his beard and cried 'Allah Akbar', thirty times over. The audience ended with a rendering of 'God Save The Queen' from the *nagorakhana* orchestra.

Bolo Khauz Mosque (мечеть Боло-Хауз)

The emirs worshipped in public across the Registan (now cut in half by Ulitsa Afrasiab) in its only surviving monument, the **Bolo Khauz mosque**. Built in 1718, with a roof extension supported by *karagachi* pillars added in the 19th century, its elegant west side is reflected in the 16th-century *khauz* (pool) of its name, and the whole complex is shaded by the trees of former Lenin Park. The minaret to the right was built in 1917.

Samani Park (Парк Самани)

Approaching the Ark by road from any of the hotels you pass a pair of 16th century *kosh* madrasas, facing each other nonchalantly across Ulitsa Mirakon, near the east end of Samani (ex-Kirov) Park. On the left facing east, the **Abdullah Khan madrasa** (1588–90) was architecturally daring for its time because the cells radiating off its north and west *iwans* cause the overall shape to depart from the standard madrasa rectangle. The **Modari Khan madrasa** opposite was dedicated by Abdullah Khan to his mother in 1567 (974 in the Islamic calendar), according to a verse in majolica over the main entrance. In any other city these buildings would be the object of huge curatorial fuss. In Bukhara two other *kosh* ensembles outshine them. They are padlocked, unrestored and not open to visitors.

Ismail Samani Mausoleum (мавзолей Измаила Самани)

When Samani park was laid out in the 1930s, a Russian archaeologist called Shishkin rediscovered an architectural gem that had languished under two metres of sediment for the 400 years of the khanate. The Ismail Samani mausoleum is one of the world's oldest monuments to famous Muslims. Samani built it for his father and grandson in 907, and was later buried here himself. It is unique in bearing traces of pre-Islamic, Sogdian culture while pioneering architectural and decorative techniques that were to be used for the next five centuries.

Its cubic base, representing the earth, supports a heavenly hemisphere to form a Sogdian metaphor for the universe. Built before ceramics came to Central Asia, the mausoleum consists entirely of clay bricks bound with egg yolk and camels' milk—but no ordinary bricklayer was at work here. In Geoffrey Moorhouse's words, 'someone obsessed with the possibilities inherent in brick had been trying to push variety to its limits.' The bricks are arranged in 18 different two- and three-dimensional patterns which make the massive walls look featherweight, creating in some places 'the texture of elaborate basketwork', in others 'a lattice through which an evening breeze might cool the summer heat inside'.

The lower part of the mausoleum has survived in all its intricacy for a thousand years. Shishkin restored the dome and corner cupolas in the 1930s with egg-and-milk bricks which are virtually indistinguishable from the originals. He also cleared away the sediment to reveal the building's full height, and moved to another cemetery the graves which had crowded around when this was a fashionable place to be buried. Now you can walk right round the mausoleum. If you do three circuits and make a wish, the wish will come true.

Chashma Ayub (Чашма Аюб)

A short, shady walk northeast from here, past a stretch of ruined city wall beyond a pond on the left, is Chashma Ayub, the Spring of Job, where curative water miraculously gushed from the desert at the Old Testament prophet's behest. The spring is still there and a *mazar* (shrine, not mausoleum) was built over it in the 12th century. It was rebuilt in the 1380s, according to an inscription over the entrance, with cells, dormitories and dining-rooms for pilgrims and dervishes. The large and incongruous conical dome was designed by architects brought from Khorezm by Tamerlane. Nowadays there are unhouse-trained doves inside, and a small museum, open daily, on the history of Bukhara's water supply. Photos show how it was cleaned up and some of its less desirable effects. You are encouraged to drink of the Spring of Job from the bucket attached to the well.

The entrance to the new **kolkhoznaya bazaar** is opposite Chashma Ayub and not far from the site of the old slave market (vaguely located by Soviet literature as 'beyond the Registan'). It opened at dawn on Mondays and Thursdays for three hours only, until the

Russians forced the abolition of slavery in the late 19th century. Slaves were only exhibited here; deals were struck in the traders' caravanserais. The modern bazaar is good for Uzbek snacks, has a fair on Sundays and Thursdays and a wall-less but shady *chai-khana*.

A 4-km section of ruined **city wall** comes to the edge of the bazaar. Bukhara's first defences were built in the mid-9th century, reinforced in the 12th and 13th, destroyed by the Mongols and rebuilt by the Sheibanids. What survives is a section of the inner wall, all 13km of which was intact when Alexander Burnes visited in the 1830s. Built of packed clay faced with adobe brick, it stood 11 metres high, tapering towards the top from its massive base. Behind the battlements was a firing gallery, and rounded buttresses enabled the defenders to pour lateral fire on an attacking force. Despite these defences, the walls were no match for the Bolshevik artillery which reduced them to their present ruinous state in 1920. On Sundays this area is again under attack. This time by a frenzied army of vendors who sell everything from car parts and 'gold' embroidered Uzbek caps to camel milk from plastic cups. Beat your way through with the best of them.

KNIFE - GRINDER
BUKHARA

Poi-Kalyan (Пой-Калян)

Kalyan Minaret (минарет Калян)

The road from the Registan to the Kalyan minaret was called Ulitsa Kommunarov by the Soviets (now Ulitsa Nur Abad); its north side is now being rebuilt as a tourists' bazaar. No one is now allowed to re-name or rebuild the minaret (though its nick-name is the Tower of Death) because it is on the UNESCO world heritage list. But it was rebuilt, or at least repaired, under the Soviets. On the south side that work is visible where the bricks don't exactly match. To see why it was necessary, look at the black-and-white photo in the museum at the Uleg Bek madrasa.

The first minaret here was wood-framed, and burned down. The second, built early in the Karakhanid Arslan Khan's reign, was of brick but after 'someone bewitched it with an evil eye' it fell on and largely demolished the adjacent mosque. Second time round Arslan Khan took no chances. His surviving colossus is nearly 14m wide at the bottom and has cubic foundations 10m deep. At 47 m high, it was probably the tallest building in the world when completed in 1127. The idea may have been for its 16-arched brick lantern, from which the people were called to prayer, to be on a level with Samarkand 250km away. It was certainly used as a lighthouse for caravans travelling at night—a fire would be lit in the lantern—and can still be seen from miles out on the flat approaches to Bukhara.

There are 14 bands of kufic calligraphy round its tapering neck (one names the architect as 'Bako'), interspersed with as many bands of decorative brickwork, all of them different. The turquoise 'necklace' at the top is the first use of glazed tiles in Central Asia.

When Genghis Khan spared this building he was probably as impressed by its punitive potential as its height. He and subsequent khans threw people off it, faithless wives as well as common criminals, hence the name 'Tower of Death'. The official Soviet guidebook dates the last death by jaculation as 1884, but escaped Austrian POW Gustav Krist claimed the tower still served this purpose in the 1920s. In pre-Soviet times, no one else was allowed up it, except the khan; it was too good a vantage point for spying on womens' balconies. Today tourists are allowed up for 100 cym. Enquire at the door of the Kalyan Mosque.

Kalyan Mosque (мечеть Калян)

The paved plaza at the foot of the tower is called Poi-Kalyan, 'Pedestal of the Great One' and is flanked by Bukhara's two most imposing facades. One of these, moored by a bridge to the tower, belongs to the **Kalyan mosque**. First built in the 12th century, it was badly damaged by the Mongols and restored in 1514–15, according to an inscription under the main entrance arch, by the Sheibanid Ubaydullah Khan with booty from a military campaign the previous year. A marble plaque on the entrance dated 1541 announces the lifting by his successor Khan Abdulaziz of a tax which may have paid for the mosaic on the mosque's main *mihrab*.

The Kalyan mosque is huge, matching Samarkand's Bibi Khanym mosque in scale if not decoration. A colonnade of 288 cupolas rests on nearly as many columns to form a 127-by-78-m courtyard. At the west end a mighty blue dome called Kok Gumbaz supported a stork's nest until Bukhara's pools were drained and storks stopped migrating here from Egypt. Colonnade and courtyard between them can hold 10,000 people although the mosque was not used for worship from 1920 to 1989. Non-Muslims may go inside. The well under the fourth arch on the left is extremely deep.

Mir-i-Arab Madrasa (медресе Мир-и-Араб)

The **Mir-i-Arab madrasa** (1535) across the plaza forms, with the mosque, Bukhara's main *kosh* ensemble. One of only two working madrasas allowed in the Soviet Union (the other was in Tashkent), it has never closed to students and never opened to tourists – who can glimpse from outside the calligraphy and mosaic round the drums supporting its two blue domes, but still miss out on some of the finest ceramic decoration in Bukhara. Its 120–130 students study Islamic law and literature and Arabic for five to seven years, and live in two storeys of cells with balconies round the central courtyard. Their main assembly hall is under the dome to the right of the *pishtak*. Under the left dome are buried Ubaydullah Khan (one of the first Bukharan royals not to have his own mausoleum) and Sheikh Mir-i-Arab after whom the madrasa is named. He is variously described as an architect, a Yemeni merchant, and 'spiritual mentor of the early Sheibanids'. He may have been all three. He certainly seems to have been foreign, to have founded the madrasa and to have paid for it with money made by Ubaydullah from the sale of 3000 Persian slaves, or Shi'ites branded slaves for belonging to the wrong Muslim sect in a Sunni city. The building site next door was originally intended to be a new dormitory.

Next to and south of the madrasa, the **Amir Alim Khan madrasa** was built near the start of the 19th century. With separate courtyards for living and working it breaks all the architectural rules for madrasas and was always more important as a library, which it still is, though now for children.

Khodja Zain-al-Din Ensemble (ансамбль Ходжа Заин-ал-Дин)

For an antidote to open-air museumitis walk west past the minaret down a narrow, mud-walled dog-leg to **Khodja Zain-al-Din**, a compact, introverted ensemble of working parish mosque, small *khanaga* and the city's oldest (and most sewer-like) surviving *khauz*. Inside the mosque, which is known as the Blue Mosque, the decoration starts with an eye-level feast of mosaic and proceeds via intricate gilt designs on light blue on the upper walls to a dark (Heavenly) blue cupola. Ask before going inside, and ask for the lights to be switched on. The walls of the near-empty *khauz* are faced with marble and the design on the marble spout, which one wishes would actually spout something, is of a dragon's jaw. This was one of only three functioning mosques left after the Revolution. Today there are forty.

Downtown in the Old Town

Return to Poi-Kalyan, continue for half a minute along Ulitsa Nur Abad and you come to old Bukhara's Hatton Garden, **Taq-i-Zargaran** (1569–70). This was the biggest of the city's famous multi-domed bazaars and is one of three to have survived. The idea was to exploit the bedlam of a busy crossroads by turning the crossroads itself into the bazaar. A high cupola 14m across rises over the intersection on a drum. Trade-heated air escapes through high windows, drawing in cooler air from the streets. The drum, surrounded by myriad smaller domes, rests on an octagonal hall, four of whose sides are shop-fronts while traffic flows in and out through the other four. Taq-i-Zargaran still trades, but in tourist trinkets rather than Asia's costliest gemstones.Before you enter the third dome from Ulitsa Nur Abad, look for the **bronze casting** workshop of Inojatov Abdukadir, famous for its bronze bells.

Abdulaziz Khan and Ulug Bek Madrasas
(медресе Абдулазиз Хана и медресе Улугбека)

Beyond the bazaar, still on Nur Abad, there is another impressive *kosh* ensemble. The **Ulug Bek madrasa** (1417) on the left (north) is the oldest in Central Asia, celebrated its 600th anniversary in 1994, and was the prototype for its more extravagant namesake built three years later in Samarkand. 'To strive for knowledge is the duty of each Muslim man and Muslim woman,' says the—for Ulug Bek—typically enlightened inscription over the entrance. The architect, Ismail ibn Takhir ibn Makhmud Isfagani, was probably related to an Iranian captured by Tamerlane to work in Samarkand and Shahrisabz.The proportions and decoration of the façade, including the ceramic plaiting on its main lancet arch, contain much that was later associated with the 16th-century 'Bukhara school' of architecture. Now fully restored it is open to the public and houses a small museum whose most intriguing exhibits are the black-and-white photos: one shows the Samanid mausoleum under snow; another a mausoleum that has since disappeared, in front of the Ark; and there's a picture of the Kalyan minaret damaged in the 1920s by Soviet bombardment, which could not be shown prior to independence. The Tajik craftsman, Ustor Shirin Muradov, responsible for the decoration of the Summer Palace and Tashkent's opera house was awarded the Stalin Prize in 1948 and has his own corner here. Examples of majolica tiles are on display; those on the winding column at the entrance were made in Bukhara. If you look closely at these you'll see some of the Koranic inscription is painted rather than mosaic; a cosmetic trick by restorers faced with a tight deadline.

The **Abdulaziz Khan madrasa** (1651–2) faces the older one across the narrow street as if, says the Soviet guidebook hopefully, in dialogue. It is the newest big madrasa in Bukhara and was never quite finished, more cells being built according to demand. These were relatively cushy: split-level studios with fireplaces and large storage niches for clothes and bedding. Students usually rented them for their whole period of study. When the numbers fell from 200 in this madrasa, it was used as a caravanserai. In today's working madrasas the maximum number is 250, and there's electricity and free food at large central canteens.

Half-pillars line the courtyard edge; the carving on some of them is unfinished, interrupted by the *coup d'état* in 1652 so UNESCO will only partially restore this madrasa since it was never, historically, completed.

The phoenixes and snake-headed birds in the *pishtak*'s mosaics represent a brave break with the Islamic tradition of not depicting animal life. (Two other well-known porticoes that break the rule—those of the nearby Nadir Divanbegi madrasa and Samarkand's Sher Dor madrasa—are also mid-17th century.) The rebellion did not catch on and, according to one Soviet guidebook, may even have been fatal for this artist. Inside, frescoes of stylized landscapes betraying Chinese and Moghul Indian influence survive in the large ex-lecture hall on the left. The red clay patterns on the roof and niches were originally dusted with gold; the cracks are from a 1976 earthquake. To the right of the entrance a former mosque now has a small exhibition of Bukharan woodwork. Wood was always a highly prized commodity in this desert environment as the lavish carving here reflects. Among the pieces are some wooden stamps used in cotton printing, dipped in sheep's fat to ensure a good transfer of dye to the cloth. As you walk out of the door look behind you. You may catch sight of the silhouette of a turbanned man, which disappears in the light. This image was the closest the decorator could safely get to portraying human form under Islamic Law.

Return to Taq-i-Zargaran. Beneath the empty plot on the left are the foundations of an Indian caravanserai. In 1976 these were excavated in order to gauge the city's age. Bukhara is now believed to be younger than Samarkand and will celebrate its 2500 anniversary in 1997. The excavations also revealed, and were hampered by, the rising water table. Today this increasingly threatens many of the monuments. Turn left (south) down Ulitsa Hakikat, formerly Frunze, and you pass on the left **Tim Abdullahkhan** (Abdullah Khan market). Single-entrance domed arcades like this used to line the whole street. This sole survivor is now a state silk shop.

A little further down on the left an ancient frontage with steps to a raised entrance has been rebuilt in yellowish brick. It's presently being renovated, but when it reopens, men should try Central Asia's oldest (16th-century) working **public baths**, though as a foreigner you may be amiably overcharged. The only light in the series of semi-subterranean stone caverns is natural and dim, filtering down from tiny skylights through the steam. You fill your basin to wash, then sit around on stone benches using the place as a mild sauna. Soap, shampoo, back-scrubber, basin, towel, locker and tea afterwards cost about 5 cents in rubles. The barber in the entrance can give directions to the women's baths near the Kalyan mosque at 4 Hamon. Open daily except Tuesday, this maze of tunnels, domed skylights and archways were previously used by the emir's harem. There used to be eight baths for women, nine for men and one for both. The latter still operates on 19 Dzhubori Kalon, fomerly Oktyabrskaya, and is a great bonus to those staying in bed and breakfasts without shower facilities.

Beside the bathhouse is **Mirfaiz's spice counter**. Resembling a pirate and with esoteric knowlege passed down the generations, he'll mix you the house special from eleven different spices; this curry powder is in a class of its own. So is the hollowed-out vegetable container you take it away in.

More family tradition is in evidence across the road. Tucked insiode Shokir Kamalov's workshop is the **Museum of Blacksmiths**. It's easily identified by the Stork scissors which Shokir designed and for which he was awarded first prize at the first Islamic Festival for Artisans in 1995. Bukhara adopted the stork as its symbol when the birds were prolific in the town, attracted by the frogs in its many ponds. But as the ponds were reduced, so were the frogs and the storks began to find dinner more easily elsewhere. Through a small door in the back of the museum you can see, for the first time, one of the most ancient and complete caravanserais of Bukhara.

Ulitsa Hakikat now disappears into the twelve-sided **Taq-i-Telpaq Furushan**, the capmakers' bazaar. Astrakhan hats and gold-embroidered skull caps are sold here as they have been since the 16th century. The main dome is lower but wider than at Taq-i-Zargaron, spanning the junction of five streets.

The **Magok-i-Kurpa mosque** (1636–7), facing the bazaar's south-west corner, is unusual in having prayer halls on two floors, but is usually closed to visitors.

Ulitsa Mehtar Ambar leads past the mosque, round the bazaar and along the top of a shady square whose west side consists of a row of jewellery and antique stalls which will diddle the dozy but may interest coin collectors. Round the square's southwest corner the 19th-century building which housed Central Asia's first Russian bank now houses an **art museum** (*closed Tues*) and a tourist information office.

Gaukushan Madrasa (медресе Гаукушан)

Continuing west on Ulitsa Nakshabandi you come to another pleasant green square, though this one used to be unpleasant and red; the Gaukushan madrasa (1570) is on the site of an earlier open-air abbattoir (*gau*=cow, *ku*=kill). This 16th-century classic, built under the auspices of the great Abdullah Khan, is nevertheless overshadowed by Poi-Kalyan and Lyab-i-Khauz (*see* below) and has been given over to engravers of copper plates to attract its share of tourists. The plates (from $15) are dipped in acid to give them a black coating which is then etched, artistically, off again. A Friday mosque was added to the madrasa in 1598. Folk-dancing displays and concerts are held here in the summer. Across the square is an old foundry.

Magok-i-Attari (Магок-и-Аттари)

Open half-day Tues; closed Wed.

Back east, beyond the art museum but before the next covered market, Central Asia's oldest mosque stands among trees on the north side of the street. Magok-i-Attari was half buried when the Russian archaeologist Shishkin got to it in 1939 after excavating the Samanids' mausoleum. He revealed its most precious component, a 12th-century south-facing portal with immaculate incised alabaster panels, but also found traces of a 5th-century Zoroastrian temple and an even earlier Buddhist one. People have worshipped most things here at one time or another, including the moon. In pre-Arab times it served as a herbalists' bazaar selling idols and drugs as well as herbs and spices. A fire destroyed whatever stood here in 937. The first mosque went up in the 11th century; a new one, built in the 12th, was ruined bar the south portal by the 15th. Most of what survives dates from a comprehensive restoration carried out 1546–7. The brickwork of the east portal seems to imitate that of the Samanid mausoleum.

The south entrance, approached by stone steps, is now 5m below ground level and was always sunken: *magok* means 'in a pit'. Most of the interior now houses a carpet exhibition but the brick-lined pits on the east side go down to Shishkin's Buddhist depths.

The *chai-khana* opposite Magok-i-Attari occupies the 20th-century **Sarrafan mosque** and the dome over Ulitsa Nakshbandi beyond it belongs to **Taq-i-Sarrafan**, the money-changers' bazaar.

Lyab-i-Khauz (Ляб-и-Хауз)

Beneath the Taq-i-Sarrafan and parallel to the street runs a narrow canal born of malicious and high-handed intent. Around 1620 the khan's grand vizier, Nadir Divanbegi, wanted to put a reservoir in the city centre on the site of the house of a lonely old woman. She refused to move so he had a canal built under her house, dissolving its mud foundations and walls. The woman fled and Divanbegi built his reservoir.

It is the beautiful pool of Lyab-i-Khauz, beyond Taq-i-Sarrafan, where the soul of pre-Soviet Central Asia survives with greater charm than anywhere else. If you do nothing else in Bukhara, come here for tea. The pool's sides were stepped, as usual for a *khauz*, to let people get at the water whatever its level. Nowadays the water is for gazing at, not washing in. It's one of two surviving ponds in Bukhara. Around it, under century-old plane trees, *shashlyk*, *plov* and *chai* are served all day to a core clientele of turbanned neo-dervishes—and to others who are patient.

Not content with his pool, the grand vizier flanked it with two grand buildings in his own memory: the **Nadir Divanbegi madrasa and khanaga**, both completed around 1620. The madrasa was originally intended to be a caravanserai but the khan inaugurated it, probably by mistake, as a madrasa. Nothing the khan said could be unsaid so it was hastily converted. It has a barber's shop and café in its south wing, a *bureau de change* to the left of the *pishtak* on the inside, and a very striking mosaic above the entrance arch. The sun, with a Mongol face like those behind the lions of Samarkand's Sher Dor madrasa, illuminates two dazzling if strangely hybrid birds, each sheltering a grazing goat. All that remained of the mosaic in 1970 was a faint imprint from which it has been completely restored.

The *khanaga* on the opposite (west) side of the pool was once a hostel for wandering dervishes but in Soviet times became an exhibition hall. Now almost everything on show is for sale. Between the pool and the madrasa, in the middle of a small formal garden, there is a modern statue commemorating the 1000th birthday of an ancient 'wise fool'. **Khodja Nasreddin** was a Robin Hood character who starred in countless Sufi children's stories and was loved by Soviet mythologists for his instinct for the redistribution of wealth by direct action.

The north side of the complex is formed by the **Kukeldash madrasa** (1568–9), Bukhara's biggest and most austere, with 160 cells and a courtyard 80 by 60m. The builder was Kulbaba Kukeldash, whose name means 'foster-brother of the Khan' (Abdullah). The decorative art of the era formed a sober interlude between the restrained opulence of Ulug Bek and the flamboyance of the 17th century. This madrasa is said to be notable for its main cupola, supported by four intersecting arches, and the alabaster pointing on the ceilings of its octagonal corner halls. It also houses a museum to Sadreddin Aini, considered to be the founder of Soviet Tajik literature, who was whipped seventy five times by the last emir for his revolutionary ideas.

Chor Minar (Чор Минар)

A 19th-century oddity remains to be seen near the eastern edge of the old town. In 1807 Khalif Niyaz-Kul, a rich Turkmen merchant, built a large madrasa whose gatehouse survives in a maze of mud streets north of Ulitsa Mehtar Ambar and 500m east of the Kukeldash madrasa. It looks like an upside-down commode. Its name, **Chor Minar**, means 'four minarets', but its four rounded towers never called people to prayer. Before their blue tiles were restored, each one sprouted a stork's nest and now they've become victims of the rising ground water level. One collapsed in March 1995 and other towers are endangered. The storks have gone, too. But Chor Minar has attracted UNESCO who added it to their list of projects.

It's amazing what you can find in a Soviet suburban wasteland. Given more than the hitherto customary two days in Bukhara, hire a taxi for half a day and take a swing round the south circular, starting just inside it, not far from Samani Park, at the functioning **Balyand mosque**. The *imam* will not let Russians in; demonstrate your foreignness. It's worth it for the lavish early 20th-century tilework in and around the *mihrab*, and for the painted wood ceiling (which hides the beams of the actual roof). The basic structure is early 16th-century, and the corner colonnade typical for a parish mosque.

Ulitsa Havzinav leads due south to a roundabout and, facing a wall of trellised vines on the right (west), the 17th-century **Dzhubari Kalyan madrasa**. This is a rare thing: a madrasa for girls, apparently aged 16–18, on a two-year course of embroidery and the Koran. Visitors are not allowed in. The mosque across the road beyond the vines is not used as one but its *khauz* seems to be a public water source.

At the next roundabout, half a mile southeast, there is a building of grandeur and desolation; which quality dominates depends on your mood and the light. The **Namazgokh mosque** was first built in 1119–20 by Arslan Khan, the Karakhanid who built the Kalyan minaret, and some of his west wall, with precious pre-Mongol decoration in brick, terracotta and stucco, survives under the main 16th-century structure. This was a big mosque but was intended only for special twice-yearly holiday prayers. It looks best in the evening and is not far from the Hotel Gulistan.

The **Buyan Kuli Khan** and **Saif ed-Din** mausolea form half of an extraordinary double act in which medieval Islam meets obsessive 20th-century industrialization. The other half is a busy railway shunting yard southeast of the Old Town off Sholkomotalnaya Ulitsa. The Buyan Kuli Khan mausoleum (1358), resting place of a Mongol Khan killed in that year in Samarkand, is a rare survivor of Bukhara's long, depressed post-Mongol resurrection. The majolica-work round its front door rivals that of Samarkand's Shah-i-Zinda complex, and is shaken all day every day by goods trains passing a few feet away. This is in the 'new' city area, behind the houses.

The Saif-ed-Din mausoleum next door commemorates Sheikh Saif ed-Din Bokharzi (1190–1262), a popular poet and theologian who survived Genghis Khan's visitation and probably funded one of this district's many *khanagas* for the poor and homeless. The mausoleum is roofless and so plain that it was long thought to date from the 13th century, though in fact it dates from the 16th. Both buildings are surrounded by huge piles of concrete pipes.

Back on the ring road it is a short drive north to the handsome **Faizabad Khanaga** (1598–99) on Ulitsa Suleymana Muradova, which gave travelling dervishes temporary shelter on three floors of cells. It is normally closed but an Intourist guide may know where to get a key.

Sitorai-Mokhi-Khosa (Ситорай-Мохи-Хоса)

Open Thurs–Mon, 94.30; Tues 9–2.30; closed Wed.

Like Louis XVI hunting boar in the grounds of Versailles while Paris seethed, Bukhara's last emir played out his final months in power in a ridiculous summer palace north of the city, spying on his bored harem through secret peepholes and trying to incorporate Russian teapots in Islamic decorative art while the Red Army tightened its stranglehold on his heritage and people. **Sitorai-Mokhi-Khosa,** built mostly in the 19th century but still being added to in 1918, is the great and only repository of 'Bukhara Kitsch' . Reached from two blocks east of the Hotel Bokhoro by bus 7 which stops near the gate, or by taxi, most of it is open to the public, though part of the grounds now belong to what was known in sinister Soviet parlance as a neurological sanatorium.

The main gate is a puny but very garish mockery of every great *pishtak* in Bukhara and Samarkand. It leads to a modest courtyard sacrificed to the hard sell of mass-produced silk dressing gowns, which in turn leads to Said Alim Khan's palace-within-a-palace round three sides of a larger yard. Named after him and finished in 1917, this is now a branch of Bukhara's history museum. A guide will probably have attached him- or herself to you by now if you did not arrive with one.

Honoured guests were received in the White Hall, which forms the west side of the yard and was decorated by a master stucco plasterer called Ustor Shirin Muradov whose picture hangs by the entrance and whose hands were maimed on the khan's orders when his work was done—either for some trifling error or so he could not reproduce the design for anyone else. The ornate plasterwork in the hall, like most interior décor in the palace, originally had a generous garnish of gold leaf which was taken by the Bolsheviks and replaced with bronze.

The fireplace in the chess room round the corner to the left is German; the silver boxes and fish are genuine antique Bukharan. Red and blue banqueting halls follow, the first with red lighting, blue stained glass and a fine collection of daggers; the second, equally nauseating, has a mirror which reflects you 40 times. The ordeal by psychedelia ends when you reach the emir's *chai-khana*, more window than wall, containing his ancestors' priceless collection of Chinese vases.

A paved walkway leads from the male playground to the female. So, reputedly, did a secret tunnel for the exclusive use of the voyeuristic emir. Beside a large *khauz* now overlooked by the neurological sanatorium is a two-storey building, more European than Asian in style, where the emir's begums used to live. The harem was said to number 400 by 1920, when M. N. Roy, an Indian member of the Central Asiatic Bureau of the Comintern, decreed a mass divorce and allowed Red Army troops in to take their pick. According to his own account, quoted by Moorhouse,

'The storming of the harem took place under strict vigilance, and nothing unpleasant happened. The begums, of course, behaved like scared rabbits, but the sight of the husky young men scrambling for them must have made some impression on them. Able-bodied young men seeking their favour was a new experience to women whose erotic life could naturally not be satisfied by a senile old man. At the end it was a pleasing sight—the secluded females happily allowing themselves to be carried away by proud men.'

In the official guesthouse, discreetly separate from both palace and harem, there is a collection of royal robes which is outshone by the one in the Uzbek State Museum of Art in Tashkent, although the spare room itself must have rivalled any in the world for sheer extravagance. There were 4.5 kilos of gold on its walls.

Chor-Bakr (Чор-Бакр)

When all the spaces round the Samanid mausoleum were filled, the Bukharan aristocracy took itself elsewhere to be buried: to the grave of a descendent of the Prophet called Abu Bakr Sa'd, 5km west of the city walls near what is now the village of Sumitan. In 1558 the khan's philosophers announced the presence of a lucky star and foundations for a monumental necropolis were laid near Abu Bakr's grave. Paid for with endowments from the city's wealthiest families, it eventually comprised two streets of tombs, a small madrasa, and a mosque and khanaga whose huge portals, standing side by side, are visible miles away.

Chor Bakr actually means 'four Bakrs', all descendents of the Prophet and possibly all buried here. The charming old caretaker confidently identifies two of their graves, neither of them Abu Bakr's. Imam Said Bakr is buried behind the street which leads north off the main courtyard. Go through the first arch on the right, turn left, pass eight small brick arches, and the grave, surely one of the world's most forlorn places of pilgrimage, is under a pile of rubble on the right. Imam Bakr Fazl's tomb is at the end of the restored brick walkway at right angles to the main street.

Chor Bakr must have been imposing once. Now it's falling down to the sound of wind in the scaffolding which props up the *khanaga*, formerly the headquarters of an order of dervishes called the Khodjagons. A pool in the main courtyard has been filled in and gold and lapis lazuli have gone from the domes and vaults of the mosque. The road from the city, once lined on both sides with willows and canals, is now just another causeway through over-irrigated cotton fields. Few people come here nowadays, which is why it's worth the effort.

Bakhautdin (Бахаутдин)

Twenty minutes' drive due west of Bukhara a massive brown dome appears on the left-hand side of the road. It forms the roof of a *khanaga* which, when completed in the mid-16th century, was the biggest in the world. Once centre of the Nakshbandi order of dervishes, it is now part of a thriving religious centre being energetically restored while the rest of Central Asia languishes. This is what happens when local Muslims rather than western tourists flock to a place. Zeal converts to cash converts to renovation, all in local currency, at local wages, with no middlemen but the mullahs.

The lure is the tomb of Sheikh Bakhautdin, who died in 1389 without claiming descent from the Prophet but has nevertheless been revered ever since. Khan Abdul Aziz II built a vault over the grave and a carved marble fence round it in 1544. The *khanaga*, currently full of scaffolding and closed to visitors, was built soon afterwards. Its dome is held up by four great brick arches like the bendy poles of a geodesic dome tent.

In time a pond was dug next to the sheikh's grave and an unusual sacred water vessel, with four arches and four towers like a miniature Chor Minar, went up next to the pond. *Imams* under mulberry trees say prayers for visitors at 50 or so rubles a prayer. Three mosques linked by colonnades separate this inner sanctum from the rest of the complex, which consists of the *khanaga*, the graves of Khans Abdul Aziz I and II beyond it, and on its east side a minaret and small courtyard for ablutions before prayer.

Sheikh Bakhautdin was a local man. His birthplace is five minutes' walk away in the grounds of another mosque which is also the burial place of his mother and two aunts. The birth is said to have happened on the walled platform under a vine trellis by the entrance to the grounds. The graves are outside the mosque's west wall. Scared teenage soon-to-be-weds come here for counselling with another *imam* under another holy mulberry tree beside another (reed-filled) pond. A few tourists visit the tiny museum of Sufism. Without a 20th-century building or cotton field in sight, and hardly a sound bar the *imam*'s murmuring, this is as relaxing a mosque as you could wish for.

Bukhara (✆ 36522–)   **Where to Stay**

expensive–moderate

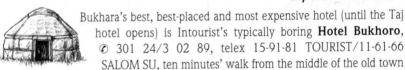

Bukhara's best, best-placed and most expensive hotel (until the Taj hotel opens) is Intourist's typically boring **Hotel Bukhoro**, ✆ 301 24/3 02 89, telex 15-91-81 TOURIST/11-61-66 SALOM SU, ten minutes' walk from the middle of the old town on the corner of Ulitsa 40 Lyet Oktyabrya and Prospekt Alisher Navoi. Technically a 'tourist complex' rather than a mere hotel it is reputed to be the best Intourist hotel in Central Asia. Rooms cost $35 for a single and $40 a double and can be paid for with Visa, American Express or dollars. The rooms are clean, comfortable and, in principle, air-conditioned. The hard-currency bar downstairs is also a casino. Intourist staff are helpful when not besieged by jet-lagged tour groups. There is an AT&T satellite credit card phone in the foyer from which you can arrange to be called back in your room. The restaurant used to be dire but has improved beyond bounds, loud music from 7pm notwithstanding. In addition, there's an express café on the first floor and a bar in the basement (*open 6pm–2am*). Air tickets can be booked at the hotel but must be bought at the airport; postcards and stamps can be purchased and posted from the lobby shop which also sells souvenirs and Konica film.

When complete (April 1996) Uzbekistan's third **Taj Hotel**, built by the Indian company, promises to compete with the Bokhoro in more than location.

The official Sputnik hotel is the no frills **Hotel Varakhsha**, ✆ 3 84 94, two blocks south of the Hotel Bukhoro. It offers hot water, fridges and a friendly receptionist with an entertaining mime about itchy guests at the Zerafshan, but no air-conditioning or heating at $15–$30.

Diagonally opposite at Akademika Muminova is the big, noisy **Hotel Zerafshan**, ✆ 3 40 67/3 41 73, where rooms start at $5–6 a night and can be paid for in local currency. But what you save in dollars you lose in sleep because of cats and midges. Guests are treated by frosty female reception staff as a necessary evil. A bar at the back of the building provides food. Bus 10 from the airport stops not far away. If everything else is full, try the privately owned **Hotel Gulistan**, Akademika Muminova 19, ✆ 3 83 10, 100m from the Namazgokh mosque and no further than the Varakhsha from the old town. 'Gulistan' means 'place of colours', which apparently refers to the rosebeds outside. Rooms are around $15 for a single and $30 a double; pay in dollars only and expect an unusually careful checking of your visa. The only bus that comes in this direction is no.7 from the bus station.

Sometimes **Kukeldash madrasa** offers accommodation, generally in the summer. For a few dollars a night you can stay in a student's room. Five are in good condition, with two or three beds in each; some have a tap but there are no other washing facilities and no heating.

Undoubtedly the best value is the bed and breakfast option. For some years **Sasha's Bed and Breakfast** business has grown in size and renown, ✆ 3 38 90/3 55 93 (English spoken). In high season accommodation costs $20 a night, in low $15 and dinner, also an option for non-residents if arranged in advance, costs $6. Airport/bus pick-ups are offered as are a laundry service and a sauna. All this unexpected comfort means that reservations are necessary. **Murbinjon**, Ulitsa Ishonpir 4, ✆ 4 20 05, close to the Lyab-i-Khauz, is a **merchant house** owned by the former Central Asian sprinter. For $15–20 you can stay in surroundings with a traditional Uzbek flavour, have dinner under the stars and a look at the collection of antique gowns. Again, booking ahead is advisable. Try also **Marvarid**, Deputatskaya Ulitsa 103, ✆ 3 15 56 ($11).

Bukhara (✆ 36522–)   ***Eating Out***

The **Hotel Bukhoro** restaurant does wholesome if sanitized Uzbek meat and salad dishes, served promptly at fixed times with cold canned western beer which you pay for in dollars. Dinner can be booked at **Sasha's** or **Murbinjon**. Or go for an **Uzbek feast** at Nadir Divanbegi madrasa—ask inside the courtyard on the left in the morning ($5). On the right-hand side of the courtyard, there is a restaurant, signposted only by the seating outside. During the day the *chai-khana* and open-air eateries round the pool at Lyab-i-Khauz win easily for authenticity, ambience and a wide variety of *manty*, *shashlyk* and bread. The **Chorsu** charges extra for the view; it gets its food from the tea-house below, which is cheaper. There is another good *chai-khana* on the left as you start heading for Samani Park from the Bolo Khauz mosque. For a cultural combination take tea in traditional Uzbek robes at the merchant house where the family of the famous revolutionary, Khojaev, lived.

Urgench (Ургенч)

Urgench is a big, new, flat, hot, dull town which should not be confused with Kunya (old) Urgench, 200km down the Amu Darya in Turkmenistan.

The only reason to come here is to see Khiva, 28km away, and unfortunately it is hard to get to Khiva *without* going through Urgench.

Getting to and from Urgench

by air

In principle there are two direct flights a week between Moscow and Urgench, on Thursdays and Sundays. In practice most people come via Tashkent, which has up to five direct flights a day, the earliest of which leaves at 6am ($86). There are flights to Namangan and Termez but not, at present, to Samarkand and Bukhara. Urgench airport is 4km from the bus stop. A connecting taxi will cost about $1.

by rail

Urgench is on the Moscow–Tashkent/Ashgabat mainline, so it has daily connections to virtually everywhere in Central Asia from Almaty to Nukus to Turkmenbashy. Moscow is two and a half days away. The once weekly direct train leaves at 7pm on Fridays.

by bus

There are daily buses to and from Tashkent (16 hours) and Bukhara (7 hours), leaving in mid-afternoon, and one a day to and from Samarkand (12 hours) and Nukus. The Samarkand buses leave in the evening whereas the daily Shahrisabz bus leaves at 8.30am. There are no direct services to Kunya Urgench and only occasional ones to Dashkhovuz. The majority going in that direction go as far as Shavat from where there are plenty of Dashkhovuz connections. If heading for Nukus, do double check the visa situation first (*see* p.197).

The daily bus from Bukhara arrives at 11.30pm and drops its passengers in the centre of Urgench rather than at a bus station. Bed and breakfast bookings can be arranged to include a pick-up. Otherwise get off the bus quickly and take one of the few waiting taxis to a hotel. These are close; pay no more than $1. Or take a taxi to Khiva, about thirty minutes away. The least you can expect to pay is $5.

Bus 3 and *marshrutnoe* taxi 3 go from the airport to the bus and railway stations on the opposite side of town, passing close to Hotels Urgench and Khorezm.

Tourist Information

Reception staff at the Hotel Khorezm speak some English and offer Uzbektourism tours of Khiva at $5 an hour, transport costs excluded. At the main tourist office, **Khorezmtourism**, Ulitsa Al-Khorezmi 26, ✆ 6 34 05, ✉ 6 76 30, German-, French- and English-speaking guides are available. Trips to Kunya Urgench can be arranged from here (*see* p.195). Also to the old **fortresses** at **Toprak Kala** and **Ayaz Kala**, 70km from Urgench, and now open to visitors. The spectacular setting of these citadels is more dramatic than Kunya Urgench. Excavation work, started by the Russians in the 1940s, has found that Toprak Kala was the 3rd century capital of ancient Khorezm, the birthplace, many believe, of Zoroastrianism. Any visit would be a lesser one without a guide but you can take a *marshrutnoe* to the pontoon bridge on the Amu Darya, across which is the Ayaz Kala fort.

The **telephone** and **post office** are next door to each other, landmarked by the clock tower, on the corner of Ulitsas Al-Khorezm and Al-Biruni. At the other end of Al-Khorezm, over the canal bridge, is the train station. *Marshrutnoe* buses to **Khiva** also depart from Al-Khorezm, on the right-hand side as you approach from the station, close to the road junction and before the canal bridge.

Urgench (✆ 36222–) ### Where to Stay

The **Hotel Khorezm** at Ulitsa Al-Biruni 2, ✆ 6 54 08 is standard, clean, spacious Intourist fare, but not particularly good value at $35 for a single, $50 a double in season (Nov–April, $25 and $40). The best value in town by far is the new **Hotel Jaikun** just off Ulitsa Al-Khorezm, close to the Uzbektourism office, ✆ 6 66 68, ✉ 6 36 70. With air-conditioning, fridges and TV in each room, huge pillars and ganche decoration in its foyer and a friendly, enthusiastic director, this modern and clean hotel is hard to beat at $17 for a single and $15 per person in a double. There's a coffee bar, souvenir shop and soon an exchange booth in reception. Pay in dollars. For bed and breakfast, call **Gulyas** and **Sveta**, Ulitsa Nekrasova 191, ✆ 6 46 58 ($20–25); they can also provide guides and cars ($4–5 per hour).

Urgench (✆ 36222–) ### Eating Out

Eat in. The Hotel Khorezm's restaurant is not bad, though not particularly Uzbek. Music starts around 7pm. At the Jaikun, head for the restaurant with a fountain or the bar for snacks and a good selection of imported liquor. There are plans for *shashlyk* on the rooftop and a *chai-khana* on the first floor.

Khiva (Хива)

Step right up to the strangest little time-capsule in Central Asia. Khiva's mud streets and inward-looking squares are so well-preserved they sometimes feel like a film set (which they were, for *Orlando*). But Khiva is an upstart; although it looks like medieval Bukhara, it is mostly no older than New York. The object of some of the most intrepid overland expeditions of the 18th and 19th centuries, Khiva was then the most remote and is now the most complete of the old Silk Route's oasis cities. Its walls are intact. The Tash Khauli palace has the finest painted ceilings in Central Asia. The Friday mosque is the strangest and most alluring in Uzbekistan. Yet Khiva is still probably more famous than it deserves.

It is merely the last in a 2000-year line of Khorezmian capitals, most of them dissolved by the continually shifting Amu Darya, some still tantalizing sun-frazzled archaeologists with their gaunt hilltop ruins. The greatest of these cities was Kunya Urgench (*see* p.194), the centre of the Muslim world before the Mongol invasion, when Khiva was nothing. Even in the 18th century Khiva was 'hardly more than a nest of caravan-robbers hidden behind the formidable barriers of the desert'. The world knew little about it, so excitable travellers' tales built it into a fearsome power. And it behaved like one, knowing little of the rest of the world.

Khiva prospered, like her predecessors, as the last great oasis on the northern caravan route to Russia. In particular she thrived on trade in Russian slaves and on their labour. But her wealth was translated into the fabric of a city only in the 19th century—and this is Khiva's fascination. The real miracle here is one of inertia, not preservation. The general appearance of Central Asian cities hardly changed in the 400 years before the Russians came, and there is no more impressive monument to this extraordinary stasis than Khiva.

History

A long time ago, when men were men and gods took a practical interest in their affairs, Shem, son of Noah, was roaming the Kara-Kum desert with his tribe. He dreamed he saw a thousand soldiers marching over the dunes bearing torches, and told his people to build a hill of sand to mark where he had dreamed. His people became thirsty. Being a full day's walk from the river they dug a hole, and struck water, and the water was sweet.

'Khei-vakh!' they cried. 'What wonderful water is in the well!'

The city that grew up round the Kheivak Well was named 'Khiva' after it; the well itself can be found at Ulitsa Abdullah a-Baltal 107, in the northwest corner of the old town.

Prehistory

Rarely do myth and reality merge so happily. Siyavush, the runaway city-founder usually associated with Bukhara, is also mentioned in connection with Khiva. The Arab historian

Al-Biruni said he turned up here around 1200 BC, but there is no archaeological evidence that old, of the man or the place.

Elsewhere in Khorezm, archaeologists tell a different story. Nowadays the Amu Darya delta shows up on satellite photos as a lonely green smudge in an ocean of brown. In 4000 BC it was a much larger smudge. The river did not reach the Aral Sea, running out instead into a vast marshland dotted with sandy islets on which man lived in big oval shelters in extended families of up to 200. The Soviet archaeologist assigned exclusively to this area reckoned the Amu Darya broke through to the Aral Sea (till then fed only by the Syr Darya) around 2000 BC. The marshland shrank, and the people of the new delta came to depend on irrigation they built themselves. Another expert, Edgar Knobloch, says these irrigation systems 'shrank and expanded in a way curiously connected with historical events, with the wealth of the country, the growth and decline of the population, the flow of world trade, internal and external security, and other phenomena'—perhaps the irrigation systems that have destroyed the Aral Sea might now shrink like the Soviet empire that built them.

Invaders and Nomads

By the 6th century BC Khorezm was controlled by a tribe of Scythian nomads called the Massagetae. Then in 530 BC Cyrus, Emperor of Persia, crushed the whole of Transoxiana and turned Khorezm into his 16th satrapy. Three centuries later, Alexander the Great heard of Khorezm, receiving a visit from a certain Farsman who claimed to be its king, but did not conquer it. Thereafter there is nothing but myth for centuries. Siyavush did found a Khorezmian dynasty called the Afrighids—coins from the 1st to 8th centuries have been found bearing his head—but no one knows where or when.

Nomadic invasions made life miserable in this already fairly desperate domain in the 200 or so years before the arrival of Islam. Everyone had to live in fortresses, which became solar crematoria if their water supplies were cut off. The Arabs found only three towns in the whole delta when they arrived at the start of the 8th century. The largest, capital of the Afrighid Khorezmshahs, was called Al-Fir and was destroyed by a flick of the Amu Darya's tail at the end of the century. The second was Urgench, now Kunya Urgench, under which Khorezm was united at the end of the 10th century. Khiva was the smallest, but two major strokes of luck were in store for her over the following 700 years.

The first was the invading Arabs' impatience with Khorezm's Jews. At first, in 712, Qutaiba ibn-Muslim contented himself with propping up the ruler of Khorezm at arm's length and exacting tribute in return. But when Khorezm rebelled, Qutaiba blamed and purged its mainly Jewish intelligentsia, who fled to southern Russia and started trading. It was a crucial chapter in the establishment of the northern trade route down the Amu Darya, across to the Caspian and up the Volga—a trade that remained the basis of Khiva's prosperity until the 1920s.

Khiva's second stroke of luck was the destruction of Urgench, first by Genghis Khan, then, more thoroughly, by Tamerlane. Tamerlane's specific aim was to bring Khorezm's trade back to Samarkand. He succeeded for a time, destroying not just Urgench but her Russian market. But trade between Central Asia and Russia was bound to rise again; when it did, it was not Urgench —by then a barley field— that benefitted, but Khiva.

The Khanate

A cadet branch of the Bukharan Sheibanids ruled Khiva from 1512 to 1804. As capital of Khorezm from 1592, her relations with Russia were governed by self-interest and mutual distrust. Khivan envoys made the trans-continental trek to St Petersburg throughout the 17th century, promising an end to the trade in Russian slaves in order that it might continue unhindered for another few years. Eight Russians went to Khiva that century. All returned with similar promises, but none with freed slaves.

It was the prospect of gold, not of redeeming lost souls, that brought the Russians out in force. Their first major expedition to Khiva, in 1717, was part of a scheme of Peter the Great's to open up an express route to the legendary wealth of India. He knew the River Oxus (Amu Darya) was navigable almost to the Asian–Indian watershed. He had heard a (false) rumour that only artificial dams caused it to run into the Aral Sea rather than the Caspian. He now reasoned that by destroying the dams he could create a continuous river–route to northern Afghanistan from Kazan on the upper Volga. It was as bold as the Soviet politburo's plan 250 years later to divert Siberian rivers to re-fill the Aral, and as doomed.

Using as a pretext an out-of-date request from the Khan of Khiva for help against troublesome nomads, Peter despatched Prince Alexander Bekovich, a former Muslim, with 4000 men and 500 horses and camels, to reconnoitre the ancient course of the Oxus. On arrival at Khiva, Bekovich was to offer the khan the czar's protection. If the offer was not accepted, he was to destroy the city. It was not accepted, because Bekovich never got the chance to make it. When his party reached Khiva, having failed to plot the czar's new route to India, it was split into small groups and butchered.

The khan sent Bekovich's head back to St Petersburg and enjoyed brief Saddam Hussein-style renown in the Muslim world for his defiance of the infidel. Then in 1740 Nadir Shah overran Transoxiana and for the second time in 2000 years Khorezm became a northern outpost of the Persian empire. Khiva was badly damaged by the invaders, but its rebuilding coincides with the first appearance on its tiles and pots of a distinct Khivan decorative style, less refined than Bukhara's but bursting out all over with flower and vegetable motifs not seen elsewhere. 'It almost seems,' says Edgar Knobloch, 'as if the creative genius of Persia, unable to express itself at home, sought and found refuge in that isolated little world behind the Kara-Kum sands. For Khiva... is a genuine oasis of art...'

A century later that isolated little world would, some believed, lead the wider world to war. It had become the focus of the hundred-year Central Asian fencing match between the two greatest empires of the 19th century, the British and the Russian. The immediate cause was another Russian military expedition to bring the nuisance khanate to heel. The ostensible aim—to end Khiva's slave trade—was merely a pretext. This time the Russian motive was security rather than booty: the British had taken Afghanistan in the summer of 1839 and seemed poised to push north.

The Russians took no chances. General Perovsky, commander of the Orenburg garrison and a Central Asian veteran, assembled 5000 men and 10,000 camels and headed south for the Aral Sea in the autumn, to avoid the summer sun. But he did not get within a month's march of Khiva. Instead of sun he got practically impenetrable snow in which, by the end of January 1840, his camels were dying at the rate of 100 a day. When the expedition returned to Orenburg four months later, only 1500 were left.

Meanwhile a one-man British expedition, Captain James Abbott, had reached Khiva from Herat in one month flat and had enjoyed many a revealing audience with the khan, who had no idea how his empire compared in terms of size and military might with Queen Victoria's. A few months later another British officer, Lieutenant Richmond Shakespear, arrived in Khiva looking for Abbott. Abbott had gone on towards St Petersburg, so Shakespear followed him there, accompanied by 416 Russian slaves whose release he had personally negotiated with the khan.

That, at least, was one version of the story. Another was that both men were spies sent to study the routes north and northwest from Khiva to Russia, and that they were accompanying slaves already freed by the Russians. Either way, the czar had been deprived of his favourite excuse for meddling in Central Asia, and Khiva retired from the headlines for a decade or two. The big picture changed little, however. British India went on menacing Russia's southern flank, Russia went on shoring it up and Khiva went on being a thorn in it. Her traffic in slaves continued, albeit on a reduced scale and with more Persians than Russians changing hands. More irritating for St Petersburg was Khivan support for the nomads of the Kazakh steppe in their running battle with encroaching Russian garrisons, and the role of leader of free Central Asia which Khiva tried to play under Mohammed Rakhim Khan II in the late 1860s and early 1870s as Tashkent, Samarkand and Bukhara succumbed to Russian force. It was only a matter of time before that force was turned on Khiva herself.

Like many an invader before him, the Russian General Kaufmann tried at first to take Khiva on the cheap, with a diplomatic offensive which started in 1868. By 1872 this had manifestly failed, and Kaufmann settled on annexation. Haunted by Bekovich and Perovsky, he planned meticulously, coordinating his own advance from Turkmenistan with others from Orenburg and from Krasnovodsk (now Turkmenbashy) on the Caspian's east coast. On 28 May 1873, with the Russian vanguard 20km miles from the city, the khan fled. Kaufmann entered unresisted, caught the khan, forced him to describe himself as 'the docile servant of the emperor of all the Russias', and reinstated him. Khiva, comprehensively humiliated, hardly gave czarist St Petersburg or Soviet Moscow another moment's trouble.

When the irresistibly glamorous Captain Fred Burnaby (six foot four, strongest man in the British Army, fluent in seven languages) battled through the worst winter since Perovsky's to reach Khiva in 1876, he found the khan 'a cheery sort of fellow', but pathetically incapable of any independent action or commitment. The most impressive thing about Khiva was its ability to serve up grapes and melons in midwinter.

The khanate died quietly with the proclamation in 1920 of the People's Republic of Khorezm, which became part of Soviet Uzbekistan in 1924.

Getting to and from Khiva

The nearest **airport, railway station** and **long-distance bus station** to Khiva are 28km northeast at Urgench (*see* p.180). Buses shuttle between them at least every half hour from dawn till about 7 pm. The fastest are the *marshrutnoe* minibuses which depart from Ulitsa Al-Khorezm in Urgench. They wait at the roadside close to the junction before the canal bridge. A ticket is under a dollar. Going to Khiva, get off when the city wall comes into view. If it doesn't come into view you are probably headed for Khiva's bus station, from where local bus 1 or *marshrutnoe* taxi 1 go to the north gate.

Taxis take about 25 minutes either way. Returning to Urgench they are easiest to pick up at Khiva's west gate. Offer about $5; it's unlikely they'll take local currency.

Tourist Information

The **Intourist Service Bureau** is at Urgench's Hotel Khorezm, ✆ 6 54 08, and on Ulitsa Al-Khorezm 26, ✆ 6 34 05, ✆ 6 76 30. The map of Khiva on sale in the bookshop inside the west gate is of limited usefulness; either the map or the numbers to which the key refers seems to be upside down.

All Khiva museums are open daily 9–6; winter opening times may be shorter.

Isak Usmanov, the curator of the Ichan-Kala history museum (ask near the West Gate) is a Russian and German speaker and a reasonable guide. His standard tour of the main sights lasts 2–3 hours and costs $3–4 in local currency. Out of museum hours he can be contacted at Kasmaobod Village, Ulitsa Zhami, dom 5, ✆ 6 11 86.

The Old Town

Khiva has never been big. At the height of its international notoriety in the mid-19th century its population was about 18,000; since then it has only doubled. The suburbs have expanded slightly, but more upwards than outwards. In places rice and cotton fields still come to within a few hundred metres of the **Ichan-Kala**, the old inner town. This covers less than one square kilometre, but seems much bigger because it is so tightly-packed. Its 16 madrasas are merely its least interesting buildings. There is enough besides to fill one very long day, or two leisurely ones.

Everything is wrapped in 2200m of unbroken **city wall**. There used to be a much longer outer wall too; its **Kosh Darvaza** gate survives at the northwest corner of the modern city. The inner wall, defying charabancs as it once defied Turkmen desert raiders, is 7–8m high and incorporates a continuous firing gallery behind the battlements and 40

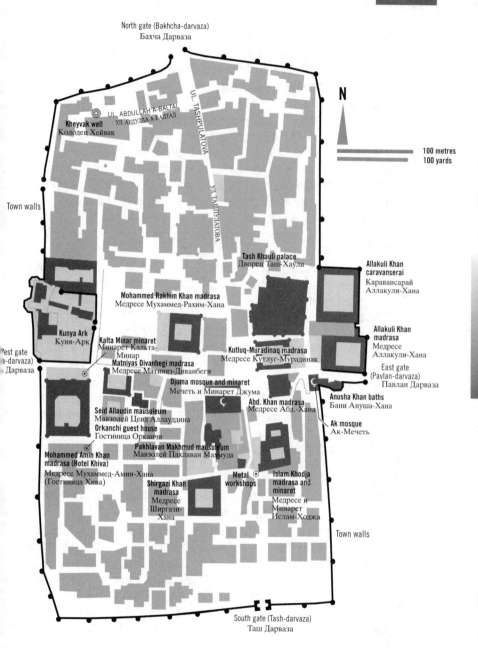

Khiva

North gate (Bakhcha-darvaza)
Бахча Дарваза

UL. ABDULLAH A-BALTAL
УЛ. АБДУЛЛА А-БАЛТАЛ

Kheyvak well
Колодец Хейвак

UL. TASHPULATOVA

УЛ. ТАШПУЛАТОВА

N

100 metres
100 yards

Town walls

Tash Khauli palace
Дворец Таш-Хаули

Allakuli Khan
caravanserai
Караван сарай
Аллакули-Хана

Mohammed Rakhim Khan madrasa
Медресе Мухаммед-Рахим-Хана

Allakuli Khan
madrasa
Медресе
Аллакули-Хана

Kunya Ark
Куня-Арк

Kalta Minar minaret
Минарет Кальта-
Минар

Kutluq-Muradinaq madrasa
Медресе Кутлуг-Мурадинак

est gate
a-darvaza)
Дарваза

Matniyas Divanbegi madrasa
Медресе Матнияз-Диванбеги

East gate
(Pavlan-darvaza)
Павлан Дарваза

Djuma mosque and minaret
Мечеть и Минарет Джума

Abd. Khan madrasa
Медресе Абд.-Хана

Anusha Khan baths
Бани Ануша-Хана

Seid Allaudin mausoleum
Мавзолей Цеид Аллауддина

Orkanchi guest house
Гостиница Орканчи

Ak mosque
Ак-Мечеть

Pakhlavan Makhmud mausoleum
Мавзолей Пахлаван Махмуда

Mohammed Amin Khan
madrasa (Hotel Khiva)
Медресе Мухаммед-Амин-Хана
(Гостиница Хива)

Shirgazi Khan
madrasa
Медресе
Ширгази-
Хана

Metal
workshops

Islam Khodja
madrasa and
minaret
Медресе и
Минарет
Ислам-Ходжа

Town walls

South gate (Tash-darvaza)
Таш Дарваза

187

massive rounded bastions, in addition to those of the gatehouses. The wall is of clay; the gatehouses of sun-baked brick. Nearly destroyed by Nadir Shah in 1740, they were rebuilt by 1785. This was to be the last major work on Khiva's fortifications until the Soviet restoration, in the 1970s, of individual gatehouses.

It is through one of these, the **Ata-darvaza** (west gate), that most visitors first enter the city. On the right, the **Amin Khan madrasa** (1852) is 300 years younger than Bukhara's Kukeldash madrasa, but looks very similar and now serves the same purpose: it's a hotel. Foreigners may stay here if they have 'Khiva' and not just 'Urgench' on their visas.

The splendid, fat bottom half of a minaret at the madrasa's far corner is the **Kalta Minar** (1855). Mohammed Amin Khan meant this to be the tallest building in the Muslim world. Had it gone on tapering from its 15-m-wide base at the rate that it does for its first 28 m, it would certainly have made Bukhara's Kalyan minaret look puny. Construction started in 1851, but after the khan died campaigning in 1855, his heir aborted the project. Nonetheless, it has some of the city's most extravagant tiling (heavily restored), in blue, white, red and Khiva's hallmark green.

Kunya Ark (Куня Арк)

Kunya Ark means 'old citadel', and the khans' stronghold has the prime site in the north-western sector of the city, as tradition says it should. Power first emanated from here in the 12th century when Akshikh-bobo, the White Sheikh, built the clay fortress which dominates the citadel, also forming part of the city wall. After the sheikh died it became his mausoleum. When the khans started building the citadel round it in the 17th century, they converted it into a gunpowder store.

By the mid-19th century the Ark was a world of its own: fortress, palace, harem, mosques, mint, stables, arsenal, barracks and parade ground, enclosed by the city wall to the west and another one almost as high on the other three sides— tyrants must defend themselves from their people as much as from their enemies. Only the summer mosque, mint and harem, reached through the twin-turreted gateway in the east wall, are deemed sufficiently restored for visitors. The **mosque** (1838) is down the first passage on the right and is smothered in dazzlingly intricate blue and white majolica patterns thick with typically Khivan plant and flower motifs. Its tall *iwan*, also typically for Khiva, faces north to catch the cool northerly breezes. As a result the *mihrab* faces south not west.

The **mint**, at the end of the same passage, is now a tiny money museum, with a mock-up of silk banknote-printing. The **harem** is opposite the gateway. Behind it the 12th-century **Akshikh-bobo bastion**, Khiva's oldest building, is closed to visitors though its roof may be accessible from the city wall. Would-be Indiana Joneses' pulses will quicken at the sight, through many a half-open door, of heaps of unsorted ancient fragments in dusty wooden trays marked only with the year of discovery: 1938, 1946, 1952. Accessible frrom the Ark is a high vanatage point from which there's an excellent view, even better in the early evening, of the Ichan Kala.

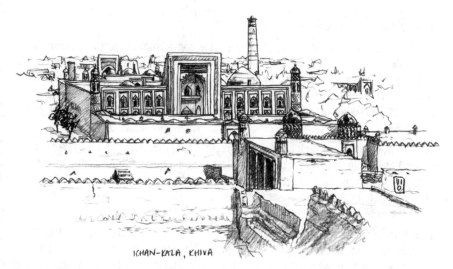

ICHAN-KALA, KHIVA

Back outside, the low bunker to the right of the gatehouse as you emerge is the **Zindan**, the khan's gaol. Ghoulish dummies show how his victims suffered and sometimes died, by a variety of means including Bukhara-style jaculation from a minaret. The woman in the sack seems to be sharing it with snakes.

The large, sterile space in front of the Ark used to be the city's most bustling square, but you would be lucky to see a kid drop a sweet wrapper there now. The **Mohammed Rakhim Khan madrasa,** known locally as the Feruz madrasa, on the far side, is now a museum devoted to the life of this khan. The **Matinyas Divanbegi madrasa** across the street, facing Kalta Minar from the east, is open as a restaurant.

Beyond it, set back on the right, Sheikh **Seid Allaudin's mausoleum** (1306) vies with the Akshikh-bobo bastion as the oldest thing in Khiva, though its most striking feature, the dense blue, green and turquoise majolica-work on the cenotaph, dates from the 14th century.

Continue past the **Kazi Kalyan** and take a look inside the **Khodjash Maggarram madrasa** (both on the right, both 19th-century). This is a woodcarver's workshop where the doors and pillars produced are destined for not only local use. Beyond is the very unusual **Djuma mosque and minaret** (1788–99). There has been a mosque here since the 10th century, and some of the 213 wooden columns supporting the roof of this latest vast, low-rise version are said to be that old. Their highly ornate capitals are certainly some of the oldest and finest wood carving in Central Asia, though they are hard to see because the whole 55 by 46m space is cast in permanent and blessed gloom. This is the coolest place in Khiva. The wood is a local kind of elm. The European carriage inside the entrance on the left was probably a gift from a Russian envoy to the khan. The minaret may be climbed for a small fee but so may the Islam Khodja minaret (*see* below), which is higher.

Tash Khauli (Таш Хаули)

Allakuli Khan (r. 1825–42) was an unstoppable commissioner of new buildings and a hard taskmaster. Soon after coming to power he set his heart on a brand new palace more lavish than the Ark, and pronto. When the first architect assigned to the project said it could not be completed in two years he was executed. The second, Kalendar Khivaki, employed thousands of slaves, peasants and craftsmen and took eight years over it (1830–38).

The result, encased in a high blind wall on a big site on the east side of the inner town, is sneered at by some purists for occasional sloppiness on points of detail. But for ordinary folk this is the most amazing piece of artistic exhibitionism to be seen in Central Asia; baroque in its obsessive treatment of every square inch, Victorian in its confidence, unmistakeably Asian in its overall impact.

Tash Khauli ('stone palace') is sometimes wrongly called a summer palace. Once it was finished the khans lived here year-round, moving into yurts on round brick pedestals in winter because they were easy to heat with the charcoal braziers used before Russian stoves arrived. The palace has three courts. Smallest and closed to visitors is **Ishrat-Khauli** (or -**Khana**) in the southeast corner, for official ceremonies and banquets. **Arz-Khauli** in the southwest corner was the court of justice and had two gateways—one of them, an exit only, was reserved for those condemned to death. Neither gateway is used today, but the rooms around the court contain an exhibition of artisans at work. To reach it, you must pass through the third and largest court, which was the **harem**. Its five north-facing *iwans* have to be seen to be believed. Their walls are covered in non-stop blue and white majolica not unlike that of the Ark's summer mosque. Their vaulted ceilings, supported by carved wooden pillars, are an orgy of colour and pattern best appreciated lying down. This was a world within a world within a world, inhabited by the khan's Uzbek, Kyrgyz, Turkmen, Persian and Karakalpak wives and their children, all waited on by eunuchs and guarded by slaves. Once sealed off from the outside world, it is now the one unmissable monument in Khiva.

Near the Eastern Gates

Steadily increasing Russian trade made Allakuli Khan's reign one of relative prosperity and peace for Khiva, and once Tash Khauli was taking shape the khan extended his munificence from his family to his people. Opposite the palace and protruding eastwards from the city wall he built, in 1835, the huge two-storey **Allakuli Khan caravanserai**, where traders would set up temporary shop outside their lodgings. It is now roofed-over as a relatively exotic ex-Soviet department store, good for cars, carpets and airmail envelopes.

Down the street on the same side, in the same year, the khan also built, and modestly named after himself, the **Allakuli Khan madrasa**, whose *pishtak* is Khiva's tallest. The path to the entrance cut in half the much older **Khodjamberdibiy mosque** (1688), which became known as a result as *Khurdjum* ('the saddle bag').

The narrow space between these giants was filled by the **Tim Allakuli Khan**, a domed arcade whose massively thick walls, high roof and lack of windows makes it cool even in mid-summer. The **Saraibazar-darvaza** gate at its east end leads to the modern **bazaar**.

The Allakuli Khan madrasa forms a *kosh* ensemble with the **Kutluq-Muradinaq madrasa** across the street, built in 1812 by the first khan of the Kungrat dynasty (1804–1920), although the decorative brickwork on the half-towers at each end of the façade recalls much earlier styles. There is a cool cistern, once used for drinking water, under the brick dome in the main courtyard. Under the raised brick apron in front of Kutluq-Muradinaq are rows of former stores and workshops with doors at street level.

At the south corner of the Allakuli Khan madrasa the city's main axis enters **Pavlan-darvaza** (the Gates of Hercules), a 60-m-long domed gateway built in 1806. On the right is the working **Seid Bey mosque**. In the café on the left a slave market was held until 1873; slaves were kept in chains in the niches under the domes of the gateway.

Back inside the old town, the **Anusha Khan baths** at the end of Pavlan-darvaza on the left have been in continuous use since 1657. The tiny **Ak mosque** (White mosque) next door was built in the same year by Anusha Khan in memory of his father, Abulkhazi, and is Khiva's oldest. The **Abdullah Khan madrasa** (1855), across the street from Mutluq Muradinaq, houses a museum of natural history.

Islam Khodja (Ислам Ходжа)

There is a herb garden on the south side of the Abdullah Khan madrasa and beyond it, across an open space, the **Islam Khodja madrasa and minaret** (1908 and 1910 respectively). Islam Khodja was Asfandiar Khan's grand vizier and father-in-law, and the khanate's last and maybe only great progressive. Visits to St Petersburg and Paris having filled his mind with the wonders of technology, he built a cotton mill, a hospital and Khiva's first European school, and linked the city to the outside world by telegraph. The clergy hated him for it. They persuaded the khan he was a menace to royal authority and had him assassinated as he returned one night by carriage to his country residence. Here was a true People's martyr. His madrasa is the honoured home of a Museum of Applied Art, which includes Lenin's face on carpets and vases but also some wonderful Arabic calligraphy. The 45-m minaret is Khiva's tallest, and the

MINARET OF
ISLAM-KHODJA
KHIVA

last notable architectural achievement of the Islamic era in Central Asia. It has 118 steps and views right out to the desert. But the surrounding metal grille makes photographs difficult. There's a small climbing fee.

Pakhlavan Makhmud (Пахлаван Махмуд)

Pakhlavan Makhmud was a wildly popular 14th-century poet-doctor-wrestler, buried in 1326 half a minute's walk west of Islam Khodja past some cheerfully percussive metal workshops. His mausoleum, completely rebuilt between 1810 and 1835 along with winter and summer mosques and a *chai-khana*, is generally considered the most beautiful building in Khiva. It is also the centre of a royal burial ground. Among the tombs whose domes and vaulted brick roofs spill down to the east from the main turquoise cupola are those of Abulkhazi Khan (r. 1644–63), Shirgazi Khan (r. 1715–30), Mohammed Rakhim Khan I (r. 1806–25) and Allakuli Khan (r. 1825–42).

That cupola sits on an octagonal base over a rectangular main chamber. The design is Persian, as are the verses incorporated into the sumptuous painted majolica which covers the interior. Mohammed Rakhim Khan II (r. 1865–1910) is buried here.

Pakhlavan Makhmud himself is buried in the smaller chamber to the left under a cenotaph whose ornamental tiling, restrained in colour but breathtakingly ambitious in design, probably represents the apogee of Khivan decorative art. The inscription over the entrance reads: 'It is easier for me to say these words 100 times, languish in gaol 100 years or climb 100 mountains of sand than to teach a single idiot wisdom.'

Legend has it that Makhmud wrote anti-religious poems (*rubais*) in Persian under the pseudonym Piryarvali. The Muslim clergy, who had canonized him as patron saint of Khiva, smothered the theory. The link was rediscovered in the 1840s by Arminius Vambery, an anglophile Hungarian orientalist who visited Khiva disguised as a wandering dervish, and subsequently taken up by Soviet historians eager to claim Makhmud as a Man of the People. They also claimed that the 19th-century craftsmen working on the mausoleum, good proto-proletarians all, surreptitiously worked his irreligious verses into its decoration.

Makhmud's record as a wrestler is less controversial. He was unbeatable, with fans and mangled challengers throughout Central Asia. Iranian professional wrestlers apparently still offer prayers to him before fighting.

The **Shirgazi Khan madrasa** (1725) across the street was built on that khan's orders by Persian slaves he had captured on a recent raid to Meshed and Russian ones who had survived the massacre of Prince Bekovich's 1717 expedition. In 1720 they killed the khan on one of his site visits. Hence the inscription over the entrance: 'I accept death at the hands of slaves'. The madrasa now contains a **museum of ancient medicine**.

To see the **Kheivak well**, where Shem, son of Noah, struck water when the Old Testament was no more than a twinkle in some Mediterranean publisher's eye, return to the Ark and follow the inside of the city wall north to its northwest corner. Turn right along Ulitsa Abdullah a-Baltal (ex-Ulitsa Uzbekistanskaya) and knock on No. 107's door. It's the well in the front yard.

The **Amin Khan madrasa** has rooms for $11, and some with private bathroom for $15 per night. It also has loud rave music emanating from a source across the courtyard. Alternatively try the **Orkanchi Guest House**. It's difficult to find, set back almost behind the Amin Khan madrasa; turn right immediately after the Kalta Minar minaret, walk straight ahead and you should see a red-lettered bed and breakfast sign on its first-floor wooden balcony. Rooms are very large, the new western-style bathrooms were added in 1995, and you can sleep out on the balcony in the summer. $20 a night includes full board; you will not go hungry but may want to bring your own bread from the bazaar. The owner's brother can drive you to Urgench or Dashkhovuz for $15.

The only restaurant as such is the **Khiva** restaurant in the central Matinyaz Divanbegi madrasa, though you may not be welcome if you are not part of a group and on time. Try dinner at the **Orkanchi Guest House** one evening. In summer you can snack at the *chai-khana* opposite the Djuma mosque, or in the café outside the east gate next to the bazaar— or just picnic.

Dashkhovuz (Дашховуз)

In Dashkhovuz you get the feeling someone decided to build a modern city for northern Turkmenistan and forgot to put people in it. They should be so lucky. In fact 125,000 people live here in endless identical blocks of flats suffering frightening levels of liver and stomach disease because of pesticides, defoliants and salt in their drinking water. Maybe this is what keeps them off the streets.

Dashkhovuz, just inside Turkmenistan and 53km from Khiva, is a reminder that Turkmenistan suffers from the Aral/Amu Darya crisis as well as inflicting it on Uzbekistan via the Kara-Kum Canal (*see* **Topics**, pp.71–3). There is not much sightseeing to be done. **Hotel Dashkhovuz**, Ulitsa Andaliba, has no phone but does have air-conditioning and facilities for you to buy your flight ticket in advance and avoid the scramble at the airport. There is an Intourist office in the hotel which can organize trips to **Kunya Urgench** 90km away, **Khiva**, **Izmukshir** (a ruined and forgotten Silk Route town 35km away) and **Lake Sarykamish**. As the Aral Sea empties, the lake fills with the toxic water drained into it from the cotton plantations. No one eats fish from Sarykamish any more, and the tigers which used to stalk its shores have gone. Official dollar prices for excursions are outrageous but negotiable.

visas

Turkmenistan did not sign the three-day transit agreement giving leeway in the other Central Asian republics. You may get across the border from Uzbekistan but flying out of

Dashkhovuz without a Turkmenistan visa is impossible. Waving an invitation and promising that you can get a visa at Ashgabat airport will not persuade the authorities here to sell you a ticket. Avoid the hassle by contacting Mr Ermukhamad Saparov in the Hotel Dashkhovuz, ☎ 2 47 37. Call well in advance; he can provide visas but is often working in Ashgabat. Alternatively speak to Uzbektourism in Urgench, ☎ 6 34 05, who are familiar with transit visas through their tours to Kunya Urgench and deal with Mr Saparov's office. *See also* **Travel**, 'Entry Formalities'.

Getting to and from Dashkhovuz

By air: There are flights to and from Moscow daily except Sundays, and at least six a day to Ashgabat ($67). At the right-hand end of the building is a large timetable. The airport is half an hour out of town. Turkmenistan Airways has an office next to the hotel. It shuts at 5pm and only sells tickets up to the day before departure. Tickets for same day flights are bought at the airport. They go on sale half an hour before the plane leaves and cause much excitement as a result.

By rail: Dashkhovuz is the next town north from Urgench on the Moscow–Dushanbe line. For services, *see* p.180.

By bus: Direct buses to Urgench are more frequent than those in the opposite direction (65km). There are also buses that run between Dashkhovuz and Kunya Urgench. These go from the bus station in town. For buses that run across the desert to Ashgabat check here or else go the airport, their other departure point.

Kunya Urgench (Куня Ургенч)

After nearly 500km of barren void, travellers crossing the Kara-Kum desert from Ashgabat begin to hallucinate. Instead of brown earth they see bushes and canalized water. Instead of Soviet suburbs, as Kunya Urgench approaches, they see the tallest minaret in Central Asia and a comic scattering of medieval mausolea. These are the remnants of old (Kunya) Urgench, known in its heyday as Gurganj.

History

The good times started with the rise of the northern caravan route to Russia and the unification of Khorezm under Mamun ibn Mohammed, Emir of Gurganj, when he assassinated his last rival in 995. They ended with the fifth coming of Tamerlane in 1388.

For these four centuries Gurganj had wealth, from international trade and as a market on the boundary between settled oasis and the steppe. It had water, but not too much. A wooden dam kept the Amu Darya at bay a mile to the east. It had people—2 million of them along this part of the river's left bank on the eve of the Mongol invasion. It had learning; Avicenna, Al-Biruni and Ibn Battuta all spent time here. Its leaders ruled Central Asia and, for brief periods, the whole Islamic world. Mamun did so partly by luck. His reign followed Baghdad's pre-eminence and preceded Cairo's. Then in

1040 the Seljuk Turks overran Transoxiana from Khorassan (roughly modern Afghanistan) and Khorezm suffered for 100 years as an isolated colony. A new dynasty of Khorezmshahs, ethnic Seljuks themselves, wrested independence from Khorassan in the mid-12th century and set about empire-building. Emir Tekesh (r. 1172–1200) conquered Khorassan and Iraq. His son Mohammed II (r. 1200–20) strutted from China to the Euphrates calling himself a second Alexander. In 1218 Genghis Khan sent an envoy with a lump of gold 'as big as a camel's hump' and the condescending message that he was ready to love Khorezm as he loved his sons. Mohammed murdered the envoy and two years later paid the price.

The Great Khan's sons Dzuchi and Chaghatai beseiged Gurganj for seven months before taking it house by house, driving out the population, splitting it into women, children and craftsmen (who were taken into slavery), and the rest (who were slain, 24 by each Mongol soldier). They then broke the wooden dam and let the river wash through the city. 'Gurganj became the abode of the jackal and the haunt of the owl and the kite,' wrote one local historian. Still, Gurganj rose again. Ibn Battuta described it in 1333 as 'the largest, greatest, most beautiful and most important city of the Turks, shaking under the weight of its populations, with bazaars so crowded that it was difficult to pass'. It must have been a fun place to visit; social status is still earned here, people say proudly, by spending money on guests rather than accumulating it for yourself.

Tamerlane mounted five separate campaigns against Gurganj between 1372 and 1388. All he left standing was the five rather forlorn ruins that draw a trickle of tourists today. By the time Khorezm recovered in the 16th century, Khiva was its new capital.

Getting to, from and Around Kunya Urgench

There are frequent buses from Dashkhovuz, one a day from Nukus, and occasional long-distance ones across the desert from Ashgabat. For Intourist day excursions from Urgench go to the main Uzbektourism office on Ulitsa Al-Khorezm 26, ✆ 6 34 05. They will arrange the transit visa that you'll need at the Turkmenistan border ($12). *See* pp.193–4 if travelling from Dashkhovuz. Everything in Kunya Urgench can be seen on foot but in hot weather it may be wise to hire a taxi by the hour.

The Ruins

The monuments start about 1km south of the modern centre on the trans-Kara-Kum road to Ashgabat. First on the right is the **Turabeg Khanym mausoleum** (c.1370). It was probably the burial place for the Sufi dynasty who ruled Khorezm between the Mongol and Timurid invasions, but is also linked to the wife of **Kutluk Timur**, Mongolian governor of Khorezm after Genghis Khan's death. The multi-coloured mosaic on the underside of the dome is unrestored and in perfect condition. Its 365 geometric figures each represent a day of the year. Most of them are stars, so the overall design may represent the sky at night. The rest of the design is equally meaning-laden: 24 windows below the dome for the hours in a day, four more small ones further down for the weeks in a month and four larger ones for the seasons. The idea was to impress on men their lowliness before creation.

Kutluk Timur Minaret

Already grabbing the attention across the road is the **Kutluk Timur minaret** (1320–30), at 62m the tallest in Central Asia and 15m taller than Bukhara's Kalyan minaret, whose bands of ornamental brick it imitates but doesn't equal. Thought to have been part of the city's Friday mosque, it survived an earthquake in 1982 and leans 1.5m to the west.

Tekesh, the conquering Khorezmshah, was buried a short distance down the track which passes in front of the minaret, on the right. His mausoleum's conical herringbone brick dome (early 13th-century) is very Khorezmian. There is nothing like it anywhere else, but there probably used to be a lot more like it here. A jug containing 813 Mongol-era coins now in the city museum was discovered here in 1991. So was a Kaaba, complete with sacred black stone, for those who couldn't make it to Mecca. Tekesh's father (r. 1156–72) lies further down the track under the **Il-Arslan mausoleum**, whose 12-sided conical dome is unique in Central Asia. Beyond it, the high portal fronting some recently excavated foundations is from a 14th-century **caravanserai**.

The rectangular mound opposite the Tekesh mausoleum is **Forty Mullahs' Hill**, named after some visiting Koranic teachers buried on top of it. Thought to contain priceless 10th- and 11th-century scientific manuscripts, its excavation has only just begun.

Nadjmaddin Kubra Mausoleum

Nadjmaddin Kubra, the holiest man in the history of Gurganj, was born in 1145 in Khiva and educated as a Sufi mystic in Egypt, Persia and Iraq. He taught philosophy and the Koran in the madrasas of Gurganj, and wrote popular four-line *rubais* on love and life. When the Mongols came, he was already 75 years old. This did not prevent him putting up an heroic fight—so the story goes—but they beheaded him all the same. He was buried in two coffins: one for his head and one for his body.

His mausoleum (1320–30), near the centre of modern Kunya Urgench, is the most hallowed spot in town. The aquamarine and terracotta decoration of its portal is, again, remarkable in being unrestored. Its original doors are thought to have been covered in gold leaf. The current carved mahogany ones came from Khiva in 1992.

The design of the 16th-century **Sultan Ali mausoleum** opposite was based on the Turabeg Khanym mausoleum. But before it could be finished, the Khivan khan who had commissioned it fled to Persia, probably pursued by Bukhara's Abdullah Khan. The whole structure rests on a sandwich of reeds and wooden beams, which may have been intended to absorb earthquake thrusts and keep out rising saline groundwater.

Between these two mausolea what looks like one tree is actually two, joined in beautiful bio-symbiosis. The trunk is a 125 year-old *karaman* with roots that go 15 m down and obviate the need for special watering. Out of it grows a *gudzum* tree, whose drooping branches give shade to weary pilgrims.

A minute's walk east the **Dash mosque and madrasa** (1908) now house a museum. It is open on request, and contains as yet unstudied 13th–15th century Arabic texts and a pair of bridal boots said to have been worth a whole camel.

Eating Out

There is a restaurant at Kunya Urgench, pleasantly situated opposite the museum. The staff like to make a fuss of tourists, but need a little notice.

The Aral Sea (Аралское Море)

The enduring image of the Aral Sea in its death-throes is not of the sea at all, but of rusting trawler hulks, high and very dry on sand dunes which a decade ago were beaches. This ships' graveyard is at Muynak, once the Aral's major port, now the lonely and eerily fascinating victim of a world-class environmental disaster. In September 1995, a UN sponsored conference met and attempted to solve this problem brought about by irrigation. President Karimov recommended the revival of a Soviet-era plan to divert Siberian rivers; environmentalists recoiled in horror and the final, eight-point, World-Bank-drafted plan promised to monitor resources and tackle health problems. Meanwhile, the sea, 100km away and further each year, is impossible to reach without a helicopter or very serious off-road vehicle.

Getting to Muynak is not straightforward either. In Soviet times the entire Aral and its shore was a closed zone. The authorities were embarrassed at causing a sea to disappear. They were also anxious no one saw the biological weapons factory on Vozlozhdenie Island. Many thought that independent Uzbekistan would want the world to see how Soviet planning abused its territory. Not so. Tashkent was reluctant to issue Muynak visas. To complicate matters this territory is actually Karakalpakstan, a nominally autonomous region within Soviet Uzbekistan that is now desperately confused about its status. Karakalpaks are proud of their language, culture and nomadic ancestry. Some want full independence from Uzbekistan, but their bureaucrats in Nukus still defer to Tashkent on protocol. If both parties start claiming it is for the other to grant permission to visit Muynak, don't give up. Play them off against each other (*see* 'Red Tape', p.9).

Nukus (Нукус)

The capital of Karakalpakstan is at its most dramatic during one of the sandstorms which frequently whip through its wide, desolate streets. It is a windy place; one of the CIS's foremost wind-power researchers builds his prototypes in the garden of its Academy of Sciences. Otherwise Nukus is undramatic; a 100 per cent Soviet city on a spur of the Moscow–Dushanbe railway line and a problematic rising water table.

Getting to and from Nukus

By air: There are up to four flights a day from Tashkent, but they can be heavily booked.

By rail: Through-trains to Moscow, Dushanbe and Ashkhabad and everywhere in between go through Khodzhenli 14km away across the Amu Darya, though there are four trains a week from Nukus itself to Tashkent.

By bus: The overnight bus from Samarkand arrives about 3 am and leaves about 3 pm. In principle there are three buses a day to Muynak. In practice there is often only one. Bus and train stations are next to each other on the west side of the city.

A Stroll Around Town

The **museum** at the west end of former Lenin Prospekt, 15 minutes' walk in a straight line from the Hotel Tashkent, contains traditional Karakalpak dress and jewellery, flora and stuffed fauna from the Amu Darya estuary, and reasonably honest display on the Aral's shrinkage from 67,388 sq km in 1960 to 37,330 sq km in 1989.

To see the Amu Darya, take a taxi or local bus to Takiatash, 15km southwest of Nukus (off the Khodzenli road once it has crossed the river). The bridge is also the last major barrage across the Amu Darya before the Aral Sea. In a bad year the trickle that gets this far is all diverted into canals like the enormous one that runs through the middle of Nukus. In 1992 heavy rains in the Pamirs meant the river broke its banks here.

Nukus (© 36122–)   **Where to Stay and Eating Out**

The *liux* rooms at the top of the 10-storey **Hotel Tashkent** at the east end of Lenin Prospekt have the best views of this bleak place, but no air-conditioning and water from 6pm. Prices are negotiable, if outrageous, down to $40–60. It's preferable to the **Hotel Nukus**, half way down Lenin Prospekt; as you hand over a minimum of $30 here, hang onto your sense of humour. Eat bortsch at the Hotel Tashkent which also offers breakfast in the fly-blown cafe underneath.

Muynak (Муйнак)

Until 1957 Muynak was an island and a place of exile. Marshal Tukachevsky, modernizer of the Red Army in the 1930s, is thought by locals to have escaped Stalin's purges here (in fact he was shot in 1937). In 1943 the place was swamped with Kalmyks, an ethnic subgroup of steppe stock from the Volga basin accused by Stalin of helping the Germans on their way to Stalingrad. The old men of Muynak remember those times, when the town was administered and supplied direct from Moscow. But it was a friendly sort of prison, they insist, not like the Gulags. But the Aral Sea has not been full since 1957. The low-lying mainland was flooded that summer, and it was a bumper year for fish. Then vast irrigation and lake-building schemes were begun throughout Uzbekistan and the sea began to recede in earnest. The problem was aggravated in 1961, when Gary Powers flew over the Aral in his U2 spyplane, and revealed to the world the existence of the biological weapons factory on Vozrazhdenie. As a result, the radius of the exclusion zone round the island was increased from 7km to 37km. The main symptoms for Muynak have been: salt- and sandstorms, around ten a year, blowing in off the dried-up bed; extreme seasonal variation from a January low of -40° Celsius to a July high of +40°, where the sea had been a moderating influence; and the collapse of the fishing industry. Back in the fifties, 160 trawlers worked out of Muynak, and the cannery churned out 23 million tins of fish a year.

As the sea continued to dwindle, the cannery turned to canning fish from the Baltic and the Pacific. It soldiered on until the end of the Soviet Union, but is now closed. Most of the boats have been broken up and the steel taken to Kazakhstan to be melted down. In addition to the economic effects of the Aral disaster, the population has to contend with declining life expectancy and rising infant mortality and cancer rates, caused by the poisoned fresh water supply. And although Muynak's fishermen have turned to animal husbandry and mink-farming, the animals are as poorly as the humans and the (caged) mink are too self-sufficient to create many jobs.

Getting to Muynak

There are up to 2 buses a day from Nukus (the first leaves at 9am and the return bus departs Muynak around 3 pm; 3–4 hours). To go by taxi from Nukus you must be a tough negotiator or wealthy. Taxis start the bidding at $100.

red tape

Permission to visit Nukus or Muynak used to have to come from the Foreign Ministry in Tashkent (Information Department, Ministry of Foreign Affairs, Mustakkalik Maidoni, Tashkent, ✆ 3712 39 18 82/39 18 84 (English spoken), ✉ 3712 39 43 48.

A formal, typed invitation, addressed to you, from an individual or (preferably) organization in Nukus, stating the purpose, length and date of your visit and taking responsibility for your welfare, was the standard requirement. Today, apparently, this process is unnecessary. Visitors from countries such as the UK for whom an internal visa is not required can visit as and when they wish. Otherwise ensure that you get Muynak and Nukus written on your visa. This is the story from Tashkent. Stick to it.

The Ship's Graveyard

The ships' graveyard is half an hour's walk from the bus station. Ask for the *niftibaza*. Five minutes' drive (hitch?) west of town on what was Muynak island's north shore road, a searingly lonely war memorial points to the empty Communist heavens from a promontory. Footprints lead away through scrub and tumbleweed where the Aral Sea used to wash against the foot of the cliff. The water in the ex-bay south of the Muynak peninsula is not a mirage, but a project by the Ministry of Irrigation and Water Utilization to create a mild micro-climate by moistening the surrounding air.

There is a **hotel** on Ulitsa Berdakha, and by now you should not need 'Nukus' on your visa (and special permission for Muynak) to stay here. Without it, the authorities used to pay a visit within hours of your checking in and would ask you to leave town on the next bus.

The Fergana Valley

The Fergana valley ought to be a wonderful place. Fringed by the Tian Shan mountains to the north and the Alai Pamir to the south, drained by the Syr Darya, traversed until the Middle Ages by silk caravans from Kashgar, this is the biggest, lushest oasis between Xinjiang and the Caspian. But it was also meant to be the economic powerhouse of Soviet Central Asia. The Syr Darya's floodplain labours under the most intensive cotton cultivation in Uzbekistan. The old trading towns of Khŭjand, Kokand, Fergana, Andizhan and Osh have been largely rebuilt this century in anti-seismic steel and con-

Fergana Valley

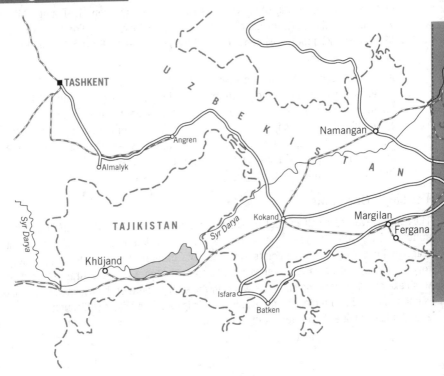

crete. And from their suburbs, which in places have merged, a dense skein of factories and power stations produces a chemical haze which permanently hides the mountains.

Yet as conspicuously as the Soviet system tamed the place, it failed to tame its people, 85 per cent of whom are Uzbek. Nowhere does a foreigner without a black and white skull-cap feel so conspicuous as in Andizhan's enormous, teeming bazaar. Nowhere was Islam practiced so defiantly throughout the Soviet era as in its mosques and those of Margilan. This is the Uzbek heartland. Anyone who wants to govern modern Uzbekistan must carry Fergana with him, as surely as anyone who wants to understand modern Uzbekistan should come here. A huge natural hothouse, 170 by 300km, it holds more than its fair share of the people, wealth and inter-ethnic tension that make Uzbekistan the most important, and potentially the most volatile, Central Asian republic. Islamic influence has grown since independence but it remains weak politically.

When you tire of the heat and dust, the mountains of Kyrgyzstan are never more than three hours away by bus or truck.

Khŭjand (Хужанд)

Khŭjand (population 120,000) straddles the Syr Darya river in the 'Fergana Gate' between the Fergana valley and the rest of Uzbekistan, but is actually the second city of Tajikistan. It has a long history. During his conquest of Central Asia in 329 BC the modest Alexander the Great founded no fewer than nine Alexandrias. Khŭjand stands on the site of the easternmost of these, Alexandria Eskhate. The name Khodzhent (the former name of Khŭjand) first appears in Sogdian texts of the 7th century. By the 10th, according to Edgar Knobloch, the town ranked among the major population centres of Transoxiana, with a citadel, inner and outer suburbs, a cathedral mosque, and a palace. All these were destroyed by the Mongols, who understood the town's strategic importance at the entrance to the Fergana valley and were irritated by its unusually determined resistance.

After enduring in relative obscurity the conquests of Tamerlane, the Uzbek khans and czarist Russia, the people of Khŭjand sparked an uprising that spread throughout Central Asia in July 1916 by refusing to be mobilized for the

Eastern Front. In 1929, the Soviet Union fixed the borders to give Tajikistan a lowland lobe north of the mountains, which included Khŭjand. The city's name was changed to Leninabad in 1936, and its history largely smothered by 20th-century industrialization. Although the city had more in common with the rest of Fergana than with the rest of Tajikistan, this meant less in Soviet times than it does now; people and goods came and went heedless of what were then only internal borders.

Since 1991, however, Tajikistan has split along thinly-disguised clan divisions. Civil war breaks out sporadically in the south of the country and Khŭjand has become the power-base of the 'communist' old-guard. For visitors this means transport links in all directions are unreliable, though Khŭjand remains the only overland gateway to the Fergana valley from the rest of Uzbekistan by public transport. And though the city is generally safe, you must have 'Khŭjand' on your visa to stay here.

Getting to and from Khŭjand
by air

The problem is the lack of flights from Tashkent, which the operators regard as a way of containing the civil war and, in any event, are reckoned too close to be worthwhile and too dangerous if violence flares in Dushanbe. The two daily flights to and from Dushanbe (leaving early in the morning and late in the evening) are at the mercy of intermittent Uzbek fuel embargoes. In principle there are flights to Moscow each week.

by rail

One solution is to use the train. But Uzbekistan, for the same reason as it does not schedule flights here, does not provide direct train services either. To come from Tashkent to Khŭjand by train, you have to catch the Moscow–Dushanbe service that stops in Tashkent.

by bus

Bus services are scarcely more reliable, as they tend to be suspended at the first sign of trouble in Tajikistan. When they run, most Fergana valley services go from the new or East bus station on the southern outskirts, half way to the railway station. The rest go from the old or West station on Ulitsa Kamoli Khudzhandi (formerly Kosmonavtov). There are three scheduled buses a day to Pendzhikent, and, in theory, one to Chimkent and Tashkent.

by taxi

This is the most reliable way to enter Tajikistan. Negotiate with a taxi driver in Uzbekistan or call a reliable travel company like Sam Buh in Tashkent, ✆ 63 75 85, who regularly provides transport to Khŭjand. In Khŭjand itself, Kasim Islamov who runs the River Business Apartments, offers transport to Tashkent airport for $90.

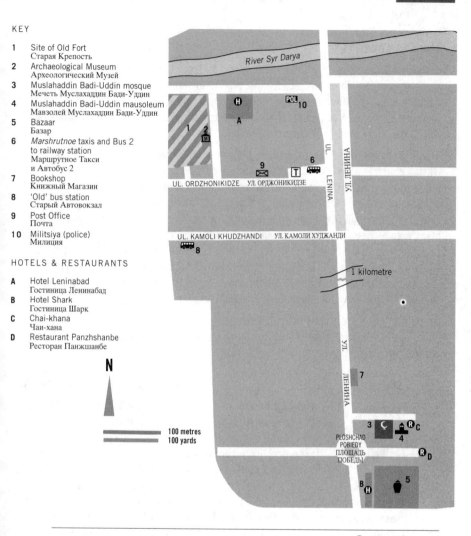

KEY

1 Site of Old Fort
   Старая Крепость
2 Archaeological Museum
   Археологический Музей
3 Muslahaddin Badi-Uddin mosque
   Мечетъ Муслахаддин Бади-Уддин
4 Muslahaddin Badi-Uddin mausoleum
   Мавзолей Муслахаддин Бади-Уддин
5 Bazaar
   Базар
6 *Marshrutnoe* taxis and Bus 2
   to railway station
   Маршрутное Такси
   и Автобус 2
7 Bookshop
   Книжный Магазин
8 'Old' bus station
   Старый Автовокзал
9 Post Office
   Почта
10 Militsiya (police)
   Милиция

HOTELS & RESTAURANTS

A Hotel Leninabad
   Гостиница Ленинабад
B Hotel Shark
   Гостиница Шарк
C Chai-khana
   Чаи-хана
D Restaurant Panzhshanbe
   Ресторан Панжшанбе

N

100 metres
100 yards

Getting Around

The airport, railway station and new bus station are south of the city and linked to it by Bus 2, which stops at the central Aeroflot office, Ulitsa Lenina 56 (8am–12pm and 1pm–7pm) and near the Hotel Leninabad. *Marshrutnoe* taxi 3 runs between the airport and the Univermag bus stop on Ulitsas Lenina and Ordzhonikidze a block south of the Hotel Leninabad. The *Pakhtakhor* trolleybus serves the old bus station from the same crossroads.

Ulitsa Lenina is the city's axis, running north-south with the Syr Darya bridge at its north end and the bazaar at its south end on Ploshchad Pobiedy. A car for the day in Khūjand costs $50.

The Old Town

Khūjand celebrated its 2500th anniversary in 1990, but there is nothing that old left. One block west of the Hotel Leninabad, three high mud walls of an old **fortress** now enclose a militia car park. The history museum inside is in the process of moving to unspecified premises in the old town and is closed. The archaeological museum outside seems to be closed too, and is definitely closed on Sundays.

The **'old' town**, centred on the huge, purpose-built **bazaar** 20 minutes' walk south on Ulitsa Lenina, is not very old. Half a block before the bazaar, down a narrow lane on the left, a mosque named after **Sheikh Musslahaddin Badi-uddin Nuri** is expanding to accommodate a growing congregation. The prayer hall on the left of its vine-shaded courtyard, behind a wall of numbered wooden shoe boxes, is new. The one on the right is being reconverted for worship having served as a museum since 1973. Through the gate at the far end of the courtyard, you come to the sheikh's mausoleum, completely rebuilt and a Mecca for pigeons. The complex probably dates from the 19th century but no one who works here knows for sure. The madrasa opposite was built in 1991 and has 140 students. At the end of the lane there is a shady *chai-khana*.

In the bazaar look out for honey in every hue of gold, and honeycomb to chew while choosing. The *lepeshka* loaves sold outside make unusually good *shashlyk* plates because of their distinctive high rims.

Khūjand (℗ 37922–)   ***Where to Stay and Eating Out***

The **Hotel Leninabad**, one block west of Ulitsa Lenina on the river's south bank, ℗ 6 69 27 has grand views across the river from north-facing rooms on its upper floors, a restaurant liable to be taken over for wedding feasts, and a dungeon of a bar selling port and sausage (by the kilogram) to drunkards. The police headquarters is next door. This used to be the number one hotel in town, but standards have slipped in the face of competiton from the private accommodation complex, **River Business Apartments**, ℗ 67 529, @ 65 824. These modern apartments have air-conditioning, hot water, TV and kitchens. Breakfast is served in your apartment ($5) and European and Tajik dishes in the main restaurant (lunch $12; dinner $8). A one bedroom apartment for two costs $30 per person, or $50 per flat. The small business centre attached to River Business Apartments provides interpreters and E-mail facilities.

Next to the bazaar at Ulitsa Lenina 3, the fine, white façade, reminiscent of the sea-front at Dieppe, belongs to the **Hotel Shark**, where the traders stay.

The **Panzhshanbe Restaurant** near the bazaar's northeast corner sits on top of a café and *chai-khana* to which people bring *shashlyk* from the stalls outside. The more traditional *chai-khana* next to the nearby Musslahaddin Badi-Uddin mosque looks more relaxing.

Kokand (Коканд)

In the middle of Kokand you find one of the defining images of Soviet and post-Soviet Central Asia. The garish palace of the despised and maverick Khudayar Khan stands shoulder to shoulder in a public park with a ferris wheel, sundry other fairground rides and a full-size Yak 40 airliner. The palace itself is given over to improving museums of natural and local history. The cult of the individual, you infer, was to be shamed by that of the proletariat. But nowadays, as the bewildered proletariat struggles with hyper-inflation and returns to Islam for solace, the sheer personality of the palace lights up the park while the grounded Yak 40 outdoes it only in comic absurdity.

Kokand is the Fergana valley's most famous city; 19th-century Bukhara's deadliest rival, imperial Russia's most tenacious Central Asian opponent, and a serious player in the Great Game. Apart from the palace there is little evidence of this momentous history, nor of Kokand's pre-revolutionary role as the second most important religious centre in Central Asia after Bukhara with, according to a local *imam*, 56 madrasas and 500 mosques. There are now a mere handful of each. All the same, Kokand still merits a visit more than Fergana (the nearest official tourist base in Soviet times). And, situated at the junction of the two main routes into the valley—one over the mountains from Tashkent, the other via Khŭjand—she is not hard to get to.

History

Kokand seems to have had a khan before it had a khanate. The only sources to hazard dates on such matters are Soviet ones, and they are baffling. A Sheibanid called Shahruk-bey is credited with founding Kokand's ruling dynasty after splitting from Bukhara's in 1710. But only in 1732 did he found a new city, on the site of the fortress of Eski-Kurgan, and only in 1740 did he call it Kokand and proclaim the khanate. Bukhara, meanwhile, did not recognise the Fergana valley's independence under Kokand until the reign of Shahruk's grandson Yodan-bey, who died in 1774.

However it was born, the khanate gained power and territory with amazing speed. Under Alim Khan (r. 1800–1809), Omar Khan (r. 1809–1822) and Mohammed Ali Khan (r. 1822–42), it annexed Khŭjand and Tashkent and established a northern frontier way beyond them in the middle of the steppe with forts at Aq-Meshit (today's Kzyl Orda, near the Baikonur cosmodrome), Aulie-Ata (Dzhambul) and Pishpek (Bishkek).

Bukhara had known nothing like it in 300 years of virtually unchallenged Central Asian hegemony. In 1839, 1841 and 1842 Nasrullah Khan launched expeditions against Kokand, putting a viceroy on its throne and retaking Tashkent and Khŭjand. He did not gloat for long. Within three years Shir Ali Khan of Kokand, Mohammed Ali's heir, had reversed Nasrullah's gains and turned his attention to the Russian threat from Orenburg.

Kazakh nomads suspected of collaborating with the Russians would find their herds driven away from grazing near Kokandian forts. Kokandian troops under Yakub Beg, a charismatic commander who was to establish his own fiefdom based on Kashgar, harried Russian detachments along the lower Syr Darya in 1852. The result was a determined Russian assault on Aq-Meshit the following year, led by General Perovsky (taking no chances after his Khivan debacle of 1839) with a ten-to-one superiority in men and a steam launch called the *Perovsky* anchored in support in the river. Thus, 230 of the 300 Kokandian defenders died and the fort fell.

It was the beginning of the end for Kokand, but the end was a long time in coming. For 13 years the Russians advanced across the steppe and down the Tian Shan, forcing Kokand continually to retreat and re-establish its defensive northern frontier. In 1864 Chimkent and Turkestan fell and Kokand applied in vain to British India for help. In 1865 General Cherniaev took Tashkent with the help of local merchants who resented Kokand's taxes, and in 1868 General Kaufman forced Kokand into economic dependence on Russian Turkestan with a humiliating commercial treaty.

Meanwhile Khudayar Khan was at his most extravagant, equipping his new palace with Russian stoves, Japanese vases and the usual abundance of gold leaf. His only remaining subjects were the people of the Fergana valley. Rather than pay his bills they rebelled. For the last three years of the khanate the Russians sat back while the khan faced insurrection from Andizhan to Margilan, and eventually from his own sons. In April 1875 he fled to Tashkent and sought Russian protection. (He was given it and, to judge by a ball he hosted for Russian officers and wives in Orenburg the following winter, he enjoyed it.) The rebel leader Polat-bey briefly assumed his throne, becoming Polat Khan, but was driven out, captured and executed by General Skobelev in January 1876. Within a month the khanate was abolished and its lands absorbed within the Turkestan Governorate General. The Russians were within 50 miles of what British India regarded as her sphere of influence in the Pamirs.

Restoration of the khanate was a rallying cry for sporadic uprisings throughout Fergana during the 40 years of colonial rule. But the next time Kokand enjoyed independence it was as a socialist republic. The 'Kokand Autonomy' lasted three months. Proclaimed in November 1917 with an elected council of Muslims and Russians, it was ignored by the British (who were accused by Moscow of supporting it), and tolerated—briefly—by the Bolsheviks while they struggled for control of Tashkent. Then the Red Army moved in, crushing the autonomy and sacking Kokand on St Valentine's day 1918.

Getting to and from Kokand

by air

There are two flights a day from Tashkent, and once a week to Dzhambul. There are now none to Dushanbe. The ticket office is near the Hotel Kokand on Ulitsa Iman Ismail Bukhary. Or else buy tickets at the airport.

All trains on the Andizhan–Dzhalalabad line pass through Kokand, giving three times a week departures to Moscow and daily to Bukhara, three a day to Tashkent. There are three a week to Bishkek but none to Dushanbe.

by bus

Kokand has hourly bus services to and from Andizhan (until 5pm) and even more frequent ones to Fergana and Margilan. Three buses a day go to Namangan (last one at 6pm) and two to Osh.

There are none across the Tajik border to Khūjand. The three daily buses that make their way to Tashkent (last bus 3pm; 4 hours) do not take the shorter, more scenic mountain route via Angren, but taxis might and hitching should be possible. A new bus station is being built on the outskirts of town.

Tourist Information

Uzbektourism has two offices: one in the Hotel Kokand and a larger one on Ulitsa Nariman Alimov 116, ✆ 41 78 82, ✉ 2 27 00 (*open 8am–6pm*). Mr Mukim Muninov, who works at the latter, speaks some English. A group or an individual tour of the city will cost $10. Trips further afield are possible and English, German or French guides provided.

For shops and a supermarket head to Ulitsa Istiklol. Everything from spare car parts to painted Uzbek cribs can be found near or in the **bazaar** on Ulitsa Furkhat, (close to the bus station).

Khudayar Khan's Palace (Дворец Худаяр Хан)

Open 9–5; closed Mon.

'The last truly monumental building in Central Asia' (Edgar Knobloch) is an easy walk up Ulitsa Istiklol from the Hotel Kokand in Mukimi Park. The palace took eight years to build (1863–71), was badly damaged by Russian shells in 1876 and 1918, and has been under restoration since 1961 with the help of a detailed 1871 description of it by the Russian geologist Fedchenko. The kaleidoscopic tiling on its long, low façade is certainly 'as new'. So is the lavish carved and painted plaster in the khan's war minister's office behind the right-hand end of the facade—though this is said to be unrestored. The room now houses an exhibition of Kokandian fruit. The door leading to what was the Chief Secretary's office (now full of stuffed birds) used to be a *mihrab*. This room was redecorated in 1972 but a patch has been left in the top left-hand corner as you enter, to show how it was.

Under the colonnade on the far side of the main courtyard (left of the entrance) there is a carved wooden column from a 15th-century mosque which Tamerlane had built in Shakhimardan, an Uzbek enclave in the mountains 60km south of Fergana. The strange narrow-bore cannon is Chinese. Opposite the main gate, Khudayar's throne room was used as a chapel by the czarists (there is an icon on the wall behind where the khan sat) and now contains antique jewellery, samovars and musical instruments. In the khan's bedroom, which he shared with his pick of 43 wives, there are 17th-century Japanese Kyoto vases and, according to one guide, some 8th-century Chinese ones.

As more rooms are restored (there were originally 113) the plan is to use them for a new, non-Soviet history museum.

The Yak 40 (see above) points at the palace's façade from the far end of the park. From outside the police station behind it, buses 7 and 8 cross a canal and pass the **Djuma mosque**, Kokand's largest, on Ulitsa Khamza. Up to 10,000 men attend Friday prayers under the towering trees in its enormous courtyard.

The Grave of Kings (мавзолей Дахма-и-Шахон)

Narbutabek madrasa is closed to non-Muslims. The key to the Dakhma-i-Shakhon mausoleum can be obtained from No. 59 Ul. Nabieva, or the man at the cemetery gate.

Ulitsas Khamza and A. Islamova meet at a large roundabout where buses 7 and 8 turn left towards the **Narbutabek madrasa** (ask for the *Chorsu* stop). Finished in 1799 and working ever since, it has 200 students mostly aged 18–25. The main reason for coming here, however, is to see two mausolea built in the cemetery behind for the family of Omar Khan (r. 1809–1822). The larger and more obvious one is **Dakhma-i-Shakhon** ('the grave of Kings'), whose painted roof, reminiscent of Khiva, was restored in 1970. Omar's mother was buried under the blue-domed **Modari-Khan mausoleum** (1825), hemmed in by modern graves next to a tree over to the right. Tourists are able to visit this To reach the cemetery, pass the madrasa on your right and follow the curving Ulitsa Nabieva to the end.

Museums with a literary theme have multiplied. For the general picture (displays of the works of all Kokand poets) visit the **Hudayar Hon Museum** on Ulitsa Istiklol, near the Mukimi Park (*open 9–noon and 1pm–5; closed Mon*). For the more specific, browse in **The House Of Khamza** on Ulitsa Khamza (*opening times as above*) devoted to the works of the eponymous Uzbek composer and revolutionary poet (1870-1930).

Where to Stay and Eating Out

If you arrive by bus, it is worth resisting the hotel between the station and the bazaar for the **Hotel Kokand**, Ulitsa Iman Ismail Bukhary (formerly Ulitsa Kirova) 1, ✆ 3 64 03, which is across town but a good deal more salubrious and, likely to improve still further after its renovation. Even so, before accepting a room, check the acoustics of the plumbing. Pay in local currency only; a single will cost the equivalent of $9, a

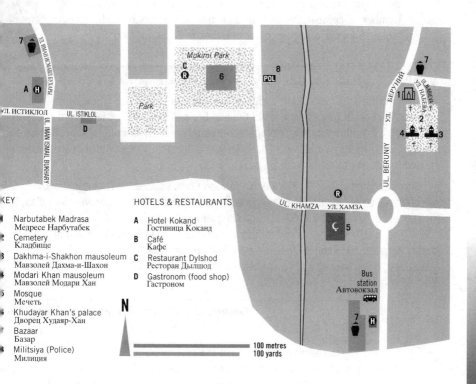

KEY

1. Narbutabek Madrasa
   Медресе Нарбутабек
2. Cemetery
   Кладбище
3. Dakhma-i-Shakhon mausoleum
   Мавзолей Дахма-и-Шахон
4. Modari Khan mausoleum
   Мавзолей Модари Хан
5. Mosque
   Мечеть
6. Khudayar Khan's palace
   Дворец Худаяр-Хан
7. Bazaar
   Базар
8. Militsiya (Police)
   Милиция

HOTELS & RESTAURANTS

A. Hotel Kokand
   Гостиница Коканд
B. Café
   Кафе
C. Restaurant Dylshod
   Ресторан Дылшод
D. Gastronom (food shop)
   Гастроном

N

100 metres
100 yards

double $5 per person. You can book international calls through reception or go to the telegraph office which is only a short walk away. Buses 14 and 21 come here from the airport. Buses 1, 2, 3, 4, 7, 8 and 21 and *marshrutnoe* taxis 8, 7 and 17 come here from the bus and railway stations.

Kokand's premier restaurant seems to be the cavernous **Dylshod**, behind the palace in Mukimi Park. There is a café opposite the Djami mosque and a *chai-khana* outside the madrasa. The Hotel Kokand's restaurant is closed by 7.30pm and doesn't open for breakfast till 9am; a snack bar in the building entered from Ulitsa Istiklol opens earlier and serves tepid sweet white coffee and *blinchiki*.

Nilufar, across the square from the Hotel Kokand, is a better alternative; its Uzbek fare is among the best in Uzbekistan and you can't argue with the price (50 cents per person). The beef stroganoff is even cheaper. *Open 10am–11pm daily.* On the road leading out of Kokand to Margilan/Fergana, Ulitsa Navoi, turn left towards the pale green Moslem school and in a similarly pale green building on the right hand side you'll find the **Noubahor** restaurant, easily identifiable by the elaborate mirrors on its exterior. Inside, off a central bar area, are a number of compartments with TVs and padded walls. Hide here for around $4 a person and a choice of Uzbek or European food.

Fergana and Margilan (Фергана и Маргилан)

The town of Fergana (population 195,000) is a miniature Tashkent; young, Russian-built, industrialized on its fringes, verdant in the middle, and proud of it. Margilan (population 123,000), 11km to the north, is older, quieter and devoutly Islamic. The population of each reflects the town's history. Margilan was a separate town until industrialization caused its suburbs to merge with Fergana's.

Fergana was founded in 1876 as a Russian garrison town. Its streets fan out from the old fort, which is still army property and very closed to visitors. Known at first as New Margilan, it was renamed Skobelevo in 1907 after the conqueror of Kokand, but has been Fergana since 1924. This is Uzbekistan's second industrial city after Tashkent, with a 78-fold increase in output between 1925 and 1975 and giant plants producing cement, nitrogen fertilizer, sulphuric acid, nylon from oil and power from coal. The air in its leafy central pedestrian zone is miraculously breatheable, considering.

Getting to and from Fergana and Margilan
by air

Fergana has the airport and Margilan the railway station. The long-distance bus station is in between at Yermazar. There are three Tashkent flights a day ($50), plus one a week to Moscow. Buses from Fergana to the airport (numbers 3, 4, 22, 21) can be found lined up, opposite the bank, on the road which joins Kuvasoi Kuchasi diagonally and leads to the pedestrianized shopping area. Those buses lined up on Kuchasi, right next to the *chai-khanas* and not far from the Hotel Ziyorat, go to the west part of town and to the countryside. Tickets must be purchased at the airport.

by rail

Margilan, on the Andizhan–Dzhalalabad line, has daily rail links with Moscow, Dzhalalabad, Bishkek and Bukhara/Samarkand and at least two a day with Tashkent and Andizhan.

by bus

Buses between Yermazar and Kokand go every 20mins (journey time, 3hrs); those to Namangan, Andizhan (2 hours) and Osh are also fast and frequent. Those to Tashkent and Khŭjand run at least three times daily (5–6 and 4hrs).

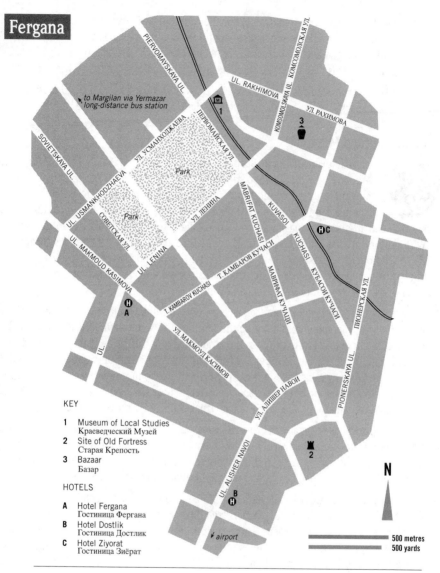

Fergana

to Margilan via Yermazar
long-distance bus station

KEY

1 Museum of Local Studies
  Краеведческий Музей
2 Site of Old Fortress
  Старая Крепость
3 Bazaar
  Базар

HOTELS

A Hotel Fergana
  Гостиница Фергана
B Hotel Dostlik
  Гостиница Достлик
C Hotel Ziyorat
  Гостиница Зиёрат

500 metres
500 yards

N

Getting Around

From the airport, Fergana's buses 3 and 4 go along Ulitsa Makmoud Kasimov, close to the Hotel Fergana. To get to the Hotel Fergana from Fergana's local bus station walk through the bazaar onto Ulitsa Mustakkilik (formerly Lenina) and down it for about 1km. The Hotel Ziyorat is a short walk south along Ulitsa Kuchasi, following the river. It's easily seen once past the row of *chai-khanas* and has a small bridge to the footpath passing its entrance. The centre of Fergana is walkable, green and enjoyable. For the museum walk back up Ulitsa Mustakkilik from the hotel, down the first street on the left after the park, and over the bridge. Buses shuttle every 20 minutes between Fergana's local station and Margilan's bazaar. Taxis take about 20 minutes and should charge less than $1 in rubles.

To get from central Margilan to the railway station take buses or *marshrutnoe* taxis marked *voksal* south down Ulitsa Karla Marxa from near the bazaar.

Silkworms and Minarets

The **Museum of Local Studies**, Ulitsa Usmankhodzhaeva (*open Mon–Sat, 9–5; closed Sun; small entrance fee in local currency*) has undergone some transformation since independence. For a glimpse of pre-Soviet Fergana, look at the black-and-white photos here. Many of the buildings in the pictures, particularly the mosques, have now gone. There are 19th-century pictures of camels with cotton bundles and a display marking *Navroos* in March (*see* Festivals, **Practical A–Z**) only openly celebrated since 1991. Afghan, Tajik and Uzbek musical instruments and paintings by local artists depict traditional Uzbek life. All this is presided over by photos of Karimov on tour in the Fergana Valley.

Uzbektourism at the Hotel Ziyorat can arrange trips to **Shakhimardan**, an Uzbek enclave in the (Kyrgyz) Alai mountains 60km to the south which is also served far more cheaply by public bus. These leave from the bazaar bus station every half hour in summer, and 8–10 times a day in winter. For $20 per person Uzbektourism offers lunch and a visit to the famed **Blue Lake** by cable car (some discount is available to those staying at the Ziyorat). A group trip to Kokand includes the Uzbek cemetery where Khudyar Khan is buried and his palace ($24 for the group). Ask for Sergei at Uzbektourism. He speaks excellent English.

Fergana's **park** was originally the Russian governor's garden and was planted with trees from around the world. Just off the street bisecting it stands an ornate Russian-built **theatre**. Today Uzbek plays are performed here, particularly those depicting the history of Uzbekistan, unified under Timur, and which, until recently, were banned.

Fruits grown in the Fergana Valley are distributed throughout the republic. The exchange is on the first-floor balcony of the hanger-sized **bazaar**, where the trade is in rice, much of which is grown in Karakalpakstan. This bazaar is one of the best in the Valley and there is an almost biblical atmosphere here as the competing sellers of *lepeshka*, pomegranates and melons climb the ramp and pass, two by two, into the covered bazaar. For other goods, try the growing number of commercial shops that surround the bazaar, the tempting store at the edge of the park or the shops in the pedestrianized shopping area. The **post and telegraph office** is on the corner of Ulitsa Mustakkilik and Makmoud Kasimov, close to the Hotel Fergana.

Near the centre of Margilan on the south side of Ulitsa Burkhaneddin Margilani, its main street, two towering minarets and the **central mosque** behind them symbolize the current resurgence of Islam. The minarets are brand new and the mosque, on the site of a

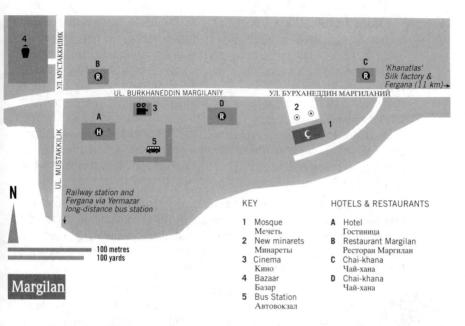

Margilan

KEY

1 Mosque
  Мечеть
2 New minarets
  Минареты
3 Cinema
  Кино
4 Bazaar
  Базар
5 Bus Station
  Автовокзал

HOTELS & RESTAURANTS

A Hotel
  Гостиница
B Restaurant Margilan
  Ресторан Маргилан
C Chai-khana
  Чай-хана
D Chai-khana
  Чай-хана

16th-century original, has been rebuilt in the last two years to accommodate up to 5000—all at the believing public's expense. Meanwhile ten more mosques of similar capacity have gone up in the suburbs. During Friday prayers (12.30–1pm) Margilan's streets are almost deserted.

The largest silk factory in the CIS is in Margilan (*open Mon–Sat, 10–4; closed Sun; $11 a group with Uzbektourism*). The **Khanatlas plant** directly employs 15,000 and depends on household silkworm cultivation by thousands more who fatten the worms on mulberry twigs and kill them by steaming before they break out of the cocoons. Since mid-1995 the factory has branched out to make carpets as well. There is a shop where you can pay in dollars and local currency.

Fergana/Margilan (© 37322/37333–)   ***Where to Stay and Eating Out***

The **Hotel Fergana**, Ulitsa Makmoud Kasimov 29, © 26 95 01, used by Intourist, is in three buildings, the earliest parts dating back to 1940: reception, Intourist's office and the restaurant serving Uzbek and Russian food, which closes at 10pm. Foreigners are usually put in the middle block, where the second-floor rooms are decorated in traditonal Uzbek style. Each room has a telephone and the seating areas on the landing overlook the park. Doubles are around $32 and singles, $25. Under the corner building, reached from Ulitsa Mustakkilik, there is another 'restaurant' where you might get lucky with a bun and a brandy. Buses 3 and 4 go to the airport from across Ulitsa Mustakkilik. Bus 15 goes to the long-distance bus station.

The **Hotel Dostlik**, Ulitsa Alisher Navoi 30, ℰ 6 86 06, is south of the centre near the old fort. The hotel was built for sportsmen in 1978 and trade has suffered considerably since independence as travel is an expense that many CIS citizens now find beyond their means. However, the staff are friendlier than those at the Fergana, the café serves coffee, the restaurant is vast and clean (*open 8am–11pm*) and there's a roof-top nightclub in the summer. Make a saving by sharing a room for three people at $10 each or else visiting in the winter when prices are lower—in season singles are $26 and doubles $17 per person. If you pay in vouchers, purchased from Uzbektourism in the Hotel Uzbekistan, for example, all meals are included. Dollar payers expect a cost of around $4 for breakfast and $7 dinner.

Next to Fergana's bazaar the eight-storey, three-star, hard-currency **Hotel Ziyorat**, ℰ 26 86 00, ✉ 26 85 02, was opened in 1994 and has taken the top slot. All rooms are clean, modern and have TV and phone; front-facing rooms have views of willow trees and the River Margilansai. Prices start at $30 per night. Phone calls are paid for daily at reception in local currency.

The restaurant serves good Russian and Uzbek food at a reasonable price. The best value is the buffet bar on the 6th floor—it's bright and cheerful, particularly if you're listening to the bird, and open 7am–11pm.

Cheap canteen-style Uzbek fare is available from the **Margilansai Café**, situated at the edge of the river virtually opposite the Museum of Local Studies on Usmankhodzhaeva Ulitsa (*open 8am–7pm*). It has seating inside and out and is a favourite with the younger population. Still on the café theme, there are various options in the park, after the Russian theatre building, and on Kuchasi towards the bazaar. They all, however, shut by 7pm.

En route to the airport, opposite a power station is the **Court Restaurant**. Built for the April 1995 Silk Road Tournament, the restaurant still has adjoining tennis courts. It's clean and bright and offers good cheap Uzbek food and loud European music. But all this is surpassed by the ingenious tennis racket/ball lamps at the complex entrance. Catch any airport bus.

The **Central Margilan Hotel** on Ulitsas Burkhaneddin Margilani and Mustakkilik diagonally opposite the bazaar and next to the local bus station claims to accommodate locals only. Suggestions to the contrary bring directions to the local OVIR office. Unless you are offered private board, your best bet is to stay in Fergana.

Directly opposite the hotel is the **Restaurant Margilan**. The best food, inevitably, is *shashlyk*, *lepeshka* and *chai* from the *chai-khanas* near Fergana's bazaars and opposite Margilan's central mosque.

Namangan (Наманган)

Namangan (population 275,000), 80km north of Margilan near where the Naryn and Kara Darya rivers join to form the Syr Darya, has nearly quadrupled in size since the Russian Revolution. Various monuments have been restored including the **Mulla Kyrgyz madrasa** (1912), the **Hazrabi Mavlan mosque** and the 17th century **Hodja Amin mausoleum**. There is a new mosque and the large Babur Park does its best to make this large city green. Namangan is the best place to find tranport to Sary-Chelek (*see* below). There are fast, easy bus connections from all over the Fergana valley and regular flights from Tashkent, occasional ones from Moscow.

Namangan (✆ 36922–) ***Where to Stay and Eating Out***

There are also numerous hotels: close to the bazaar, department store and restaurants is the **Orzu**, Ulitsa Nodira, ✆ 3 16 51. Singles cost $22 and doubles $17 per person.

The **Namangan**, Ulitsa Abdulla Khojaev 6, ✆ 6 21 54, in the business part of the city, is more expensive at $30 single and $60 for luxury double. Not far from the airport is the **Fazo** at Mikrorayon 2, ✆ 2 51 43. All rooms cost $50. **Umarjon Isanov** runs a small private hotel, Ulitsa Navoi 11, Apartment 1, ✆ 6 22 43. Otherwise try the **Chorsu** on Chorsu Square, ✆ 3 85 01.

Sary-Chelek (Сары-Челек)

There are places any writer with an ounce of conscience should refuse to write about, and this high-altitude nature reserve in Kyrgyzstan's Katkalski mountains, centred on a pristine, trout-filled lake surrounded by walnut and apple groves stalked by bear, boar, mountain goat, badger, porcupine and marmot, is one of them.

Fortunately it is hard to get to and protected by the Soviet total-exclusion approach to nature conservation. Besides Kyrgyz government VIPs and their guests, and the ranger and his family, only two people in the world are allowed to camp here—a journalist from Tashkent and a former Gorbachev-aide friend of his—and then only because they have been coming here since before it became a nature reserve in 1959.

Getting to Sary-Chelek

Approaching from Namangan, get a bus to Karavan (76km north) then another bus, or hitch, to the Sary-Chelek *turbaza* where you may be able to join a day-trip to the lake. Otherwise make your own way to the entrance to the reserve, get in by saying you are going to see the director, go and see the director and ask for written permission to continue to the lake. Approaching from Bishkek, make the 12-hour journey over the mountains to Tash-Kumir, turn right and continue for 80km to the *turbaza*, and proceed as above. It's also possible to take a bus to Sary-Chelek from Osh (*see* p.221).

The bazaar in Andizhan is the only place in Central Asia where you feel you might stumble on a whiskered dervish sharpening scimitars for the coming *ghazawat.* Fergana's last holy war, carefully organized and amply financed by the Nakshbandi Sufi brotherhood, was crushed near here by the Russian 20th Line Battalion in 1898. It jolted the Russians into Russifying the local Muslim elite and coincided with the arrival of their railway from the Caspian. Four years later old Andizhan was destroyed and 4500 were killed by an earthquake later put at 9 on the Richter Scale.

The orderly Russian city built from scratch on the rubble quickly grew into the industrial and administrative centre of east Fergana. Its population doubled between the earthquake and World War I, and has trebled since then to 275,000. Cotton production in the Andizhan oblast is the most intensive in the CIS. But the bazaar remains utterly un-Russian, virtually unmodernized, worth a long detour.

Getting to and from Andizhan

by air

There are four flights a day from Tashkent and two a week from Moscow. There are occasional flights to Samarkand and Bukhara in the summer, and a once weekly flight to Almaty also limited to the summer months.

by rail

Andizhan is a major rail terminus, with daily services to and from Tashkent, five services a week to Moscow, and trains on alternate days to Bishkek/Dzhalalabad and Bukhara.

by bus

Buses come and go all the time between Andizhan, Osh, Fergana, Margilan and Namangan. Of the 4–5 buses to Tashkent (10 hours) only the morning one is reliable. In summer only, buses go three times a day to Arslanbob (*see* below), three hours away. In the winter this mountainous route is snow-covered.

Getting Around

Railway and bus stations are five minutes' walk apart on Ulitsa Amir Timur and the air ticket office (*open 10am–1pm and 2pm–4pm*) is in the former. Hotel Zolotaya Dolina is eight stops from the bazaar by trolleybus 2.

A Stroll Around Town

What sets Andizhan's **bazaar** apart from countless others in Central Asia is Ulitsa Bazarnaya. Wriggling round the fairly conventional vegetable market from Ashur Khaydarov Ulitsa, it is saturated with skull caps and lined with

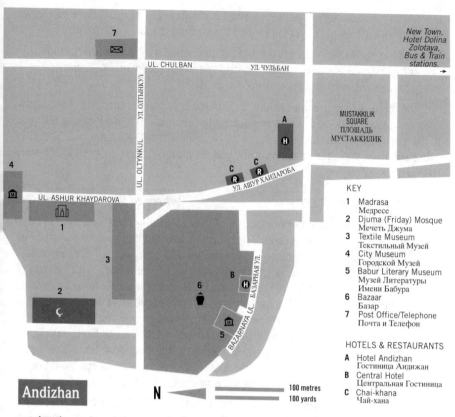

metal and wood-workshops producing orange sparks, a mighty din, sickles, axes, painted wooden cradles—and surely the odd scimitar.

The **Babur Literary Museum** (*open weekdays, 9–5*) at Ulitsa Bazarnaya 21, honours someone more famous for empire-building than literature. Zaherredin Mohammed Babur, fifth in line to the throne of Tamerlane, born in Andizhan in 1483, succeeded his father Umarshayekh Babur as sheikh of Fergana at the age of 12 and lost all his territory trying to re-conquer Samarkand by the time he was 22. He fared better in India, taking Khandahar (in modern Afghanistan) in 1522, Delhi in 1526, and there founding the Mughal dynasty which ruled until 1858. His great-great-grandson Shahjahan built the Taj Mahal. Babur spoke Uzbek, Arabic and Persian, wrote poetry, history, geography and mineralology and died in 1530. This 'museum', in a restored 18th-century madrasa on the site of his residence, was opened in 1989 apparently to mark the 460th anniversary of the publication of *Baburname*, his encyclopaedia. Nothing in it is old. The large painting in the first room on the right is of the young Babur in Osh about to leave for Afghanistan. There are also rooms about Babarakhim Mashrab (1640–1711), a local dervish and poet hanged for attracting the ardour of a religious

Andizhan   217

leader's wife, and an Andizhani poetess called Nadira (1792–1842), in whose honour the nearby town of Shakhrikan was founded by her husband the Khan of Kokand.

Not far from the Babur Museum is what is known locally as the **Khunarmandchilik** open-air museum. Here Uzbek craftsmen display and sell their work. A local speciality is miniature painting on pumpkins and wooden cribs.

The enormous **Friday mosque** behind a trouser factory on the other side of the bazaar accommodates 10,000 and can be reached via the entrance arch of a working madrasa. It has been heavily restored but its caretaker claims it is 300 years old. The **City Museum** (*open 9–5 daily except Mon*) next to the madrasa has a display on local history and costume.

Andizhan (✆ *37422–*)　　　　　　　　　　　　　　　　　***Where to Stay and Eating Out***

Hotel Zolotaya Dolina ('Golden Valley'), Ulitsa Mashrabi 19, ✆ 6 87 08, is dismal, with dirty rooms, sputtering yellow water and no floor ladies—and all this for $17 a single, $13 per person in a double. But the hotel is undergoing renovation which should be completed in late 1996. A Korean company is providing a new telephone system which, it is claimed, will allow international calls. At present a double room is the same size as a single and the only finished refurbishment is the Uzbek-decorated dining-room reserved, according to the restaurant manager, for foreigners. This is through the main, dark cavern of a restaurant. Breakfast is $4, lunch and supper $6. Alternatively, eat at any of the abundant *chai-khanas* near the bazaar or try one of the growing number of private restaurants (trolleybus 2).

The **Hotel Andizhan**, Ashur Khaydarova 241, ✆ 5 87 07, also near the bazaar, looks cleaner and friendlier than the Golden Valley, is much better placed and run by a private company. If neither appeals you could put yourself into the hands of the Andizhan branch of Uzbektourism and request a home stay. Their office is in the Golden Valley Hotel. Ask for the deputy chairman, Toulkin Akbarov ✆ 6 10-69, ✉ 4 20 13.

Arslanbob (Арсланбоб)

Alexander the Great is said to have planted the walnut forests for which this mountain resort three hours north-east of Andizhan in Kyrgyzstan's Fergana range, is famous. From May to September it throngs with Andizhanis on cures and walnut-gathering expeditions. The vertiginous waterfall an hour's breathless walk above the *turbaza* is also a place of pilgrimage. The mountains around are generally gazed at, not explored, and would make wonderfully lonely trekking country.

Buses come here in the summer season from Andizhan and Dzhalalabad. It should be possible to hitch year-round. Besides the *turbaza* 2km above the town at the roadhead there is a hotel signposted from the central crossroads by the bazaar. The local honey is exquisite—not unlike Golden Syrup. One place to buy it is 5km below the town on the main road near *Pensianat Gumkhana*. Ask for *myod*. Kzyl Unkur, at the head of the valley off which you branch to get to Arslanbob, is also a recognized resort but less visited and some say more beautiful than Arslanbob.

Dzhalalabad (Джалалабад)

This is one of the more civilized staging posts on the epic 1870-km M41 Bishkek–Dushanbe highway via the Tian Shan and Pamir ranges. Just inside the Kyrgyz border at the eastern end of the Fergana valley, Dzhalalabad (population 60,000) is a very arduous day's drive from Bishkek or an easy bus ride from Osh. It used to be a place of pilgimage, but in the Soviet era Muslims were encouraged to make their obeisance to the cult of human health instead, at a spa (*kurort*) atop a parched hill sparsely covered with pistachio trees 5km north of the centre and 980m above sea level. Mud-baths for nervous, digestive, renal, dermatological and gynaecological disorders are by special arrangement only, but the warm spring water in the pavilion (*open 6.30–8am, 10.30am–1pm, 4–6.30pm*) is free, the breeze blissful and the general ambience pleasantly surreal.

Getting to and from Dzhalalabad

by air

There are up to five planes a day to Bishkek and four a week to Cholpan-Ata, but none to or from Uzbekistan. The city Aeroflot office (*open 8 am–12pm and 1–5 pm*) is 3 minutes' walk north of the bus station and across the street at Ulitsa Lenina 180.

by rail

Trains go daily to Tashkent and less frequently to Bishkek, Moscow, Dushanbe and Tomsk—all via the Fergana valley; there is no railway over the mountains. The station is near the hotel at Ulitsas Toktogula and Vokzala.

by bus

Buses from Osh arrive, three per hour, at the *avtovokzal* (bus station) at the end of Ulitsa Lenina. For Arslanbob take a Burgendu bus (departures roughly every hour) and change at Bazar Korgon. For Sary-Chelek take the afternoon bus to Karavan. For Bishkek go to Toktogul (two departures each morning), and change there.

Getting Around

To reach the hotel from the *avtovokzal*, take any local bus marked *bazar*. *Marshrutnoe* taxi 138, which is actually a bus, also runs to the bazaar, continuing on to the spa.

Dzhalalabad (℡ 33231–) **Where to Stay and Eating Out**

The **Hotel Dzhalalabad** at the foot of the hill, on Ulitsa Lenina, ℡ 3 21 31, is run with rare pride and efficiency, takes rubles only, and has a groaning buffet open from 7am till late.

For dinner try the **Kosmos** restaurant two blocks west and one south on Krasnaya Armeyskaya Ulitsa, with a rocket in front and cosmic interior décor. The food and management are Russian and feel downright sophisticated after a few days in a *turbaza*. You may be able to stay in a bungalow at the spa, even if you are fit.

Osh (Ош)

Eighty minutes south of Dzhalalabad by bus and 35km from Andizhan, Osh spills down a valley and round the base of a sacred hummock in the brown and alarmingly seismic foothills of the Pamir Alai. This is Kyrgyzstan's second city (population 200,000), and the oldest in the Fergana valley; at 2500 years, it is as old as Samarkand. Not a single ancient building survives as evidence, but that is no reason not to come here. Osh is also the gateway to the CIS's highest mountains. The road over the 'Roof of the World' to Khorog—technically the Tajik section of the M41—starts here, and off it branches the even more rugged route to Karamyk under Pik Kommunisma. Expeditions fly into Osh to catch trucks and helicopters to the permanent base camps of the High Pamirs, and sometimes they don't come back. History's worst mountaineering accident happened on 18 July 1990 when an avalanche swept down the north face of Pik Lenina and killed 43 climbers in their tents.

There is no memorial to the 200 people who died in six weeks of street fighting in Osh in June and July 1990; nothing to remind you of the state of emergency imposed to keep Uzbeks and Kyrgyz apart. If you raise the subject you are told it is history, then encouraged to drop it.

Since the 10th century pilgrims have visited **Suleiman Gora** the 'Throne of Suleiman', the craggy hill in the middle of the city where, according to unfounded legend, the Prophet once prayed. Many visitors are childless women who hope that by praying here they may conceive. In silhouette the hill is supposed to look like a pregnant woman lying on her back. The easiest way up is from beside a geodesic aluminium dome on Ulitsa Isanova. The **Museum of Local Studies** (**Краеведческий Музей** *closed Mon and Tues*), hewn out of rock at the far end of the hill, contains Kyrgyzstan's most absurd urban yurt.

The lively **bazaar** is situated on Alishernavaya Ulitsa, opposite the bus station.

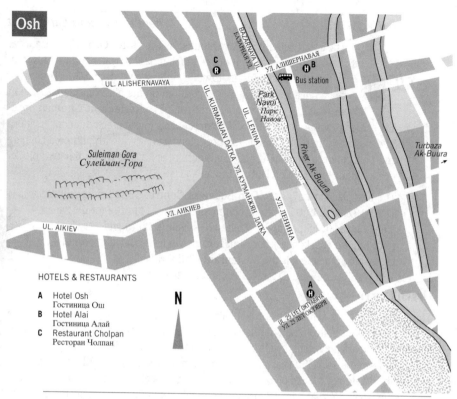

Osh

UL. ALISHERNAVAYA
БАЗАРНАЯ УЛ.
УЛ. АЛИШЕРНАВАЯ

C **R**

H **B**
Bus station

Park Navoi
Парк Навои

УЛ. КУРМАНЖАН ДАТКА
UL. KURMANJAN DATKA

UL. LENINA
УЛ. ЛЕНИНА

River Ak-Buura

Suleiman Gora
Сулейман-Гора

Turbaza Ak-Buura

УЛ. АЙКИЕВ

УЛ. ЛЕНИНА

UL. AIKIEV

HOTELS & RESTAURANTS

A   Hotel Osh
       Гостиница Ош
B   Hotel Alai
       Гостиница Алай
C   Restaurant Cholpan
       Ресторан Чолпан

N

A **H**

УЛ. 25 ЛЕТ ОКТЯБРЯ
UL. 25 LYET OKTYABRYA

Getting to and from Osh

by air

Flights from Bishkek are frequent (4–6 a day) and spectacular. You can also fly from Moscow, Almaty and Cholpan-Ata. Aeroflot has offices in the Hotel Osh and next to the Hotel Alai on Ulitsa Alishernavaya. You can also get them through the Osh Business Centre, Ulitsa Lenina, Building 331, room 113.

by bus

There are daily bus services to and from Tashkent (via Kokand and Fergana) and Toktogul (for Arslanbob, Sary-Chelek and Bishkek); hourly ones to Andizhan (for the nearest railway station); three a day to Uzgen; and three an hour to Dzhalal-abad. The main bus station is opposite the bazaar on Alishernavaya, five minutes' walk down the hill from the Hotel Alai. Andizhan departures are from a separate station north of the centre reached from opposite the main one by bus 6.

The smart hotel, used by Intourist, is the **Hotel Osh**, Ulitsa Isanova, ℗ 2 47 17 , which is not central but has hot water and the least raucous restaurant in town. Doubles cost from $30. Ten times cheaper (rubles only) and 200m up the hill from the bus station is the grimy, noisy **Hotel Alai**. The **Restaurant Cholpan** opposite serves good *laghman* and *beshbermak* but its music precludes conversation. The closest thing to nightlife is the opportunity to dance with plastered soldiers and policemen to skull-splitting Asian house music at the **Disco Bar** two blocks north of the Hotel Osh on Ulitsa Kurmanjan Datka.

The best place to stay is the **Osh Business Centre**, Ulitsa Lenina, Building 331, ℗ 27 187, ✉ 24 605. Here accommodation comes in the form of apartments for $10–15 per night. There are e-mail facilities and very helpful staff. English speakers ask for Almaz. Conveniently located opposite, and highly recommended, is the **Restaurant Chilnara**.

Uzgen (Узген)

Three mausolea and a minaret are all that remain of the 11th-century capital of the Karakhanid Turks, situated 55km northeast of Osh on the Kara Darya river. The **south mausoleum** (1186) has the most intricate decoration of the three, with incised terracotta plaques inside the *iwan* imitated 300 years later at Shah-i-Zinda in Samarkand. All three were pioneers of the ornate *pishtak* and of exterior decoration in general. The minaret, originally 40m high but now only 17, was a model for the Kalyan minaret in Bukhara. Today the mausolea and minaret are featured on the Kyrgyz 50 som note.

Uzgen is a typical Uzbek city located within Kyrgystan. The best value *karalpaks* are found in the bazaar here and Uzgen's pink rice makes the *plov* here a colourful experience.

Getting to and from Uzgen

Buses and *marshrutnoe* serving Uzgen from Osh leave all day from the old bus station; as soon as they're full, they go. Tickets cost around $1 and the journey takes 1–2 hours. Abulbek Tolonov at the Turbaza Ak-Buura can organize excursions here.

YAKS IN THE PAMIRS, TAJIKISTAN

If yetis exist, they exist in Tajikistan. Ever since a meteor smashed into the high Pamirs 10 million years ago and left a crater lake now known as Kara-Kul, Tajikistan has known better than to separate the natural and the supernatural. Nine tenths of this untamed frontiersland is mountain. Half of it, including nearly 10,000 square km of glacier, is over 3000m high, the domain of the yak, the eagle, the snow leopard and, mountain-dwellers solemnly attest, *snezhny chelovyek*—the abominable snowman. Some claim that a hirsute child of yeti-human parentage works as a street-sweeper down in Dushanbe, the capital.

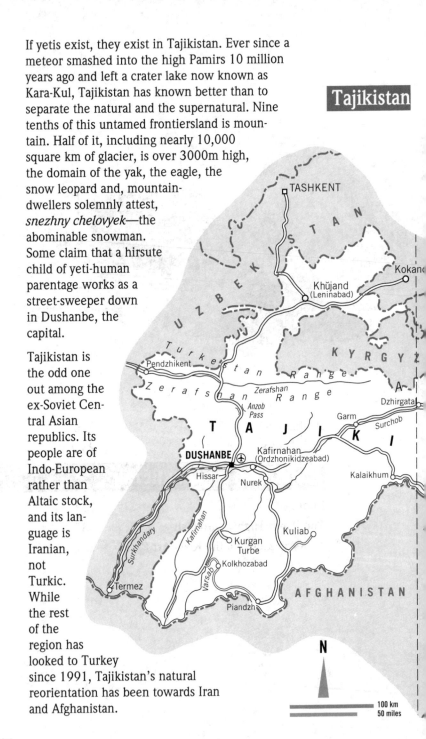

Tajikistan is the odd one out among the ex-Soviet Central Asian republics. Its people are of Indo-European rather than Altaic stock, and its language is Iranian, not Turkic. While the rest of the region has looked to Turkey since 1991, Tajikistan's natural reorientation has been towards Iran and Afghanistan.

It has also been torn by fighting. With the failure of Moscow's August 1991 coup in Moscow, the Tajik Communist leader, Kakhar Makhkamov, resigned. His successor was another Communist, Rakhman Nabiyev. Unlike his counterparts in the Turkic republics, he legalized an Islamic opposition party—and in September 1992 it ousted him in a coup. Since then there has been almost continuous fighting in the fertile valleys south of Dushanbe, boiling over intermittently into civil war. It is clan war, fuelled by religious fervour - stronger than any political party- and camouflaged by imported labels like 'nationalist' and 'democrat'. In February 1995 the first post-independence parliamentary elections gave a nominal victory to President Rakhmanov which was boycotted by his opponent, Abdullojonov. Uzbekistan, meanwhile, is determined not to be infected by the violence brought about by Tajik politics. In the past it has frequently and without notice closed its Tajik borders and cut off supplies of petrol. And vehicles bearing Tajik number plates have been refused entry. The UN-sponsored peace talks in Ashgabat, Turkmenistan, drifted inconclusively through early 1996.

So the bad news for travellers is that Tajikistan can be hard to get to. The good news is that the fighting is limited to certain regions: the Afghan Tajik border where the CIS forces are largely deployed and the Kurgan Turbe area; Garm and the eastern region of Gorno Badakhshan where Islamist guerillas and Pamiri activists are active. There have been occasional attacks on state buildings in Dushanbe by anti-government forces. The sudden action that brought the

225

rebels to outskirts of this city in February 1996 is a reminder of uneasy calm, rather than peace, enforced by mainly Russian CIS troops since the end of 1992. Northern Tajikistan however, has been familiar and safe territory to various trekking companies for many years.

Tajikistan consists of two different worlds. In the western one, where the fighting is contained, a fast-growing population of 5 million competes for space on the valley floors with hydro-electric dams and intensive cotton cultivation. The eastern one is Gorno-Badakhshan; vast, very high and scarcely populated. This is the Roof of the World, bordered by China to the east and Afghanistan to the south. Despite being linked to Osh and Dushanbe by the 750-mile (1200-km) Pamir Highway, it remains a virtually untracked wilderness, where Afghan smugglers can melt away after crossing the Pyandzh on inflated inner-tubes and intrepid visitors can realize the more innocent dream of the adventure of a lifetime.

Dushanbe (Душанбе)

Dushanbe is a clean, green European city three hours' drive from Afghanistan. Until 1991 its location beneath the snow-capped Hissar range in the wide valley of the Varsab river, a tributary of the Amu Darya, was its greatest asset. Now it has a refugee problem because of the fighting further south, and is all too easily cut off from Uzbekistan.

At the time of the 1917 revolution Dushanbe was a village called Dushiambe, known only for its Monday market (Dushiambe is Tajik for Monday). The revolution found no echo here, and Soviet power was not proclaimed until 1923. But in 1929 a circuitous branch line of the Transcaspian railway reached Dushiambe from the southwest, via Termez and the Surkhandaria valley, and put the place on the map.

Renamed Stalinabad, it was made the capital of the new Soviet republic of Tajikistan. Tens of thousands of Russians were resettled here before and during World War II, so that the city's population grew by a factor of 45 between 1926 and 1959. It is now 55 per cent Tajik, 23 per cent Uzbek and 11 per cent Russian, with significant German and Korean minorities. In 1961, as part of Khrushchev's de-Stalinization programme, its name was changed back to something like the original: Dushanbe.

The city served as a base for Brezhnev's 1979 invasion of Afghanistan, and since independence a big CIS (i.e. Russian) garrison has kept an uneasy peace on the streets. Iran has kept well clear of internal power struggles while quietly opening an embassy and book-shop, and funding a madrasa. The response of ordinary people to troubled times ranges from the set grimace of a Russian *babushka* queueing for rationed cheese, to the devil-may-care delight of the taxi-driver raking in inflated fares from foreign correspondents.

Dushanbe has a charming ethnographic museum and is one end of a spectacular plane ride to Khorog. In current circumstances, though, it doesn't warrant a trip by itself, since Osh (*see* p.220) provides an alternative gateway to the Pamirs.

Getting to and from Dushanbe

Public transport is almost non-existant. There are no regularly scheduled bus services or trains from Uzbekistan into Tajikistan. The most reliable mode is private and it is important to have all your visa paperwork arranged before you attempt to to cros the border. A useful organisation that has solid experience with Tajikistan transport is **Sam-Buh**, ✆ (3712) 63 75 85.

by air

Fuel permitting, there are four flights to and from Moscow each week, one to Almaty, Bishkek and Ashgabat. There are none to Tashkent. Tajikair and Khŭjand Airlines operate daily from Khŭjand.

Weather permitting, there may be one flight a day to Khorog, capital of Gorno-Badakhshan (45 minutes, around $50). The planes are 40-seater only and usually very full—book ahead if possible. They do not take off if there is any cloud in Khorog. You need permission from the Foreign Ministry to go there (*see* 'Tourist Information' below).

Air tickets are sold at the Intourist Service Bureau at the Hotel Tajikistan, ✆ 21 68 92.

by rail

There are departures every evening to Moscow via Volgograd (80 hours) and Tashkent via Samarkand (29 hours), and in the afternoon to Termez (11 hours). On even-numbered days a train goes to Ashgabat via Bukhara (35 hours). Incoming trains all arrive in the early morning, except the one from Tashkent (early afternoon). All journeys start or finish with a time-consuming detour to Termez and the Afghan border to avoid the mountains.

by road

Buses in Tajikistan are largely local services confined to operating within the republic. There is one daily connection with Samarkand. Services have been disrupted not only by the civil war but also because of the influx of Tajik refugees into Uzbekistan; to contain it, the Uzbekistan government has virtually closed the border.

Within Tajikistan buses, like the trains, defy unrest when humanly possible. Swashbuckling drivers take pride in taking risks, though Kuliab services were suspended in 1992 because the Vakhsh bridge at Nurek had been blown up. Buses go to Kurgan Turbe and on to Kolkhozabad and Piandzh as long as the road is open, though not necessarily to a strict timetable.

Khorog-bound **trucks** wait for fuel in front of the airport on the left hand side—sometimes for weeks. When they go, drivers expect to take paying passengers; open the bidding at $5 in Tajik rubles. If time is short and planes are grounded you may be able to get a truck quickly by paying for all its petrol on the black market. The driver will obtain it; the necessary 300 litres shouldn't cost you more than an air ticket. Non-stop, the journey to Khorog takes 14 hours.

Taxis congregate outside the Hotel Tajikistan. Negotiate with one to travel locally or to other towns in the republic. Bear in mind that they may not be able to take you across the border into Uzbekistan. At times, the Uzbek authorities refuse entry to vehicles with Tajik licence plates.

Getting Around

Most hotels, shops and government buildings are on or near Prospekt Rudaki (formerly Prospekt Lenina). The railway station is at the south end of this central artery, which has kinks at Ploshchad Lenina and Ploshchad Aini. Trolleybuses 2 and 10 and buses 1, 15 and 25 connect these streets. To get to the airport from the Hotel Tajikistan, take bus 9; from the bus station to the railway station, take bus 15.

Tourist Information

For visa stamps to places like **Khorog**, call the Ministry of Foreign Affairs, ✆ 39 86 23. For **permission to visit Gorno-Badakhshan** approach Takhir Akhmedov or Nazar Abdullov of the Ministry's Protocol Department, ✆ 22 76 78; go through the middle door of the pink building on the east side of Ploshchad Lenina. Latofat Zagurova of Intourist can help. She usually does so by enlisting a private tour firm called **Badakhshan**. It is run by a dapper Pamiri called Kara-Kul, who is friendly with the minister for Gorno-Badakhshan and whom Latofat Zagurova informally represents. **Firdaus Shukurov** is chairman of Dushanbe's Esperanto Club and can provide visa support and accommodation, ✆ 34 64 72/21 50 51.

A private outfit specializing in climbing and trekking in the northern Pamirs is **Alp-Navruz**, ✆ 24 53 73, at the Baza Alpinistov near Dushanbe's Institut Fizkultury on the east side of the city. Run by Vladimir Mashkov, ✆ 35 91 72, Alp-Navruz's trips all start from the upper Garm valley north east of Dushanbe. Special permission is not usually needed for this valley, which gives access to the CIS's highest mountain, the 7505-m giant that still, for the time being, rejoices in the name Pik Kommunisma. Treks in Northern Tajikistan which aim to combine the physical and the cerebral, can be arranged through a German organisation, **BISS**—Berliner Informations und Studienservice, Freiligrathstrasse 3, D-10967 Berlin, ✆ (4930) 693 6530, 🖷 694 1851.

Pakistan, Iran and China have embassies in the Hotel Tajikistan. There is an Israeli embassy nearby at Ulitsa Nasim Khikhmet 32. The American embassy on the 4th floor of the Hotel Oktyabrskaya is sometimes evacuated to Tashkent.

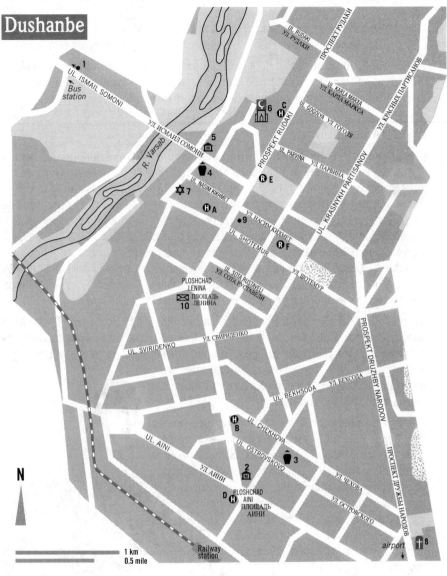

Dushanbe

KEY

1 Baza Alpinistov
   База Алпинистов
2 Tajikistan Unified Museum
   Объединённый Музей Таджикистана
3 Bazaar
   Базар
4 Bazaar
   Базар
5 Ethnographic Museum
   Этнографический Музей

6 Mosque and madrasa
   Мечеть и Медресе
7 Synagogue
   Синагога
8 Russian church
   Русская Церковь
9 Beryozka
   Берёзка
10 Post Office
   Почта

HOTELS & RESTAURANTS

A Hotel Tajikistan
   Гостиница Таджикистан
B Hotel Vakhsh
   Гостиница Вахш
C Hotel Oktyabrskaya
   Гостиница Октябрская
D Hotel Dushanbe
   Гостиница Душанбе
E Chai-khana Rohkat
   Чаи-хана Рохат
F Restaurant Vostochny Express
   Ресторан Восточный
   Экспресс

229

You can change money, buy stamps and post letters downstairs at the Hotel Tajikistan. Residents can make international phone calls with surprising ease.

The **Tajik ruble** was introduced in May 1995 at approximately 50 to the dollar but inflation struck and by October there were 300 to the dollar. Meanwhile, the Russian ruble remains acceptable currency in the provinces.

A Stroll Around Town

The **Tajikistan Unified Museum** (**Объединённый музей Таджикистана** /*Obyedinyony muzey Tajikistana—closed Mon*) on the north side of Ploshchad Aini has stuffed snow leopards and Marco Polo sheep on its ground floor; the closest most people get to seeing the real thing. Its prehistoric section on the first floor is short on artefacts but long on captioned etchings, one of which claims there was palaeolithic life at Kara-Tau, north of Kurgan Turbe, 200,000 years ago. The modern history section includes a mock-up of the Zindan gaol at Bukhara (*see* p.165). Most entertaining are the Soviet anti-capitalist cartoons on the first floor and the rare extant exhibition of breakneck Soviet-led industrialization on the second—though these exhibits may not last much longer.

There is a small **bazaar** a block north of Ploshchad Aini at its junction with Ulitsa Ostrovskovo, but the main one is on the south side of Ulitsa Ismail Somoni (formerly Putovskaya, now named after the great Samanid Khan of Bukhara who—Tajiks claim—was himself a Tajik, and whose name they spell with o's instead of a's). Walk three blocks north of Ploshchad Lenina, then west towards the river.

Continue over the bridge for the **Ethnographic Museum** (**Этнографичский музей**/*Etnograficheski muzey— open 10–6; closed Sun*), Ulitsa Ismail Somoni 14, on the north side of the street. It has fine collections of traditional (but not antique) clothes, jewellery, teapots and musical instruments, including a Swiss-looking Alpine horn. There is also a beautiful *chilim* for the smoking of intoxicating substances, and a hard-currency shop.

Dushanbe caters for all creeds. The principal **mosque** and adjoining, new, Iranian-funded **madrasa** are at Ulitsa Sholmoni 58, near the Hotel Oktyabrskaya and west of Prospekt Rudaki. The 100-

year-old **synagogue**, whose congregation has halved since emigration became easier two years ago, is in Ulitsa Nasim Khikhmet. From the Hotel Tajikistan turn right, right again at once and then first left.

There is a lovingly maintained **Russian church** half way to the airport on Prospekt Druzhba Narodov.

Dushanbe (℅ 3772–)   **Where to Stay**

expensive

The Intourist **Hotel Tajikistan**, Ulitsa Shotemur 22, two blocks north of Ploshchad Lenina, ℅ 27 51 27, is still operating despite the toll taken by the last few years civil war. The floor ladies have hearts of gold. There's even a laundry service and hot water. International phone calls can be booked at reception and made from your room. Singles cost $66 and double $81. Buses 3 and 9 come here from the airport. Trolleybus 1 comes from the railway station as does bus 15 which goes to the train station.

The **Hotel Oktyabrskaya**, Prospekt Rudaki 105a, ℅ 24 63 03, is discreet, expensive and used mostly by diplomats including the American Embassy. A single here is $78; a double $103.

inexpensive

The **Hotel Dushanbe,** Prospekt Rudaki 7, ℅ 23 36 60, is cheap (about $2 in rubles for a double) and within walking distance from the railway station. The quieter rooms are at the back. All are excellent value, with local phones, TV, fridges, baths and hot water most of the time. From the airport take trolleybus 2,3 or 4; from the bus station bus 15, trolleybus 8 or *marshrutnoe* taxi 15.

Two blocks up Prospekt Rudaki on the south side of Ploshchad Rudaki is the dingy **Hotel Vakhsh**, even cheaper than the Dushanbe and bewildered at the idea of putting up a foreigner.

Dushanbe (℅ 3772–)   **Eating Out**

For a fast Tajik lunch and good people-watching, join the throng at the famous, two-storey, concrete **Chai-khana Rokhat**, two stops north of Ploshchad Lenina by trolleybus 1, on the right hand side of Prospekt Rudaki. Tajik and Uzbek *laghman* seem to be identical.

The Hotel Oktyabrskaya's restaurant is hushed and rather grand. The men of the Iranian embassy eat here together every evening. The food is Russian, filling, dull. Under the Hotel Dushanbe there is a very basic café and a life-saving *shashlyk* grill. Service and food are bad at both the Hotel Tajikistan's restaurants. Its first-floor buffet is the best bet for breakfast.

Around Dushanbe

At Hissar, 30km west of Dushanbe, is the restored gateway of an 18th-century Bukharan fort destroyed in a rearguard action between the Basmakhi and the Red Army during the Civil War. Facing it are two plain madrasas of the same period which are unlikely to scintillate those who've already been to Samarkand. Buses go to Hissar from the main bus station. Intourist does half-day trips for $8 per person in a bus or $67 for three in a car. They also do half- and whole-day trips to the Varsab gorge in the Hissar mountains.

To get high quickly, contact Badakhshan (the firm) through Intourist, and ask to visit their boar-hunting base north of Dushanbe in the Hissar range.

The Pamirs (Памир)

The Pamirs are not just the Roof of the World, they are the hub of Asia. A blob-shaped mass of mountains from which radiate three tremendous natural frontiers: the Karakorams, the Hindu Kush and the Tian Shan, separating the Indian subcontinent, the steppes of old Russian Turkestan and the deserts of Xinjiang. Impossibly remote, always strategic, seldom visited, the Pamirs attract a special breed of explorer: Alexander the Great, Marco Polo and the great Great Game-player Francis Younghusband.

The jaggedest Pamir peaks are the northern ones. Pik Kommunisma (7505m) and Pik Lenina (7248m) seem to tower over Kyrgyzstan, from where they are most easily approached. Further east, towards the Chinese border, the mountains are smoother, the valleys higher, the air fiercely dry as well as thin. In the southwest the Afghan border is formed by the deep gash of the Piandzh river valley; in the southeast by the Vakhan corridor, established in 1895 to keep the British and Russian empires apart—in places less than 40km apart.

Less than one tenth of one per cent of Tajikistan's population live in the Pamirs—a mere 180,000 people. Most of them are Ismaili Muslims, speakers of an East Iranian language not unlike ancient Sogdian and followers of the Aga Khan like the people of Gilgit and Hunza in northern Pakistan. The Ismaili religion, which has no mosques or official clerics, was brought here in the 11th century by a mystic poet called Nasir-i Khosrov. It survived the Soviet era, in Alexandre Bennigsen's words, 'as a kind of secret society', but its followers now pride themselves on their openness, and want full independence.

A 1.5-million-hectare Pamir National Park is planned, to attract more foreign mountaineers and trekkers; numbers fell after 43 were killed by an avalanche that wiped out Pik Lenina's poorly sited base camp in 1990. The park will also protect wildlife. Gorno-Badakhshan has by far the world's largest population of wild Marco Polo sheep—an estimated 8000 adults. Their curly horns are up to 2m long and beloved of millionaire hunters, mostly from the USA and Germany, who pay $18,000 per trophy.

The Pamirs are not quite of this world. Their largest lake was created by a meteor. A smaller one was formed in 1911 by an earthquake which heaved a mountain into the path of the Murgab river. In the 1950s *Komsomolskaya Pravda*, the Communist youth newspaper, sponsored a series of expeditions to find and photograph the yetis they firmly believed existed here.

Khorog (Xopor)

The capital of Gorno-Badakhshan has a population of 20,000 and one main street. At the confluence of the Piandzh and Gunt rivers on the Afghan border, it is the closest thing to a major town on the Pamir Highway. The mountainsides are barren but apples, onions and potatoes are grown along the rivers. Poplars abound in the town, and the Gunt is deep and clear. But the best thing about Khorog is...

Getting There

by air

Aeroflot says the 45-minute flight from Dushanbe is the most difficult in the world, and pays its pilots danger money. The planes used are twin-jet Yak 40s, with 40 seats but sometimes more than 40 passengers. The descent into Khorog begins after clearing a snow-covered pass by a few hundred metres and swerving to avoid the north face of Pik Vudor, which at this point is approaching at 450 mph (700kmh). You then dive for the runway at the bottom of the Piandzh valley, swinging out at the last moment over Afghanistan, from where the *mujahedin* have been known to take potshots at incoming aircraft. Ask to sit in the cockpit and look out for pale green patches of heroin poppies on the Afghan side just before landing.

There used to be up to 15 flights a day, weather permitting. Fuel shortages mean there is currently one at most. By paying for your seat in dollars you stand a good chance of getting on. Planes don't leave Dushanbe when there is cloud at Khorog.

by road

The truck journey from Dushanbe is even more spectacular than coming by plane, and takes one long day or two more leisurely ones. In theory there are two options. One goes southeast from Dushanbe, following the Afghan–Tajik border from Kalaikhum, where truckers usually recommend spending the night. The River Piandzh forms the Afghan border and, at this point anyway, defences are *de trop*; reddish-brown water runs fast, deep and treacherous down the great cleft it has drilled for itself between the Pamirs and the Hindu Kush. Cross-border skir-mishes here between CIS frontier troops and Afghan supporters of Tajik rebel forces sometimes close the road and account for the numerous checkpoints along it. Southeast towards Rushan (178km further on) the gorge widens and the clear waters of the Bartang river meet the Piandzh. The Dushanbe–Khorog road is closed by snow from December to March. The alternative route starts in Osh, Kyrgyzstan, and is no less spectacular for being the safer of the two (*see* p.220)

Red Tape

You must have Khorog on your visa before you arrive. No amount of persuasion, articulate or otherwise, will get you one after you leave Dushanbe. Go to the Ministry of Foreign Affairs, ℂ (3772) 39 86 23, before you leave.

Getting Away

Weather permitting, planes from Dushanbe turn straight round and go back there. Fuel permitting, there are flights straight across the Pamirs to Murgab. To go there and on to Osh by road, hitch. There are no buses. The petrol shortage has reduced traffic on the trans-Pamir highway to a trickle, but Badakhshan may be able to help find a vehicle making the trip. The Khorog–Osh road is open year-round.

If you already have an Afghan visa you are, in theory anyway, allowed to cross the border at the Piandzh bridge 15km upstream of Khorog.

Getting Around

The airport is beside the Piandzh. The town is round the corner on the Gunt. Buses usually meet incoming planes, but if you have to walk turn right from the airport and keep going for about an hour.

Tourist Information

Badakhshan's Khorog office is at Ulitsa Lenina 7, ℂ 6086, on the second floor of the former Communist Party 'Abcomparti' building.

For permission to go **trekking**, contact Azorabek Lailibekov at Ulitsa Lenina 36, ℂ 5068—the big government building across the road behind Lenin. Lailibekov is an ex-hunter, now in charge of nature protection in the Pamirs and of planning the national park.

The United Nations' World Food Programme has an office further up the street on the same side (ℂ 4913), staffed by two former English teachers whose job is to deliver grain exclusively to Afghan Badakhshan even if Khorog is going hungry.

There is a quaint museum 500m down Ulitsa Lenina from Lenin's statue, on the left-hand (river) side. It has stuffed animals, relics from a 3rd-century BC fortress up the Piandzh beyond Ishkashim, and a wall of black-and-white photographs of Lenin.

Where to Stay and Eating Out

The only public hotel is the cheap, basic **Hotel Druzhba**, a block towards the river from Ulitsa Lenina at Ulitsa Aini 3. There is a government guest house with rooms overlooking the river behind the Abcomparti building (Ulitsa Lenina 7). Badakhshan can get you in here. However, it's more than likely that someone, with typical generosity, will invite you into their home. Try hard, without offending, to offer payment in return.

Opposite the post office at Ulitsa Lenina 45 there is a gloomy Soviet café with a much pleasanter *chai-khana* attached.

Near Khorog

The road which follows the Piandzh to the Vakhan corridor, rejoining the Pamir Highway half way to Murgab, is now open to foreigners. A left fork about 50km south of Khorog climbs to curative hot springs at **Garmchashma**. Ishkashim's ruined **Kaakhka fortress** is at Tajikistan's most southerly point, where the Piandzh swings away from Pakistan having come virtually within shouting distance. There is another ruined fort further up the road at Yamchun.

Trekking

Locally-recommended treks start not at Khorog but 60km north at Rushan, where the Bartang river meets the Piandzh. About 150km up the Bartang a track branches southeast to Lake Sareskoye, the one formed by the 1911 earthquake. The track continues south to Lake Yashyl-Kul, 3500m above sea level. Badakhshan has summer camps here and at Yul Masar, in the mountains to the north at 4000m.

The Pamir Highway to Osh

The first 60km up the Gunt valley from Khorog are some of the most beautiful on the Pamir highway. The harshness of the mountains is relieved by snow on their summits and terraced fields in the valley floor. Along the way there are many villages of one-storey adobe houses, adorned in autumn by tall, pointed haystacks on their flat roofs.

By the time you reach Dzilandi (3500m), a truck-stop 123km from Khorog, moonscape is already taking over. The terrain is bald. The nights are bitter.

Where to Stay

At Dzilandi, there is a very humble hotel and a dining-room which may not have any food. If so, walk back a short way to two amazing greenhouses which are superheated by a hot spring, and ask to buy some tomatoes. You can also bathe in the spring water here.

To Murgab

Between Dzilandi and Murgab there are two passes, Koitezek (4272m) and Naizatash (4137m), an army listening post and a lonely Kyrgyz settlement in a breathtakingly high plain grazed by yak. This is as close as the road gets to what Great Game-players called the Pamir Gap.

Just over the southern horizon, in 1891, Lieutenant Francis Younghusband was surprised in his tent by a party of cossacks and Russian officers claiming this romantic campsite for the czar. Younghusband entertained his rivals with a bottle of Kashgari wine, took dinner with them that evening, then high-tailed it back to Srinagar to report the hostile Russian presence on the Indian watershed.

It was the critical moment of the Game. Britannia rattled her sabre in London and St Petersburg. The czar backed down and four years later the Vakhan corridor was established as a buffer between the two empires.

Southwest of Murgab, 40km before you reach the town, is the Shakhty grotto, which contains some 15,000 year-old mesolithic cave paintings. **Murgab** itself is a new and desolate town, home to frontier troops, Kyrgyz herdsmen and a minority of Uighurs.

Lake Kara-Kul

The Akbaital pass north of Murgab is the highest in the CIS at 4655m. There follows a long descent beside a barbed-wire border fence to **Lake Kara-Kul**—at a mere 3915 m it is still too high for any aquatic life.

After accompanying what he called 'the last ride of the free Kyrgyz', Gustav Krist, an escaped Hungarian POW, spent a winter with them here during the Russian Civil War. With only the felts of a yurt to protect him from temperatures down to –60° C, he still spurned the offer of a Kyrgyz wife.

'One reason for my refusal,' he wrote, 'was that I was afraid of infection, for all the dwellers in Central Asia are riddled with venereal disease. Morover, the Qirghiz womenfolk hardly come up to our standards of either beauty or cleanliness. I often used to watch them sitting in the sun obligingly picking the lice out of each other's hair and popping them into their mouths with manifest enjoyment. This filled me with such uncontrollable disgust that I should gladly have banished them from my yurt even by day.'

Pik Lenina (7248m), visible beyond the lake from its south side, disappears from view as you enter Markansu. The name means Death Valley, and refers to the aridity and lack of oxygen, not the uranium deposits discovered nearby. This is the approach to the 4280-m Kizyl-Art pass and the Kyrgyz border.

Kyrgyzstan is instantly greener than Tajikistan. As you swoop down into the valley of the Kizyl-Su, the white rampart of the High Pamirs is behind you and the lower, craggier Alai range is ahead. Up the valley, 100km to the west, is **Daraut Kurgan**, a possible location of the Stone Tower mentioned in the writings of both Pliny and Ptolemy, where Chinese and Persian Silk Route traders met, exchanged goods and headed home.

Daraut Kurgan is the last major settlement before Pik Kommunisma's international mountaineering camp at Ashik Tash. The road there leaves the Pamir highway at Sary Tash, which is six tortuous hours from Osh.

Non-stop, the journey from Khorog to Osh takes 18 hours.

A rough track that leads north from Daraut Kurgan to Fergana once served as a caravan route between Eastern Bukhara and the Khanate of Kokand. But then, in the years before the Russian Revolution, caravans began to go astray—or so Gustav Krist relates, demonstrating once again a healthy and uncritical appetite for the grotesque.

Tarantula Schnapps

While traversing these wild mountains himself, Krist sheltered for a night in a forester's hut. The hut, according to its owner, stood on the site of an old caravanserai that had been taken by the Bolsheviks only after bitter fighting. When it fell, its keeper boasted before a revolutionary tribunal of having killed 411 men:

'His procedure was ingenious,' wrote the credulous Krist. 'He entertained the newly arrived guests with drink, including always tarantula schnapps. When they were thoroughly drunk on this poisoned liqueur he threw them into the cellar to feed his bear. He used to keep the bear for weeks without other food till it was reconciled to human flesh.'

'After this gruesome confession, a detachment of the Red Army was sent back into the mountains and—sure enough—under the ruins of the bombarded caravanserai they found the cellar with a great savage bear and the bones of hundreds of its victims covering the floor in thick layers.'

Tarantula schnapps, the forester told Krist, 'had been known and used in Turkestan from time immemorial. If you want to brew it you catch a number of the poisonous spiders, put them in a glass, and throw in some scraps of dried apples or apricots. The furious brutes fling themselves on the food and bite into it. They thus inject their poison into the dry fruit, which you then mix with fermented grapes. Thirty or forty tarantulas make about a quart of the deadly brew. A tiny glass of this liqueur is enough to drive a man insane. Half an hour after he has drunk it the victim is so paralysed that he cannot move; an hour later he is raving mad.'

'The caretaker of the caravanserai used to dope his guests with this tarantula schnapps, and as soon as paralysis set in he threw them to the bear, who did the rest. The Russians condemned the man to death, but in the night the Sarts [local Uzbeks or Tajiks] broke into the prison and fetched him out into the desert. They tied him with ropes to the saddles of two swift camels [and] stuffed pepper in their behinds so that the infuriated animals dashed out into the desert dragging the body of the hundredfold murderer after them. A few days later his skeleton was found, picked clean by the vultures.'

KYRGYZ
WEDDING PARTY

Kyrgyzstan Кыргызстан

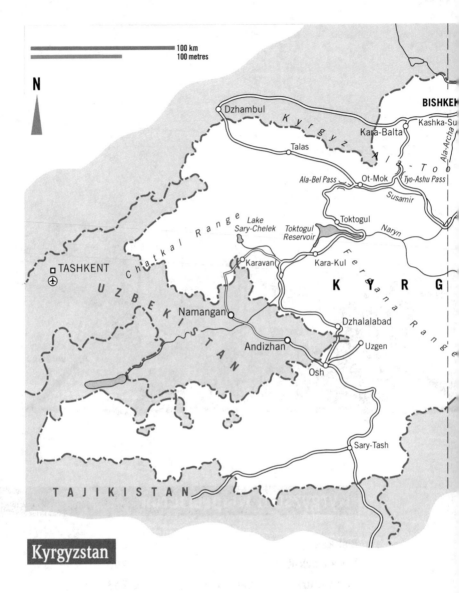

Kyrgyzstan

*The wondrous beauty of nature and the knowledge
that my journey was taking me into the fastnesses
of the mountains, far from Communist experiments,
brought a profound peace to my soul.*

Paul Nazaroff, 1919

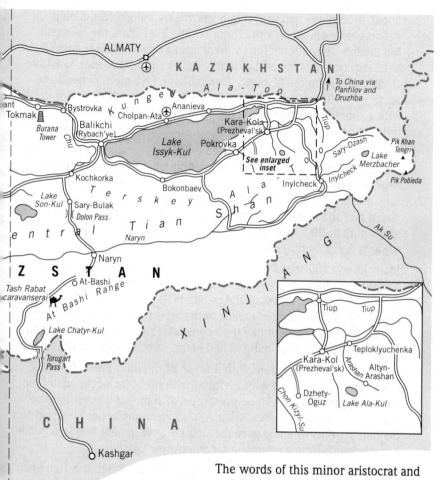

The words of this minor aristocrat and counter-revolutionary, written after fleeing from the Bolsheviks into Kyrgyzstan, hold good today. Nearly 75 years on, nature here still has a wondrous beauty. A sense of escaping the bleak mess left by Communist experiments still brings peace to the soul—or wild exhilaration, depending on your disposition. Kyrgyzstan is a mountain paradise surrounded by deserts, and the homeland of nomads whom Soviet power never quite tamed. It is also a friendly, open country that actually seems to be enjoying independence. Not to put too fine a point on it, Kyrgyzstan is a revelation.

Between the Kazakh steppe and the Tarim basin, the earth's crust has been pushed up in giant waves that catch the scarce moisture of the upper atmosphere and turn it into snowfields and glaciers, mountain streams and rich, green alps. These are the Tian Shan, the Heavenly Mountains. They stretch for 1500km from Kazakhstan deep into China, but Kyrgyzstan has the best of them. Their central knot rises to 7439m at Pik Pobieda (to the Chinese, Tomur Shan). Five more ranges have peaks over 4000m, and two of them flank Lake Issyk-Kul, an inland sea with a shoreline so long and serene that even abundant concrete sanatoria cannot spoil it.

The Tian Shan's wildest valleys used to be out of bounds even to Kyrgyz citizens, falling within a 100-km wide frontier zone alongside China. Now they are open, and you are free to explore some unspeakably romantic territory; to walk through juniper and walnut forests to a glacial lake that vanishes in summer, to climb a marble mountain that glows pink in the evening, or ride out from a medieval *caravanserai* towards Asia's continental divide.

Many Kyrgyz still spend the summer in remote yurt encampments, tending vast flocks of sheep and breeding horses for transport, milk and meat. Gustav Krist, an escaped Austrian POW, met some of their ancestors in 1918. They hunted gazelle with eagles trained to go for the eyes, and struck him as 'not unlike their own yaks, sinister and terrifying to look at, but just as good-natured and harmless on nearer acquaintance.'

Now, as then, Kyrgyz men with a sense of tradition wear the *ak-kalpak*, a distinguished white felt hat with black (or occasionally red) trimmings and tassels. To be presented with one as a guest is to be highly honoured. President Askar Akayev went one better on a visit to Beijing in 1992, when he gave the Chinese government two semi-wild snow leopards from a mountain sanctuary near Osh.

The Kyrgyz have not, as some brochures claim, inhabited the Tian Shan for 2000 years. They originally came from the headwaters of the River Yenisey, between Lake Baikal and the Altai mountains in southern Siberia. Until the 9th century, pure-blooded Yeniseyan Kyrgyz people were, according to a contemporary Chinese account, fair-skinned, green-eyed and red-haired. The gene pool has been stirred considerably since then. Mongols overran the Yeniseyan lands in the 10th century. They seem to have cohabited peacefully with the Kyrgyz until the mid-13th, when Kyrgyz warriors then began to harry the northern fringe of Genghis Khan's declining empire. In 1293 Genghis's great grandson Kublai Khan responded by driving them away, forcing an epic eastward migration to Manchuria and the Pacific coast. But some Kyrgyz escaped westwards, eventually reaching the Tian Shan in the late 16th century. It was the only place left to them; the quintessential mountain refuge.

The Kyrgyz lived here unmolested for 300 years, until the Russians came. Growing pressure from Russian and Ukrainian settlers, who planted wheat, beet and potatoes on the lushest pastures of the Chu valley, drove the Kyrgyz to rebellion in 1916. The traumas of collectivization and political purge hit Kyrgyzstan along with the rest of the Soviet Union in the 1930s—but that of industrialization did not. There are factories along the edge of the steppe and power stations on the lower reaches of the River Naryn, but the mountains and high pastures (*dzhayloo*) have been spared.

Kyrgyzstan is the place that many dared not hope existed; one that has emerged from the Soviet era still recognizable in the rose-tinted descriptions penned just as that era was beginning. Its different ethnic groups (50 per cent Kyrgyz, 30 per cent Russian, with Uzbek, Uighur, Ukrainian, German, and Korean minorities) seem, after a month of bloody rioting in Osh in 1990, to have chosen to live and let live. President Akayev, a physicist who never held a Communist Party post, outlawed the Party in August 1991. His own position looks rather more secure. Victorious in the December 1995 elections he should remain in office until 2001. Under Akayev, the Kyrgyz press, once among the most conservative in the Soviet Union, is now one of the most outspoken in the CIS. But the economy is in a hole. The government has pinned its hopes on drastic market-oriented reform and so have numerous international organizations that have pledged financial assistance. But the country's mountainous topography and lack of natural resources make the transition slow and painful. Compounding this is the same problem that besets other republics: the emigration of ethnic Russians and their vital expertise. The country's main export is hydro-electricity, its most promoted business, foreign tourism. One can only hope that what Stalin left relatively untouched, economic drive and an influx of tourists will at least respect.

Bishkek (Бишкек)

The Kyrgyz capital is the likeable younger brother of the Kazakh one. A cool, tidy, Soviet-built city 806m above sea-level at the foot of the Tian Shan, Bishkek has all the natural advantages of Almaty without the smog or the hustle. The permanent snows of the Kyrgyz Ala-Too range are almost as close as they look, 40km from the southern outskirts and four vertical kilometres higher. Meltwater rushes down the canalized Ala-Archa river into town, where a network of aryks sends it gurgling along the streets to feed the trees which are said to provide 100 sq m of shade for each of the 670,000 inhabitants.

In fact the trees and buildings often obscure the view of the mountains, which are best seen from the footbridge over the railway tracks to the left of the station. The fine-looking soldier on a horse among the trees in front of the station is the Bolshevik general Mikhail Frunze, who gave his name to the city during the Soviet era.

Bishkek is young—built almost entirely since World War II—and mellow; rather than fret about the endless petrol shortage, people walk to work and enthuse about the air. When the heat and hassle of Uzbekistan's oases get too much, this is the place to come.

History

The Khan of Kokand built a clay fort here as part of his defensive northern frontier in 1825, and called it Pishpek. Russians destroyed it in 1862 and founded a city on the site in 1878. White settlers followed the soldiers, lured by grants and free parcels of land. Judging by Stephen Graham's highly subjective 1916 account, they prospered:

'The Russians seemed thriving and everyone seemed to have plenty of horses and cattle. In this country, where wishes are horses, even the hawker of bootlaces in the bazaar has his nag tied to a poplar tree near by.'

There was also a municipal ambulance towed by a camel.

Pishpek, known briefly as Bishkek after the Soviet takeover, was re-named Frunze in 1926, and reverted to Bishkek in 1991.

Getting to and from Bishkek

by air

In the spring of 1993, Kyrgyzstan ran out of money for aviation fuel and the airport closed. When operative, Kyrgyzstan Airlines is the only carrier and provides four flights a week to and from Moscow ($198/$400 rtn) and two to Tashkent, one in conjunction with Uzbek Airways ($92) and the other with Kyrgyz Airways ($100). There are no regular scheduled flights to Almaty, but up to seven flights per day to Osh ($70). Ticket prices, including those quoted above, are subject to 5% tax and a $3 charge per ticket. Tickets are sold at the old airport building on Prospekt Mira 95, and at a new Kyrgyz Airways office, centrally located at Soviet-skaya Ulitsa 105, ✆ 42 29 22 (*open daily 8am–noon 1–7pm*). Tickets for Almaty can be bought no more than 15 days before flying (for Osh, 3 days beforehand).

If the airport closes, the nearest alternative is at Almaty, four–five hours away by bus. This also used to be the closest option for international flights. But from spring 1996 Turkish Airways will add Bishkek to its Central Asian itinerary. At present there's a company called Neufeld Reisen, Ulitsa Bokonbaeva 199/81, ✆ 24 83 64, or, in Germany, ✆ (052) 612 271, which operates a Kyrgyzstan Airways charter to Hannover, Germany, every Wednesday. For the airport information desk call ✆ 25 07 47, and for international flights, ✆ 42 29 22.

Check-in at Manas airport, Bishkek, is completed forty minutes before take-off. Arrive one and a half to two hours beforehand. Foreigners have to check in at the three-storey *mezhdunarodnoe* building, not at the main airport building. If coming by bus, get off at the penultimate stop of the same name; or walk 500m back from the main airport.

by bus

Departures to Almaty are almost hourly (the fare is $5). Journey time is about 5 hours unless you catch the scenic option which stops at almost every town *en route*. Four buses a day go to Tashkent ($10) and take 11 hours. Older, slower machines go up to 18 times a day to Kara-Kol (formerly Przheva'lsk) at the far end of Lake Issyk-Kul (journey time, 9 hours), via Balikchi (4 hours). Kara-Kol buses usually take the spine-shattering south shore road round the lake. To take the longer, smoother northern one, change at Balikchi. On any bus, be prepared to pay extra for each piece of luggage you bring.

There are no longer state buses to Naryn. Go instead to the west bus station and take a private one, which will take 4–6 hours. A *marshrutnoe* leaves daily at 7.15am to make the 9-hour journey to Toktogul, from where there are onward buses to Dzhalalabad and Osh. Tickets for the Toktogul transport often sell out three days in advance. There is also a bus to Talas, which takes 8 hours.

All these buses use the west (*zapadniy*) or long-distance bus station. It has some of the cleanest public toilets in Central Asia and a snooker table for those who tire of bus spotting. Tickets for night buses are purchased from the driver. The east (*vostochniy*) station has short-haul departures only, to Kant and Tokmak in the Chu valley and to Issyk-Ata, a spa in the foothills of the Kyrgyz Ala-Too. There are no buses from here to Ala-Archa. Instead these leave from the Osh bazaar.

Marshrutnoe minibuses also make the trip to Kara-Kol and take six hours. Catch them from the other side of the road at the long distance bus station.

Commercial buses wait in the car park of the west station. The usual rules apply. A more reliable alternative is the Kyrgyz Concept bus company, offering a choice of vehicle (anything from a Lada to a mini-bus). This option is better value than a taxi, particularly if you take advantage of their discount arrangements at certain hotels, including the Dostuk, Bishkek Business Centre and The Pynara. They also offer airport collection and visa provision. The hardest part is finding their office at Ulitsa Razzakova 100, ✆ 21 05 56/21 06 22/26 58 22, 🖷62 07 46/21 05 54. Approach a block that looks more like residential flats than an office and go down the steps to basement level. After 7pm, you can call the manager, Ainura Sydykova, at home, ✆ 21 00 02. She speaks excellent English.

by rail

There is a train to and from Moscow every day, joining the main Syr Darya line near Chimkent and taking the best part of three days. Three days a week there are services to Dzhalalabad via Tashkent, to Novokuznetsk and Sverdlovsk on even dates and daily to Balykchy. If the airport is closed all these tend to be very full. In the station's ticket hall, the old Soviet emblem is prominently displayed encircled by traditional Kyrgyz design; it's the centrepiece of the painted ceiling and quite a surprise. For the new emblem of independent Kyrgyzstan, go to the Hotel Ala-Too and buy a sticker in the foyer shop.

In summer, holiday specials go up Kyrgyzstan's only internal line to Balikchi (formerly Rybach'ye) at the west end of Lake Issyk-Kul.

Trolleybus 48 links the railway station to the west bus station.

by jeep

This is the only foolproof way of getting to the Chinese border at Torugart. Note that the Torugart Pass is open only from May to September. Transport can be arranged through Dostuk Trekking or Tian Shan Travel (*see* p.250). A cheaper but unreliable option would be to take a (private) bus to Naryn and then hitch. For details on the border itself, *see* pp.7–8 and 343–4.

Getting Around

The city's axis is Prospekt Erkindik (form erly Prospekt Dzherzhinskovo), with the railway station and the Hotel Ala-Too at its south end, Lenin and parliament near its north end, and gardens between its carriageways. The way to get from one end to the other is to stroll. Sovietskaya Ulitsa, parallel and two blocks east, is the commercial centre of Kyrgyzstan. Bishkek's east–west artery is Prospekt Chu (formerly Leninsky Prospekt) and Ulitsa Kievskaya, one block south, with Osh bazaar at its west end.

The long-distance bus station is north of the centre on Ulitsa Zhibek Zholu (formerly Ulitsa 50 Lyet KSSR), linked to the Hotel Ala-Too and the railway station via the bazaar by bus 48, to Ulitsa Sovietskaya by bus 35 and to Prospekt Chu by bus 7. The east station is at the opposite end of Zhibek Zholu, reached from the centre by trolleybus 1. Buses cost around 10 cents in som; pay the driver as you get off.

Manas airport is down on the plain, 20km north of the city. Bus 153 goes to the airport and picks up from the bus stop at the Manas sculpture near the Philharmonic Building on Prospekt Chu. It can take up to an hour. A quicker alternative is the *marshrutnoe* (30 minutes), the first of which passes the Philharmonic stop at 5.30am. Other *marshrutnoe* minibuses shuttle to and from the long distance bus station.

For taxi rides within the city, fix the fare in advance, opening the bidding at $1 in som. Women are advised not to travel around the city on their own at night.

Bishkek

Airport and
← long-distance bus station
УЛ. ZHIBEK ZHOLU

УЛ. ЖИБЕК ЖОЛУ

East bus
station →

UL. FRUNZE   УЛ. ФРУНЗЕ

UL. IVANITSINA   УЛ. ИВАНИЩИНА

UL. FRUNZE   УЛ. ФРУНЗЕ

UL. ABDUMAMUNOVA   УЛ. АБДУМАМУНОВА

PLOSHCHAD
ALA-TOO

ПЛОЩАДЬ
АЛА-ТУ   UL. PUSHKINA   УЛ. ПУШКИНА

PROSPEKT CHU

ПРОСПЕКТ ЧУ

Osh bazaar

KIEVSKAYA UL.

КИЕВСКАЯ УЛ.

UL. TOGOLOKA MOLDO

UL. OROZBEKOVA

TOKTOGULA   УЛ. ТОКТОГУЛА

MOSKOVSKAYA UL.

UL. ENGELSA   УЛ. ЕНГЕЛСА

UL. PANFILOVA

PIERVOMAYSKAYA UL.

PROSPEKT ERKINDIK   ПРОСПЕКТ ЭРКИНДИК

UL. BOKONBAEVA   УЛ. БОКОНБАЕВА

MOSKOVSKAYA УЛ.   МОСКОВСКАЯ УЛ.

UL. BELINSKOVO

UL. 40 LET OKTYABRYA

UL. LOGVINENKO

KRASNOOKTYABRSKAYA UL.

SOVIETSKAYA UL.

SHOLKOVA

UL. PRAVDY

Railway station

UL. LVA TOLSTOVO   УЛ. ЛЬВА ТОЛСТОГО

UL. GORKOVO   УЛ. ГОРЬКОГО   LINEA

UL. VOSTMAADGSEDAU

HOTELS

	History Museum	**8**	Tsum Store
	Музей Истории		Цум
	Frunze Museum	**9**	Dubovy Park
	Музей Фрунзе		Дубовый Парк
	Fine Art Museum	**10**	Panfilov Park
	Музей Искусств		Парк Панфилова
	Circus	**11**	Philharmonic Building
	Цирк		Филармония
	Post Office	**12**	Zoology Museum
	Почта		Зоологический Музей
	Telephone and Telegraph office	**13**	Jyrgal Baths
	Телефон и Телеграф		Баня Жыргал
	Dostuk Trekking		
	Достук Треккинг		

A Hotel Ala-Too
Гостиница Ала-Ту

B Hotel Bishkek
Гостиница Бишкек

C Hotel Kyrgyzstan
Гостиница Кыргызстан

D Hotel Ak-Sai
Гостиница Ак-Сай

E Business School Hotel
Гостиница Колледжа
Бизнеса

F Dostuk Hotel
Гостиница Достук

G Uighur Hotel
Гостиница Уйгурская

RESTAURANTS

H Restaurant Son-Kul
Ресторан Сон-Куль

I Restaurant Naryn
Ресторан Нарын

J Mi-Na Restaurant
Ресторан Ми-На

K Sary-Chelek
Сары-Челек

L Automatic
Автоматик

M Belasugin Restaurant
Ресторан Беласугин

N Phoenix
Ресторан Фунукс

O Nooruz
Ресторан Нооруз

City maps are sold at bookshops throughout the city, for instance on the corner of Prospekt Erkindik and Kievskaya Ulitsa, and in the foyer shops of the main hotels. Additionally, in the Hotel Ala-Too, ✆ 22 56 43, through the entrance hall and along the corridor to the right of the stairs, is the **Intourist service bureau** (*open Mon–Fri, 9–5*). Cholpon, the helpful, English-speaking assistant, can arrange city tours for $10 for individuals or $5 per person in a group; and group excursions to the Ala-Archa gorge ($15 per person for a 6-hour tour), Burana tower ($10 per person for a 5-hour trip; *see* p.252), Lake Issyk-Kul ($50 per person for a 12-hour tour) and the Torugart Pass. They can also make reservations at the Hotel Aurora in Kara-Kol.

The Dostuk Hotel's **Business Centre** (2nd floor), hires out cars and drivers for $4–5 per hour in town, and translators for $7 per hour. Trips from Bishkek to Almaty cost $99, to Manas airport, $15, and to Lake Issyk-Kul, $110.

A map of the **city bus routes** can be bought from the small sales counter in the foyer of the foreign ministry building, Ulitsa Kirova 205. Dostuk Trekking is a good source for large-scale topographical **maps** for walking and climbing. And the formerly top-secret State Geodetic and Cartographic Agency, Kievskaya Ulitsa 107, provides detailed Russian maps. Whether or not you purchase anything, it's worth going to the agency for an interesting browse.

The main **post and telephone** offices are on Sovietskaya Ulitsa, on the block between Prospekt Chu and Kievskaya Ulitsa. The post office closes at 4pm. Local phone calls cost a few cents in the form of a one som token purchased from kiosks. **E-mail** can be sent or received via Dostuk Trekking for a small fee, and from a more central location, El Cat, Piervomayskaya 54, near the junction with Ulitsa Toktogula, ✆ 22 75 85.

City visas for travel within Kyrgyzstan are no longer strictly necessary as long as you have one for Bishkek, but many hotels and police don't know this. For their benefit, OVIR (**ОВИР**) will happily write your itinerary onto your visa form. Their office is in the Interior Ministry building on the south side of Kievskaya Ulitsa, half a block east of Sovietskaya Ulitsa and opposite the post office. Through the left door go up half a flight of stairs and turn right. *See also* **Travel**, 'Entry Formalities', pp.10–16. There are, however, still a few places that you must have permission to visit: Inylchek and the Pamir region. And if you want to stay in the Karakol area, you should pay a tourist tax. Three days cost $8, longer $15. For 'permissions' go to OVIR. For tourist tax, the Ministry of Tourism on Ulitsa Frunze and Ulitsa Togoloka Moldo.

Official **interpreters**, who can also work as general fixers for business people and journalists, can be hired at $8 an hour from their office on the third floor of the Hotel Ala-Too and from Kyrgyz Concept, ✆ 22 23 68. The latter can also sell Kyrgyz invitations for $10 each.

A monthly magazine, published by the **Aksent Information Agency**, contains the most up-to-date information on life in Kyrgyzstan from politics to culture. The same company also publishes a weekly digest of the Kyrgyz national press. For these go to Kievskaya Ulitsa 96a, ✆ 22 16 04. The office is on the seventh floor, room 728 and not easy to find: arriving from Prospekt Chu, enter the Ministry of Agriculture building on the left-hand side. On the seventh floor, turn left from the lift, left along the corridorand proceed to room 728 but beware, the doors are not numbered consecutively.

Exchange booths are numerous and easy to find both on the street and in hotels. Rates improve throughout the day and, not surprisingly, the best ones come from the street booths. Of these your budget bargain is on the corner of Prospekt Chu and Sovietskaya Ulitsa. Stand with Prospekt Erkindik to your left and the post office on Sovietskaya, to your right. Up a few stairs adjacent to the wall is a small window. There's credit card **cash withdrawal** at the Orient Bank (commission 6%), Moskovskaya Ulitsa 161, and the Union Bank (7% commission), Ulitsa 40 Lyet Oktyabrya (*open 8.30–12 noon*), but here you must wait 20–30 minutes while a call is made to Almaty's Alem Bank. At the Bank of Kyrgyzstan, Ulitsa Molodaya Gvardiya 27, travellers' cheques can be cashed into som at 2% fee. If you want to transfer funds, the lowest fee is charged by the commercial bank Kyrgyz Kramnsbank, Ulitsa Lermontova 35. Or if you require a safe for valuables go to the Kurulush Bank, Ulitsa Berlinskovo and Ulitsa Toktogula. The cost of a safe is from 10 cents to just over a dollar per night.

Embassies

China: Ulitsa Toktogula 196, ✆ 22 24 23. Visas are issued here for travel to China. But only if you have an invitation from one of the two Chinese state travel companies. If you don't have one already go to Intourist, Hotel Ala-Too, with your passport and money to pay for a telex. Kyrgyzintourist will contact the CITS firm in China and pass on your travel details. Take the return telex from CITS to the Chinese Embassy. The consular department is open Mon, Weds and Fri 9–11.30am, ✆ 21 67 62.

Travel to China is also possible through Dostuk Trekking and Tian Shan Travel. Kyrgyzintourist can provide transport to the Chinese border at the Torugart Pass and arrange for you to be met by CITS.

Germany: Piervomayskaya Ulitsa 28, ✆ 22 48 11, ✉ 22 85 23

India: Prospekt Chu 164, ✆ 21 09 77/21 08 75 (consular dept)

Kazakhstan: Ulitsa Togoloka Moldo 10, ✆ 22 54 63

Russia: Piervomayskaya Ulitsa 17, ✆ 22 16 91/26 17 62 (consular dept)

Turkey: Moskovskaya Ulitsa 89, ✆ 22 78 82

USA: Prospekt Erkindik 66, ✆ 22 27 77

Dostuk Trekking, Vosemnadsataya Ulitsa 42–1, not far south of the railway station, ✆ 42 74 71/41 91 29, ✉ 41 91 29, is a private travel company run by a geologist called Nikolai Shchetnikov, who has access to the State Geological Survey's under-used trucks, boats, guest-houses and helicopter pilots. He would love to plan your entire trip, but will also undertake specific commissions such as providing transport to Torugart, Tash Rabat or Inylchek. There's no sign on the building, but a Landrover in the courtyard provides a clue. The firm has its own base camp in the Central Tian Shan, and its own ski base 50km from Bishkek. There's a translator at the office who speaks English as does the guide called Shamil. Prices start around $50 a day per person including all necessary equipment. **Tian Shan Travel**, Ulitsa Panfilova 105, ✆/✉ 42 98 25, is the privatized climbing and winter sports branch of Intourist. It runs the old Soviet International Mountaineering Camp (IMC) in the Central Tian Shan, half an hour up the glacier from Dostuk Trekking's new one. The brochure lists numerous activities from treks to heli-skiing to horse riding. The English-speaking director, Vladimir Komissarov, is also the president of the Federation of Alpinism and Rock Climbing in Kyrgyzstan. **Genrih Cruise**, Ulitsa Lva Tolstovo 70a, ✆ 22 23 68, ✉ 22 55 18, offers various trips, including trekking, with prices that start at $80–100 per person per day. For a six-hour horseback trek that includes lunch and a *banya* by a glacial stream for $40 per person, call **Rafael Slaski**, ✆ 33 56 87 or 20 97 59.

History Museum

Open 10am–1pm and 2–6 pm; closed Mon; adm a few som.

Lenin still stands on his pedestal in former Ploshchad Ala Too because the government cannot afford to move or replace him. The white marble extravagance to his right is the government building. Behind him stands what used to be the Lenin Museum, but has become the **History Museum (музей Истории)**. The ground floor has taken on a Manas theme with a new display to the epic hero and early copies of the poem in various languages. All set in the context of traditional Kyrgyz costume, jewellery and weapons. The east wing of the first floor is used for temporary exhibitions. Most of the second floor is as it was pre-1991: a sumptuous shrine to Lenin and the revolution, finished in brass and mulberry-coloured marble at unimaginable cost. The plan is to turn the space over to Kyrgyz history as funds allow. This has already happened on the top floor where the display cases have been stripped and filled with local artifacts.

Frunze's House and Museum

Open 10am–6pm; closed Mon.

A block north of here on the corner of Ulitsas Frunze and Piervomayskaya, the **Frunze Museum (Дом-музей Фрунзе)** is less easily rearranged, since it is built over Frunze's house itself. The man who took Central Asia for the Bolsheviks was born in 1885 in the humble whitewashed cottage which now occupies most of the museum's ground floor. You can go inside, but only when the sullen woman in charge says so. A pupil of Lenin's in Moscow before the 1917 revolution, Mikhail Frunze was dispatched to Tashkent in an armoured train in 1919 to prevent a counter-revolution taking hold in the Uzbek khanates. He commanded the Red troops which drove the last khan from Khiva and the last emir from Bukhara, and gave his name to Bishkek in 1926. The top floor of the museum contains a hall of fame of Kyrgyz socialist hero workers, an exhibition on the city's contribution to Soviet victory in World War II, and another on Soviet space exploration.

Fine Art Museum (Музей изобразительных искусств/ *Muzey izobrazityelnikh isskustv; open 10am–6pm; closed Mon.*)

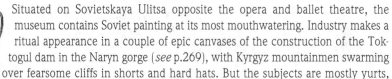

Situated on Sovietskaya Ulitsa opposite the opera and ballet theatre, the museum contains Soviet painting at its most mouthwatering. Industry makes a ritual appearance in a couple of epic canvases of the construction of the Toktogul dam in the Naryn gorge (*see* p.269), with Kyrgyz mountainmen swarming over fearsome cliffs in shorts and hard hats. But the subjects are mostly yurts, horses, rivers and mountain-shaped mountains with snowy summits and verdant flanks. There are also interesting collections of *glasnost* posters, Kyrgyz rugs, and, bizarrely, reproduction Egyptian and classical statues.

The **Opera and Ballet Theatre** (Театр оперы и балета), with its marble-tiled colonades and recent repaint, offers tickets for $1. It's worth a visit just to look at the decoration of the hall and the ceiling paintings, overseen by People's Artist, Gapar Aitiev. Information is posted outside the entrance as it is for the **Russian Drama Theatre,**Krasnooktyabrskaya Ulitsa 116 , the **Kyrgyz Theatre**, Ulitsa Panfilova 273, and **Circus**, on Frunze between Sholkova and Sovietskaya. For Kyrgyz music played on traditional instruments, spend an evening at the white marble **Philharmonic** building on Prospekt Chu and Ulitsa Belinskovo. Nearby, a sculpture commemorates the epic hero, Manas, slaying a dragon. Walk east from Prospekt Erkindik along Ulitsa Ivanitsyna, and you'll pass the **Wedding Palace**, on the left-hand side after the junction with Ulitsa Krasnooktyabrskaya. Anyone with wedding jitters or second thoughts will appreciate the long flight of steps to the entrance—there's plenty of time to change your mind on the way up. At the summit, follow the red carpet past the psychedelic stained-glass windows. Wedding kit is available from the basement shop. At the **Hippodome** on Termechikoava 1, horse races and games demonstrate the equestrian prowess of the Kyrgyz people. Or visit the animals at the **Zoology Museum** (*open 10–1, 2–5; closed Mon*), Ulitsa Pushkina 78.

Osh Bazaar

At the opposite end of town, a travelling circus from Osh sometimes performs in front of **Osh Bazaar** on Kievskaya Ulitsa, where the spices are as exotic and the meat stalls as grotesque as in any of Uzbekistan's more famous bazaars. A now permanent adjunct to this one is an acre or so of kiosks selling shoddy Chinese shoes and electronics.

Manas Village

1995 marked the Manas millenium and the opening of the Krygyz Aiyl by Pdt Akayev in the presence of guests from all over the world. This complex, close to the Issyk-Kul hotel, might be made of concrete but its design is based on an ancient nomad encampment. There are seven traditonal yurt dwellings, the Burana Tower and the Square of people's Friendship. In '95 it was filled with folk dancers and musicians for the celebrations, and is intended to be a permanent tourist site.

Excursions from Bishkek

The quickest way into the mountains is to go with Intourist or Dostuk Trekking, or by taxi, to **Ala-Archa** (**Ала-Арча**). Despite being less than an hour's drive from the city, this valley is less spoiled than most of the Alps. You climb imperceptibly through fields and *dachas* to a toll booth at the entrance to the Ala-Archa nature reserve, then more steeply for 12km to the roadhead. A climbers' chalet burned down here early in 1993 but is being rebuilt. Walks of any length are possible in any direction. The main path up the left (east) side of the valley leads to a waterfall at the head of the higher Ak-Sai valley, and from there past the snout of the Ak-Sai glacier into an impressive amphitheatre of technical (non-trekking) peaks, all over 4000m. A long day's walk on up the Ala-Archa valley from the roadhead brings you to a ski base so high that it's only open in summer. There are two drag lifts. The lower one starts at 3435m and the top one goes up to 4000m. The cheap way to get to Ala-Archa would be to take a local bus to Kashka-Su, then hitch or even walk.

The **Burana Tower** (**Бурана**) makes a more sedate day trip from Bishkek, though as Kyrgyzstan's only easily-accessible Silk Route relic this restored 11th-century Karakhanid minaret is over-promoted. The 25-m burnt-brick tower is all that remains of a Karakhanid city called Balasagun which the Mongols spared and renamed Gobalik ('Good City') in the 13th century. There is also a collection of about 80 6th–10th-century stone figures here from Turkish graves in Kyrgzstan and Kazakhstan. They usually represent the dead man or someone he killed. The site museum claims Balasagun was the centre of a Karakhanid state stretching from Kashgar to Urgench, but insofar as the semi-nomadic Karakhanids had a capital it was actually Bukhara. Still, the tower's position is quietly idyllic. In sloping fields beneath the mountains 10km south of Tokmak and 60km east of Bishkek, it can be included in a trip to Lake Issyk-Kul. Arrange transport with Intourist or Dostuk Trekking. Alternatively, take a bus to Tokmak from Bishkek's east station and then use a local taxi.

Shopping

Souvenirs, from rugs to ak-kalpak hats, are stocked at the Central Department Store, or **Tsum**, at Prospekt Chu 155. Felt slippers and other products of local craft, are sold at the **Kyrgyz Concept** office and, when open, **Kiyal**, Prospekt Chu 202, close to Osh bazaar.

For jewellery try **Samosvety** at Prospekt Erkindik 35. Several **galleries** sell local art: one at Ulitsa Manas 57; the Khudozhestvenny Salon, Ulitsa Belinskovo 57; and the Great Silk Road Gallery on the second floor of the Dostuk Hotel. Also at the Dostuk, just outside the south door of the hotel, is the **Adai Shop**, and on Ulitsas Bokonbaeva and Sovietskaya is **Taberik**. For books, some of which are in English, try **Nuska** at Prospekt Erkindik 43, by the intersection with Kievskaya Ulitsa. Replenish your supplies of Kodak film at either the **Tsum** department store (on Prospekt Chu and Ulitsa 40 Lyet Oktyabrya) or the Ai-Peri beauty salon, on Sovietskaya and Moskovskaya. The twenty-four hour developing service costs around 50 cents a print.

Bishkek (℗ 3312–)   *Where to Stay*

expensive–moderate

Bishkek's three business hotels are at the top end of the price scale. The **Dostuk**, Ulitsa Frunze 429, ℗ 28 42 11, ✉ 28 47 11, has the facilities to make international calls (book them with the floor lady, or else pay more for the satellite phone at the business centre). It has a restaurant and several snack bars including one open until 2am, and a sauna. Non-residents may use this and for $14 have breakfast. Payable in hard currency or by credit card, singles cost $79 and doubles, $138, including breakfast.

The fourth floor of the building at Ulitsa Panfilova 237, is the **Bishkek Business Centre Hotel** (a joint Kyrgyz–Canadian venture in the same building as the business school), ℗ 22 28 43/22 25 85, ✉ 22 13 20. Rooms are extremely comfortable, the size of suites, with kitchenettes and western-style bathrooms. The rate is $80 per person; for each week of your stay after the first there's a $10 reduction.

South of the centre, 6km towards Ala-Archa, next door to the Manas village, is the third business hotel. There are two parts to the **Issyk-Kul**, Prospekt Mira 103. One remains the Kyrgyz state hotel, ℗ 44 81 68, where single rooms are around $47, breakfast included. The other is Korean-run, ℗ 44 88 55, ✉ 44 88 58; its advantages over the Business Centre include the Belly Ollen restaurant, better service and satellite TV, but it's slightly more expensive, starting at $55 for rooms with TV.

The **Hotel Bishkek** (part of the Issyk-Kul Hotel and Trade Complex), Prospekt Erkindik 21, ℗ 44 81 43, is more expensive; singles with shower cost $60, including breakfast.

The **Hotel Ala-Too** opposite the railway station, Prospekt Erkindik 1, ℗ 22 60 41, is somehow just as it should be: solid, unpretentious and quiet—like Bishkek. Some rooms facing the street have balconies with views of the mountains. All have hot water in the evenings but not the highest standards of cleanliness. A double with a shower costs $40.

On the corner of Ulitsas Frunze and Orozbekova, the **Sary-Chelek** charges $30 for a single with a bathroom ($40 for a double) in local currency.

The huge, boring **Hotel Kyrgyzstan**, diagonally opposite the art museum at the east end of Ulitsa Abdumamunova (formerly Ulitsa Kirova) is still in refit limbo.

inexpensive

Better for those on a budget is another option in the same building as the **Business School**, ✆ 22 04 14, and belonging to the International Business School of Management. On the third floor, you'll find twin-bed rooms with small balconies and a shared bathroom. The floor lady with red hair brings *chai* for a few som, speaks some English and is in a class of her own—a contrast to the surly receptionist on the ground floor through whom you must book and pay. Unfortunately, there's little evidence of heating. Rooms cost the equivalent of $15 in som.

Cheap rooms are found at the **Ak-Sai**, opposite the Circus building, ✆ 26 14 65. Rooms sleep up to four people and a few cockroaches, showers are communal and the cost is around $5 in local currency. At the same price the four-storey **Kyrgyz Altyn**, ✆ 26 94 41, offers clean rooms and communal showers with hot water, and will hire you an electric teapot for a few som. It's not sign-posted; the entrance is from the courtyard immediately after the Apteka on Ulitsa Manas, close to the junction with Kievskaya. There are even cheaper rooms in another multi-functional building: a **clinic** on the corner of Ulitsas Panfilova and Kievskaya. The 2nd floor charges $2 per person for accommodation.

Anyone interested in arranging a **home-stay** should call Aigul, ✆ 28 45 65, who works for the international educational company, Jurta Ak-Tilek. This is a non-profit-making organisation that arranges Kyrgyz–German and French exchanges. Aigul speaks good German and some English. **Private apartments** can be booked through Dostuk Treking and Intourist and cost $7–10 per person per night.

Bishkek (✆ 3312–)   **Eating Out**

moderate

Opposite the Turkish embassy is the Turkish and European restaurant, **Nooruz**, Moskovskaya Ulitsa 73. The food and the ambience are good but the price ($10–20 a head) means this is a place for foreigners only. So is the Belly Ollen Korean restaurant on the seventh floor of the Issyk-Kul Hotel; but the food is worth the price, the service attentive and in the summer you can dine on the balcony.

At the basically Korean **Mi-Na**, Ulitsa Alma Atinskaya 115, close to Alamdein bazaar, the combined opening times of the restaurants on its two floors ensure that it's open almost twenty four hours a day. And the raunchy floor show, live bands and plentiful alcohol ensure that you need the same length of time to recover. The European–Kyrgyz restaurant **Naryn**, close to the Dostuk Hotel and Circus, also offers shows and live music; it's tucked between the casino and a nightclub. The Arizona restaurant at the Dostuk serves overpriced American food.

inexpensive

Eating in at the **Hotel Ala-Too** can be a pleasurable journey into retro-chic. The dining room is elegant, in a muted Stalinist sort of way, and so are the female Kyrgyz vocalists singing pop hits in shimmering full-length gowns. The menu is short and mainly Russian. Try 'salat Intourist' as a starter and expect to pay in the region of $4 for grilled chicken and the same for 50g of caviar. Omelettes and borscht are under $1.

Copious quantities of Chinese food and a beer cost $6 at **Belasugin**, next to the Russian film theatre off Chu. For $2 you'll get a good-value Kyrgyz meal at the **Ak-Sakal** *chai-khana* in Dubovy Park (in the circular building); for the same price, try the excellent *shashlyk* at the **Astrakhan** café by the History Museum. *Open lunchtimes only.* Excellent chicken dishes are served at the **Phoenix** on Sovietskaya next to the Fine Art Museum (*open 9am–8pm*), and the **Altyn Kush** near the corner of Ulitsas Sovietskaya and Toktogula. **Flash Pizza**, Prospekt Chu 36, offers a meal for $6, and the bright, novel **Automatic** diner, towards the other end of Chu, even offers veggie burgers, for $2 a head. Here you don't line up for your burger, you are served by solemn waiters.

Less bright, in fact extremely dark, is the **Tête-à-Tête**, the ground-floor restaurant of the Bishkek Business Centre building. The food is varied and reasonable but the waiters take advantage of the lighting when adding up your bill, or perhaps they're distracted by the disco lights flashing in sync with the music. Expect to pay $3–5. The *laghman* and *besh-barmak* have lost their edge at the **Son-Kul** restaurant on the corner of Prospekt Erkindik and Prospekt Chu. You're better off at the café next door.

Talas

Talas, in northwest Kyrgyzstan, is further off the beaten track than Bishkek and towns near Lake Issyk-Kul. Settled since the 9th century, this area became part of Russia in the mid-nineteenth, after which it was cultivated by Russian, German and Ukrainian immigrants. The town was founded in 1877, beside the River Talas.

As the reputed birthplace of **Manas**, Talas claimed a place on the tourist map in 1995, the Manas millenium year, and hosted its own celebrations to complement those in Bishkek. While visitors won't be treated to the sight of thousands of traditionally clad Kyrgyz horsemen thundering across the steppe (the highlight of the 1995 commemoration), they will see the Manas mausoleum (an ancient burial place named in honour of Manas) and a new museum built with UN assistance. Among its exhibits are reconstructions of Kyrgyz nomadic life. Close to the mausoleum is a large rock bearing a horse-shoe imprint, supposedly left by Manas's winged horse, and its tethering post.

In the centre of town is the Intourist hotel, previously reserved for VIPs. More hotels are under construction. Buses take eight hours from Bishkek (the fare is around $7) and pass through Dzhambul which also has its own Talas bus service.

Issyk-Kul (Озеро Иссык-Кул)

There are two major depressions in the Tian Shan. The Fergana valley is one of them. The other is filled to a depth of 702m by one of the world's largest bodies of fresh water. Issyk-Kul means 'warm sea', as does its Chinese name Ze-Hai. Despite being 1600m above sea level, its 6200-sq km surface never freezes, baffling scientists but not those who have always lived here. They know that the lake's true depths, never plumbed by man, are heated by the centre of the earth. Surrounded by snow-capped mountains, fed by 80 streams and rivers but drained by none, domain of the world's smallest, smartest navy, this inland sea is the pride of Kyrgyzstan and probably its heart and soul as well.

Turkish and Mongol nomad armies used to winter on its shores because the snow lies thinner here than elsewhere in the mountains. Tamerlane is said to have built a fort on an island and to have banished there some Tartars he captured in Asia Minor. The story is unprovable because the island has since vanished, probably in an earthquake. But bits of brick and pottery are periodically washed up on the lakeshore, fuelling tales of an entire city, not just an island fortress, lost beneath the waves.

The Chinese always coveted Issyk-Kul but never conquered it, unlike the Russians, who built a fort at its east end in 1864. Settlers began arriving from Siberia and European Russia in the 1880s, and their low, whitewashed compounds still lend an old-fashioned air to towns like Balikchi (former Rybach'ye) and Kara-Kol (former Przheval'sk). The lake was closed to foreigners throughout the Soviet period, from which it has emerged relatively unscathed. There are some predictable concrete carbuncles near the main resort town of Cholpan-Ata, but the lake itself is pristine and the mountains behind them are virtually unexplored.

To Balikchi

The main road east from Bishkek edges gradually closer to the mountains for 110km until, beyond Bistrovka, it swings south into them up the gorge of the river Chu. In case you are in any doubt, you know by the moulded silver snow leopard beside the road that you are entering wild country. But the defile is short, soon turning east again and giving way to the long, dry saddle which holds in the lake.

The road that forks away to the right, 20km short of Balikchi, leads to Naryn and China. At this point, it seems that the river must be the outflow of the lake, as indeed it once was. But the topography is deceptive. Soon after a checkpoint at which cars pay a toll and have their emissions analysed, the lake comes into view some way below and the river can be seen making a slow turn towards the gorge from the south.

On a clear day you can see the mountains on both sides of the lake from here. The northern ones, separating Kyrgyzstan from Kazakhstan, are the Kungey ('sunny') Ala-Too. The southern ones are the Terskey ('shady') Ala-Too. Beyond them, sometimes visible from hundreds of kilometres away, are the glaciers of the Tian Shan's central knot.

Most holiday traffic zooms through Balikchi bound for Cholpan-Ata and Kara-Kol, which leaves Balikchi's beach relatively uncrowded. This is the only town of any size at the west end of the lake and is named after the fish for which a small fleet of skiffs lies in wait not far offshore on summer evenings. Its Russian name, Rybach'ye, was replaced in 1991 by Issyk-Kul, which was too confusing to stick and was replaced in 1993 by Balikchi, a Kyrgyz translation of Rybach'ye (balik = ryba = fish).

Getting to and from Balikchi

by rail

The railway line from Bishkek was completed in 1948. There are twice daily depatures, early morning and mid-afternoon, taking four hours to get to Bishkek 2 station, at the extreme west end of town.

by bus

The bus station is closer in, a block east of the roundabout on the main north shore road. Eight buses a day take the northern route to Kara-Kol (217km of good road); eight more take the southern one (197km of bad road). Arrive in good time to get a seat and don't be surprised at how cosy the journey becomes. Only two buses start here for Bishkek but many more pass through going that way, taking 3 ½ hours. The quickest way to Bishkek is by long-distance *marshrutnoe* taxi from outside the bus station for about $3 in *som*.

Issyk-Kul (© 33144–) ### Where to Stay and Eating Out

A double room with no shower at the **Ak Kyy**, away from the lake amid apartment blocks, costs $12–14 in local currency; for around $30 you get a *lyux* version. If you lurk in the vicinity of the post office you may find a Krygyz homestay. If you don't, share your happiness with those at home; make an international call from the telegraph office next to the post office. There are several restaurants in town.

Cholpan-Ata (Чолпан-Ата)

Half-way along the north shore and closer to Almaty than to Balikchi, this is the fashionable place to take a cure; the Montreux of Issyk-Kul without the style, the hotels or the rock festival. The root of the hotel problem is that most visitors stay in soulless sanatoria owned by factories and trade unions; for this reason Cholpan-Ata is eminently missable.

The mountains behind it are a different matter. These are the highest and snowiest in the Kungey Ala-Too, and are traversed by at least four recognized trekking routes, all of which start and finish at Medeo above Almaty, and take about eight days. Large-scale maps of each route are available from the Chimbulak ski base on the Kazakh side—but apparently not in Cholpan-Ata.

Getting to and from Cholpan-Ata

by air

Cholpan-Ata's is the busiest airport on the lake, with planes approaching low over the water and landing uphill. In season there are three flights a day from Osh, two from Almaty and Tashkent and one from each of Bishkek, Dzhalalabad and Dzhambul (all those from within Kyrgyzstan being subject to fuel supplies). Antonov biplanes seem to do pleasure flights over the lake. The airport is situated to the west of the town.

by bus

There are two express buses to Bishkek per day, taking 5 hours to make the journey, three a day to Almaty via Bishkek, and one to each of Dzhambul, Chimkent and Kara-Kol in addition to the Balikchi–Kara-Kol stopping services. The bus station is near the west end of town, set back from the main road on the lake side.

Cholpan-Ata (© 33143–)   *Where to Stay*

The only ordinary (i.e. non-sanatorium) **hotel** is beyond the airport in a satellite suburb called *Mikro-Raion PMK*. Those intent on spending the night in Cholpan-Ata could try instead the 10-room hostelry above **Café Zhuldyz** (*open 11am till midnight*) in the town centre. This can be a little chilly, lacking hot or cold water but compensating with friendly staff ($7).

To Kara-Kol

Twenty kilometres east of Cholpan-Ata what was formally the sanatorium and is now the **Hotel Aurora**, © 44 8 70/44 2 59, blots out the lake like a concrete QE2 in dry dock. It has less success with the mountains that rise to well over 1,700m on the south side. Formal gardens lead from the hotel to a beach and a jetty where a steamer occasionally loads up for pleasure cruises. Here the clean rooms have hot water and balconies, and there's also a tennis court. As in all former Soviet spas, meals are at set times. The buffet breakfast, however, is a feast including fresh fish, and you can order pizzas for picnic lunches. It's advisable to book in advance; this can be done for you in Almaty, ✆ 21 49 55, or Bishkek, ✆ 22 17 20, ✉ 62 03 65. The rate for singles is $25–30, doubles $30–40.

Others should move on—to **Ananieva**, for example, another 30km east. The town is unremarkable, but it has a pleasant new *turbaza* 2km south of the centre on the lake, with bungalows, sauna, disco, camel and its own beach.

The lake's east end consists of two long inlets. Into the northern one flows the River Tiup, much of whose catchment area was, it is said, given over in Soviet times to heavily-guarded marijuana plantations which the upstanding new regime has torched. At Tiup, the place, the main road to Kara-Kol turns south while a minor one continues east up river and over a low pass into Kazakhstan. Tiup has a café, a *chai-khana* and a basic hotel, all near the main road's right-angle bend.

Kara-Kol (Кара-Кол)

A picturesque Russian church and gracious colonial houses on tree-lined streets sloping up towards glaciers and pine forests are rare in the former Soviet Union—but Kara-Kol has them. Rarer still, the shop-fronts near the bazaar are 19th-century wooden colonnades; a cross between small-town Bavaria and the Wild West.

Soviet architects were let loose on the main square because Kara-Kol is an administrative centre and because you can't have everything. But the older parts of Kara-Kol are a blessed relief from rectilinear concrete. This old-world Russianness belies the town's ethnic diversity. Apart from Kyrgyz and Russians, there is a significant minority of Tungans. Like the Uighurs, they are regarded here as Chinese, though in China they consider themselves as anything but.

History

Founded as a Russian garrison in 1864, Kara-Kol was renamed Przheval'sk in 1888 after Nikolai Przhevalski, the legendary explorer, misogynist and spy whose memorial park and museum occupy an entire promontory down by the lake. In 1916 Andizhan's anti-czarist rebellion spread to Issyk-Kul, where Kyrgyz herdsmen feared that Russian settlers, who were already farming the lakeshore, would soon take over their high pastures as well. Some estimates claim 2000 Russians were killed and those who weren't took refuge in Przheval'sk while Russian troops took their revenge. Whole Kyrgyz villages were burned and those inhabitants who survived were deported to Naryn, whence many fled to China. With the fall of the Soviet Union, Przheval'sk's Kyrgyz name was quickly re-adopted.

Many Russians, third- and fourth-generation immigrants who left after the fall of the Soviet Union, have since come back. This place exerts a powerful nostalgia.

Getting to and from Kara-Kol

by air

Fuel allowing there are three flights a day from Bishkek. The airport is on the east side of town near the bus station, selling tickets for both flights and bus journeys.

by bus

Numerous buses come each day from Bishkek via the north shore (journey time, 8–9 hours and cost $9 in som) and up to 16 more from Balikchi—Kara-Kol is not hard to get to. Leaving town, last buses are at 3pm for Bishkek, 4.30pm for Balikchi, 5pm for Bokonbaev on the south shore and 5.50pm for Cholpan-Ata. There is one bus a day to Naryn, leaving early. It's worth double checking bus departure times here.

Tourist Information

Valentin and Gallia Dyerevyanka run their own **Karakol Tourist Agency Ltd**, but no longer from the ground floor of the Hotel Kara-Kol. Ask the receptionist at the hotel for details of their flat. Though neither speaks English and both would prefer to sell you their excursions (*see* below), they are bursting with energy and genuinely keen to help. Valentin is a former moto-cross trainer who sometimes has motorbikes for sale or hire.

The **post office** is one block north of the Hotel Kara-Kol on Ulitsa Kalinina, and sells postcards.

In and Around Kara-Kol

The main **bazaar** or *rynok* begins diagonally opposite the Hotel Kara-Kol across the central square. To see the elegant two-storey villas of colonial Kara-Kol, walk south from here, towards the mountains, up Ulitsa Gorkova.

The rest of Kara-Kol's attractions are not actually in the town. The **beach** is 9km northwest, reached by buses marked *dacha* (дача) from the *rynok* stop on Ulitsa Gorkovo. Two thirds of the way there a right fork leads to the **Przhevalski Museum and Memorial**. The museum is worth a visit; if you find it closed, ask at the memorial. Since Przhevalski was an ardent czarist, the Soviet curators could not turn him to ideological advantage and have properly concentrated on his tireless exploration and mapping of Siberia, Xinjiang and northern Tibet in the 1860s, 70s and early 80s. One of the finest exhibits is his beautiful portable theodolite. The town is peaceful and worth a visit, but be sure to bring a picnic—there's no food here.

Moored beneath Przhevalski's memorial by the beach road are the two grey cutters which constitute the Kyrgyz navy.

Dzheti-Oguz (Джети-Огуз)

Some 25km inland from Kara-Kol, seven peculiar red cliffs, endlessly photographed, stand guard over the spa of Dzheti-Oguz. The cliffs were once wild bulls, immobilized by the gods to stop them terrorizing local yurt-dwellers. The spa, 15km west of Kara-Kol on the south shore road and then 10km into the mountains, is as pleasant a place as any to study the mass-produced silver statues of healthy young men and women which were the official icons of the cult of the proletariat.

To get there, take any south shore bus and ask to be let off at the Dzheti-Oguz turning, then hitch or walk. Alternatively let the Karakol Tourist Agency take you there. They also offer excursions to another mineral spring 19km southeast of Kara-Kol on the Ak-Su river, and highly recommended **honey-tasting trips.**

Trekking

Dostuk Trekking in Bishkek has large-scale maps covering two well-trodden but very beautiful 4–5-day treks from **Pokrovka (Покровка)** to Kara-Kol, 38km to the east, via some of the highest passes of the Terskey Ala-Too. Both routes start heading southeast from Pokrovka up the Chon-Kizyl-Su valley, and end by following the Arashan river past some hot radon springs at Altyn-Arashan down to the village of Teploklyuchenka a few kilometres east of Kara-Kol. The easier trek (map: **к Лидинкам Терскей Ала-Ту**=*K Lidnikam Terskey Ala-Too*=To the Glaciers of the Terskey Ala-Too) crosses the Archa-Tor, Teleti and Ala-Kul passes at 3800, 3800 and 3860 m respectively, skirting on the penultimate day Lake Ala-Kul, filled by glacial meltwater. The more advanced one (map: **по Центральному Тиан-Шаню**=*Po Tsentralnamu Tian-Shanyu*=In the Central Tian Shan) crosses the SOAN, Archali-Tor and Skalnyi Zamok passes at 3900, 4200 and 4200m respectively. This trek is not strictly in the central Tian Shan, which begins further east (*see* over), but it is very strenuous, and only those with climbing experience should attempt it unguided. Recommended campsites are mostly in wooded, valley bottoms but are not permanent; bring all your own equipment.

Where to Stay

Cubism seems to have been the chief architectural influence on the central **Hotel Kara-Kol**, Ulitsa Kalinina 118, ✆ 2 41 55, seems to have problems with its hot water and charges $28 in som for a double room. Front-facing versions have balconies.

There's a public *banya* half a block north of the post office where for under 10 cents you can thaw out.

The **Hotel Intourist**, Ulitsa Fuchika, ✆ 2 07 11/2 17 21, is hidden in its own park opposite the *Rot Dom* stop on bus route 1, northwest of the centre. Definitely the luxury option, good for recuperation after mountain exertions, it feels like a former preserve of Party top brass. There are two buildings. Both have restaurants and the bigger one has a sauna. Rooms cost $20–30; more if you take the biggest suite which is the size of a squash court.

Sergei Pyshnenko, ℂ 2 64 89, ✉ 2 34 43, who works as a guide both independently and for **C & P Ltd** treks, sometimes offers accommodation at $50 per night with meals included. Sergei can also provide transport into the Ala-Too mountains ($120 return) and speaks good English. But prices don't always remain the same as the original quote. Be warned.

The cheapest place is the small hotel at the bus station for $1–2.

Eating Out

Eating out possibilities are limited. The Hotel Kara-Kol's **restaurant** has its own entrance on Ulitsa Piervomayskaya. But if nothing appeals, turn right out of the hotel and first right again to a silver-and-blue dome where you can find fried eggs and mashed potato. At the Intourist hotel restaurant the menu is basic; bread, soup and salad will cost $3.

Fast food at the **bazaar** consists of noodles with opaque white jellied potato starch; a Uighur dish also popular in Kashgar. Fresh fish does not seem to be available anywhere. The Karakol Tourist Agency can arrange a spectacular Tungan feast in a private Tungan home.

The Central Tian Shan

Enter a different world, where rain is rare but blizzards can come every day, where feral Russian climbers outnumber the local Kyrgyz, and where—except on one spectacular road—the only means of transport are mule and helicopter. This is one of the world's least explored high mountain regions. Clustered near the remote junction of the Kyrgyz, Kazakh and Chinese borders are the CIS's second-highest mountain, an 80-km glacier, a disappearing lake, and an entire range of unclimbed peaks.

The gateway to the central Tian Shan is the disused but not quite deserted tin-mining town of **Inylchek (Иныльчек)**, 200km southeast of Kara-Kol. Before the advent of the plastic bag and the consequent collapse of world tin prices, Inylchek received lavish central government investment. As a result the road from Kara-Kol is good. It follows the northern edge of the Terskey Ala-Too east for 50km before turning south into a wide and very beautiful valley. At the entrance there is a checkpoint; until recently, only specially-authorized expeditions could go beyond it. Near the far end of the valley a yellow bulldozer on a giant boulder commemorates the sacrifices which went into the next 100km. The road hairpins up the left side of the valley and into a still higher one, leading to a bleak and often snowbound watershed. South of here eveything drains into the Sary-

Dzhash river, which feeds the Aksu oasis over the Chinese border and then disappears into the scorching Taklamakan desert.

Soviet engineers surpassed themselves on the descent into the mind-boggling Sary-Dzhash canyon. The sheer red cliffs left the roadbuilders with no option but to follow every twist of the river. Six hours' drive from Kara-Kol, the road emerges suddenly into the flat-bottomed Inylchek valley. At this point the Sary-Dzhash is joined from the east by the grit-laden Inylchek river, product of the Tian Shan's longest glacier. Inylchek itself stands at the confluence of these rivers, and consists mostly of ugly, empty blocks of miners' flats.

Maidadir (2800m), 17 rough km further up the Inylchek valley, is little more than an army base, a line of tents and a helipad. Higher up, gravel covers the valley's flat floor and colossal buttresses of brown rock form its northern side. The south side is less forbidding. Steep lateral valleys between the peaks of the Inylchek range support modest populations of marmot, ibex and mountain partridge. The trees are mainly Tian Shan spruce.

The **Chon Tash** campsite is 35km from Maidadir at the snout of the glacier. On the glacier itself, 15km further on, you come to the unique, inaccessible **Merzbacher Lake**. For most of the year, the 6-km-long, 1-km-wide lake is contained by the north side of the glacier, but every summer, usually in August, an ice-plug melts and the entire lake drains in three days. A Russian expedition of 1931 witnessed this effect:

'It was an extraordinary sight, with water shooting up in various places and making a terrible noise... Our horses were so frightened that we hardly managed to force them down the slope. The animals seemed transfixed by the tremendous roaring and shaking of the glacier. Involuntarily we also became seized by fear, and there was a moment when the glacier seemed to be on the point of breaking away and rushing downward, destroying everything in its way.'

Discovered in 1903 by Gottfried Merzbacher, a Bavarian geographer and mountaineer, Lake Merzbacher fills the entrance to the seldom-visited North Inylchek valley, which is separated from the south one by the short but very high Khan Tengri range. **Khan Tengri** is what Merzbacher was actually looking for. This supremely handsome marble mountain (6995m) is one of Kyrgyzstan's two principal attractions for climbers. The other is **Pik Pobieda** (7439m), the world's northernmost mountain over 7000m, facing Khan Tengri from the south side of the South Inylchek glacier.

Getting to and from the Central Tian Shan

Until 1992 most visitors to the central Tian Shan were climbers whose journey from Bishkek or Almaty to base camp was prearranged and often entirely by helicopter. This is still possible, though Kazakh kerosene supplies are more reliable than Kyrgyz. Contact Dostuk Trekking or Tian Shan Travel in Bishkek (*see* p.250), Kramds Mountain Company in Almaty (p.293) or OTT ('Specialist Holidays', pp.8 and 9).

by air

The Mi-8 MTB is a five-rotored beast of a helicopter specially adapted for high altitudes. Consuming nearly a tonne of fuel an hour, it can take 15 people and a mountain of luggage to 4500m. Without the luggage, its ceiling is a staggering 6000m.

These awesome machines thunder up and down the South Inylchek glacier almost daily in July and August, ferrying climbers to and from base camps at $400 an hour. Gorky and Zvezdochka camps are supplied from Maidadir; a straightforward 45-minute, 80-km flight up the Inylchek valley. The Kazakh IMC is supplied from an acclimatization camp at 1700m on the Karkara river north of the Khan Tengri and Sary-Dzhash ranges. This flight is a truly unbelievable experience. To clear the Khan Tengri ridge when flying from the South Inylchek glacier into Kazakhstan the helicopter spirals up an ice-filled cwm and heaves itself over a 5500-m pass before descending nearly 4 vertical kilometres in 20 minutes, passing in the process from arctic to sunbathing weather.

Heli-hitching is possible. A couple of crisp $20 notes should get you onto most flights if there is room.

by road

There are no regular buses to Inylchek. Dostuk Trekking uses Geological Survey trucks from Kara-Kol's *baza geologov* on the road to the Przhevalski memorial. Tian Shan Travel has its own. The Karakol Tourist Agency at the Hotel Karakol can also arrange transport. Otherwise, hitch.

on foot

It is possible, and apparently unforgettable, to trek across the Terskey Ala-Too from the headwaters of the River Tiup, east of Lake Issyk-Kul, to Chon Tash at the foot of the Inylchek glacier. This takes about nine days and would be very difficult unsupported. However, Dostuk Trekking, Tian Shan Travel (*see* p.250), OTT and Exodus Expeditions (*see* pp.8 and 9) have all organized supported treks along this route in the last two years.

Walking from the roadhead at Maidadir it takes two days to get to Chon Tash, camping after 20km on the south side of the valley at the confluence of the At-Dzhailu and Inylchek rivers. The At-Dzhailu should be crossed early next morning before it fills with meltwater.

Lake Merzbacher is a long day's walk up the glacier's south lateral moraine from Chon Tash. The lake is on the north side but you should make first for *zilyoni polyana* (green clearing), a heaven-sent grassy campsite on the opposite side of the glacier at 3500m. The glacier can be crossed the following morning, but sometimes crevasses make it impossible to reach the lake.

The base camps for Khan Tengri and Pik Pobieda are another two days up the glacier. There are three camps. The official Kazakh International Mountaineering Camp (IMC) is on the south side of the South Inylchek glacier with the best views of Khan Tengri and the best access to Pik Pobieda. The Kyrgyz IMC (also known as Gorky Camp), run by Tian Shan Travel, is opposite the Kazakh one facing Pik Pobieda. Dostuk Trekking's *Zvezdochka* camp is a short walk down the north lateral moraine from Gorky Camp. All are at about 4200m.

Note: the glacier is not safe without a guide, even for experienced trekkers.

Red Tape

Since the end of the Soviet Union, access to the central Tian Shan has theoretically been unrestricted. But the guards at the checkpoint on the road from Kara-Kol can still ask for documentation, so it pays to have been to OVIR in Bishkek (*see* p.248) and had Inylchek added to your visa.

To China via the Torugart Pass

The new high road to China passes through the lonely heart of Kyrgyzstan, within striking distance of one of the last true strongholds of the yurt and near to the most evocative piece of Silk Route architecture in Central Asia. It may not be as spectacular as the other mountain route to Kashgar, the Karakoram highway, but it is still little known to westerners.

Entering China via the Torugart Pass is more complicated and expensive than via Khorgos or Druzhba (see pp.356–357). However, three quarters of the Bishkek–Kashgar road are within Kyrgyzstan, and they are the easiest, fastest and most rewarding quarters; worth covering even if only to turn back before the border.

To Naryn

For the first 150km, follow the road from Bishkek as if you were going to Lake Issyk-Kul. At the top of the Chu gorge, most Naryn traffic turns south and takes a short-cut across the extreme east end of the Kyrgyz Ala-Too to join the Balikchi–Naryn road above the Orto-Tokoiskoye reservoir.

The next town is **Kochkorka**: one broad street, two dining-rooms and a bazaar, set in a lush green basin with distant snow in all directions. Kochkorka, one has to admit, looks like the paintings in Bishkek's fine art museum of traditional Kyrgyz life enhanced by enlightened Soviet settlement policies.

South of here the road begins a long climb to the 3030-m Dolon pass. After about 45km, just beyond the village of Sary-Bulak, there is a signed right turn to **Ozero Son-Kul**. Lake Son-Kul is a magical place, very high (3020m), very shallow, hard to get to and without a single tree or permanent dwelling on its shore. Every spring several hundred herdsmen drive their sheep and horses up to the smooth grasslands above the lake, pitching their yurts beside the streams which feed it. Son-Kul is 50km from the turning above Sary-Bulak. Another road joins this one at the lake, having approached from nearer Naryn, mostly following the Son-Kul river. Both are unpaved. To get to the lake from Bishkek take a Naryn bus as far as the turning above Sary-Bulak, then hitch. Alternatively arrange transport all the way there through Intourist, Dostuk Trekking or Tian Shan Travel in Bishkek. Bring a tent, a warm sleeping bag and all your own food.

Naryn (Нарын)

Do not expect too much of Naryn. Founded in 1868 as a Russian garrison, it is now a long, thin town of 40,000 built mostly since World War II between the fast-flowing Naryn river and the steep sides of the river valley. In winter the snow lies a metre deep. In summer Naryn is by turns dusty and rainy.

Getting to and from Naryn

Naryn is 115km south of Kochkorka, and about 50km south of the junction between the main road and the more southerly of the two roads to Lake Son-Kul. Seven hours from Bishkek and five from Torugart (where there is no hotel), this is the main staging-post on the Bishkek–Kashgar road.

by air

This is currently impossible owing to fuel shortages, though there is an airport east of the town centre.

by bus

State-run buses between Bishkek and Naryn have now ceased, and you must go to Bishkek's west bus station and take a private bus, which will leave only when it is full. Journey time: 7 hours. There are also no scheduled buses to Torugart, but if improvising your way to the border it would be worth asking at the bus station about any *spetsialny* (special) or *chastny* (private) buses that may be going there. The bus station is near the east end of former Ulitsa Lenina, not far from the main Naryn river bridge.

hitching

Ten minutes' walk south of the bus station, the Torugart road leaves town up a narrow side valley with a cemetery on the right hand side. There is a local bus stop here, and usually an assortment of would-be passengers to At-Bashi and beyond. All China-bound traffic has to go this way. Drivers will expect at least the equivalent of a bus fare, but may ask for much more.

The **Hotel Ala-Too**, at the junction of Ulitsa Bishkek and former
Ulitsa Lenina, © 2 18 72, is the only one in town. It's filthy and
basic with an appalling café, and costs 15 som for a single or
30 som for a double, both with bath. It would be better to
talk to local people about a homestay, and better to eat on the street.

To Torugart

Eleven kilometres south of Naryn, the road descends into what—by Kyrgyz standards—is
a fertile plain, between the Naryn and At-Bashi mountains. At-Bashi is 30km from Naryn,
and is the last town of any size before the border. The At-Bashi range runs north-east to
south-west, and the road tracks it in an almost straight line for about 60km. Then there is
a signed left turn to the **Tash Rabat caravanserai (Таш-Рабат)**. Having come this far it
would be a waste not to take it; 15km into the mountains, up a valley so perfect that it
leaves you flailing for superlatives, this massive stone shelter, half-embedded in the slope
rising behind it, was protecting Kashgari silk caravans from snowstorms and bandits
before Tamerlane or even Genghis Khan was born. Its exact date is not known but there
has been a caravanserai here since the 10th century. This one was restored in the early
1980s, though you wouldn't know it but for the surreptitious use of mortar in the domed
ceilings, which were originally a gravity-defying marvel of intuitive design, using only dry
stone. There is a dismaying car park at the roadhead, but it is hardly used and the whole
area is otherwise completely unspoilt; the only way to get to it is to take a bus to Naryn
and then hitch, or to arrange your own transport all the way here from Bishkek, as for
Lake Son-Kul.

There is a gate in the road, where a thoroughly unofficial charge of 5 som per person is
made. At the caravanserai, ask for the key at the white house opposite to see inside (3

TASH RABAT CARAVANSERAI
KYRGYZSTAN

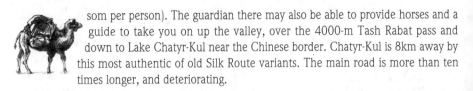

som per person). The guardian there may also be able to provide horses and a guide to take you on up the valley, over the 4000-m Tash Rabat pass and down to Lake Chatyr-Kul near the Chinese border. Chatyr-Kul is 8km away by this most authentic of old Silk Route variants. The main road is more than ten times longer, and deteriorating.

Getting to the Torugart Pass

It takes three hours to cover the remaining 90km from the Tash Rabat turning to the Chinese border at Torugart.

To be sure of getting to Torugart, charter a jeep in Bishkek from Dostuk Trekking or another agency. This will cost you between $130 and $250 dollars per person, depending on the size of the vehicle, the number of people, and whether food and accommodation in Bishkek and *en route* is included.

Getting across the Torugart Pass

At the pass, new CIS customs and immigration facilities are now nearly complete to cope with the expanding volume of traffic, but as yet that traffic is mostly Kyrgyz and Chinese; the authorities are not used to Westerners. The only fool-proof way of getting out of Kyrgyzstan and into China is to be met at the border by a Chinese jeep (although by the time you read this it may become possible to take the newly instituted twice-daily bus service on the Chinese side). This means phoning, faxing, telexing or writing ahead to one of the Kashgar outfits that can arrange this: CITS, Xinjiang Kashgar Travel Agency or John Hu (for details, *see* p.338). A crossing will set you back at least ¥2000 ($250) per vehicle.

No-man's land is about 5km wide at the pass, and you can't walk it. CIS border troops won't let you out until their Chinese counterparts have told them that whoever is meeting you has arrived on the Chinese side.

The Chinese side is a controlled military zone. Chinese vehicles and drivers entering it need special documents, and it is worth reminding whoever is meeting you of this when contacting them in advance. Foreigners entering the zone pay a fee of 165 FEC at the main army checkpoint in Tuo Yun, 10 minutes' drive below the pass. More may be demanded if you look rich or if the duty officer is in a bad mood. Customs (interested mainly in cameras and electronics) and the health inspectorate (25 FEC fee) are across the road.

visas

It is impossible to get Chinese visas at, or anywhere near, the border. Officials have no hesitation in turning visa-less travellers away. Visas are currently available only in national capitals (*see* 'Entry Formalities', p.15).

The first three quarters of the 620-km mountain route to Osh are almost never flat or straight. This road, itself merely the first third of the epic M41 to Dushanbe, begins in earnest 30km west of Bishkek at Kara-Balta. From here it climbs nearly 3000 m to the 3586-m Tyo-Ashu pass and then drops down into the long, high valley of the Susamir river, which it follows westwards. Most human life along the Susamir is in yurts, but at the head of the valley there is a truck stop called **Ot-Mok**, with a dining-room and a dosshouse. The road forks here, with the northern branch going over the 3330-m Ot-Mok pass to Talas and the Osh road, climbing to 3184 m at the Ala-Bel pass. The high-voltage power lines are from the Toktogul dam, 180 gruelling kilometres away by road.

Toktogul (Токтогул)

Most of that distance is accounted for by going the long way round the Toktogul reservoir to cross the Naryn river, which is its main water supply. But first the road descends a dramatic gorge, part of a nature reserve, to the town of Toktogul. Created in 1970 at the same time as the lake, Toktogul is named after a reformer known to history as the first Kyrgyz democrat, who was born nearby in 1870.

Getting to Toktogul

The town is served by one bus a day from Bishkek (journey time: 9 hours) and two from Dzhalalabad (also 9 hours).

Where to Stay

At Uish-Bulak, 20km back up the road, a former Communist Young Pioneers' camp is open to the public, and would be a more interesting place to spend the night than the municipal hotel near Toktogul's bus station.

Kara-Kul (Кара-Куль)

Not to be confused with Kara-Kol (former Przheval'sk), Kara-Kul is sited near the west end of the Toktogul reservoir, and exists to serve the Toktogul dam. Both reservoir and dam are invisible from the town, separated from it by a tapering, rocky ridge. This forms one side of the gorge filled by the dam—a phenomenal concrete wedge 215m high and almost as wide at its base. Permission to visit the generator room underneath it (*mashin zal* or *ma. zal*) can be obtained from the director's office on the second floor of the administration building in the centre of Kara-Kul. Ask for the *biuro kaskada* ; everybody knows it.

The only functioning hotel in town is the secluded **Hotel Turist**, ℡ 5384, on the western outskirts. If you are coming from the direction of Bishkek, you'll see it signposted to the left at the 390km post. The hotel has no restaurant. In the evening, try the **Restaurant Edelweiss** near the *biuro kaskada*. For breakfast and lunch the best bet is a café set back to the right of a food store opposite the Edelweiss.

Tash-Kumir (Таш-Кумир)

For most of the 64km from Kara-Kul to **Tash-Kumir**, the road rides high above the River Naryn. There is no room beside the river, which is swollen by a series of smaller barrages producing electricity mainly for the Fergana valley. Tash-Kumir has two separate halves, both across the river on its north side, one upstream of the river, one down. The only hotel is in the lower half near the railway station and only four of its rooms have keys.

Getting to Kara-Kul and Tash-Kumir

Both towns are served by Dzhalalabad–Toktogul buses. Tash-Kumir, at the end of a branch-line from the Tashkent–Dzhalalabad mainline built for the local coal mines, has infrequent trains to and from Namangan. For transport from the Fergana valley, *see* Sary-Chelek, p.215.

ZENKOV CATHEDRAL, ALMATY

Kazakhstan* Казахстан

Kazakhstan is big: four times the size of Texas, five times that of France, as big as the whole of Western Europe or half the continental United States. It stretches 2000km from the Volga delta to Mongolia and 1200km from the Urals to the suburbs of Tashkent, filling a void in the middle of Asia— and in most mental maps of the world. With 16 million inhabitants, Kaza- khstan is the third most populous republic in the CIS. It is also, in terms of the number of warheads on its soil, the world's fourth nuclear power.

Nine tenths of the country is steppe; a vast, flat, kidney- shaped grassland that separated Russia from her Asian empire as oceans separated Britain from hers. That was until Stalin's Five Year Plans. Then what had been a mere tran- sition zone, virtually unpopulated except by nomads, became the scene of frenzied industrialization and two catastrophic experiments with the land. Between 1920 and 1940 Kazakhstan's industrial output increased by a factor of 40. Brand new industrial cities sprang up on the northern steppe, mining coal, drilling for oil, rolling out steel. The biggest of them, Karaganda, quickly became the republic's second city. Hundreds of thousands of Russians and Ukrainians were resettled to populate this brave new world. They

RUSSIA

Orenburg

Volga

Astrakhan

Caspian
Sea

Aral
Sea

Turkmenbashy

TURKMENISTAN

Kazakhstan

easily outnumbered the Kazakhs, who meanwhile slaughtered their livestock rather than see it collectivized. Thus died some 24 million sheep and goats, 5 million cattle and 3 million horses, in 1933 alone. It was, wrote Ian Murray Matley, 'the most serious economic blunder made by the Russians in their entire hundred-year rule of Central Asia'.

*Kazakhstan has been spelt throughout with an 'h' according to current British practice.

A comparable one was to follow. To make the Soviet Union self-sufficient in wheat, 30 million hectares of virgin Kazakh steppe were ploughed up to the accompaniment of a propaganda blitz between 1954 and 1962. The Virgin Lands campaign produced two bumper harvests and then collapsed. It turned out that a thin covering of grass was the most the semi-arid steppe could support, as the nomads who had grazed it for centuries might have pointed out, had they been asked.

Convenient, empty Kazakhstan was also chosen as laboratory-cum-playground for the cream of Moscow's nuclear physicists and rocket-builders. From 1948 to 1992 an average of 15 atom bombs a year were exploded over and under the Semipalatinsk test site, while all Russia's space rockets blasted off from the Baikonur cosmodrome, falling to earth on a sealed-off range the size of England.

The current president, Nursultan Nazarbayev, an ex-Communist with an ambitious privatization programme, has signed a deal with the American oil giant Chevron, allowing them to extract apparently vast reserves in the Tengiz oil field in the north of Kazakhstan. He has been slower to do deals with opposition, even locking them out of parliament. 1995 saw his presidency extended, by 'referendum', into the next century and a new constitution approved a bicameral parliament. All this, plus progress made towards establishing a legislative and bureaucratic framework, makes Kazakhstan appear more liberal than at least one of its neighbours, and its mineral resources make it one of the most attractive of the ex-Soviet states to foreign business.

The steppe may have taken a beating, but Kazakhstan's southeastern fringe is different. Most of the country's history and natural beauty are concentrated along the great natural frontier formed by the Tian Shan and the Altai. Here are all of Kazakhstan's 2700 glaciers and many of its 48,000 lakes and 85,000 rivers.

Here is the transition zone between Russia and Asia in vivid cross-section, from the brown bears, log cabins and Siberian winters of the Altai to the wild geese of the Balkash wetlands and the saxaul scrub of the Kizyl-Kum desert; from Dostoyevsky's house in Semipalatinsk to the ski-lifts of Chimbulak and the timeless Timurid mausoleum of Turkestan. Here is all Kazakhstan's ethnic diversity, from the minority Uzbeks of Chimkent to the Korean businessmen of Almaty and the Russian nuclear technocrats of Kurchatov.

From Chimkent to Semipalatinsk, the cities on the TurkSib railway and the mountains behind them are the most accessible part of the country, the most interesting to non-specialist visitors and the most Central Asian. They may not be Central Asia proper (the Soviet designation for the region as a whole was 'Kazakhstan and Central Asia') but like Fitzroy Maclean approaching Almaty by train in 1937, let us not split hairs:

'Far to the south, dimly seen in the remote distance, towering high above the desert, rose a mighty range of mountains, their lower slopes veiled in cloud and vapours, their snow-clad peaks glittering in the sunlight, suspended between earth and sky... All day we trundled across the desert towards those distant peaks. Then, suddenly in the early afternoon, we found ourselves once again amid cultivation: apple orchards, the trees heavily laden with fruit; golden fields of Indian corn ripening in the sun; plantations of melons; rows of tall poplars growing by the side of canals and irrigation ditches... Already we could see the white houses of the town. Beyond it the tree-covered foothills of the Tian Shan rose steeply towards the snow-covered peaks behind them. I was in Central Asia.'

Chimkent (Чимкент)

Welcome to ammunition city. The satanic black tangle of chimneys and furnaces on the southern edge of Chimkent smelts lead from ore mined in the nearby Karatau hills, and makes bullets from it. Chimkent, population 369,000, is the CIS's biggest lead producer. It also has a tyre factory. Brownish-grey fumes hang over the apartment buildings and mothers wish their children were elsewhere.

It was not ever thus: 'Chimkent is a miniature of Tashkent, but without the great buildings and shops,' wrote Stephen Graham in 1914. 'It is a beautiful little town, however... [with] its mountain background, its white-stemmed, magnificent poplars, its old ruins, its fortifications.'

No such ruins remain. Chimkent was founded in the 11th century and later prospered from trade between steppe nomads and the settled subjects of Kokand. But it was heavily shelled by the Russians in 1864, and has been entirely rebuilt since World War II. Except to get a bus to Turkestan's Khodja Ahmed Yasavi mausoleum (*see* p.277), there is little point in stopping here.

Getting to and from Chimkent

by air

Chimkent's airport has at least three flights a day to and from Almaty ($94); Moscow (two flights per week go to, $175). There are no flights to Tashkent.

The central **ticket office** (*open 8.30am–12 noon and 1–7pm*) is at Ulitsa Dzhiltakhan 4 (formerly Ulitsa Dolores), from where bus 12 goes to the airport.

by rail

Chimkent has two TurkSib trains in each direction each day, serving Tashkent, Novosibirsk and everywhere in between. In addition there are two trains a day to Moscow—one from Almaty and one from Bishkek. The station is east of the centre, linked by buses 5 and 20 to the Hotel Chimkent and by buses 2 and 6 and trolleybuses 3 and 6 to the Hotel Voskhod.

by bus

Buses go to Tashkent every 30 minutes between 7am to 7.25pm (the journey of 160km takes 3 hours). There are ten a day to Kentau via Turkestan, ten to Dzhambul and four to Almaty. Tashkent–Bishkek buses stop here. The bus station is on the south (Tashkent) side of town. Cross into Uzbekistan from here, by bus. Border formalities are less daunting than at Tashkent airport and near the bazaar is an interesting spaghetti junction of trucks from Asia and Eastern Europe.

Chimkent (℗ 3252–)   **Where to Stay**

The **Hotel Voskhod**, former Sovietskaya Ulitsa 1, ℗ 3 19 20, is the closest to the stations. It means well but is afflicted by traffic noise at the front and giant mosquitoes from a stream at the back.

Hotel Chimkent, Prospekt Taukikhan (former Prospekt Lenina) 6a, ℗ 18 55 41 is the Intourist hotel in the centre of the city. Foreigners get the best rooms on floors 2 and 5 but all seem to suffer from unreliable hot water. *Lyux* rooms are $25, 'half-*lyux*' $18 and plain doubles are $8. The service bureau is closed at weekends. There is a post office downstairs (*open 9am–12 noon and 1–7pm*).

Preferable to either if you can get in is the **Hotel Druzhba**, Ulitsa Chernishevskaya, ℗ 46 84 90. Sited on a green rise above the smog, it is run by, and mostly for, the tyre factory.

Chimkent (℗ 3252–)   **Eating Out**

The giant, yurt-themed restaurant at the Hotel Chimkent smells of the lavatories near its entrance. The Hotel Voskhod's restaurant is better, and closer to the fresh fruit and *shashlyk* of the **bazaar**, two blocks up the hill to the southeast.

From Chimkent the M32 trunk road strikes out bravely along the northern edge of the Kizyl-Kum desert towards European Russia. Two and a half hours (160km) down it, between the Syr-Darya river and the end of the Karatau hills, stands the **Khodja Ahmed Yasavi mausoleum** (**мавзолей Ходжа Ахмед Ясави**) (1397); *open every day, 10am–2pm and 3–7pm.* Still a place of pilgrimage, it dwarfs the otherwise unremarkable town of Turkestan (population 76,000) and is presently enjoying a period of restoration, thanks to Turkey's assistance.

Turkestan was founded as Shavgar in the 10th century, became an important religious centre under the Karakhanid Turks in the 11th, and from the 16th to the 18th centuries was centre of the Kazakh Khanate of the Lesser Horde. Khodja Ahmed Yasavi was a Sufi poet and teacher who lived in Turkestan and died here in 1146; his mausoleum is all that remains of the ancient city. Tamerlane commissioned it in 1394, on the grand scale of the one built for his favourite son Jehangir in Shahrisabz.

It is not clear why; Tamerlane never acknowledged a particular debt to Yasavi's teachings. He may simply have been seeking a pretext for an intimidating exhibition of wealth in the northern reaches of his empire. He certainly ensured it bore his name; apart from its dome, which is the largest in Central Asia, the mausoleum's most impressive element is a sacred two-tonne bronze water vessel, returned from the Hermitage in 1988, in the main chamber, bearing the Arabic inscription: 'This is a gift from Timur for having built this mausoleum.' The gift was to Abd al-Aziz Sharif ad-Din at-Tabrizi, the Persian master-craftsman who cast the vessel in 1399.

The mausoleum was actually a self-contained religious complex with 35 rooms on two floors reached by corridors leading off the central chamber, which served as a mosque, and spiral staircases in the three-quarter columns flanking the *iwan*. First on the left, with a high ceiling and huge brick ovens, was a kitchen to feed pilgrims and wandering dervishes. In the corridor through the far left hand door there is a ghoulish and unexplained collection of Marco Polo sheep skulls and horns. It leads to a small mosque whose exquisite tilework has recently been restored. **Yasavi's tombstone**, visible through a carved wood screen, is directly behind the chamber and reached through the far right hand door. The **tomb of Abulkhair**, the khan of the Lesser Horde who pledged allegiance to the czar in 1730 and died in 1746, is adjacent to Yasavi's.

Tamerlane intended the outside of the building to be covered entirely in blue and green tiles, but when he died the glaziers stopped working. The tiling remains unfinished to this day, although the dazzlingly-restored rear elevation shows what the front should have looked like. The ribbed cupola over Yasavi's burial chamber was the first of its kind in Central Asia, famously imitated at Gur Emir in Samarkand.

The smaller mausoleum facing Yasavi's was for **Rabiya Sultan Begin**, a niece of Ulug Bek's (some sources say it was for Yasavi's daughter). This is a replica of the 16th-century original. A nearby 16th-century **bath-house** has been turned into a museum.

Getting to and from Turkestan

by rail

Up to five trains a day go through towards Moscow: two from Tashkent and one each from Almaty, Bishkek and Andizhan.

by bus

Buses come nearly every hour from Chimkent. Going back there, the first one each day is at 6.30am, the last at 6.30pm. Three buses a day go to Kzyl-Orda, 286km down the Syr Darya.

Getting Around

Buses 1, 2 and 5 ply between the bus and railway stations and the Hotel Turkestan.

Where to Stay and Eating Out

The **Hotel Turkestan**, facing the back of the mausoleum on former Prospekt Lenina 88, ✆ 5 11 72, appears to have closed down at present. The town's principal eatery is the **Restaurant Nauryz**, a block north of the hotel on the corner of former Ploshchad Lenina. The canteen next door is basic but open longer hours. Facing the mausoleum there is a line of avoidable *chai-khanas*. The best option is the abundant fresh produce in the bazaar.

Baikonur Cosmodrome (Байконур)

The financial mayhem gripping the CIS extends even unto space travel. The word on space street is that while NASA charges $70 million to put a satellite in orbit, Baikonur will do it for a recession-blasting $1.5 million.

And you can see it happen. Shrouded in secrecy until 1991, the cosmodrome is now open, with certain conditions, to the public. Launches are literally earth-shaking, and they let you get closer here than at Cape Canaveral. The cosmodrome is near the military city of Leninsk on the Syr Darya, 490km beyond Turkestan and 230km beyond Kzyl-Orda; a network of launch-pads, gantries and tracking stations in an otherwise eerily empty part of the planet. (The village of Baikonur is 300km north of here and has nothing to do with space travel. The cosmodrome was named after it as a decoy.)

Red Tape

The space programme is still run and funded by Russia and mission control is still at Star City outside Moscow. Nikolai Simionov, ✆ (095) 972 3755, is in charge of scheduling there, speaks some English, and can tell you when the next launch is.

Since the cosmodrome is now on sovereign Kazakh territory, however, permission to go there must be obtained from the Kazakh Foreign Ministry in Almaty, Ulitsa Aiteke Bi 65, ✆ (3272) 63 25 38/63 13 87.

Plan ahead. If the authorities at Leninsk do not receive at least 20 days' notice from the Foreign Ministry that you are coming they will bar you from the cosmodrome and send you back to Almaty. A Leninsk visa stamp is not sufficient. To increase your chances of permission give the ministry at least two months' notice, the most impressive-looking credentials you can muster and if possible a formal invitation from a Kazakh sponsor.

Getting to and from Baikonur

There is no public airport at Leninsk, which does not exist on most maps and whose mainly Russian personnel still regard it as closed, even though the Kazakh media announced in 1991 that is was open.

The nearest public airport is at Kzyl-Orda, to which there are frequent flights from Almaty ($90). From here it is 4 hours by taxi to Leninsk (offer $15 in rubles), or 6 by train. All Moscow-bound trains from Tashkent (17 hours and $23), Andizhan, Bishkek (26 hours and $22) and Almaty go through Kzyl-Orda and Leninsk.

Leninsk proper is separate from the station and walled, with an army checkpoint at the entrance. The entrance to the cosmodrome is about 5km away on the other (north) side of the railway line, with another checkpoint.

Security has become lax since Soviet times. The soldiers at the checkpoints are bored and friendly. If in doubt about the validity of your documentation, play dumb and enlist their support rather than walk into the arms of the equally bored but habitually suspicious ex-KGB personnel who monitor comings and goings at Leninsk's two hotels; this will ensure a short stay.

Group Trips

Ask around; four to five years ago **Intourist** in Almaty, at Hotel Otrar, Ulitsa Gogolya 73, used to arrange trips for the press. Rumours that tours were also offered to sightseers are usually denied. But it's worth asking, even if the going rate at their affiliated Hotel Interkosmos and the cosmodrome excursion used to be a suitably astronomical $1200, excluding the obligatory return flight, specially chartered, to Leninsk.

Kramds Mountain Company in Almaty,Ulitsa Michurin (Karasat Batyra) 68b, ✆ (3272) 62 38 50, ✉ 63 90 20 arranges Baikonur trips through, Vasily Fedotavich Oniskov, ✆ (3272) 44 75 30, who works for a state organization called Inkos.

Try also **Ian McNeill** ✆ (3272) 69 41 18, ✉ 69 42 18.

Where to Stay

The **Hotel Interkosmos**, on the left inside the entrance to Leninsk, is where Gagarin used to stay. With marble everywhere and chrome models of rockets along the bar, this is the acme of Soviet chic and very expensive. Intourist clients will be put here automatically. There is an overflow hotel for non-VIPs nearby. Modest compared with the Interkosmos, it is still spruce, comfortable and bedecked with space memorabilia.

Dzhambul (Джамбул)

A branch of the Silk Route and the old czarist post road wound their way over the Karatau hills from Chimkent to Dzhambul, as the M39 does now. It descends into the elbow formed by the Karatau and the Kyrgyz Ala-Too ranges, where the Talas river waters an ancient oasis.

Founded in the 6th century as Taraz, Dzhambul claims, like Bukhara and Balasagun (of which only the Burana tower near Bishkek survives), to have been a capital of the Karakhanid Turks in the 11th century. The Mongols destroyed most of it in the 13th, and the Russians named it Aulie-Ata in 1864. 'Dzhambul' is a Kazakh name but a Soviet idea. Dzhababayev Dzhambul was a local folksinger, and Aulie-Ata took his name when Kazakhstan gained the status of republic in 1936.

Dzhambul's past, like Chimkent's, is mostly buried beneath the new Soviet city (population 307,000). There is some genuine 11th-century brickwork on a nearby mausoleum, but the 'scores of mosques, lifting their slender minarets above the verdure of the trees,' which Stephen Graham saw in 1914, have gone. In their place are 11 numbered districts, each consisting of 65 apartment blocks, each block being home to 120 families. Three chemical combines on the outskirts turn phosphate ore from the mountains into fertilizer, employing 17,000 people while fouling the air and causing frightening levels of cancer and lung disease in nearby homes. The good news is that the current economic crisis has left no money for wages, halving production and pollution since 1991.

Dzhambul is twinned with Fresno, California.

Getting to and from Dzhambul

by air

There are two flights a day between Almaty and Dzhambul, four a week to Moscow, three a week to Tashkent and two a week to Semipalatinsk. The ticket office at Ulitsa Tole Bu 43 (formerly Kommunisticheskaya Ulitsa) has a foreigners' window (*open 8am–1pm and 2–5pm; closed weekends*). Bus 9 goes from here to the airport.

by rail

There are daily services to Moscow, Almaty, Bishkek, Tashkent and Novosibirsk.

by bus

Buses go regularly during the day to Chimkent and Bishkek, both day and night to Tashkent and Almaty.

Getting Around

Bus 29 runs to the Hotel Taraz in the town centre from the bus station, bus 1 from the railway station, bus 9 from the airport and bus 3 from the bazaar, which is two blocks southeast of Lenin Park.

Buses for the Aisha Bibi mausoleum at Golovachovka (**Головачовка**), 18km to the west along the Chimkent road, leave from Dzhambul's bus and railway stations. To get there by taxi, offer the driver $4 in rubles for the return trip.

Tourist Information

The **Intourist office** at the Hotel Taraz (open 9am–1pm and 2–6pm, ℃ 3 19 18/3 15 59, exists mainly to sell city tours which take in the Aisha Bibi mausoleum and—at about $75 ($25 an hour)—are absolutely not worth it.

They also do wine-tasting trips to the I. V. Michurin grape *kolkhoz* back up the Chimkent road, and excursions to a stud farm 120km towards Bishkek, where flat-racers and show-jumpers are bred and local boys and girls may be persuaded to play *kiss-ku*. In this horseback kiss chase, when a boy catches a girl he kisses her and when a girl catches a boy she hits him over the head.

Remains of Old Taraz

The **Karakhan mausoleum** (*open 9 am–1 pm and 2–6 pm; closed Mon*) in the city centre's former Lenin Park, is a 20th-century reconstruction of an 11th-century original. It contains a small exhibition of finds from old Taraz.

The plain **Daudbek Shahmansur mausoleum** nearby is also a reconstruction, this time of a 13th-century original.

To find any actual remnants of the ancient city, you must leave Dzhambul for Golovachovka. Here, in a glass box, stands the restored 12th-century **Aisha Bibi mausoleum** (**мавзолей Аиша Биби**). Little is known about this Karakhan woman besides her name. The carved terracotta stars and rosettes in its east wall are original, and more intricate than anything of the same period in Bukhara. The glass box is to protect them from polluted air—but is far from air-tight. Next door is the rebuilt 11th-century **Babadzi-Khatun mausoleum**, with a very unusual straight-ribbed pointed roof.

Dzhambul (✆ 3262–)   ***Where to Stay and Eating Out***

The **Hotel Taraz**, Prospekt Dzhambul 75, ✆ 3 27 50/3 34 91, is an Intourist hotel and predictably oblong from the outside, but clean, comfortable and friendly on the inside. There are hot showers, TVs, a sauna, and an air ticket office; accommodation ranges from apartments at $35 to doubles at $11 (with phone $12) and singles at $9–1. The restaurant serves Russian and Kazakh food, and seems to make an extra effort for foreigners.

Another Intourist-run hotel is the **Dzhambul**, Ulitsa Tolebay 40, ✆ 4 25 52, 📠 4-17 50. It also offers apartments for $35–80; doubles and singles cost the same at $25. At the airport is the **Sokol**, ✆ 5 21 89.

The **bed and breakfast** option (maximum capacity 15 people) is run by a private firm, **L.A.T.**, at Ulitsa Beyzak Botira 8, ✆ 4 48 49, 📠 4 74 29. The director is Loigev Aleksandr and rooms cost $10 for *lyux* and $8 for half-*lyux*. For $10 you can use the sauna.

The bus station has Dzhambul's best fast food.

Almaty (Алматы)

To get the feel of Almaty, leave it. Go instead to Medeo on a Sunday afternoon. Every one of Almaty's 1.2 million inhabitants who can skate, and thousands more who can't, will be up here, swirling and tumbling round an enormous white oval in the stadium: Korean families in matching Sunday best, Ukrainian hippies in Y-fronts only, ex-Soviet ice dance champions and ice-hockey bruisers. The Medeo speed-skating rink is the world's largest, and the pride of Almaty. Filling a beautiful valley in the Zailiisky Ala-Too 16km from the city centre, it symbolizes the Russification and modernization of Kazakhstan.

In a not much subtler way, so is Almaty itself, laid out neatly below under a near-permanent brown haze. Somewhere down there in Panfilov Park, old Kazakh men in homburg hats play chess in the shadow of a pastel-painted wooden Orthodox cathedral. Across the road the Intourist hotel's restaurant is shaped like a yurt. Two blocks in one direction, *koumis* (fermented mares' milk), the great gastronomic invention of the steppe nomad, is sold from the ground floor of a Soviet office block. Two blocks in the other, an orgy of reinforced concrete houses so-called 'oriental baths'.

In the Soviet era Almaty did not so much defer to local customs as absorb them, remaining essentially a Russian outpost. Geoffrey Moorhouse, passing through in one of the city's last Soviet winters, found it depressing: 'a city of relentlessly grandiose public architecture without a trace of charm, and of concrete barrack blocks for the proletariat which were even meaner inside than without; and there they were stultifying enough.'

Poor Mr Moorhouse. It must have been the time of year. In spring and autumn, dull buildings notwithstanding, Almaty is an invigorating place, with cool air, wide streets, trees everywhere and views of glinting glaciers even closer than those above Bishkek. Fitzroy Maclean, in 1937, thought it 'one of the pleasantest provincial towns in the Soviet Union', and Laurens van der Post, in the early 1960s, was quite carried away by its setting between mountain and plain:

'This contrast, this opposition between two irreconcilable principles of earth, reached its most dramatic expression at Almaty, for there in front of us the "Mountains of Heaven" rose sheerly out of the low land of Kazakhstan like a wall with watchtowers of 15,000 and 17,000 feet high under permanent snow.'

Almaty has changed faster since *perestroika* than any other Central Asian city. Its fabric is the same, but there is a new cosmopolitanism and a whiff of Klondike spirit in the air. The cheap hotels are full of Chinese Uighur traders from Ürümqi, come to sell plastic luggage and fake designer tracksuits in the burgeoning bazaar. The expensive ones are becoming used to Western businessmen attracted by Nursultan Nazarbayev's relatively red tape-free regime. High-rollers from Chevron, British Gas and Elf-Aquitaine fly in to bid for drilling rights on the northern steppe, staying in a $140-a-night former Communist Party guest-house. Taxi-drivers and interpreters grow worldly-wise and dollar-rich while their counterparts in Tashkent, under a more conservative regime, miss out on the gold rush.

History

Like most other cities along the northern edge of the Tian Shan, Almaty stands on the site of a former Silk Route town which was besieged by the Mongols and of which nothing remains. The Kazakhs called it Almaty, after the apple trees for which it was famous. The Russians established a frontier post here in 1854 and called it Verney.

Verney was to be a substantial presence, not just a garrison; a signal to the Kazakhs, the Chinese and the Khanate of Kokand that the czar meant business in Central Asia. Cossacks and Siberian peasants farmers were settled here as soon as a fort was built, and by 1877 Verney's population was 12,000.

A Place of Exile

But in 1887 and 1911 it was all but flattened by earthquakes, and Stephen Graham wrote dismissively after his 1914 visit: 'It is not necessary to say much about Verney, the capital of Seven Rivers Land. It is so subject to earthquakes that it is difficult to see in it a permanent capital. No houses of two storeys can with safety be built... In order to look imposing, shops and stores have fixed up sham upper storeys.'

Verney was at this time a place of exile, but it cannot have been too miserable. 'Verney has its bazaar, its inns and doubtful houses,' Graham continued, 'its baths, dance halls, clubs, restaurants... It has its frivolity and sin and small crime.' But: 'It has no electric cars. It has no Bond Street or West End.'

Nor would it. Soviet power arrived in 1921 and Verney was renamed Alma-Ata ('father of apples'), presumably to acknowledge the original Kazakh name and then go one better. In 1929 Almaty took over from Kzyl-Orda as capital of Soviet Kazakhstan, and the following year the TurkSib railway connected it to the Trans-Siberian. During World War II, entire communities of Koreans from the Soviet Far East and Germans from the Soviet Volga German republic were deported here, where it was thought they could do least to undermine the Soviet war effort were they so minded. Heavy engineering plant was also relocated to Almaty during the war, and formed the basis of its manufacturing industry afterwards.

Kazakhs have always been in a minority in their own capital, and for most of the Soviet era they submitted quietly to alien rule because they had no choice. But within a year of Gorbachev's accession, Almaty's students were on the streets in an unprecedented public protest at the replacement of the Kazakh first secretary of the local Communist Party with a Russian. And in 1989 a Kazakh poet called Olzhas Suleimanov led a public campaign in Almaty to force an end to nuclear testing at Semipalatinsk. Testing stopped that year. The campaign, Nevada-Semipalatinsk, is the subject of a permanent exhibition in Almaty's central state museum, and Suleimanov is a national hero. Shortly after independence in 1992, Alma-Ata reverted to its Kazakh name of Almaty.

Getting to and from Almaty

by air

Starting or finishing your trip at Almaty is fairly straightforward. Almaty's airport now rivals Tashkent's as an international hub. Lufthansa, ℂ 34 47 20/34 44 75, flies direct from Frankfurt four times a week and Turkish Airways, ℂ 50 62 20/34 01 70, from Istanbul once a week direct and twice via Tashkent. Amsterdam's KLM has two weekly flights as has CAAC from Ürümqi.

Austrian Airlines/Swiss Air, ℂ 50 10 70/50 10 69, have two airbus flights per week to Vienna and connections from there to all major cities worldwide. Pakistan Airways, ℂ 34 42 97, fly once weekly to Almaty from Islamabad and Iranian

Airways, ℗ 34 49 49, once weekly from Tehran. For $200 (single) you can arrive from Ulaan Bataar courtesy of the Mongolian national airways, MIAT. Turkish Airlines fly from Istanbul with connections to Europe and North America. Air France offer connections via Paris.

Flights within the CIS have been hit by rising fuel prices. This, in addition to seasonal variations, makes it worth checking the schedule upon arrival. In general, there is at least one flight a day to and from Moscow (4 hours, $200).

Flights go to Tashkent three to four times a week ($83), three times a week to Novosibirsk ($109), once a week to Irkutsk ($150), and twice a week to Ashgabat ($124). There are no flights to Samarkand or Bishkek. The state airline, Kazair, offers connecting flights throughout Asia as well as to various European destinations.

The main Kazakh cities are all well served by frequent flights: Chimkent (4 per day, $94), Dzhambul, Kzyl-Orda, Karaganda, Akmola (formerly Tselinograd), Pavlodar, Semipalatinsk and Ust-Kamenogorsk. In the absence of a flight to Tashkent, consider flying to Chimkent and completing the journey by bus. Buses are frequent and the Uzbek border formalities are often less arduous than those at Tashkent airport.

Intourist at the Hotel Otrar no longer sells Aeroflot tickets. The tickets sold in the office, ℗ 33 00 07/33 00 37, to the left of the main entrance are for Transaero, KLM and Air France.

Transaero competes with Aeroflot, flying to all the main cities of the CIS and internationally under the name Riga Air. Tickets for Kazair and Aeroflot can be purchased at the main ticket office, ℗ 54 15 55, located in the *aerovokzal*, six blocks west of the park on Ulitsa Zhibek Zholu (formerly Ulitsa Gorkovo) and Ulitsa Zheltoksan. The large murals on the building to the right of the *aerovokzal* are a useful landmark. (Alternatively, try the international/Intourist section of the airport (*open 24 hours*), at its left-hand end as you approach from the city.

The *aerovokzal* is more than a ticket office. It also provides a bus service to the airport and deals with flight registration. Arrive at least one hour prior to your flight departure. Go to the opposite side of the hall to 'ticket sales' and find the door with the appropriate flight information above it. Your baggage will be checked in and the bus departure announced. Flight information is displayed on a large electronic board in the centre of the hall. Otherwise, catch state bus 92, which also stops at the main hotels, and proceed to the airport. Taxis charge in the region of $10.

by rail

Competition from the state bus has resulted in, at times, half-empty trains. There are two railway stations: Almaty I, ℗ 36 33 91, and Almaty, II ℗ 60 55 44. The

Almaty

KEY

1	Zenkov Cathedral Зенковский Собор	**8**	Circus Цирк	**15**	Bus stop for Medeo Остановка для автобусов до Медео
2	Museum of Kazakh Instruments Музей Казахских Инструментов	**9**	Zelyony Bazaar Зелёный Базар	**16**	Post Office Почта
3	St Nicholas Cathedral Никольский Собор	**10**	Nicholas Bazaar Никольский Базар	**17**	President's Palace Резиденция Президента
4	Art Museum Музей Искусств	**11**	Arasan baths Бани Арасан	**18**	Chinese Uigur and Korean Theatres Китайский, Уйгурский и Корейский
5	Central Museum Центральный Музей	**12**	Almaty II railway station Железнодорожный Вокзал II	**19**	Theatre of Opera and Ballet Театр Оперы и Балета
6	Archaeology Museum Музей Археологии	**13**	Aeroflot booking office Агенство Аэрофлота	**20**	Lermontov Theatre Театр имени Ю. Лермонтова
7	Glory Memorial Памятник Славу	**14**	Aeroflot city terminal Городской Аэровокзал	**21**	Tsum Цум

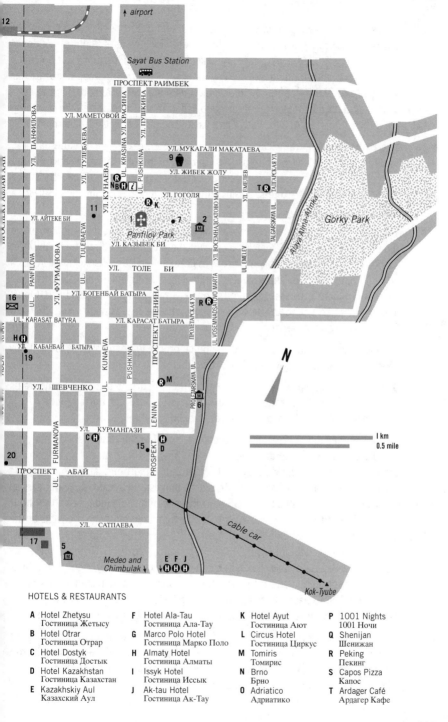

HOTELS & RESTAURANTS

A Hotel Zhetysu
Гостиница Жетысу

B Hotel Otrar
Гостиница Отрар

C Hotel Dostyk
Гостиница Достык

D Hotel Kazakhstan
Гостиница Казахстан

E Kazakhskiy Aul
Казахский Аул

F Hotel Ala-Tau
Гостиница Ала-Тау

G Marco Polo Hotel
Гостиница Марко Поло

H Almaty Hotel
Гостиница Алматы

I Issyk Hotel
Гостиница Иссык

J Ak-tau Hotel
Гостиница Ак-Тау

K Hotel Ayut
Гостиница Ают

L Circus Hotel
Гостиница Цирк ус

M Tomiris
Томирис

N Brno
Брно

O Adriatico
Адриатико

P 1001 Nights
1001 Ночи

Q Shenijan
Шенижан

R Peking
Пекинг

S Capos Pizza
Капос

T Ardager Café
Ардагер Кафе

closest to the centre is Almaty II, at the north end of Prospekt Ablai Khan. Most trains that start or finish in Almaty do so here. Trolleybuses 5 and 6 run down Ablai Khan to Almaty II. You can buy tickets here for all departures, but do check which station your train goes from. Pay in local currency at the counter at the far left-hand side of the station. The mechanical card indexes in Almaty II are a better source of up-to-date departure information than the big departure boards, which are only summaries. An alternative and useful source of tickets is the airport.

The daily Moscow train leaves Almaty II at noon, except on Wednesday and Friday when it it leaves at 4pm. It goes via Dzhambul, Chimkent and the Syr Darya, and takes three days. The fastest train on the TurkSib is the Tashkent–Novosibirsk express, passing Almaty each day in each direction ($30 for a *kupe* from Almaty).

There is a direct train to Novosbirsk leaving Almaty at lunchtime on even days of the month. Daily services to Semipalatinsk include both transit and direct trains and take 22 hours. Direct trains run on even days, as does the service to Bishkek, which takes 10 hours and costs $23. There are less frequent services to and from Mezhdurezinsk (southern Siberia), Irkutsk, Barnaul, Tomsk, Krasnoyarsk, Ekaterinburg, Omsk and Saratov. To get to the Fergana valley, change in Tashkent. Andizhan no longer has any direct service.

If booking a berth on a train, go to the office on the left-hand side of the station. There should be a window labelled Ürümqi here.

Almaty I, ✆ 36 33 91, is north of the centre on the TurkSib mainline. Some trains between the southern republics and Siberia stop here but not at Almaty II. If marooned at Almaty I, catch the express bus 30 or 34 into town.

In the summer the international express no.14 (a Kazakh train) departs Almaty I for Ürümqi on Saturday and Monday evenings, and its Chinese sister, no.13, arrives from there on Monday and Wednesday mornings at 8.05am (going through Almaty II at 8.25am). A dining-car makes only erratic appearances, so bring plenty of provisions for the 35-hour journey, which includes an 8- or 9-hour wait at the border for bogie changing. And be prepared for lengthy checks at the Chinese border; your belongings will certainly be searched and don't be surprised if your passport is held for several hours. Departing Almaty for Ürümqi on the last day of your visa is possible—so says the head of the visa department at the Ministry of Foreign Affairs and Intourist, although staff at the train station may claim otherwise. The Almaty–Ürümqi fare is the equivalent in local currency of $84 per person in a *lyux* two-berth cabin, $50 for the same in *kupe*, or economy class.

On the Chinese train, which costs slightly more, the cars with 'hard sleeper' (*yìngwòchě*) on the side are actually the usual soft sleepers, and the ones with 'soft sleeper' (*ruânwòchě*) are ultra-soft, with two beds and a comfy chair per compartment, like the Chinese Trans-Manchurian train.

The main bus terminal, ✆ 26 26 44, is west of the city centre on Ulitsa Tole Bi and Mate Zalka, and can be reached by trolleybus 19, which runs up Prospekt Lenina, along Abay, and down Mate Zalka. Quicker are buses 126 and 43 which go along Tole Bi and can be caught from near the Hotels Otrar and Zhetisu.

Bus travel along the north edge of the Tian Shan is quicker but more cramped than the train. Tickets are easier to get and less expensive. For a $50 ticket catch the bus to Ürümqi via Khorgos leaving at 7am (*Mon–Sat*); it's quicker (24 hours) than the twice-weekly train via Druzhba—but occasionally Almaty bus station claims you need an HIV negative certificate to get on it (no such thing is needed coming from China).

There are four buses a day to Tashkent (16 hours, about $25), one to Ust-Kamenogorsk (*not* via Semipalatinsk; 21 hours, about $30) and four to Panfilov (7 hours). Buses depart hourly from 7am to Bishkek (5 hours, $5–7) and also to Dzhambul (10 hours, $15).

Getting Around

Central Almaty is a grid on a slope, 650m above sea level at its northern edge and 950m at the foot of the mountains. Walking north is thus a pleasure while walking south can be hard work. A point reinforced by locals who refer to 'up' or 'down' Almaty when giving directions. Blocks are long—four or five to a kilometre—and the whole city is on a larger scale than similarly-shaped Bishkek.

The principal north–south artery is Prospekt Lenina, starting at Panfilov Park, passing the Hotel Kazakhstan and becoming the road to Medeo. Further west, Prospekt Ablai Khan leads down from near the Presidential Palace past the *aerovokzal* and the Hotel Zhetsu to Almaty II station. Crossing these a block apart from west to east are Ulitsa Gogolya and the partly pedestrianized Zhibek Zholu ('Silk Road'). Gogolya passes the Hotel Otrar and forms the north side of Panfilov Park. Zhibek Zholu passes the *aerovokzal* and the bazaar. Both end at Gorky Park.

Public transport consists mainly of buses and trolleybuses; Ablai Khan and Gogolya are the streets best served by trolleybuses. So it is easy, for instance, to find your way from Almaty II to the *aerovokzal*. Less easy to find are bus numbers that stay the same. What follows is a hopeful guide. Buses and bus stops generally list their destinations in Cyrillic. Bus 92 comes to the *aerovokzal* from the airport and buses 43 and 126 and trolleybuses 4 and 3 sets out from the long-distance bus station on the western outskirts. Bus 6 goes to Medeo from the stop opposite the Hotel Kazakhstan on Prospekt Lenina.

Prospekt Abay and the parallel Ulitsa Gogolya with their intersecting streets (Prospekt Ablai Khan and Ulitsa Furmanova) are all well served by buses. Two useful options are no.61, whose route includes the Central Museum, along Furmanova past the embassies and onto Karla Marxa for the Arasan Baths. And no.151 from Prospekt Lenina (Hotel Kazakhstan), the Zelyony (green) bazaar and the *aerovokzal*. If you stay sitting on either bus 4 or 2, you can't go far wrong since both follow circular routes. Enjoy a city tour.

Commercial buses offer an alternative to the state variety and are distinguished only by having three not two numbers on them. For a slightly higher fare (less than 50 cents) you buy the privilege of being picked up or set down at your request. State buses go by the bus stop. If in Almaty for more than one month, a state bus pass is a good investment. Purchase these for approximately $5, at newspaper kiosks or from the bus conductor. Otherwise pay per journey on the bus; either the driver or conductor.

Ever hopeful and ever obliging private cars/taxis are much in evidence as a means of general tranport. At night, however, it's advisable to stick to the official taxis which can be called by dialling 058 or call Alem Taxis, ✆ 30 49 73.

Hertz rent-a-car has offices (*open 9am–6pm*) at the airport and on the ground floor of the circular business centre opposite the Hotel Kazakhstan; Prospekt Lenina 85, ✆ 63 18 32/62 25 15, ✉ 63 18 32. Cars and prices are western; credit cards are accepted.

Tourist Information

Intourist in its old, Soviet guise, is no more; it has joined the ranks of the numerous independent travel companies. Still operating from its office at the Hotel Otrar, Ulitsa Gogolya 73, ✆ 33 00 45, its trips are linked to the service provided by the hotel although they can be joined by non-residents. Their city tour (excluding museums, which cost extra) and Medeo excursion each take three hours and cost $60 for up to three in a car ($20 an hour). The same hourly rate applies for a seven-hour trip to Lake Issyk, which was obliterated by a mudslide in 1963 and should not be confused with Lake Issyk-Kul.

For the individual, a tour to Medeo including lunch in the Kazakh Aul Restaurant will cost $30 or you pay a more modest $10 to visit the Central Museum and $8 for a trip to the Museum of Kazakh Instruments. Credit cards and travellers' cheques are accepted for excursions. Intourist claim not to be able to arrange trips to Baikonur Cosmodrome, but there's nothing to lose by asking them anyway, and they may, at least, be able to find out when the next launch is.

Bear in mind that permission to visit is needed from the Ministry of Foreign Affairs. The hotels Marco Polo and Almaty (business centre, ✆ 63 02 02) also offer city tours with a guide. The district **post office** is a block west of the Hotel Kazakhstan on Ulitsa Kurmangazi. The main one is on the southeast side of Ulitsa Bogenbay Batyra, on the junction with Prospekt Ablai Khan.

Queues at the central **telegraph and telephone office**, on the south side of Ulitsa Zhibek Zholu opposite no. 81, are interminable. A less time consuming alternative is to use one of the business centres attached to the large hotels, which also offer fax and e-mail services. Try the Dostuk, Marco Polo and Kazakhstan, all open to non-residents and payable in hard currency or by credit card. (Residents at these hotels and the Otrar can make international calls from their rooms.)

Or try the International Business Centre at Prospekt Lenina 85, opposite the Hotel Kazakhstan. The entrance faces Kurmangazi street. *Open Mon–Fri, 9am–6pm.*

For **visa support**, including **extensions** and extra **city stamps**, call OVIR, ✆ 62 44 36, Ulitsas Vinogradov and Masanchi. If you have more money than time, it's well worth getting a travel company to do it for you, for instance, **Checkpoint Business Services**, ✆ 65 17 42/64 32 48, **C.A.T.S**, ✆ 63 90 17/62 50 33, or **Kuppava Consultancy**, ✆ 53 59 66. The fee varies.

Gone is the day when Kodak film was hard to find. On the corner of Ulitsas Zhibek Zholu and Pushkina is a one-day **photo lab** with a Kodak sign. At the other end of town, try the shop in the foyer of the Hotel Kazakhstan, or, for film and developing, the shop opposite the Dostuk Hotel on Ulitsa Kurmangazi. This has the added advantage of taking credit cards.

When getting film developed, bear in mind that unless you specify otherwise, you will receive negatives only. The cost of prints is extra, displayed at the counter against the size of print available. As a guide, expect to pay around 50 cents, in local currency (tenge), per regular-sized print.

Of all the republics, Kazakhstan has one of the most stable currencies. There's little to be gained by exchanging money on the black market. **Change kiosks** are numerous and easy to find—on street corners and in department stores as well as hotels and banks. American Express **travellers' cheques** can now be cashed at the Alem Bank of Kazakhstan, Prospekt Lenina 39 (*open 9am–12.30pm*), and TexaKaBank, Ulitsa Zenkova 4 (find it by going to the huge building facing the 'eternal flame' in Panfilov Park; the entrance is to the left of the arch). *Open Mon–Fri, 9am–1pm, 2–4.*

There's also a branch of the Alem Bank in the foyer of The Dostuk Hotel, but a costly 10% commission is charged for dollar exchange and travellers' cheques there.

Austrian Airlines/Swiss Air: C.A.T, Amangeldi 52, ✆ 63 90 17, @ 63 90 20

Lufthansa: near the airport hotel Aksynkar, Malina 2, ✆ 34 44 75, @ 34 40 49

PIA: near the airport hotel Aksynkar, Malina 2, ✆ 34 42 97

Turkey: Aiteke Bi 81 (Zheltoksan junction), ✆ 50 62 20

Xinxiang Airlines: Timiryazeva (Aurezova junction), opposite the exhibition centre, ✆ 50 94 85

Embassies

China: Ulitsa Furmanova 137, ✆ 63 49 66/63 92 91, @ 63 92 91. In theory the consular department can issue visas for China but only does so with an invitation from one of the state tourist agencies like CITS. Allow at least 5 working days to process. *Open 9am–12 noon and 3–6pm.*

France: Ulitsa Furmanova 173, ✆ 50 77 10/50 62 36/50 62 37, @ 50 61 59

Germany: Ulitsa Furmanova 173, ✆ 50 61 56, @ 50 62 76

Iran: Hotel Kazakhstan, ✆ 67 50 55, @ 54 27 54

Italy: Samal 2-69, 6th floor, ✆ 63 98 04/63 98 14, @ 63 96 36

Kyrgyzstan: Hotel Kazakhstan, suite 1310, ✆ 61 92 03, @ 50 62 60

Pakistan: Ulitsa Tulebaeva 25, ✆ 33 15 02/33 35 48/33 38 31, @ 33 13 00

Russia: Ulitsa Dzhandosa 4, ✆ 44 64 91/44 76 01, @ 44 82 22

Tajikistan: Ulitsa Emelev 70, ✆ 61 17 60, @ 61 02 25

Uzbekistan:Ulitsa Barybaeva 36, ✆ 61 83 16, @ 61 10 55

Turkey: Ulitsa Tole Bi 29, ✆ 61 39 32/61 81 53, @ 50 62 08

UK: Ulitsa Furmanova 173, ✆ 50 61 91and 92, @ 50 62 60

USA: Ulitsa Furmanova 99, ✆ 50 76 21/50 76 63, @ 63 38 83

Trekking

To be in Almaty and resist the mountains is hard. For those after more than a Sunday stroll at Medeo, there are now a host of trekking companies happy to assist. All levels of experience and adventure are catered for, but remember that to venture far afield without some guidance is inadvisable.

A good source of maps, not only the linear trekking variety, is the **A.P.S.** (Adventure, Protection and Survival) company. Experienced in rock-climbing, ski-mountaineering and trekking, they will provide all necessary kit for either the individual or the expedition tempted by the Tian Shian, Alatau and Jun ranski ranges.

For a helicopter trip into the Central Tian Shian, excluding guide cost, budget to spend around $50 per person per day. The company also offers visa support, transport and generally a helping hand to those baffled by red tape (very useful for first-time visitors). Since 1995, it has also run a Mountaineering and Conservation Club. Contact Ian Mcneill, ✆ 69 41 18, ✉ 69 42 18.

Another private operator, **Kramds Mountain Company**, now at Ulitsa Michurina 68b, ✆ 62 38 50, ✉ 63 90 20, started commercial guiding for climbers in 1989 and has since branched out into trekking, ski-touring, rafting, riding, mountain-biking, ballooning, paragliding, hunting and fishing trips, excursions to Baikonur, Silk Route tours, botanical, zoological and bird-watching tours. Helicopters to, from or during any of these cost from $200 an hour. Trekking and other guides cost from $30 a day, mountain guides from $150 a day. English, German and French are spoken.

For trips to Kyrgyzstan's Lake Issyk-Kul or those lakes closer to Almaty try **Zhetisu Travel** at Eisenberlinya 36, ✆ 62 42 18/34 92 62, ✉ 63 12 07, near the Sayahat Bus Station. Trips typically last 3–6 days and all-inclusive costs per person per day start at $70. Helicopter tours and one-day charter tours to Turkestan are also offered; English, French and German are spoken.

C.A.T.S. (Central Asia Travel Service), Amangeldi 52, ✆ 63 90 17, ✉ 69 70 55, offers different hikes each week, all lasting 7–8 hours and costing $30, including trips to the Bolshoy Almatinski Lake, Kok Zhailau Gorge and Manshuk Mametova Glacier for groups of two to twenty. Bookings must be made by the Thursday before you go. C.A.T.S also organize trips to Western China. English, French, German and Spanish are spoken.

Eric Elinsky, who can be found at the Central Army Club on Ulitsas Satpaeva and Furmanova, ✆ 64 17 59, or Zharokova 208, ✆ 48 47 09/48 19 42, or can be called at home, ✆ 69 44 60, if given ten days' notice, will arrange for you to ride a camel across the Kazakh steppe.

Other possiblities include: **Tourcentre Asia**, ✆ 49 79 36, for the adventurous, and **Kazinter Service Ltd**, ✆ 62 38 50, ✉ 63 90 20, if weekend trips near Almaty hold more appeal. **Alexander Khemelevsky** speaks excellent English and works independently as an interpreter or guide; contact him through Barracuda Trips, ✆ 48 27 79. As with other tour companies throughout Central Asia, his itineraries are very flexible (if you have a specific trip in mind, ask). So are his prices, within reason.

Panfilov Park (Парк Панфилова)

Almaty's most central park is dominated by one of the world's tallest wooden buildings. **Zenkov Cathedral**, named after its architect, was put up in 1904 without a single nail. With its 56-m west tower and magnificent painted exterior, it no doubt inspired reverence then. Not least because it survived the severe earthquake of 1910. Now it's a rare reminder of a time when grown-ups could be superstitious and buildings could have personalities. It served under the Soviets as a concert and exhibition hall. Today it has resumed its role in the Orthodox community and services are held daily despite current renovation work. Almaty's Orthodox Christians, Kazakh as well as Russian, also worship at **St Nicholas Cathedral** near the junction of Ulitsas Kosmonavtov and Baitursynova, on the west side of town. The original bells were restored to the cathedral in the summer of 1995 in the presence of the Orthodox Patriarch from Moscow.

At the east end of Panfilov Park is the city's most unusual building, a cross between Noah's ark and a Chinese pagoda, also built by the Almaty architect Andrei Zenkov and formerly the Russian Army Officers' Club. Now it's home to the **Museum of Kazakh Instruments** (*open 10 am–6 pm; closed Mon*), a unique collection of traditional instruments, some of which have been restored using references in old books and archaeological finds. The generic term for the most common type, a kind of long-necked lute, is *dombira*. The older ones have horsehair strings; the later ones silk. There's a sound recording of each; you are not supposed to play the recordings yourself but if the *devushka* in charge doesn't do it for you, start reaching under the cabinets for the switches and she probably will. For the nomad Kazakhs, *kyuis* (instrumental pieces) and songs ensured their traditions were passed from one generation to the next; forming a body of wisdom by which they lived. Each seasonal migration was blessed by a song, performed by the *aksakal* (white-bearded elder). Consider yourself blessed, if your visit includes an encounter with the museum's resident equivalent. With an impromptu concert he'll transport you to the Kazakh steppe and, for around $7, he'll provide a souvenir cassette.

The alarming bronze sculpture which accosts passers-by between the cathedral and the museum is the **Glory Memorial** to 28 Almaty men of General Ivan Panfilov's division who in 1941, so the carefully-nurtured legend goes, repulsed 50 Nazi tanks from the outskirts of Moscow. The eternal flame in the slab of black marble beneath their mighty muscles used to be guarded day and night by platoons of children.

Across the street at the west end of the park, the **Arasan baths** (meaning 'warm spring'), ✆ 62 68 88, are divided into Turkish, Finnish and Russian sections, each with male and female sub-sections, all variations on the sauna theme. The ticket window is below street level under the main entrance on the south side. The standard option, recommended if your hotel is stingy with its hot water, can be a treat for $1–2 in local currency (for a small additional charge, towels can be hired in the changing rooms). Or you can splash out on a luxury mineral bath and underwater back-massage for $8. For the entrance to the luxury, private rooms, go to the east side of the block, on Ulitsa Kunaeva. *Open Tues–Sun, 8–8, but some facilities have different closing times and take a break 1–2pm.*

Theatres in Almaty reflect its varied ethnic composition. At Nauryzbay Batyra, you'll find Chinese, Uighur and Korean theatres. The Russian theatre is the **Lermontov**, Prospekt Abay 43;the German one is at Ulitsa Satpaeva 64. Auezov's famous trilogy about Kazakh life is performed at the theatre named in his honour at Prospekt Abay 103, a venue, like the Russian Drama Theatre, that's not adverse to the odd Shakespeare play. At performances in Kazakh, a Russian translation can be supplied through headphones. The **Theatre of Opera and Ballet** at Ulitsa Kabanbaya Batyra 112, has a good central location and a repertoire that embraces resident Kazakh as well as Muscovite and European companies. Information on performances is posted outside all the theatres.

For a rather different spectacle try the **State Circus,** located further along Abay (*performances most weekends*). Resembling the space ship in the film *ET*, it's easily identified. Kazakhstan shares with Turkmenistan and Kyrgyzstan a justified reputation for horsemanship and another weekend pastime, although confined to the summer months, is **horse racing**. The race track is located at Lesnaya Ulitsa 10 and Belinsky, in the older part of town.

Manhattan Disco (*open until 4am nightly; except Sun*) is Almaty's new hot spot, near the corner of Ulitsas Kunaeva and Zhibek Zholu. This is almost as unexpected as the Florida in Ashgabat. Gyrate under flashing lights to the latest western groove. Almaty's slick set is out in abundance and visiting business suits are on the prowl. Admission is more expensive on Fridays and Saturdays ($16–22).

Central Museum (Центральный музей)

Open 10 am–6 pm; closed Tues; adm under $2; photography is forbidden.

This marble megalith facing the east side of the Presidential Palace on Ulitsa Furmanova, is a no-expense-spared showcase of Soviet curatorial technique. Natural history, ancient history, modern history, contemporary history and ethnography are all here, mostly sanitized, nonetheless impressive.

The lower ground floor recreates a time when dinosaurs stalked the steppe and sabre-toothed dolphins frolicked in the Caspian and Aral seas. There is also a model of the Mongols sacking the ancient Kazakh city of Otrar in 1218. The golden suit of armour belonging to a *zolotoy chelovek* ('golden warrior') is a copy of the 5th-century BC Scythian original found near Lake Issyk, now the property of the Academy of Sciences.

The museum's domed central lobby is done out as a colossal yurt. There is a real one to the right, with a full-size stuffed camel tethered outside. Such was the timeless idyll of Kazakh nomadic life. We then see its defenders, 19th-century warriors with bows and arrows and chain-mail; and faded daguerreotypes of their czarist foes. Machines made the

Russians invincible. Those on display include a Singer sewing machine and a Smith Premier Simplex typewriter.

The second floor covers the Soviet era. After the inevitable revolutionary hall of fame (1917–45) there is a yurt adapted for propagandizing—hence the books and gramophone—and a collection of photographs of haggard old men and women building the TurkSib railway (1926–30). Less haggard faces peer from posters depicting Kazakhstan's role in the Second World War. Rosy-faced women work on the land and in factories; a reminder that Soviet industry was moved to Central Asia for 'safety'. And there's also a reminder of Kazakhstan's ethnic diversity, an exhibit on the Jewish community. With the emigration that has followed independence, such communities are growing smaller.

Until 1991 the north wing of this floor was given over to space travel, including Soviet space food. Now it is half-filled with a display commemorating the joint US–Kazakh Peace Walk in 1990 and memorabilia from the Nevada-Semipalatinsk anti-nuclear testing campaign. The campaign's symbol is a silhouette of a Shoshone Indian from Nevada smoking a peace pipe with a Kazakh herdsman. There is a picture of its leader, Olzhas Suleimanov, with the mayor of Hiroshima, and a T-shirt with the message, 'stay warm, eat garlic, sip red wine, peace and health,' from Doug of California.

As you pass from nuclear testing to sporting achievement, you'll find, by the exit, a cut-away model of a metro planned for Almaty. If the souvenir shop and handmade Kazakh rugs leave you, as well as your wallet, in need of refreshment, try the café. Those interested in traditional jewellery should ask to visit the vault, which is opened on request.

Opposite the museum is a pristine white square building. This is the **new President's Palace**, tucked behind the old one that faces the Square of the Republic on Ulitsa Satpaeva. Originally planned as the Lenin Museum it was converted by a French company and opened this year.

Art Museum (Музей искусств)

10am–1pm, 2–6; closed Mon; adm around 50 cents.

West of here on Ulitsa Satpaeva near the Bolshaya Alma-Atinka river, the State Art Museum has an applied art section with traditional Kazakh rugs, jewellery and clothing. There are also Chinese, European and Soviet Kazakh paintings. The development of figurative fine art in Kazakhstan is relatively recent since Islamic belief ensured more attention was paid to ornamental design. In this collection, the works of the exiled Ukranian painter, Taras Shevchenko, provide a visual record of 19th-century Kazakh life and there are also a number of paintings by the Russian Vereshchagin, famous for his battle scenes. Look out for the idealized images of collectivization and the Virgin Lands by people's painter Abylkhan Kasteyev, who knew how to dress up propaganda as art. A gift shop in the foyer sells work by local artists as well as Kazakh and Russian crafts.

Kazakhstan's first private gallery can be found in the foyer of the Russian Drama Theatre on Prospekt Abay 43. The **Tengri Umai's** collection (*open 10–6, Mon–Sat*) is varied, ranging from sculpture and paintings to folk art and jewellery. Exhibitions change monthly. There's also opportunity to meet local artists. Admission is a few dollars.

At the east end of Prospekt Abay, parallel to Ulitsa Satpaeva and a block north, the cable car up **Kok-Tyube** (green hill) is more or less permanently under repair. The original costume of the Scythian 'golden warrior' found at Lake Issyk, of which the central state museum has a copy, is two blocks down from here, past the Hotel Kazakhstan, in the vault of the **Archaeology Museum of the Academy of Sciences**, Prospekt Lenina 44. On-going digs throughout Kazakhstan constantly swell this collection, which is displayed in the museum rooms above a cinema.

The **Museum of Books** is at Kabanbay Batyra 94, ✆ 62 11 04, at the intersection with Prospekt Lenina. Nearby is the **Geology Museum** at Kabanbay Batyra 69a, ✆ 61 58 83. Recently renovated, both have large and interesting collections, well worth a browse.

There are also several smaller museums. A visit to the Academy of Science **Nature Museum**, Ulitsa Shevchenko 28, would be an interesting complement to any trek. The Academy's main building on Schevchenko was designed by Alexi Shchusev, the architect responsible for Moscow's Lenin mausoleum and Komsomolskaya metro station.

For the literary minded, there are the **house museums** of the Kazakh writers Muchtar Auezov, Ulitsa Tulebaeva 185, and Sabit Mukanov, Ulitsa Tulebaeva 125. And there's an exhibition at the **Ceramics Factory** (*open Mon–Fri, 9am–5pm*), Ulitsas Karasat Batyra and Muratbaeva.

Gorky Park

The city's biggest and leafiest park is three blocks east of the bazaar. This was Verny's municipal garden, laid out in 1856, and well worth a visit. Go through the splendid entrance on Ulitsa Gogolya and choose a ride, from camel to pedalo. You can enjoy a lazy picnic amongst the 2000 different species of plant, or there are tennis courts for the more active, and an impromptu Sunday market for the bargain hunter. A fifteen-minute walk will bring you here from Panfilov Park, or trolleybuses 25,16,1 and 12 all of which, apart from number 25, stop at Panfilov Park *en route*.

Zelyony Bazaar

The **Zelyony bazaar** (green bazaar), is north of Panfilov Park, occupying most of a large block between Ulitsas Zhibek Zholu and Mukagali Makataeva, towards their eastern ends. The apples are large and happily justify the hype; Korean salads are colourful and tasty. Bring your own carrier bag and be prepared to buy by the kilo; a request for two tomatoes will be met with blank incomprehension. Kiosks, *lepeshka* and furniture sellers all jostle for attention at the bazaar fringe. And along Zhibek Zholu, there's a line of women, all anxious to sell the same imported clothes and shoes.

Shopping

Almaty is no souvenir-hunter's paradise, but the streets around the **bazaar** look more like the new free-market China with every train that pulls in from Ürümqi. Thanks to the entrepreneurial spirit unleashed since independence, every other shop is a private *kommercheski magazin*. These days there's a greater range of goods on the shelves, but still very little sense of stock continuity. Elbow in among the thronging browsers and stock up on toothpaste, deodorant, lipstick, soap, shampoo and miscellaneous western goodies including alcohol and chocolate biscuits. If ice-cream is top of your list, wander along the partially pedestrianized Zhibek Zholu. Abundant ice-cream, pop corn and candy floss are as much a feature of winter as of summer.

The two largest **department stores** are Tsum on Ulitsa Zhibek Zholu and Prospekt Ablai Khan and Universam at Zhibek Zholu 67.

Opposite the Dostuk Hotel, is the credit card **Aksept** shop, Ulitsa Kurmangazi 31; it does a good line in Lemsip and other basic medical supplies. The best selections of **postcards** and Kazakh **souvenirs** also lurk in the Aksept shop and in the foyer shops of the hotels Dostuk and Kazakhstan.

There are three good **supermarkets**: Samal at Prospekt Ablai Khan 96; the Galaxy shop close to Panfilov Park at Ulitsa Kazybek Bi 45 and Kunaeva; and west of here, Tilek on Nauryzbay Batyra and Aiteke Bi.

Three blocks west of the Hotel Otrar on Ulitsa Gogolya, the Korean **clothes** shop now competes with designer boutiques like BSB at Ulitsa Furmanova 87—a sign of the growing polarization of wealth among the population.

Kiosks, numerous and open late, remain a useful source for biscuits, Mars bars, drinks and cigarettes. For **handicrafts**, try the Central Museum and Art Museum. Alternatively, visit the gallery located in the Kazakh Business Centre, Prospekt Lenina 85, or the art shop at Ulitsa Shevchenko 44.

Almaty (© 3272–)   **Where to Stay**

The numbers of foreign experts and large company businessmen flooding into Central Asia, and the secondary wave of foreigners providing services to the first lot, have driven prices up to levels higher than those in many Western European cities. The expense-account mentality leads to prices being paid for goods and services out of all proportion to value given, or to the real cost of providing them.

At any level of budget, very few hotels in Almaty represent value for money. Singles are often the same price as doubles, or no more than 15% cheaper, except in the older Soviet hotels that were built with single rooms, which are half-price. Of course, the prices are lower for citizens of other CIS countries and lower still for Kazakhs. Prices quoted in dollars are often still payable in tenge; ask.

expensive

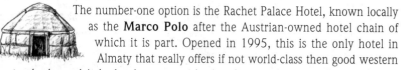

The number-one option is the Rachet Palace Hotel, known locally as the **Marco Polo** after the Austrian-owned hotel chain of which it is part. Opened in 1995, this is the only hotel in Almaty that really offers if not world-class then good western standards, and it looks the part, with glass-fronted elevators sliding up and down the inside of the atrium. It offers all the usual facilities including hot and cold running everything, direct dial satellite phones from each room, access to the health club, the swimming pool and the business centre, and massages. All rooms open off the 11-storey atrium and prices are correspondingly sky-high: $1500 for the two-bedroom Presidential Suite, plus 20% VAT (sales tax); $275 for a single; $325 for a double. The hotel accepts all major credit cards.

Prices are likely to drop when a larger, Turkish-owned five star hotel, the **Ankara**, opens soon near the presidential palace on Satpaeva, ✆ 81 16 20, ✉ 81 16 35; toll-free ✆ (0800) 960501 from the UK, and ✆ (1 800) 735 5740 from the USA and Canada. Former guest house for Communist Party top brass, **Hotel Dostuk**, Ulitsa Kurmangazi 36, ✆ 63 65 55, ✉ 63 68 04/63 66 12, retains its selective atmosphere and solid old-world charm. The imposing frontage with its array of flags says embassy rather than hotel. The lobby is soberly done in marble, stucco and dark wood panelling. Rooms have CNN and BBC. The Business Centre and Finnish sauna ($25) are both open to non-residents. International papers and stamps can be bought in the foyer shop which faces the hard currency food store, Bazarlik. The hotel has restaurants, bars and a sauna. The English-speaking receptionist is pleasant and happy to accept hard currency and major credit cards. The rate for a single is $135, a double $160, a suite with two rooms and a bathroom is $215 and a *lyux* suite $300. From the US, bookings can be made through The Fair Winds Trading Company, which now owns the hotel, ✆ (602) 748 1280, ✉ (602) 748 1347.

The state-owned **Almaty**, Kabanbay Batyra 85 (corner of Ulitsa Panfilova), ✆ 63 09 43, ✉ 63 02 02, is a monolithic, building with a somewhat Soviet atmosphere, opposite the Opera and Ballet Theatre; not all rooms have air-conditioning. Payment can be made by credit card or, if in cash, tenge only and 50% of your first night's stay must be paid for in advance. Doubles are from $80, including breakfast.

The **Peking Hotel**, Ulitsa Zenkova 52, ✆ 54 31 10, 📠 54 31 18, is a smaller and more comfortable place, central and with air-conditioning. There are hints of its Chinese ownership in the long-case clock in the hall, and the thermos of boiled water in every room. Rates are $80 for a single, $100 for a double.

The **Kazakhstan** is a 26-storey Korean-run tower at Prospekt Lenina 52, just north of the junction with Abay, ✆ 61 99 06, 📠 61 96 00/50 61 11. It's the tallest building in Almaty and, like other hotels in the city, subject to the renovation epidemic. But with so many floors to play with, the Kazakhstan remains open throughout the works. Rooms have good views over the city or towards the mountains, but little else to recommend them. Those rooms on the 14th and 15th floors already renovated by a German company cost around $120 a night. Singles cost $68 and $72, doubles $88, three-bed rooms $104; you can pay in hard currency, tenge or with American Express. From the airport take bus 92 to the *aerovokzal*, then bus 151.

If you're considering the $60–$80 range, one of the best value hotels is the **Issyk**, Bogenbay Batyra 140, ✆ 69 90 57. Turkish run and located two blocks west of Ablai Khan, it is clean and has helpful receptionists. Beware of the cunningly placed step close to the flight of stairs in the lobby. Any lack of coordination creates a rather public spectacle. Singles cost $60, doubles $70 and breakfast is included. Take trolleybus 5 or 6 from Almaty II train station and buses 92 and 97 from the airport.

The **Hotel Otrar**, Ulitsa Gogolya 65, ✆ 33 00 76, 📠 33 20 56, is the official Intourist hotel. All rooms have air-conditioning and bathroom; room service is prompt and courteous. The central location is its main advantage; many rooms have a view over Panfilov Park to Zenkov Cathedral and the Zelyony Bazaar is just a block to the north. There's a basement spa, a karaoke bar and a new marble floor in the entrance, of which the receptionist is very proud. A news stand and post office can be found in the lobby. Some English is spoken. Prices include breakfast and one airport transfer but you must pay 10% of the first night's stay when you make a reservation. Pay in local currency for only one night and thereafter in dollars or with a credit card; doubles are $90, singles $56. From the airport take bus 92 to the *aerovokzal*, then walk a block south to Ulitsa Gogolya and go two stops on any eastbound trolleybus. From Almaty II railway station take any trolleybus two stops south on Ulitsa Abilai Khan, then any eastbound one two stops on Ulitsa Gogolya.

moderate

The **Kazpotrepsoyuza** is tucked away on Ulitsa Kunaeva and Zhambul, in the southwest corner, ✆ 62 04 09. You enter through a small door decked out with various signs including two pharmacy green crosses, just south of the junction. Turn right along the passage and right again to the stairs; the reception is one floor up. Expect to pay $80 for a comfortable sitting-room, bedroom and bathroom, with fridge and TV; $33 will buy you the same but without the sitting room. This is probably the best value hotel for the middle-budget traveller.

Further up the street towards Medeo, the **Hotel Ala-Tau**, Prospekt Lenina 105, ✆ 64 35 09, was renovated in 1995. It is served by buses 52 and 151 from the *aerovokzal*, bus 151 from Almaty II station and trolleybuses 19 and 25 from the long-distance bus station. Take them as far as Prospekt Lenina, then go south on bus 22, 52, 151 or 6.

The **Zhetsu** on Prospekt Ablai Khan between Ulitsas Zhibek Zholu and Mukagali Makataeva, ✆ 39 22 22, 🖂 33 00 66, is next to the *aerovokzal* and almost opposite the Tsum department store. It's another state-owned hotel with a wide range of rooms from upwards of $9, but foreigners (if admitted) are likely to be bundled into the $35 rooms which have private baths. There are rooms taking six people for $27, and you may be able to talk your way into one of these if you arrive in a group. The reception thinks that the Soviet era is still with us, and will not serve you until good and ready. There is a restaurant on the second floor. Take bus 92 from the airport, any trolleybus from Almaty II, and buses 126 and 43 from the long-distance bus station. If logistics demand, the **Aksunkar** is Almaty's airport hotel, ✆ 34 09 94.

inexpensive

A more appealing alternative may be a **private flat**. Ask one of the people who sit outside the Zhetisu waiting for foreigners. In Almaty, **Aunt Valja**, ✆ 39 63 68, comes highly recommended. Ask for her daughter who speaks very good English. Or try **Xakuma**, ✆ 67 53 18. Typically, a room and use of a bathroom with three meals a day will cost $20, with little room for haggling (but try). Given the cost of eating out, this is a bargain, although you may be a little way out from the centre

Of the other cheap hotels, the **Ayut**, on the corner of Gogolya and Ulitsa Nauryzbay Batyra, a block south of the *aerovokzal*, is the cleanest. The communal shower is in the basement, rooms have their own toilet and cost $12.

The **Hotel for Circus Artists** is directly behind the circus at 50 Prospekt Abay, ✆ 67 47 67. As you face the Marco Polo, it's the building on the right-hand side, at a lower level. A gorgon guards reception. Fairly basic rooms without a bath will cost around $17.

The **Altyn Den**, Ulitsa Timiryazeva 42, to the right of the Exhibition Centre, ✆ 44 78 30. Take trolleybus 11 along Prospekt Abay or Lenina. The reception is on the fourth floor of the building to the right of the exhibition hall main gates. If you stay here you are more interested in economy than comfort; rooms are not very clean but do have a bath. The only foreigners that stay here are Pakistani traders, who know a good cheap deal when they see one. A single costs $15, a double, $33.

Inside the football stadium, close to the Khan Tengri Travel Agency, and likely to be completely full, is the **Sport Hotel**, 48 Prospekt Abay, ✆ 67 40 33. Rooms are for three people and the shower on the first floor. A single costs $4, a double $8.

The recently refurbished **Hotel Medeo** in Medeo itself (*see* p.306) is a perfectly feasible base for seeing Almaty. Buses take 20 minutes going down there and 30 coming back.

Almaty (✆ 3272–)   **Eating Out**

Note that as with other services in Almaty, prices may be in dollars but payment is always in tenge. English is rarely spoken, but pointing at dishes and waving a number of fingers usually produces the right results. Some restaurants have photo albums of their dishes. Opening hours are like those of stores with a break in mid-afternoon except that restaurants stay open later. New restaurants are opening all the time, and word goes round the small ex-pat community very quickly if a new place is managing to serve something resembling good quality western food.

Typically things start well, then after six months either the foreign chef leaves and is not replaced, or the place simply closes at the height of its popularity for hidden political or mafiosi reasons. Others, such as the restaurant at the Ala-Tau, the Peking (Chinese) Restaurant, and the Tulbo Korean restaurant have begun to adopt strippers and even more explicit floor shows, which tend to bring a slightly threatening atmosphere along with the new clientele.

Anything costing $10 or more for a main course will only be frequented by ex-pats, mafiosi, and a few genuine local businessmen. But Almaty does offer opportunities to enjoy authentic and cheap Kazakh food, from the numerous street vendors and the smaller cafés.

expensive

Prices are as varied as the international cuisines on offer. For those on expense accounts, the **Tomiris** restaurant is a favourite, one block north of the Hotel Kazakhstan near the corner of Ulitsas Lenina and Shevchenko. It has good Turkish/European food and English-speaking staff. The desserts and cakes are excellent, and in summer outdoor seating is available. The ample lighting is a bonus when it comes to reading the bill, which will be $25–50.

Hotel restaurants at the **Dostuk** and **Marco Polo** are good and varied but not cheap. The Dostuk has two restaurants, offering everything from veal saltimbocca to pork chops calvados, at around $16 for a main course, $3 for side dishes. For those craving the comforts of home there is a hot and cold breakfast buffet for

$10. In the competition to produce western food, no-one can compete with the **Marco Polo**, but then no one can compete with their prices either: $25 for a main course, $3 for a cup of tea, $4.50 for a coffee. The main advantage of these hotels is that you can pay by credit card, as you can at an up-market, joint-venture Italian, the **Adriatico**, Ulitsa Mechnikova 90, close to Zhambula.

Standards in all the restaurants attached to the Kazakhstan Hotel have fallen, or perhaps, now that there is more choice, the food simply seems poor by comparison. The Korean food at the **Tulbo** restaurant is not worth the $20 upwards it costs. A standard cold drink here will cost $3, or six times what it costs at a pavement café, so expect your final bill to be substantially more. The floor show, which often includes strippers, starts at 9.30pm.

Better value and locally recommended but less central is the **Circus Hotel** restaurant. The **Hotel Otrar** has a restaurant like a giant yurt, with a domed, painted ceiling, carpeted walls, and a variety of western, Russian and local dishes, accompanied by loud music, for about $15. Hardly surprisingly given the distance from Almaty to the ocean, the sushi bar in the basement has no sushi. But it does attempt some basic Japanese dishes, such as *tsoba*, *ramen*, and *kariraisu*, at $10–12.

moderate

A more unexpected venue, behind the Hotel Otrar, Zhibek Zholu 64, with its entrance on Krasina, is the popular Czech restaurant, **Brno**. Service is good and the draft beer plentiful. The menu in English can be gentle on the budget.

Both the snack bar and the more formal dining-room of **1001 Nights**, Nauryzbay Batyra 37a, offer inexpensive Lebanese food. Expect your pitta and lamb accompanied by a live band and some enthusiastic dancing.

Chinese options include the **Shenijan** on Bogenbay Batyra 136, near the corner of Prospekt Ablai Khan and the **Peking**, Ulitsa Zenkova 52. Both of these have Chinese management but the Shenijan has a much more pleasant atmosphere and a more varied menu.

The once popular **Shaggie's** Burger Bar, also attached to the Kazakhstan, is now to be avoided. This is about as far from McDonald's as Almaty is from New York. Far superior and very substantial real beef burgers can be found at **Bar-B-Q**, Ulitsa Shevchenko 44. The hot dogs are excellent. A cheeseburger with French fries and a small salad, plus a beer will be around $10. For sheer volume this may be the best value in town. Pizzas are inexpensive at the **Italian Café**, on the 2nd floor of the Kazakhstan Business Centre, Prospekt Lenina 85; and at the **Pizza Bar** in the Circus building. The prince of pizzas is found at **Capos Pizza Bar**, set back off the south side of Prospekt Abay, one third of a block west of Seyfulina. It's a popular place, not only with ex-pats, and offers all the bustle and bottled beer you'd expect, and meals at a reasonable $12–14. Officially, you should have a membership token to gain entry but explain that you are not a local resident. *Open Mon–Sat, 6pm–1am.*

cheap

Kazakh food is like Kyrgyz, with *laghman* and *beshbarmak* the standard main courses. The best place to try them, and also Russian fare, is in the cafés. Those with a devoted local following include **Café Light**, on Prospekt Lenina and Ulitsa Bogenbay Batyra, where salads cost from $1, and meat dishes under $5—the beef Stroganoff is particularly recommended—and **Café Solyanka**, close to the embassies and government offices at Ulitsa Panfilova 100, where a beer is $3, and a main course $4. Such cafés are most easily spotted by the tables outside. There's also one by the Hotel Issyk and another, larger eaterie on the right of Prospekt Ablai Khan as you walk south, after the Parliament building and the park with the Lenin statue. *Koumis* (fermented mare's milk) is available in spring and summer at the **Ardager Café**, Ulitsa Gogolya 15, halfway between Panfilov and Gorky parks, where you can also find good *laghman* and *plov* for $2–3.

The highest restaurant in town is the **Aul** on top of Kok-Tyube. This has the best city panorama of the various cafes that cluster here. During the day they can be reached by bus 557 from Ulitsa Kurmangazi and Prospekt Lenina. If a bus ride doesn't appeal, try the **Café Cosmos** on the 26th floor of the Hotel Kazakhstan. It offers a limited menu of smallish meaty Russian dishes at around $5, but is almost deserted in the summer in favour of the newer pavement restaurants. The staff speak some English and are friendly.

Vegetarians overwhelmed by the meat hanging in the bazaar will find sanctuary at the **Hare Krishna Kafe**. At Seyfulina 54/4, this is quite far from the centre but on the way to the airport, next to the Cinema Shugla. There's a small sign on the right; be sure to arrive before 7.15pm, when last orders are taken. Your taxi ride will be the most expensive part. *Closed Mon.*

If you feel hungry while waiting, look for the stalls by the bus stops opposite the Otrar Hotel. *Shashlyk* snacks abound at the **Zelyony bazaar** and bread is available in a variety of shapes and sizes. Butter and cheese are sold by weight, and tomatoes provide the basis of chunky, filling sandwiches, which can be followed up with a wide choice of fruit. The peaches, for instance, look a bit rough compared to the picture-perfect varieties at home, but taste far better than many and are raised without chemical assistance because no one can afford it, and are no more than 45 tenge per kilo for the very best. For those in an apartment with access to cooking equipment, there's also a wide variety of vegetables and meats, and some canned foods.

One of the city reservoirs, **Bolshoy Almatinski Lake**, set high in the mountains and in the same area as the seismological station, can be visited from Almaty. The road is poor and tourists sometimes need permission to visit, so check first. C.A.T organises a trek here with lunch on the lake shore. It's also possible to drive from the lake up the Dzhusaly Keden Pass. A not-too-taxing climb will then bring you to Almatinsky peak with views of the Zailiisky Ala-Too mountain range, Bolshoy Almatinski Lake and Almaty itself. Return via the Alma-Arasan Gorge.

As an alternative to the mountain scenery, take a taxi the one and a half hours to the **River Ili**. This is steppe country. To see the old Buddhist cliff paintings four hours downstream, ask a travel agent in Almaty. At **Lake Kapchugai**, east of the Ili, boats can be rented from the lifeguard station on the lake's north side. It's possible to camp here or rent a small cabin.

To find the ancient **rock carvings** on the postcards sold in the Hotel Kazakhstan go to Tamgaletas, North of Kopa, two hours drive from Almaty. Alexei, ✆ 611548, 61115 is recommended as a guide to these as well as the tenth-century Silk Road capital, **Talgar** and burial mounds at **Issyk** where the Golden Man was found. For English-speaking guides, try the Archaeology Institute, ✆ 61 56 11.

Medeo (Медео)

To skate, ski, walk, climb and breathe real air, go to the bus-stop opposite the Hotel Kazakhstan. Bus 6 and others marked **Medeo** leave all day from here and take half an hour to get there. Medeo's ice-rink is a ten minute walk from the last stop. During the week it is used by ice hockey teams and world-class speed skaters and on Sundays 10am–2pm, open to the public. In 1995, the rink was closed for renovation. When operational, skate hire is underneath the rink at its downhill end.

Another twenty minutes' walk from here will bring you to the dam and a view that makes the arduous steps worthwhile. But don't expect to find any water. The dam exists to protect Almaty from any springtime deluge.

Having worked up a healthy appetite, you could try the Kazakh food at the Medeo restaurant, guaranteed to leave you, and not your wallet, feeling full. Or else, stop for *shashlyk* at a mountainside café.

In late August, Medeo hosts the 'Voice of Asia' song festival with competitors coming from Europe as well as the CIS.

Where to Stay

The **Hotel Medeo**, ✆ 64 87 16, ✉ 64 84 30, was renovated in 1995 by a Turkish company and is now run as a joint Kazakh–Turkish venture. Phoning in advance of arrival requires perseverence. The mountain location poses quite a challlenge to telecommunications. Bus route 6 terminates near here, below the Medeo ice rink.

Chimbulak (Чимбулак)

Those depressed by the sight of a giant stadium in an alpine valley should not despair. Most of the Zalayisky and Kungey Ala-Too ranges between here and Kyrgyzstan are still unspoilt. To see them, start by walking up the grass-covered ramp behind the rink (which protects it from mud-slides and avalanches). Turn right at the top and follow the metalled road up the west side of the valley for an hour or so, to the **Chimbulak Ski Base**. From here a very slow Yugoslav chairlift goes up to 3150m, year round, for about $5 in tenge a ride.

In summer there are marked walks all round here. Topographical maps covering at least four different trekking routes to Lake Issyk-Kul in Kyrgyzstan (*see* p.256) are usually available from a kiosk on the ground floor of the Hotel Chimbulak at the foot of the lift. The treks take at least a week, and you need to carry all your own equipment and food. From November to May Chimbulak offers some of the world's most recherché downhill skiing, with fine, powdery snow. Heliskiing is also possible; contact a travel company in Almaty (*see* pp.292–3). Ski and boot hire from the Hotel Chimbulak costs about $10–25 a day in tenge. Lifts cost around 50 cents a ride.

Getting to and from Chimbulak

Apart from private cars, the only vehicles which use the steep road from Medeo are Chimbulak's own trucks. To arrange transport from Medeo or Almaty, phone the Hotel Chimbulak (*see* below).

Where to Stay

A former road-builders' hostel in the trees below the hotel has been turned into an expensive private *pension*. Luxury apartments at the **Pensionat Polistrom**, ✆ 33 70 76/32 18 13, cost $120 a night. The simpler, more attractive rooms under the eaves are about $10 in rubles.

The none-too-rustic **Hotel Chimbulak**, ✆ 33 86 24/33 84 63, has rooms for around $10 a night. and a good restaurant with chicken, chips and a beer costing around $6. Trekking maps are available from the hotel kiosk.

*He sat down on a pile of timber by the shed and began looking
at the wide, deserted expanse of the river. From the steep bank
a wide stretch of the countryside opened up before him… There
in the vast steppe, flooded with sunlight, he could see the black
tents of the nomads, which appeared just like dots in the
distance. There was freedom, there other people were living,
people who were not a bit like the people he knew; there time
itself seemed to stand still as though the age of Abraham and his
flocks had not passed. Raskolnikov sat there, looking without
moving, and without taking his eyes off the vast landscape
before him; his thoughts passed into daydreams, into contem-
plation; he thought of nothing, but a feeling of great desolation
came over him and troubled him.*

Fyodor Dostoyevsky, *Crime and Punishment*, 1865–6

Nowhere has Russia's encounter with Asia been touched with such poignancy as in Semipalatinsk, where Dostoyevsky exiled the anti-hero of *Crime and Punishment*, having
been sent here himself in 1854. For Russians, exile in Semipalatinsk meant suffering and
isolation. Their arrival, for the nomads in their black tents, meant expropriation and,
much later, the terror of living on the edge of a nuclear test site.

Semipalatinsk is 1000km from Almaty and only 30 from Siberia. Summer temperatures
can rise to 45° C, but in January they average –23°. The first cold snaps in November can
freeze the River Irtysh overnight and treble the price of fur hats in the bazaar.

This is a Russian-looking place, from its surviving log houses and its Soviet smoke-stacks
to the haunting beauty of the woods along the river under snow. Indeed, the Russians
founded Semipalatinsk, but you only have to see the faces of the Kazakhs who come in
from the surrounding villages to trade at the bazaar to be reminded that this is very Asian
territory—a mere two days' bus ride from the Mongols' ancestral homeland in the Altai.

History

The first Russian fort here was actually 18km downstream, built in 1718 in the
reign of Peter the Great. Called Semipalatka because of the tented village which
grew up round the fort (**палатка**=*palatka*=tent), the settlement moved here
and took its modern name in 1776.

What started as a military outpost became a significant trading town. By 1854
it had four banks and in 1914, according to Stephen Graham, 'there were at
least six department stores, with handsome clocks, vases, bedroom furniture, mandolins,
violins, guitars, Vienna boots, American boots, gay hats, silk dresses, wrapped chocolates,
promiscuous and lavish supplies of all manner of European goods.'

White Russians controlled the town during the Civil War (1918–20), but it was knitted firmly into the Soviet system by the TurkSib railway in 1930. Nuclear testing, organized from a secret town 200km southwest of Semipalatinsk, began in 1949 and ended, in a triumph for the Nevada-Semipalatinsk anti-testing movement, in October 1990.

The people of Semipalatinsk have emerged by no means unscathed. Cancer rates are higher than average for the CIS, and some grim genetic mutation has been attributed to radiation from the tests.

Visitors are very unlikely to be affected, though. Background radiation is now easily within internationally accepted norms, and is acually lower than in mountain areas where exposed rocks push up the natural background level.

Getting to and from Semipalatinsk

by air

This is easiest from Almaty, with two flights a day. There are daily flights from Novosibirsk and Ust-Kamenogorsk, four a week from Moscow and less frequent ones from Tashkent, Bishkek (in principle), Dzhambul, Chimkent, Karaganda, Krasnoyarsk, Omsk and Tomsk. The central ticket office at Prospekt Shakarima 38, 10 minutes' walk from the Hotel Irtysh, is open 9am–1pm and 2–8pm, closing at 5pm on Sundays.

by boat

Stephen Graham ended his 1914 trip by meandering up the Irtysh to the Altai:

'I left Semipalatinsk and went in a little steamer up the narrowing and rocky river, past wooded islands, grey moors, and emerald marshes... We stopped at elementary wooden landing-stages beside small hamlets, bought eggs, fish, fruit from peasant women and children, backed out into midstream again, making our big wave that went washing along the banks and drenching incautious boys and girls...'

Nowadays, the only river trips are local. They go from the river station (*rechnoy vokzal*) on the south bank next to the Hotel Turist, but only in summer.

by rail

Daily services to Novosibirsk, Tashkent and all stations in between. The station is north of the centre, linked by buses 11 and 33 to the Hotel Irtysh and bus 11 to the Hotel Turist.

by bus

Two buses a day go to Ust-Kamenogorsk, which has connections to Almaty and the Altai. Local buses 2 and 35 go to the Hotel Irtysh from near the central bus station, which is on Ulitsas Proletarskaya and Chokana Valikhanova. For the Hotel Turist take buses 3, 36, 39 or 42.

Tourist Information

Intourist is no more. In Semipalatinsk it has been eclipsed by **Bogas Inturservice**, run by volleyball coach Vladimir Bazaev from the ground floor of the Hotel Irtysh, ☎ 66 77 09, ✉ 44 67 83. Bazaev mainly sells foreign travel to Kazakh citizens, but given sufficient notice he can fix trips to the nuclear test site (*see* below).

Ask here for the street map (*turisticheskaya skhyema*) which shows bus routes and is sometimes also available at news-stands.

Dostoyevsky's House

Ulitsa Dostoyevskovo 118, closed Sun and Mon.

Dostoyevsky lived from 1857 to 1859 in a wooden house on what became Ulitsa Dostoyevskovo, three minutes' walk across former Ploschad Lenina from the Hotel Irtysh. He had already spent five years in a prison camp near Omsk, 700km downriver.

In Semipalatinsk he served as an army officer, earning 18 rubles a month and living in reasonable comfort. The **F. M. Dostoyevsky Memorial Museum** covers his whole life, not just his sojourn in Semipalatinsk, and includes the house as he lived in it.

There are copies of notes and doodles for *Crime and Punishment* and *The Idiot*, and a letter written to his brother in 1854 in which he says, almost cheerfully, 'I am almost on the Kyrgyz [now called Kazakh] steppe... open steppe... pure steppe...'. The statue outside the museum is of Dostoyevsky with his admirer Shokan Valikhanov (1835–65), a Kazakh officer in the Russian army and a prominent orientalist, who died of TB aged 30.

Abay Museum

A more famous Kazakh Russophile, **Abay Kununbaev** (1845–1904), has his own museum not far from here on former Ulitsas Lenina and Kalinina. Abay was born in the Chingis-Tau hills south of Semipalatinsk, came here initially to spend three years in a madrasa, then taught in schools, translated Russian literature into Kazakh, and wrote poetry.

Dismissed as 'semi-feudal' by the Soviet iconoclasts of the 1930s, his writings were later reinstated as progressive for their time. His brainwave was to idealize traditional Kazakh life while at the same time advocating progress through collaboration with the Russians.

History Museum

Ulitsa Abay 90 (formerly Sovietskaya Ulitsa); closed Sun and Mon.

 The **History Museum** is back towards the Hotel Irtysh, a block northwest of Ploshchad Lenina. It contains some 3-m mammoth tusks and an explanation of how a local meat factory was converted to produce surgical instruments during the war. There is a new display on anti-nuclear testing protests, including a book first published in 1990 called *The Day The Earth Shook*, about the first tests in the 1940s. One of the staff would love to practise her English by giving you a guided tour.

Old Semipalatinsk

All that survives of old Semipalatinsk are some charming low log houses round the **bazaar** (*rynok*), north of here near the bus station on Ulitsa Chokana Valikhanova, and a 19th-century **mosque** which looks like a white clapboard New England church but for its twin minarets and is now an exhibition hall. It is four blocks east of the Hotel Irtysh near the junction of former Sovietskaya Ulitsa and Ulitsa Sverdlova.

Specialists seeking information on local health problems linked to radiation should contact Dr Urazaliv Marat, the local Nevada-Semipalatinsk representative, at the *Medinstitut* (℡ 62 73 49) two blocks northwest of the Hotel Irtysh on the river side of Ulitsa Abay.

Where to Stay and Eating Out

 There are two hotels. The obvious first choice is the **Hotel Irtysh**, Ulitsa Abay 97, ℡ 66 64 17. Quiet but centrally located between Ploshchad Lenina and the east bank of the Irtysh, it also has the best restaurant in town with, apparently, *no live music*. Foreigners get so-called Intourist rooms on the 4th floor, where the floor-ladies have hearts of gold and there is an excellent café (*bufet*). Double rooms here cost about $5 in rubles. Bus 33 comes here from the airport via the railway station. Buses 2 and 35 come from the bus station.

The **Hotel Turist**, Ulitsa Dzhambula 9, ℡ 44 75 01, just across the river, offers rooms from about $3 in rubles.

The Polygon

This is what they call the test site; 18,000 sq km of steppe and low hills southwest of Semipalatinsk, given over in 1949 to a physicist called Kurchatov, father of the Soviet atom bomb.

Nuclear tests were carried out at a rate of 12–15 a year until stopped by Gorbachev, under pressure from Nevada-Semipalatinsk, in 1990. Until 1963 most were air tests. Thereafter all were underground. The site was run from a neat, closed town, named after Kurchatov, on the banks of the Irtysh. Its very existence was denied until the late 1980s.

Such is the depth of the economic crisis that has set in since then that the mayor of Kurchatov and the military personnel still responsible for the site are turning it into a tourist attraction. The standard tour will, they say, take in Kurchatov's hitherto secret military museum, the first (1949) test site, and Lake Shagan, created by a shallow underground explosion in the path of the River Shagan in 1963. Incredulous visitors will be invited to catch and eat fish from the lake.

The two-and-a-half-hour drive to Kurchatov captures the full eeriness of the steppe, and the town itself is not so much sinister as surreal. 'May peace prevail on earth,' says a sign at its entrance in four languages. Background radiation levels in Kurchatov, as in Semipalatinsk, are lower than in Almaty.

Red Tape

Permission to visit the Polygon must be obtained from the Ministry of Defence in Almaty, but Bogas-Inturservice (*see* p.309) can help. They need at least a week's notice. Another possible source of help is Oleg Popov, a manager on the fifth floor of the regional government building on the south side of Ploshchad Lenina in Semipalatinsk, two minutes' walk from the Hotel Irtysh. As for Baikonur, a Kazakh sponsor and official-looking credentials increase the chances of gaining permission.

Getting to the Polygon

Once permission is granted, transport is usually provided. If it is not there is a bus to Kurchatov every afternoon from Semipalatinsk, but don't get on until the mayor's office at Kurchatov has been warned by telex of your arrival. The mayor's name is Nikolai Feodorovich Yelnikov. The bus station may still use *Konyechnaya* ('the end') as a euphemism for Kurchatov.

Lake Shagan is actually outside the polygon and permission is not needed to go there. There are three buses a day to Shagan and the journey takes two hours. Otherwise go with Bogas-Inturservice.

Ust-Kamenogorsk (Усть-Каменогорск)

Ust-Kamenogorsk, 200km east of Semipalatinsk, is the gateway to the Altai mountains. Apart from that, it is grim. Founded in 1720 as Peter the Great's easternmost steppe fort, it hardly expanded until 1939. Then its population jumped from 20,000 to 149,000 in 20 years. The newcomers were almost all Russians and Ukrainians sent here to mine and smelt heavy metals for Stalin's military-industrial complex. Ust-Kamenogorsk is also thought to have enriched much of the uranium and plutonium used in the Semipalatinsk polygon. Locals say that rain which has fallen through Ust-Kamenogorsk's air turns tomatoes brown.

Getting to Ust-Kamenogorsk

The airport has flights from Almaty (up to four a day), Novosibirsk (two), Moscow (one) and less frequent ones from other Kazakh and Siberian cities. The central ticket office is opposite the river station (*rechnoy vokzal*) near the east end of Prospekt Lenina, reached by buses 9, 10 and 19.

Two buses a day come here from Semipalatinsk and one from Almaty (in 27 hours). For the Altai, take the Katon-Karagai bus which leaves every morning around 8am and takes all day. You have to spend the night in Katon, continuing next morning.

Getting Around

Bus 12 runs from the airport to the Hotel Ust-Kamenogorsk. From the bus station, bus 6 or 21, or any tram going over the river. Get off after the bridge at the Ulitsa Kirova stop and walk down Ulitsa Kirova to the hotel.

Where to Stay and Eating Out

Stay at the **Hotel Ust-Kamenogorsk**, former Proletarskaya Ulitsa 158, ✆ 66 18 01. If the restaurant staff ignore you, try the canteen outside.

Sport

In Ust-Kamenogorsk with time to kill, visit the *ice-hockey rink* next to the bus station across the bridge from the hotel. If Ust-Kamenogorsk are playing at home, you are at the equivalent of a Premier League game in England.

The Altai Mountains (Алтайские Горы)

Siberia, Mongolia, China and Kazakhstan rise very gradually to meet each other at one of the lushest nodes in Asia. The Altai are the gentler sort of mountain, with more woods and meadows than ravines and rock. They occupy the very middle of the continent, roughly equidistant from the Arctic Ocean and the Indian, and from the Caspian and the Pacific. They stretch for a thousand kilometres into Mongolia, but break out into alpine peaks and glaciation only around Pik Bielukha (4506m) on the Russian/Kazakh border. Bielukha's foothills are on the same latitude as Brussels, and get nearly as much rain.

The place to head for is Rakhmanovski (**Рахмановски**), a *turbaza* in its own snug wooded valley, with bath-houses over natural hot springs, and cross-country skiing circuits where the Russian national team trains in winter. Accommodation, in wooden chalets, is full board and very cheap. To see Pik Bielukha, walk up the north side of the valley and look over the ridge.

Take the Katon-Karagai (**Катон-Караган**) bus from Ust-Kamenogorsk (*see* above). On arrival, ask to get off at the *stolovaya* (canteen). This is the only place to eat and it closes at 7.30pm. There is a basic hotel a block away, uphill.

It is another 111km up the valley of the Bukhtarma river to the roadhead at Rakhmanovski. Buses in that direction leave Katon-Karagai by 8am. To reach the bus station from the hotel, walk back to the canteen, turn right, continue to the river, take the first left turn after it and walk downstream about 1km. It pays to be at the station by 7am.

If there is no bus to Rakhmanovski there should be one to **Berel** (**Берел**), a village of log cabins and maral deer enclosures 30km back down the road near the head of the main Bukhtarma valley.

ALTIT FORT
HUNZA VALLEY

The Karakoram Highway and into Xinjiang

Southeast of Tajikistan the rolling Pamirs give way to the sharpest peaks on the planet. Words are too puny to describe the mountains of northern Pakistan. This area, no bigger than Ireland, takes the brunt of the Indian subcontinent's collision with Eurasia and witnesses the meeting of the world's four greatest mountains ranges in a dizzying, deafening, unending geological hurricane. They are the Himalayas, the Hindu Kush, the Pamirs and the Karakorams—and the greatest of these, contrary to popular belief fostered by the fame of Everest, are the Karakorams.

Forming the Sino-Pakistan border north of the upper Indus and east of the Pamirs, the Great Karakoram comprise five peaks over 8000m, including K2, the world's second highest at 8611m; some 50 peaks over 7000m; and the world's longest glaciers outside the sub-polar regions, five of them over 50km long. The Karakorams have not settled down. Earth tremors here are almost daily occurences, major earthquakes are all too frequent and glaciers can move 600m in a day.

Unbelievably, a road cuts straight through these mountains. The Karakoram Highway began as a political project. In the early 1960s China sought an Asian ally with whom to counter Soviet-Indian dominance of the continent. She settled on Pakistan, which was already serving as a conduit for secret diplomatic messages between Washington and Beijing. In 1964 the previously disputed Sino-Pakistan border was fixed with the cession of 2000 sq km of mountainous territory to Pakistan, and a Friendship Highway linking Gilgit and Kashgar was mooted.

Building started in 1966. Pakistani workers, up to 15,000 at a time, built the southern half of the road from Havelian to Gulmit. At least 400 of them died in landslides, rockfalls and blasting accidents. The Chinese hacked their way through the least geologically stable section, from Khunjerab to Gulmit, and built all the bridges.

The highway was finished in 1980, opened to trade and official traffic in 1982 and to tourists in 1986—though the Chinese were still working in the Ghez river canyon in 1988. Begun in the depths of the Cold War and finished at the height of glasnost, it is 1200km long and required the blasting of 20 million cubic metres of rock. Its highest point is the Khunjerab Pass, 4730m up on the Chinese border.

Beyond here, far below, are the deserts of western China (Xinjiang). The most dreaded of these is the Taklamakan—a local word meaning 'go in, but you won't come out'. This warning to humans not in air-conditioned buses applies equally to rivers. Billions of cubic metres of meltwater from the Tian Shan to the north and the Kunlun to the south simply vanish into the Taklamakan. Pilgrims, Silk Route traders and Chinese invaders have always skirted warily round the edges of this giant oval oven dish, the size of France but with a good deal less inside. The extreme dryness preserved buildings, frescoes and unembalmed corpses in the oases on its fringes for fifteen centuries. In the Turpan depression, second lowest point on earth, some of these have even escaped plunder by 19th-century western 'explorers', and the vandalism of Mao's cultural revolution.

The Karakoram Highway links two regions which, against the odds, have much in common: their position straddling the Silk Route, a Buddhist past and an Islamic present, a fiercely arid climate and a shared antipathy to foreign empire-builders. With the opening of China's Kazakh and Kyrgyz borders the highway has also become an unforgettable overland route to former Soviet Central Asia.

Geology

The diamond-shaped continental plate we know as India was once a part of Antarctica. Some 70 million years ago it detached itself and began drifting northward towards Asia at a speed of 5cm a year. This was fast; 2000km in 40 million years. Then, 30 million years ago, it met the Asian plate and began to slide underneath it, pushing it upwards. The part of the southern edge of the Asian plate which took the full force of the collision became the Karakorams. Tibet, which had been a fertile habitat of hippo and giraffe, some 1000m above sea level, rose four vertical kilometres to became a freezing, lifeless plateau.

The collision is still happening and is not straightforward. While the deeper layers of the Indian plate become submerged beneath Asia, the top ones are being scraped off it as if by a monstrous planing machine. The shavings, curling up even higher than the Karakorams, are the Himalayas, whose extreme northwestern tip is Nanga Parbat (8126m). Meanwhile, between the two continental plates, an arc of oceanic volcanoes has been squashed and upended. Known as the Kohistan Island Arc, this is now a buffer zone between the Himalayas, the Karakorams and the Hindu Kush. Gilgit sits in the middle of it and the Indus gouges its way through it. The former ocean floor forms the south of the arc, while one-time volcanic summits form the north.

'It is now possible,' writes the leader of the Royal Geographical Society's 150th anniversary International Karakoram Project, 'to travel from the surface of the earth down towards the centre of the earth simply by travelling south from Hunza through Gilgit to Patan, along the Karakoram Highway.'

For the latest immensely detailed wisdom on the geology and geography of northern Pakistan, see the two-volume *Proceedings of the International Karakoram Project*, ed. Keith Miller (RGS, 1984) or his layman's summary, *Continents in Collision* (Time Life Books, 1983).

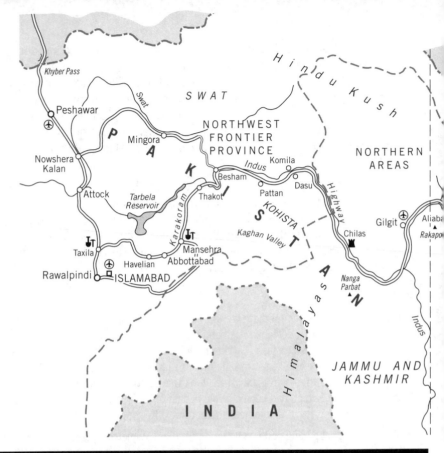

The Indus Gorge

Pain before pleasure. All who would marvel at Nanga Parbat and the Karakorams must first be pulled through the gargantuan grey-black mangle of the Indus gorge. Unless you fly, that is, or take the jeep track over the Babusar pass to Chilas. But the KKH follows the Father of Rivers, sometimes within earshot of the water, more often as a white-knuckle notch in the cliffs above it. The gorge can be desperately hot and intimidating. Its truck-stops are neither attractive nor safe, peopled as they are by historically ungovernable Shins and Pathans who live in continuous fear of being swept by a landslide, along with their meagre livelihoods, into the thundering, silt-laden flow. But then going to Gilgit is not like going to Tunbridge Wells. It is somehow right that one should suffer getting there, not least because this section of the KKH claimed more lives in construction than any other.

In practice the KKH starts at the twin cities of Rawalpindi and Islamabad (Pakistan's capital), 230km south of where it enters the Indus valley. You leave Rawalpindi north-westbound on the Grand Trunk Road and turn right after half an hour into the broad Taxila valley, cradle of the Gandharan Buddhist culture that percolated over the moun-

318

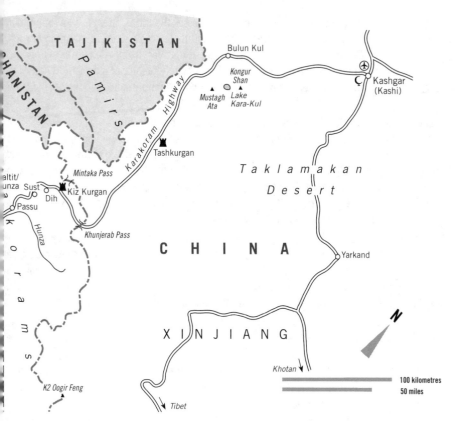

tains to the most distant oases of Xinjiang between the 3rd century BC and the 3rd century AD. **Taxila** itself thrived as a religious centre under the Mauryan King Ashoka (273–235 BC), and served as capital of the Kushan empire from the late 1st to mid-3rd century AD. It's heavily promoted as a day-trip destination from Islamabad and Rawalpindi.

The foothills of the western Himalayas begin beyond the railhead at **Havelian**, official southern terminus of the KKH. From here the road climbs swiftly to the cool air and faded colonial elegance of **Abbottabad** (1220m), founded by the British in the 1850s and named after James Abbott, its first district commissioner. Abbottabad is 122km and three hours by bus from Rawalpindi. The Pakistan Tourism Development Corporation (PTDC) information centre is on Jinnah Road, ✆ 4946.

Mansehra, half an hour beyond Abbottabad, is famous for the **Ashoka rocks** on its northern edge, on which Ashoka inscribed some edicts in the mid-3rd century BC. At the junction of the KKH and the road to the beautiful 161-km **Kaghan valley**, Mansehra is also a regional transport hub. It is possible to by-pass the entire Indus gorge via the 4145-m Babusar Pass at the north end of the Kaghan valley, but only between mid-July and late August, and only on foot or in a jeep.

Opposite **Thakhot**, where the KKH meets and crosses the Indus, there is a low mountain confidently but not necessarily correctly identified in 1926 by Sir Aurel Stein as Aornos, captured by Alexander the Great in 327 BC. Fugitives from Alexander's previous conquests are supposed to have fled here, and to have worshipped goats and Dionysius, or an equivalent local deity, in a rite called the *shin*. The mountain's modern name is Pir Sar (2164m).

The bridge at Thakhot is the southernmost one built by the Chinese. The contours here are relatively gentle, but by **Besham**, 40 minutes later, 255km and seven hours from Rawalpindi, they are beginning to close in. This is where the Swat road (the southern end of the old Indus Valley road) joins the KKH. Branching off the Grand Trunk road 110km north-west of Rawalpindi at Nowshera Kalan, it makes a longer but more scenic approach to the Indus gorge than the KKH. Buses and vans shuttle all day over the Shangla pass between Besham and Mingora in the Swat valley.

Besham is the place to break your journey if arriving late northbound, and hoping to pass through the gorge in daylight. There are several cheap hotels near the bazaar, where all through-buses stop for refreshment and you can buy a reconditioned Lee Enfield sniper's rifle at any hour of the day or night. The PTDC motel and tourist information centre, ✆ 92, are out of town on the Rawalpindi side, between the highway and the river.

North of Besham vertigo sufferers should sit on the left. The gorge is on the right until Dasu, beyond the half-way point, where the road crosses it. For the next three and a half hours there is hardly a patch of level ground visible from the road. The river, often more than 300m below, is cast in almost permanent shadow. Peaks rise to between 3000 and 5000m either side, but their verdant upper flanks are seldom seen from the sheer sides of this terrible gash.

At **Jijal**, half an hour north of Besham, you pass abruptly from geological India onto the Kohistan Island Arc (*see* 'Geology', above). Until now the crust around you was always somewhere near the surface of the earth. The greenish hue of the rocks beside the road at Jijal indicates that until the collision of the Indian and Asian landmasses they were perhaps 20km below the ocean floor.

The cliffs stand back briefly after another half-hour at **Pattan**, destroyed by an earthquake-induced landslide in 1974 and rebuilt since. The journey is slow and tortuous as the road makes endless detours into side valleys to avoid steep climbs. Beyond the twin villages of **Komila** on the west bank and **Dasu** on the east, the gorge straightens, and northward progress speeds up. Komila, two hours north of Besham and six or seven south of Gilgit, has cheap hotels and a bazaar from where short-haul minibuses leave throughout the day for Besham and (north on the KKH) Chilas. Rawalpindi–Gilgit buses stop here but are often full. From here to the end of the gorge the drop is on the left.

Chilas

Two and a half to three hours north of Komila the gorge opens out, river and road swing to the east, and you pass from the Northwest Frontier Province into the Gilgit-administered Northern Areas. After about an hour of gentle climbing beside a new, relaxed-looking Indus, the colossal bulk of Nanga Parbat heaves into view 50km away at two o'clock. **Chilas** is closer but less obvious, 3km south of the highway at the foot of the Babusar Pass. In 1892, intent on securing a new southern supply route to Gilgit over this pass, a Major George Robertson exceeded his authority by burning Chilas to the ground; he and his friend Algy Durand, the political agent in Gilgit, considered it a hot-bed of anti-British bandits. It was certainly unruly, or 'acephalous' (headless), as it has subsequently been classified along with the scores of other independent valley-kingdoms that made up 19th-century Kohistan. But Robertson had thought too little and acted too much. The following year most of Indus Kohistan rebelled. The new road was never built—it is still only a jeep track—and the fort which still dominates Chilas has been busy and resented ever since, imposing alien notions of law and order handed down first by Calcutta and since 1947 by Islamabad.

Chilas is also noted for its petroglyphs: rocks etched with ancient travellers' names, prayers and pictures of ibex, snow leopard and Buddhas. Some date back to the 1st century BC. Follow signs to Chilas I and Chilas II from the KKH.

Chilas is 455km from Rawalpindi and 135km from Gilgit. Upstream of it the Indus valley turns gradually north and north-west, forming a huge east-facing D. The river's smooth silver skin is deceptive. Underneath it five million tonnes of sediment are on the move in any one day. When that thick, heavy flow is blocked the results can be apocalyptic. In the winter of 1841 an earthquake nudged a cliff into its path just beyond Raikot bridge, due north of Nanga Parbat. By May a lake 60km long and 300m deep had formed, reaching back almost to Gilgit. When the dam burst a wall of water tore through the canyon and, despite warnings from the ruler of Gilgit floated down earlier on pieces of bark, wiped out an entire army encamped on the plain near Attock 320km away.

The valley floor above the dam was turned from precious farmland into a silty waste, over which the KKH romps easily to Gilgit, 590km and about 17 hours from Rawalpindi.

Gilgit

In the chill of an autumn morning a gang of black-bearded Chitralis overloads an ancient Wills jeep for the slog over Shandur top towards the Afghan border. Mist slips through the cables of the featherweight suspension bridges over the Gilgit river. Boys whose fathers could ride before they could walk are playing football on the polo ground below the mosque. The poplars on Airport Road are turning yellow but are not yet bare. Firdous Karim Khan, proprietor of the Pearl Coffee Shop, boils the milk for tourists' *capuccini* while jewellers, playing for higher stakes, lay out their ruby necklaces and eggs of lapis lazuli. Across the street the day's first Rawalpindi bus hoots its last call for southbound passengers. The skies are clear to Nanga Parbat and Islamabad, so there will be a plane or two as well.

John Keay called Gilgit 'the hub, the crow's nest, the fulcrum of Asia'. Its strategic importance may wax and wane with the bellicosity of lowland empires, but it will always generate its own inimitable bustle. Perched on a broad, stony shelf west of the KKH, the town is situated 5km above the confluence of the Gilgit and Hunza rivers and 35km above where they join the Indus. It's not idyllic, but it is the administrative centre and major market town of the Northern Areas, and gateway for thousands of tourists a year to the wildernesses beyond.

History

Gilgit was a Silk Route town; most caravans heading south from Kashgar came through here. Chinese Buddhist monks returning from pilgrimages to India in the 5th century found Buddhism widely practised. Hinduism began to filter north from India in the 8th century, and probably reached Gilgit in the 10th on the sabre-tips of a force of Shins invading from the lower Indus. The Shin language, Shina, is still the Gilgit vernacular.

The Indus Valley was forcibly converted to Shia Islam in the 11th century by Mahmud of Ghazni (971–1030), who led a total of 17 military expeditions from Afghanistan to India between 1001 and 1026. Gilgitis are now Ismaili Muslims, followers of the Geneva-based Aga Khan. They joined this branch of the Shia sect in the early 1300s, three centuries after their co-religionists further west in Badakhshan.

Regional Rivalry

With the decline of the Silk Route in the 16th century Gilgit's commercial traffic dwindled to a mere handful of Uighur traders from Xinjiang each summer. For three and a half centuries its isolation was almost complete. Then all at once three regional rivals turned covetously on it while a foreign superpower manoeuvered behind them.

Sikh troops from the Punjab captured the town in 1841, only to lose it to Kashmir in 1846. Hoping to control Kashmir and the still-unmapped mountains beyond by proxy, the British made its ruler a maharaja and paid him a subsidy. But in 1852 Gilgit fell to Gohar Aman, a rival chieftain from Yasin. These were bad times for the people of Gilgit; Gohar's favourite moneyraising tactic was to sell his subjects. By the time he died in 1857, 40 per cent of Gilgit's population had spent time in slavery.

In 1860 the town reverted to Kashmir. The maharaja took his revenge on Yasin, slaughtering 1200 of its inhabitants. Babies, it was alleged, were thrown in the air and cut in half as they fell. A British surveyor called George J. Whitaker Hayward, leaked the news of these atrocities to the outside world in the Calcutta *Pioneer*.

Ambush at the Pass

Hayward had Herculean stamina—and probably a death wish. Having made an enemy of the maharaja with his newspaper article, he returned to the Yasin valley in June 1870, intending to cross the Darkot pass at its head and map the Pamirs beyond. On the night of 18 June, as he fell asleep in his tent at the foot of the pass, he was ambushed and killed.

He was a loner, alone, a long way from home, mysteriously and treacherously murdered for exposing evil while serving his country. It was very poetic:

And now it was dawn. He rose strong to his feet,
And strode to his ruined camp below the wood;
He drank the breath of the morning cool and sweet,
His murderers round him stood...

Light on the Laspur hills was broadening fast.
The blood-red snow-peaks chilled to a dazzling white,
He turned, and saw the golden circle at last,
Cut by the Eastern height.

'O glorious Life, Who dwellest in earth and sun,
I have lived, I praise and adore Thee.'
A sword swept.
Over the pass the voices one by one
Faded, and the hill slept.

Sir Henry Newbolt, 'He Fell Among Thieves'

The Maharaja of Kashmir was proving none too pliant a client, and the Russians were bidding for influence with the Afghan chieftains further east. A clamour grew in Britain for a robust stand. A political agent, John Biddulph, was sent to Gilgit in 1877—only to be recalled when Liberals replaced the Tories back in London two years later.

But Russophobia was still on the rise. In 1883 William McNair, a British surveyor disguised as a Muslim doctor, established that Gilgit was within a week's march of no fewer than six passes on the Russian-Indian watershed. In 1889 Lieutenant Francis Younghusband learned that a Russian agent called Gromchevsky had struck a deal with the Mir of Hunza, and the Gilgit agency reopened.

Fixing the Frontier

The second agency was beefier than the first. Permanently staffed by 20 British officers, it raised and trained a force of Gilgit Scouts and served as a base for British expeditions against Hunza in 1891 and Chilas in 1892. In 1895 British India and Russia at last fixed their frontiers in the Pamirs, separated by a tongue of Afghanistan (the Wakhan corridor), and life in Gilgit quietened down.

The agent's job evolved from military campaigner to small-time diplomat. He hosted visiting anthropologists and gentleman-climbers, maintained friendly relations with local rulers, and kept the power of the Kashmiri governor merely nominal. As Ghandi and Nehru wrote the writing on the wall of the Raj in the 1920s and 1930s, Gilgit became, in Keay's words 'an anomalous and much sought-after posting' for lovers of the mountains and fresh air.

There was one more act to the drama. In August 1947, as India split into separate, independent Hindu and Muslim states, the Maharaja of Kashmir dithered. He was a Hindu. Many of his subjects, including all of Gilgit, were Muslim. Eventually in October he declared for India and a shootout between the people of Gilgit and its Kashmiri garrison seemed inevitable. At this point Major William Brown, a young Scot attached to the Gilgit Scouts, showed historic and completely unauthorized initiative by taking the new Kashmiri governor into 'protective custody' and announcing in a telegram to the new Prime Minister of the Northwest Frontier Province that, following a bloodless coup, Gilgit was now part of Pakistan. It has been ever since.

Getting to and from Gilgit

by air

PIA propeller-driven Fokker Friendships fly from Islamabad up the Kagan valley, past (and below) Nanga Parbat and over the Babusar Pass to Gilgit up to three times a day in summer, weather permitting. They don't take off if visibility is less than excellent anywhere along the route, though if Nanga Parbat is catching clouds, as it often does, they sometimes fly up the Indus Gorge. Either way, the trip makes a spectacular introduction to northern Pakistan's topography. If your flight is cancelled because of the weather you are automatically wait-listed for the next one. Flight time is 1 hour, 15 minutes, and the price Rs1700 return and Rs850 (single).

PIA in Rawalpindi is three blocks west of PTDC's Flashman's Hotel on The Mall, near its junction with Saddar Road, ✆ 591071/568071. There are several offices in Islamabad, including two in the Blue Area, one near American Express, and one in the Awami Markaz building. In Gilgit the office is in JSR Plaza on Airport Road, but seats can also be booked at PTDC's Chinar Inn by the river, ✆ 2562.

by bus

The state-run **Northern Areas Transportation Company (NATCO)** runs seven buses a day between Rawalpindi and Gilgit in both directions at 4am, 9am, 11am, 2pm, 5pm, 8pm, and 9pm. Northbound departures are from the Pir Wadhai bus station on the northeast edge of Rawalpindi, stopping at Havelian, Abbottabad, Mansehra, Besham, Komila/Dasu and Chilas. Southbound departures are from Gilgit's NATCO station opposite the Madina Hotel in NLI Chowk. Tickets are Rs180, Rs220, or Rs250 depending on the degree of comfort. Barring accidents, breakdowns and landslides the trip takes between 15 and 17 hours. Keep warm clothes handy.

Masherbrum Tours, and **Sargin Travels**, private rivals to NATCO run daily, slightly faster, buses between Rawalpindi's Pir Wadhai or Kashmiri bazaar (in Saddar bazaar) and Gilgit for between Rs220 and Rs250.

Northward on the KKH there is one NATCO bus a day between Gilgit and Sost in each direction. The northbound one leaves Gilgit at 8am and stops at Aliabad (in the Hunza valley), Gulmit and Passu. The southbound one leaves Sost at 5am. The trip takes four to five hours and costs about Rs70 one-way.

To cross the Khunjerab Pass into China, change at Sost and choose between NATCO and PTDC buses.

by private transport

NATCO's scheduled services are just the beginning. Private Suzuki and Ford passenger vans stream up and down the KKH between Rawalpindi and Sost all day every day, filling up at bazaars and stopping more or less anywhere. In addition, many hotels in Gilgit and points north run their own van services, and most can arrange private jeep transport along the KKH and up its tributary valleys.

Getting Around

Gilgit is 4km long. To get from the airport to the hotels at the west end of town, or from the hotels east of the airport to the centre, flag down any Suzuki taxi on Airport Road, which is reached from the airport terminal by following the runway to the roundabout. Otherwise walking is easiest.

Tourist Information

The **PTDC office** at the Chinar Inn, ✆ 2454/2562, is run by Riaz Ahmad Khan, who knows everything there is to know about the Northern Areas.

The managers of hotels such as the Hunza Inn and the Madina are good sources of local information, which they are careful to keep up to date.

G. M. Beg's famous **bookstore** at the north end of Jamat Khana bazaar sells English-language books, newspapers and magazines, and a schematic map of the peaks and glaciers of the Northern Areas, although some of these are cheaper in Rawalpindi or Karimabad.

Fuji, Kodak, and Agfa **film** including some slide film is available from several shops on Airport Road and in the bazaars. C41 developing and printing to a decent standard is also available for Rs25 plus Rs5 or 6 per print.

In and Around Gilgit

Most people use Gilgit as a base for forays into the wilder Northern Areas, and for recuperating afterwards. With few recognized tourist attractions, its most diverting pastimes are polo-watching (in April and the first week of November, with frequent practice sessions in September and October) and browsing in the Rajah and Saddar **bazaars**, which form the town's main shopping street at its western end. Near here, opposite the New Golden Peak Inn, **George Hayward's grave** can be seen in the old Christian cemetery. Up Bank Road towards the office of the Northern Areas Administrator, the third turning on the right leads to what was the British political agent's bungalow, now a municipal library.

The nearest evidence of Gilgit's more distant past is a 7th-century **Buddha** carved on a cliff above Kargah, 5km west of town on Punial Road.

Where to Stay

expensive

The best hotel is the comfortable **Gilgit Serena Hotel** which is well out of town in the Jutial area, ℗ 2330, ✉ 2525, but which will collect you from the airport or NATCO. Pleasantly decorated in Hunza style, with elaborately carved wooden pillars and beams and bright, multicoloured fabrics, it has good views, a garden, international telephone connections, satellite television, and an excellent restaurant. Doubles are Rs2150; singles Rs1700.

moderate

PTDC's very civilized **Chinar Inn**, Babar Road, ℗/✉ 2562, has high-ceilinged bedrooms with fans, big shower-rooms and wide verandas and offers singles at Rs650, doubles at Rs750. The **Hunza Inn**, ℗ 3814, is next door to the Chinar, and arranged round a pleasant garden courtyard. Here a double with hot shower goes for Rs500, a single Rs400. Further along Babar Road towards the airport, the spruce **Hunza Tourist House**, ℗ 2388, does a brisk trade with groups, who get a 10% discount. Doubles cost Rs470 and singles Rs350. The big, businesslike **Park Hotel**, Airport Road, ℗ 2379, has doubles from Rs300, with single occupancy from Rs185.

inexpensive

Most cheap hotels are on or near Airport Road and the bazaars, and are therefore noisy. An exception is the friendly and helpful **Madina Hotel**, at NLI Chowk, at the city end of Airport Road which has an enclosed garden. Rooms cost from Rs50 to Rs200, dormitory beds are Rs40 and Rs50. Another is the **New Golden Peak Inn,** beyond the bazaars at the opposite end of town from the airport, also more secluded, with a private garden, where singles, doubles, and triples are all Rs100. The new **Mountain Refuge Hotel** just west of the PTDC Chinar Inn has also been highly recommended. In addition to its peaceful location, it has the same friendly management as its namesake in Sost.

Eating Out

All the hotels have restaurants of sorts. The Serena Hotel has excellent all-you-can-eat buffets for around Rs200, and an à la carte menu to match. The Chinar Inn has full Western and Pakistani menus, unadventurous but unthreatening to your bowels. The Madina Hotel's set menu dinner is justly famous for its nicely spiced soups and perfectly crisp vegetables; a pleasant change at Rs50. There is also excellent local food in cheap restaurants such as the Pathan Hotel in Airport Road just west of JSR Plaza. The boneless beef masala served with piping hot bread is particularly good.

'it. All our mills and water channels were destroyed. The ice remained down for fifteen years. All our cultivation was spoilt... The Mir fed us.'

If there was ever a crack in the mountains up which man was not supposed to travel this surely is it,' wrote John Keay of the Hunza river gorge north of Gilgit. A century earlier the more understated John Biddulph called it 'a more difficult and dangerous piece of ground than I had ever traversed in a tolerably large experience of Himalayan sport'.

The only route to Hunza at that time was a mule track up the west side of the river, often crossing sheer cliffs on a scary miscellany of branches, twigs and stones jammed in convenient cracks. It can still be seen at some points from the KKH across the river.

Modern traffic leaving Gilgit rejoins the KKH either 10km back down the road to Rawalpindi or by crossing the Gilgit river on one of the suspension bridges below the Chinar Inn, then crossing the Hunza river on a third.

On the far side of this bridge the road disappears into a cliff, turns abruptly to the right, re-emerges and climbs to the village of Dainyor on the KKH.Karimabad, Altit and Aliabad, the principal villages of the Hunza valley, are some 80km up-river. Half way there the gorge turns right (east) and the road passes beneath the ruined fortress of **Nilt**, where the combined irregulars of Hunza and Nagar detained Algy Durand and the 5th Gurkhas for three weeks in the winter of 1891–92 in the single most colourful engagement of the Great Game. Three British officers won the VC for suicidal bravery with climbing ropes and explosives under heavy fire and falling rocks on a near-vertical battlefield, Durand got a lead-coated garnet bullet in the groin and E. F. Knight of *The Times*, himself commanding a platoon of Pathans, reported it all in fiercely patriotic detail.

Between the twin villages of Ghulmet and Yal, 10km further on, a sign invites you to crick your neck for a first glimpse of **Rakaposhi** (7790 m). Along this section of the KKH glaciers tumble towards it every few kilometres, sometimes moving visibly and even threatening to meet in the river. Local lore holds such meetings to be romantic. A clear-iced glacier is male, a cloudy one female, and all they want to do is kiss and then retreat.

Kisses, and consequent floods and crop damage, can be prevented by burying a piece of the intended kissee in the oncoming snout. Nowadays the Pakistan Air Force bombs advancing glaciers—but there were no planes here in 1903, when one advanced 5km in eight days.

According to a local account quoted by Kenneth Mason in *The Study of Threatening Glaciers*, 'it came down, like a snake, quite steadily: we could see it moving. There was no noise. When an obstruction got in the way the ice went round it at first and overwhelmed it. All our mills and water channels were destroyed. The ice remained down for fifteen years. All our cultivation was spoilt... The Mir fed us.'

Beyond Yal the KKH crosses to the north bank of the river at Pisan. Soon afterwards it swings to the left, the mountains stand back, and you see for the first time the terraced fields of Hunza. The next village, Murtazabad, is actually a northern outpost of Hunza's historic rival Nagar, whose territory is mostly on the southern side of the unique basin opening out ahead. This, says the bumph, is the real Shangri-La.

Hunza wastes no time with foothills. The slopes rising off the terraces and apricot groves go straight up to 7000-m peaks, including the supremely mountain-shaped Rakaposhi to the southwest. There are few places in the world where, as here, you can take in nearly six vertical kilometres of mountain in a single glance.

Hunza has always lured writers into hyperbole. A pretentious 19th-century philologist called Gottlieb Leitner called it 'that cradle of human thought as expressed in language', creating an inaccurate impression of simplicity and purity as a result of centuries of supposed isolation. In fact Hunza and Nagar were exposed to all the cultural cross-breeding brought to most of Central Asia by Silk Route caravans, and traditionally enriched themselves by raiding them.

There are plenty more myths about Hunza—that it is naturally fertile, for example, and that its people live to over 100 by eating apricot kernels. In fact Hunza's crops depend on long irrigation channels which take great skill to plan. John Staley studied them: 'If a mistake is made then several months' labour by a dozen or more strong men will be wasted, and the elder who supervised them will lose his reputation.' The longevity myth seems to have arisen from confusion about birthdays, though Hunzakuts certainly consume a lot of apricots and grow them in 29 varieties.

Baltit Fort

The ancestral home of the Mirs of Hunza is one of the most famous landmarks on the KKH. In scaffolding for five years, it looks over the tourist Mecca of Karimabad on the north side of the valley and will reopen in the summer of 1996 as a museum.

The fort is about 600 years old, and until 1891 was a jackdaw's nest full of booty from raids sponsored by the Mirs on trans-montane caravans. At that time the Mir was Sadfar Ali, who, impatient about primogeniture, had murdered his father in 1886. Or, in a colloquial translation of Sadfar's own version: 'By the will of God and the decree of fate my late father and I recently fell out: I took the initiative and settled the matter, and have placed myself on the throne of my ancestors.' It was to punish the thieving and apparently Russophile 'young Saffy', as Algernon Durand called him, that the celebrated 1891 expedition via Nilt was launched. By the time the British reached Hunza the Mir had fled to China with his choicest trinkets. Muhammad Nazim Khan was installed in his place and was still living in the fort in a certain eclectic style when Peter Fleming, brother of Ian, passed through having ridden along the deadly south side of the Taklamakan desert and over the Mintaka Pass in 1935:

'To the queer, comfortless rooms assorted bric-a-brac lent comfort if not dignity. A chandelier clashed with bows and arrows. Viceroys, Political Agents, Moslem leaders, Kitchener, the youthful Curzon stared portentously from the walls. Ibex horns were much in evidence.'

A few metres above Karimabad's Hilltop Hotel there is an unusual junction. A switchback leads to the modern residence of the current Mir (great-grandson of Muhammad Nazim Khan), which stands in ostentatious isolation on its own terraced fin. Another track departs at right angles under a mini-aqueduct and sends unwary drivers spinning into a void. Actually it turns sharp right, zig-zags down a cliff, contours in and out of a ravine and brings you to Baltit's twin, Altit.

Altit has its own fort, older than Baltit's and even more spectacularly positioned on a 300-m cliff above the Hunza river. Approached on foot through an orchard from the polo ground, it is empty but open to visitors (Rs10). Its tower gives a wonderful bird's eye view of the flat roofs of a Hunza village, and the dung, apricots and clothes that may be drying on them.

Shopping

Waistcoats and hats of Hunza wool (*patti*) are sold by tiny gift shops in all of Hunza's villages, together with cut and uncut gems, lapis lazuli and coral jewellery.

Where to Stay

Karimabad

Explosive growth fuelled by government loans at rather un-Islamic interest rates has turned Karimabad into bustling single street mini-metropolis, with new hotels and guest houses springing up everywhere, and new metalled roads linking them to the valley below. Just below where the old jeep track meets the newer metalled one at the lower end of the village is the grumpy but relatively plush **Mountain View Hotel**, ✆ 7053, with its layered concrete balconies, where singles are Rs400, doubles Rs500 and three-bed rooms Rs550. The original rock-bottom **Hunza Inn** slightly above it has been renamed the **Haider Inn**; it's one of the longest standing guest houses in Karimabad, a motley collection of buildings on both sides of the jeep track, popular for its low prices for both rooms and set menu. Dormitory beds are Rs15, doubles Rs50. Further up the **Karakurum Hotel** has a pleasant garden; here, doubles are Rs200. At the top of the village on the left just after the fork, the quieter **Garden Hotel** has a terraced garden and apricot orchard; three-bed rooms go for Rs200, doubles Rs150, dormitory beds Rs40. The prestige address, when complete, will be the **Rakaposhi View Hotel** with multiple stars and swimming pool.

Altit

It's more pleasant to stay in Altit, twenty minutes' walk from the centre of Karimabad, at the friendly and helpful **Kisar Inn**, i with frequent free jeep pickups and dropoffs at Ganesh on the KKH, and plentiful good food. Considerably quieter than the Karimbad hotels, and a short walk from Altit Fort, its vine-hung open air café has become a favourite place for budget travellers to exchange news. For those who want to get back in touch with the world, there is the option of BBC World Service TV in the restaurant. Dormitory beds are Rs35, doubles Rs100 and 200.

Crossing to China

From **Ganesh**, below Baltit on the KKH, the road follows the Hunza river for 85km through Gojal or Upper Hunza to the Pakistani border post at Sost. The valley is still cultivated where possible, but increasingly the views are of scree and naked rock. Road and river turn north 19km beyond Ganesh. A stone tablet on the opposite bank marks a visit by Lord Kitchener in 1903.

Gulmit, about 35km from Ganesh, and **Passu**, 16km beyond, are both possible overnight stops and popular trekking bases. In Gulmit the friendly **Tourist Cottage**, where doubles cost Rs280 and traditional Gojal-style dormitory beds Rs65, and in Passu the **Village Guest Houses** (dormitory beds Rs40, doubles up to Rs400) are good places to stay. Above these villages, four glaciers in the space of 30km come down from the west to within easy walking distance of the KKH. The last one, the Batura, actually crossed it and wrecked a bridge in 1976. Peter Fleming picked his way over this glacier in 1935 and decided, 'there was something unnatural about that tortured, cataclysmic place; it was as though we had invaded the surface of another world.' Gulmit is a better place to stop than Sost when coming from China, since it has an interesting tiny museum, good walks, and

several places to stay. If you can afford to charter early morning transport to get you to the border (Rs5–600 for a jeep) this is also a better place to spend your last night in Pakistan.

From Passu, it is 34km to **Sost**, where the Pakistani customs and immigration are situated (*see* below). From Sost the KKH curves gradually eastwards, leaving the Hunza river for the Khunjerab river shortly before it enters the Karakoram National Park (KNP) at Dih, a security post. After another claustrophobic, crumbling canyon, the Karakorams finally relent. As you make the final climb to the Khunjerab pass, you realize that the horizon is curving smoothly for the first time since Islamabad.

As befits a pass in the Pamirs, the Khunjerab is long, shallow and very high. At 4730m it is in fact the highest international border crossing in the world. Chinese customs and immigration—and not much else—used to be an hour inside the border at **Pirali**. In 1993 they moved three hours further down the road to Tashkurgan, passing on the left a third of the way there the high, wide entrance to the Mintaka Valley.

Perched on a rocky spur beyond where the highway meets the Mintaka river are the remains of Kiz Kurgan, a fortress founded by a Han Chinese princess who took refuge here when waylaid by robbers on her way to marry a Persian king. She never came down, forming instead a relationship with a visiting sun god which produced a child who grew into the first of a long line of Kyrgyz chieftains.

The Mintaka Valley leads to the Mintaka Pass, preferred by Silk Route traders to the Khunjerab being a more direct route south; closed by the Chinese for being too close to the Soviet Union, it is now a candidate for a mooted Tajikistan–Pakistan highway.

Getting to the Border

Whatever means of transport you use, you must set out from Sost early in the day; it is a 5-hour journey to Tashkurgan, and the 3-hour time difference between China and Pakistan means that you won't reach Tashkurgan till early evening.

Western Xinjiang

N

new railway

A

⊕ Ürümqi
Miquan ▲

Yiaohe T
Turpan

Bezeklik T
Caochang T

la

100 kilometres
100 miles

by bus

Northbound NATCO buses from Gilgit stop at Sost and take about 5 hours to get there. Onward NATCO and PTDC buses to China leave Sost each morning through the summer at about 8am, stopping at Pakistani customs on the way. A one-way ticket to Tashkurgan, where you can spend the night, is Rs740.

The PTDC bus is for foreigners only, can sometimes be a comfortable minibus, and is amenable to stops for photographs. A Chinese bus from Tashkurgan to Kashgar is ¥77.

by jeep

It is probably easiest to leave your jeep at Sost and continue by bus. Otherwise, check that both driver and vehicle can accompany you to Tashkurgan, or arrange to be met by a Chinese vehicle from Kashgar.

Border Formalities

The Khunjerab Pass is open for tourists, weather permitting, 1 May–15 Nov, 1 May–31 Oct for groups. There are now buses throughout the year, again weather permitting, but tourists may not be allowed to take them. There are routine checks for stowaways at the pass itself, and several passport checks at points on both the Pakistani and Chinese sides, but this is a much easier crossing than the Torugart Pass, and everything usually goes smoothly. At the Chinese post at Tashkurgan you will have to fill in a customs declaration; what they are really interested in is cameras and consumer electronics. This has become a formality, but be sure not to lose your copy of the declaration which you will need to leave China. You may also be required to declare that you are in good health, and may be asked for vaccination certificates, especially cholera, but if you are a Westerner it doesn't seem to matter if you don't have one.

visas

It is impossible to get Chinese or Pakistani visas at or anywhere near the border. Nationals of most developed countries are allowed to enter Pakistan and obtain at least a three-day transit visa at the border, which can be converted to a tourist visa only in Islamabad, but do not rely on this. Officials of both countries have no hesitation in sending people back where they came from, and Chinese officials may decide not to let you leave Tashkurgan without a Pakistani visa. Visas are only available in national capitals (see 'Entry Formalities', pp.15–16).

Where to Stay

Most China-bound travellers end up spending a night at Sost. Accommodation is basic but plentiful. Try the **Khunjerab Hotel**, ☏ 462 13, above the KKH on the right as you enter the village, where a single is Rs250, and a double with hot shower Rs400. At the **Mountain Refuge**, ☏ 462 19, 200m beyond it and run by the same friendly people who manage the hotel of the same name in Gilgit, a dormitory bed costs Rs35, a double with hot water about Rs300.

The last place to stay or pitch a tent in Pakistan is the KNP's rest-house near Kukshal, 35km beyond Sost and 52km below the pass (*open May–Sept only*). Trekking is possible within the KNP but only with a permit from the Khunjerab Security Force at Dih.

Tashkurgan

Tashkurgan, 3040m above sea level, is said to have nine months of winter and three of summer. China's only Pamirian town of any size, its population of 5000 is mostly Tajik. Its one street heads off at right angles from the main highway towards an enormous **Chinese fortress**, possibly 14th-century, on the only hillock in the otherwise flat-bottomed Tashkurgan River valley. Xuan Zang, a Buddhist monk who returned by this route to China in 642 after a long pilgrimage in India, wrote that there had already been a citadel here since the 4th century BC. Chinese tourist bumph calls it Stone City in an over-literal translation of 'Tashkurgan'. There's not much to see inside.

Where to Stay

The bus may stop at the **Pamir Hotel**, at the end of the main street on the left. Twin-bed rooms in the newer 'hot water' wing go from ¥180; triples in the older 'cold water' one are ¥100. The Tajik-run restaurant serves set dinners for ¥25. Typically bare but clean doubles (¥30 per bed) and four-bed rooms (¥25 per bed) are available in the newish **Khunjerab Hotel** next to the customs department on the highway, but most visitors coming from Pakistan prefer to continue on into town.

The rock-bottom **Ice Mountain** just before the Pamir is Pakistani-run and cheaper at ¥25 per bed in a carpeted four-bed room, or ¥15 without carpet. ¥50 per bed in a double. Pakistani food is available cheaply from the restaurant. The **Transportation Hotel** next to the bus station just off the highway is the same price as the Ice Mountain but grimmer.

To Kashgar

Marc Aurel Stein, indefatigable Hungarian-born archaeologist and the British Museum's greatest plunderer of far-off treasure troves since Lord Elgin, came through Tashkurgan in 1906 with 15 mule-loads of kit including 2000 photographic glass plates, 'a small armoury of surveying instruments' and a raft to be floated on inflated goatskins. Of the tough route north to Kashgar he wrote: 'I made up my mind to cover its ten regular marches in six days in spite of the baggage.'

Nowadays, with a rucksack and a bus ticket, you can do the 300-km journey in a day. This would mean driving straight past China's two isolated Pamir giants, **Mustagh Ata** (7546 m) and **Kongur** (7719 m), and between them, **Kara-Kul lake** (not to be confused with Tajikistan's larger lake of the same name, this one is called *Kalakuli* by the Chinese).

North of Kongur, the Karakoram Highway tumbles off the Pamir plateau into the Tarim basin, via the Ghez River canyon. The last 80km to Kashgar are flat and blissfully smooth, cruelly raising hopes of a comfortable ride for those going south.

The **Xinjiang Mountaineering Association** in Kashgar (for address, *see* p.338) can book you into their permanent Mustagh Ata base camp. A 5-hour trek above the lake (longer if you carry your rucksack instead of putting it on a camel), the camp consists of Kyrgyz yurts. The summit of Mustagh Ata is between four and six days' extremely demanding, oxygen-depleted plod away. The XMA also offers a ski-up, ski-down package.

Bulun Kul (*Bulunkou* in Chinese), beneath Kongur, is a Kyrgyz settlement where you can break your journey.

Kashgar (Kashi)

Commanding all the entrances to Kashgar's famous Sunday market, there is a grand, beaten-up building bearing an even grander announcement: 'Kashgar International Trade Market of Central and Western Asia'. This is no hyperbole. What's more, it could refer to the whole town. Kashgar is a triumph of commerce over both nature and ideology. Historically it was the nexus of at least four branches of the Silk Route, despite being surrounded by awesome physical barriers: the Tian Shan to the west, the Pamirs and Karakorams to the south, and the dreaded Taklamakan Desert to the east.

For much of this century it has been controlled by one of the world's two Communist giants and divided by minefields, watchtowers and double barbed-wire fences. Yet within two years of the break-up of the Soviet Union, triangular trade between China, Pakistan and the CIS has taken root in Kashgar and flourished.

From the portal of the Id Kah mosque to the Sunday market, Kashgar is thronged by traders and their goods and families and livestock. From the Khunjerab come Pakistanis in diaphanous white cotton to stay at Chini Bagh, the old British consulate, and buy silk. From Kyrgyzstan, via the more recently opened Torugart Pass, come returning Chinese in brand new Moskvich cars bought in Russia and baptized on a route that is more river-bed than road. Pioneering ex-Soviet truckers also come this way, piled high with zinc-coated plov-makers from Kazan, to be bartered for Chinese copies of Japanese electronics.

Muslim Uighurs, who account for 90 per cent of Kashgar's 280,000 population, dominate bazaar trade and the town centre. The Chinese, who claim to have been here since the Tang dynasty (AD 618–906), have built the straight boulevards, the ring road, the East Lake and the airport, and for the most part are heartily resented.

Kashgar—known to the Chinese as Kashi—is the definitive Central Asian trading oasis, far more exotic than clichéd silhouettes of caravans and minarets, not so much despite the intrusion of modernity in the form of jeeps and ghetto-blasters as because of it. Eras collide here, as well as cultures. For its variety of peoples, trades, traditions, noises, colours and smells, and for sheer street bustle, Kashgar can have few rivals in either the Chinese or the former Soviet empires.

History

The earliest inhabitants of the Kashgar oasis were probably Scythians, Indo-European nomads famous as archers and jewellers. Traces of their art dating back to the 8th century BC have been found here and in Fergana on the other side of the Tian Shan, though around this time many of them migrated west towards their future homeland in southern Russia.

Of Kashgar's current rival ethnic groups the Chinese, unfortunately for the Uighur independence movement, seem to have got here first. The imperial envoy Zhang Qian passed through around 130 BC on his way to buy some of Fergana's 'heavenly horses' with which to defend China against Mongolian nomads. Two hundred years later the Chinese arrived in force under General Pan Chao and made the Tarim basin a military protectorate.

On Pan Chao's death Kashgar fell to the Kushans under their greatest leader, Khan Kanishka, who sent an army over the Pamirs from Khorassan around AD 130. The Chinese did not regain control of Kashgar until their golden age under the Tang Dynasty (618–906). Tang troops arrived after crushing a rebellion in Turpan in 640. They consolidated their position in the oasis, named it Shu-le and pressed on westward over the Tian Shan. It seemed possible that all of Central Asia would become part of the Chinese empire, but in one of the decisive battles of history the Chinese were routed by the Arabs at Talas in 751.

Contrary to many accounts, the Arabs did not bring Islam to Kashgar; they never got this far. Even the Uighurs, who started migrating into the Tarim basin from Mongolia in the late 9th century, arrived as infidels. It was the Karakhanids who brought Islam to this eastern outpost, having learned it in their adopted capital of Bukhara.

Kashgar was one of Genghis Khan's first conquests, around 1206. It passed to his son Chaghatai, and later to Tamerlane and the Uzbek khans of Bukhara and Kokand. The Chinese did not return until 1755.

What they found was a confident, homogeneous Uighur city. The Manchurian Qing dynasty who then ruled China were alien to the Chinese—and doubly so to the Uighurs. In 1759 Kashgar rebelled. Manchu troops crushed the rebellion with unprecedented savagery, and carried off a Uighur princess called Xiang Fei. The emperor Qianlong fell madly in love with her, only to receive the ultimate snub when she committed suicide.

For centuries Kashgar's isolation had ensured it relative freedom from imperial meddling. Now not only were the Chinese resurgent in Central Asia; other powers, technologically advanced and completely foreign, were encroaching steadily from the west and south. It was inevitable that Kashgar would become a focus of the Great Game between Russia and British India.

The Russians took round one. In 1860 Count Michael Ignatiev, on a lucky streak after successful missions to Khiva and Bukhara, arrived in Beijing and cajoled the emperor into allowing a Russian consulate in Kashgar. But it was to be 20 years before the consul could take up his post. Kashgar was seething with almost continuous Muslim rebellion. In 1865 a charismatic soldier called Yakub Beg who claimed descent from Tamerlane returned from exile in Kokand, eliminated rivals for control of the city and proclaimed himself king of Kashgaria. After a decade of devious rule in which he won formal recognition from Britain and Russia despite continually playing them off against each other, Manchu armies re-took Kashgaria and Yakub Beg perished—whether by poisoning or his own hand no one quite knows.

A Russian consulate was finally established in 1882 and a British one, by George Macartney, in 1892. Macartney stayed for 26 years, becoming the linchpin of British spying and Russia-watching in Central Asia while his residence and gardens, lovingly tended by his wife Catherine, became an unlikely haven of British imperial elegance.

From the Russian Revolution in 1917 until the Chinese nationalists took over under Chiang Kai Shek in 1941, Kashgar was informally controlled by the Soviet Union. Communist China closed the road from Kashgar to Kyrgyzstan in 1960 and opened the new one to Pakistan in 1982.

Getting to and from Kashgar
by air

Throughout most of the year China Xinjiang Airways (CAAC) flies daily from Ürümqi to Kashgar and back (flight time 1 hour 40 minutes; ¥1265 one way), leaving Ürümqi at 6pm Beijing time and Kashgar at 9pm. On some days in summer there are two flights; in winter, the frequency falls to three flights a week unless there is exceptional demand. Book ahead if possible. The unhelpful Kashgar **CAAC office**, ✆ 222113 (*open 10am–1.30pm and 3.30–7.30pm Beijing time*) is next to the People's Park's south entrance on Jiefang Nanlu. An airport bus leaves here every day at 6.30pm and takes 25 minutes.

by rail

There is no railway line to Kashgar, though the Chinese government apparently intends extending the Ürümqi–Korla line this far.

by bus

Going from Kashgar to Pakistan, an international bus is supposed to leave for Sost every morning when the pass is open (1 May–15 Nov, 1 May–31 Oct for groups; tourists may not be allowed to take the bus outside the pass opening hours). It goes from the yard on the left-hand side of the main building of the Chini Bagh Hotel, and tickets are available from the foyer for ¥265. The bus is reported to leave at 11am, but this is just when the customs office opens and the fun begins.

First show your passport and your copy of the customs declaration form you received on the way into China to the person at the left window, then show your baggage to the people with the scales at the rear of the bus, and then pay ¥2 at the right-hand office inside the customs building, taking your luggage to the loaders. They will also take your ticket and passport, which will be returned as you board the bus. You will not have access to your luggage at Tashkurgan, so take essentials with you on board the bus.

There's a local bus from the bus station to Tashkurgan on Monday, Wednesday, and Friday mornings for ¥40. However, to board an international bus from Tashkurgan doesn't cost much less than from Kashgar—¥202.

To go by bus along the northern rim of the Tarim basin from Kashgar to Ürümqi via Aksu, Kuqa, and Korla, the relatively comfortable option is the 36-hour sleeper bus which leaves the bus station three times a day and costs nearly twice as much as the same journey in the opposite direction: ¥378 to Ürümqi for a bottom bunk or ¥322 for a top one. There are buses on Mondays, Wednesdays, and Fridays to Turpan directly, or daily buses to Daheyan where you can change to a local bus (or get a taxi).

There are also two buses a day along the south side of the Taklamakan Desert to Hetian (Khotan) via Shache (Yarkand) and Yecheng (Karghalik). To go from Yecheng into Tibet is forbidden, but nevertheless many people do it by private negotiation with truck drivers. To come from Lhasa by this route is permitted as long as you have one of the easily available permits. A legal route to Tibet is to continue eastwards from Hetian to Ruoqiang, and then go southeast to Lhasa via Golmud.

Getting Around

Kashgar is divided into four quadrants by Renmin Xilu and Renmin Donglu (People's Road West and People's Road East) and, perpendicular to it, Jeifang Beilu and Jeifang Nanlu (Liberation Road North and Liberation Road South). The old town is in the northeast quadrant. Further out, so are the Sunday market, the Kashgar Guest House and the Abakh Hoja tomb. The People's Park and long distance bus station are in the southeast quadrant. Further out, so is the East Lake. The Id Kah mosque is in the northwest quadrant. Further out, so are most of the hotels which take foreigners.

by bicycle

By far the best way to get about is to hire a bicycle. The Seman Hotel rents bicycles for ¥2 per hour, and some of the other nearby Western cafés also have bikes. Park in designated bike parks where possible, ¥0.20.

by public transport

The buses in Kashgar are not particularly useful to the visitor. There are also donkey carts (not in the centre), motorbikes (you ride in the sidecar), and ordinary taxis (scarce, and with 'broken' meters). Drivers mostly understand foreign manglings of local place names, but the Uighur versions are more useful than the Chinese ones. Fix the price in advance, preferably in writing, and refuse to pay a fen more. From the Seman Hotel to the Sunday market by motorbike sidecar, for instance, should be no more than ¥3 for one, ¥5 for two.

The official tourist office is **CITS (China International Travel Service)**, upstairs on the first floor of the building immediately inside the Chini Bagh Hotel compound on the left, ✆ 223087/225390 (*open 10am–1.30pm and 3.30–7.30pm Beijing time*). The last number will get you the foreign individual travel department, where Li Mei speaks good English and is very helpful. They have glossy maps of Kashgar (¥5) and organize tours by car, jeep and bus into the desert, up the Pamirs and most places in between.

Anything CITS does, the **Xinjiang Kashgar Travel Agency**, Jeifang Nanlu 1, Kashgar, Xinjiang, China 844000, ✆ (0998) 222593, ✉ 222525, telex 79123 KSBTH CN, will claim they can do too, though not necessarily more cheaply.

John Hu's Information Café, ✆ (0998) 224186, ✉ 225390 is run by John Hu and his younger brother (John II), the most switched-on English-speaking fixers in town, who can arrange a wide variety of services including short notice plane tickets, and who mostly charge slightly less than the others. The café is opposite the Seman Hotel's new entrance, and there are others opposite the Turpan Hotel in Turpan, and opposite the Hongshan Hotel in Ürümqi.

The Kashgar branch of the **Xinjiang Mountaineering Association** is No. 8 Tiyu Lu (Sports Road), ✆ 223680, ✉ 222957, telex 79123 KSBTH CN. They provide guides, interpreters, transport and, most importantly, permission, for expeditions to Kongur, Mustagh Ata, Mudztaga (in Tibet), Broad Peak, Hidden Peak, Gasherbrum and K2. They also run a programme of treks (including to these mountains' Chinese base camps) and Silk Route tours. Turn left at the first major crossroads south of the CAAC office on Jiefang Nanlu. The offices are upstairs in a two-storey white building with an English sign.

The **Bank of China** (*open 9.30am–1.30pm and 4pm–7pm in summer, and 10am–2pm and 3.30–6.30pm in winter, Beijing time*), at the extreme west end of Renmin Xilu about a kilometre from the Seman Hotel, changes most western currencies into renminbi and accepts all major credit cards for cash withdrawals in renminbi, apparently with no limit except your own credit limit. Take your passport. This branch is particularly reluctant to change renminbi back into dollars or to give dollars for travellers' cheques. Be firm and insist, especially if you are leaving via the Torugart Pass, where banking hours are erratic or non-existent.

Travel Permits and Visa Extensions

These are available from the main **Public Security Bureau** two blocks south of the Chini Bagh Hotel next to a bit of old city wall on Shengli Lu (*open 10.30am–7.30pm*). Xinjiang's list of open cities not requiring permits has lengthened in recent years to include those on the southern route around the Taklamakan.

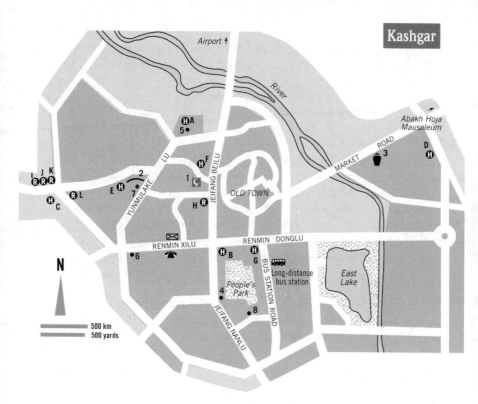

Kashgar

Airport ↑

River

Abakh Hoja
Mausoleum

MARKET ROAD

OLD TOWN

East
Lake

RENMIN XILU

RENMIN DONGLU

People's
Park

Long-distance
bus station

BUS STATION ROAD

JEIFANG NANLU

JEIFANG BEILU

YUNMULAKE LU

N

500 km
500 yards

HOTELS & RESTAURANTS

A Chini Bagh Hotel
B Renmin Hotel
C Seman Hotel
D Kashgar Guest House
E Silk Road Hotel
F Noor Bish Hotel
G Tian Nan Hotel
H Central Asia Restaurant
I Limin Restaurant
J Seman Road Restaurant
K Daniel Restaurant
L John Hu's Information Café and Seman Hotel
   Building

KEY

1 Id Kah mosque
2 City wall
3 Sunday market
4 CAAC (China Xinjiang Airlines)
5 CITS (China International Travel Service)
6 Bank of China
7 Public Security Bureau
8 Xinjiang Mountaineering Association

A Stroll Around Town

To see and inhale the essence of Kashgar, walk or ride east from the enormous red chunk of 500 year-old **city wall** near the junction of Shengli Lu and Seman Lu, through the old town to the Sunday market. For a taste of the tranquil side of imperial China, take a picnic to the **East Lake**, 20 minutes' walk east of Mao on Renmin Donglu.

Id Kah Square

A narrow, potholed street, starting to the right of an empty ornamental pool opposite the PSB on Shengli Lu, leads past the south side of the Id Kah mosque to **Id Kah Square**. This is the heart of Uighur China, perpetually full of knots of men in quilted black robes in earnest conversation or playing cards. Their Turkic features, clothes and cadences constantly remind you how much closer you are to Fergana than Beijing.

Id Kah Mosque

Built in 1442, this is Xīnjiäng's biggest mosque, with room for 20,000. A sign in the entrance has a potted history in English which declares that in 1962 it was put in the care of the autonomous regional government. When not being used for prayer, its quiet, leafy courtyards provide soothing relief from the mayhem outside. Non-Muslims, including women, are allowed in if modestly dressed. Inside the main gate on the right there is a public lavatory. To enter the main hall costs ¥3, but the interior is unspectacular. To take photographs anywhere inside the gate costs ¥5.

The Old Town

The streets of the old town east of Id Kah Square constitute Kashgar's main permanent **bazaar**. It is good for farm tools still hot from the anvil, hand-tooled cradle legs, lurid carpets and every conceivable variety of take-away Uighur food.

The Sunday Market

This takes place about 1km east of the old town, over the opaque red Tuman river on the right-hand side behind the 'Kashgar International Trade Market of Central and Western Asia' building. Even on weekdays, a vast array of useful rather than exotic goods is sold here by hundreds of neat stalls in an orderly, shaded grid. Sundays are special for the livestock market. There are not many places left in the world where horses and camels are still test-ridden with all the seriousness of the pre-internal combustion age.

Abakh Hoja Tomb

Kashgar's finest piece of Islamic architecture is 6km northeast of the Sunday market—half an hour by bike down pleasant roads lined with

MAKING 'MANTAU' IN KASHGAR MARKET

poplars and irrigation canals. The Abakh Hoja tomb, famous for its green tiled dome, is the centrepiece of a burial complex wherein lie 72 bodies from five generations of the same noble Uighur family. When it was built, no one can agree. Opinions range from 1640 to the late 18th century. Its first occupant was a Muslim missionary called Yusuf Hoja, but it is named after his more famous son, Abakh Hoja or Abkhoja, who became leader of a local Islamic sect and in some accounts ruler of Kashgar, and died in 1693. Legend has it that Xiang Fei ('Fragrant Concubine'), the princess who committed suicide after the suppression of the 1759 Uighur rebellion rather than accept the Emperor Qianlong's love, is also buried here. Her real resting place is probably much further east in Heibei province. ¥15 per person, and ¥2 per camera.

Ancient Sites around Kashgar

When Xuan Zang, the Buddhist monk, came through Kashgar in 644, he noted that Buddhism was already widely practised here at more than 100 shrines and temples. Surviving traces of these within day-trip range include the sandstone **Mor pagoda**, partly ruined but still huge, 38km north-east of town on a bad road (you need a jeep; ¥250). Unfortunately there are ticketing problems here: ¥5 per person just outside the site, but a further ¥10 per person is extorted by Uighur peasants with threats of violence at the site itself.

The caves of the **Three Immortals**, 20km north of Kashgar and not really worth the effort. They are half way up a cliff and you can't get close.

Off the Tashkurgan road, 50km to the southwest, is the **tomb of Mohammed Kashgari**, an 11th-century Uighur scholar after whom Kashgar, formerly Shu-le, was renamed. Born on the south shore of lake Issyk-Kul in today's Kyrgyzstan, he was educated in Kashgar and travelled as a young man to Baghdad. Here, between 1075 and 1094, he hand-wrote four copies of a Turkic dictionary which has become a key text for modern scholars of ancient Turkic texts. Again, a jeep is necessary; hire costs ¥250.

Kashgar (℃ 0998–)   ***Where to Stay***

All hotels except the **Kashgar Guest House** have beds in large, bathroomless rooms for as little as one fifth the price of a double with its own bathroom.

expensive

Close to Kashgar's pulsating heart is the **Hotel Biniwa/Qinibake/Chini Bagh**, Seman Road 93, ℃ 222103. The variously-spelled former British consulate has two five-storey blocks instead of Catherine Macartney's cherished gardens, and none of the leather armchairs and back copies of the *Illustrated London News* which so delighted her visitors. There is a Chinese restaurant to the left of the main building, a Uighur one behind it, and the CITS office is situated in front of it. A twin-bed room with bath in the 'international' wing costs ¥360; a bed in a four-bed room with a bath in the older wing, ¥40).

For complete seclusion and large, slightly musty twin rooms at ¥350 go to the **Kashgar Guest House**, ✆ 222368, ✉ 224679, 15 minutes east of the old town by bike. Take the first major right turn after the Sunday market then look out for the English sign on the right. There are Chinese and Western restaurants.

moderate

The closest thing to elegance in Kashgar is the **Seman Hotel**; ✆ 222192/222861, on the west side of the Seman road roundabout. Here, a twin with bath is ¥280 in the newest building, ¥160 in an older one, ¥100 in Building No. 3 across the road. It also has decaying dormitory rooms in the low, pink outbuildings which were the Russian consulate for ¥15 and in one of the newer buildings for ¥20. Downstairs, Legoland meets the Forbidden City in the very Chinese foyer, where you can buy stamps, and hire a bike or a Chinese-built Volkswagen Santana with driver. Hot water is only provided 9.30am–12 noon and 7.30pm–1am, Beijing time.

inexpensive

The **Silk Road Hotel**, ✆ 222004, is near the east end of Seman road on the south side. It has now become mainly a Pakistani hotel with two- or three-bed rooms at ¥20 per person or ¥15 in a dorm. The back rooms overlook the old city wall, but the bathrooms are primitive and the cheaper Seman Hotel dormitory beds are much better value.

Close to the bus station on the south side of Renmin Donglu, the **Tian Nan Hotel**, ✆ 222211/225692, has private rooms without private bathrooms from ¥30, with bathrooms from ¥60 per bed, and four-bed rooms without bath for ¥16 per bed. Beware the restaurant and café where you will be charged double for being foreign. Two blocks west at Jiefang Nanlu 1, the **Renmin Hotel**, ✆ 224785, is central and friendly, but not such good value as the Seman. A bed in a triple with its own bathroom is ¥53. Dorms are ¥16 per bed in a nine-bed room. Primitive but colourful, the **Noor Bish Hotel**, ✆ 223092, is a traditional Uighur building tucked away on the left as you walk from the Chini Bagh to the Idkah Mosque. Only Uighur is spoken, unless a Pakistani guest can act as a translator, but dormitory bed prices are negotiable and may be as little as ¥10 or ¥12.

Kashgar (✆ 0998–)   **Eating Out**

Laghman, as in the CIS, is thick noodles with a spicy meat sauce. *Pulau* (*plov*) is fried rice with mutton and grated turnip. Other staples include *manta* (boiled sacks of meat and vegetables, with the stress on the second syllable), *suyuk'ash* and *chuchureh* (noodle soups), *thau kebab* (bread and meat boiled in soup) and the ubiquitous, supreme *kebab*. Large flat round loaves are called *nan* in Uighur. Small bagel-like ones are *girday*.

There is sanitized Uighur food at the **Chini Bagh Hotel**, or take your chances at any of the grimy al fresco eateries in and opposite the Sunday market, in the old town, or the Idkah Square night market. A good compromise might be the **Central Asia Restaurant** with an English sign on the south side of Id Kah square. There are Pakistani restaurants opposite the Chini Bagh.

For western food, Chinese food, English menus and wicker armchairs on a wide, shady pavement, choose between the **Limin Restaurant**, the **Seman Road Restaurant**, and **Daniel Restaurant** next to each other opposite the old entrance to the Seman Hotel, and **John Hu's Information Café** opposite the new one in building No. 3. Omelettes are from ¥4.50; Chinese main courses from ¥12. The vine-hung café just inside the old entrance is the best place to eat in the Seman Hotel.

Entertainment

The Chinese do movement-to-music, tai-chi and sword dancing every morning from 8.30–9.3 am Beijing time just inside the south entrance to the People's Park on Jeifang Nanlu.

To Kyrgyzstan via the Torugart Pass

The high and lonely crossing from China into Kyrgyzstan is definitely one for connoisseurs of checkpoint drama. From Kashgar, a bone-shaking drive up into the Tian Shan will take you to the Torugart Pass (3752 m). The 160-km road is still abysmal, but has been somewhat improved. The Chinese side is a controlled military zone. Chinese vehicles and drivers entering it need special documents, and it is worth reminding whoever is meeting you of this when contacting them in advance. Foreigners entering the zone pay a fee of around $2 in renminbi at the main army checkpoint in Tuo Yun, 10 minutes' drive below the pass. More may be demanded if you look rich or if the duty officer is in a bad mood.

Getting to and across the Torugart Pass

The situation on travelling to Bishkek is changing. Until recently there was a bus to **Bishkek** every Thursday morning at 9am during the summer, if demand was sufficient, less frequently or not at all as winter approached. The bus left from the Wuzi Binguan south of the Remin Hotel, where tickets were also available. It was reported to take three hours to get to the border, approximately 160km, and to reach Bishkek late the same day for ¥90, taking advantage of the three-hour time difference. However, the company running it preferred you take their helicopter from the Torugart Pass rather than go the whole way by bus, and quoted at least US$100 for the privilege. A valid CIS country visa or at least a fax or telex of visa support was essential if the Chinese were to let you out at the border. Another telex confirming that you were being met on the Kyrgyz side also helped. Despite the difficulties, some foreigners successfully left China this way.

However, the opening of a new customs area much closer to Kashgar in late 1995 means that travelling by this route may become much easier. The post is at or near Xiangfeimu, the point at which the road to **Irkeshtam** leaves for the west and on to Osh, and the post will probably serve both routes (the Irkeshtam crossing is forecast to open in mid-1996). The new border post is reachable by local buses from Kashgar, and two buses are said to run daily over the Torugart Pass to the Kyrgyz side.

CITS, Xinjiang Kashgar Travel Agency or John Hu (for addresses, *see* p.338) will happily take you as far as the border, but Chinese vehicles cannot cross it. Prices range from $200 per person (Xinjiang Kashgar Mountaineering Association) to ¥2000 (CITS) or ¥1900 (John Hu) for four people. Sometimes Chinese vehicles meet Kyrgyz ones for a no-man's-land exchange exactly at the border line. This is about 5km wide at the pass, and you have to walk it, hitch, or pay a lot of money, although sometimes border guards will tell trucks to take you. Arrive early as the Chinese and Kazakh borders close for lunch consecutively. On the other side there may or may not be a motley collection of transport asking for absurdly high prices. As a result, the only way to guarantee getting at least to the nearest accommodation at Naryn is to be met by a Kyrgyz jeep (*see* 'Bishkek', p.246). Patience, calm determination and a valid Kyrgyz visa are essential. The border is closed on Saturdays and Sundays.

visas

It is impossible to get CIS visas at or near the border. The Kyrgyz officials have no hesitation in sending people without visas back where they came from. Visas are currently available only in national capitals, except those for Kazakhstan which are available in Ürümqi if you have visa support or an onward air ticket (*see* 'Entry Formalities', pp.10–15).

The Turpan Oasis

The Turpan depression is the second lowest place on earth and the hottest in China. Cradling the baked ruins of two ancient Silk Route cities, it is also the second most heavily-promoted tourist destination in Xinjiang after Kashgar, 1300km away to the southwest. Its administrative centre is Turpan City, where all the hotels are.

Huge gravel plains tilt down from the mountains towards Turpan and the centre of the earth. There are no rivers, but meltwater arrives via an underground irrigation system called the *karez*, to be soaked up by spectacular green valleys full of vines. Most of the grapes are white and seedless and are turned into raisins in traditional brick drying towers. They, and the brick kilns, are the closest Turpan gets to heavy industry. There is a grape festival at harvest time at the end of August.

Against the odds, Turpan is a mellow sort of place. It is a heat trap, 154m below sea level and flanked by two eastern branches of the Tian Shan. Summer temperatures can rise to 48° C, but the heat is bone dry and many of the streets are shaded with trellises. Tourists stay comfortable provided they drink enough, and unembalmed corpses like those of the Astana tombs are still identifiable after 1500 years.

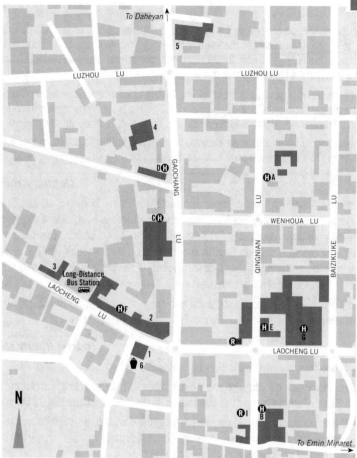

Turpan

To Daheyan

LUZHOU LU

LUZHOU LU

GAOCHANG LU

WENHOUA LU

QINGNIAN LU

LU

BAIZIKLIKE LU

LAOCHENG LU

Long-Distance Bus Station

LAOCHENG LU

To Emin Minaret

N

KEY

1 Bank of China
2 Xinhua Bookshop
3 Post and telephone office
4 Museum
5 Public Security Bureau
6 City market

HOTELS & RESTAURANTS

A Oasis Hotel
B Turpan Hotel (Binguan)
C Turpan Hotel (Fandian)
D Gaochang Hotel
E Yiyuan Hotel
F Jiaotong Hotel
G Crain Trade Hotel
H Chinese and Uighur restaurants
I John Hu's Information Café

345

Getting to and from Turpan
by bus

There are buses roughly every half an hour from Ürümqi's Turpan Affairs Office near the Erdaoqiao market in the south of the city. Journey time is 4–5 hours, and the price, from ¥11, but usually doubled for foreigners. The bus station usually charges ¥11, and ¥15 for express buses.

There are sleeper buses direct from and to Kashgar three times a week, and others to Daheyan all taking about a day and a half. There are local bus connections from Daheyan bus station (¥10 for foreigners), and taxis outside the railway station.

Daheyan, also known as Turpan Station, is on the mainline from Ürümqi or Korla to Lanzhou. The nearest **airport** is at Ürümqi.

Getting Around

Since three of the area's most important ancient sites are between 40 and 50km from Turpan City, the only practical way of seeing them is by joining a tour group or forming your own. A one-day CITS air-conditioned bus tour of all the major sites and some minor ones with an English-speaking guide costs about ¥100 per person. Private operators offering similar tours at about half the price mob foreigners at the bus station, and inside and outside the hotels.

Within Turpan City and to get to Jiaohe you can hire a bike from hotels or **John's Information Café** opposite the Turpan Hotel, or take a donkey cart.

Tourist Information

The CITS office is at the Oasis Hotel on Qingnian Lu, ✆ 522491/522478.

There are **bureaux de change** and **post offices** at the Oasis and Turpan hotels, and the Bank of China is near the bus station, but on the opposite side of the road.

You will find postcards Turpan on sale at the gift shops of various hotels and at the sites themselves, and there are two maps of Turpan on sale at the Xinhua Bookshop, east of the bus station before the roundabout.

In and Around Turpan

The set menu for sightseeing in Turpan has eight courses served up in two half-day tours, which CITS calls the East Route and the West Route. The East Route takes in the Bezeklik caves, Gaochang, Astana and a brief stop to photograph the **Flaming Mountains** which run for 100km along the northern side of the depression and in the right light apparently look as if they are on fire. The West Route's main attraction is Jiaohe. You also visit Turpan City's working **mosque**, the 18th century **Emin minaret** (at 37m Xïnjiäng's highest), and a **karez**—part of a 1600-km canal network which defeats natural evaporation 200 times greater than average rainfall by being underground. Some of it is said to date back 2000 years although most, Aurel Stein believed, was built in the 18th century along lines pioneered in Iran.

Jiaohe

The first city in the Turpan oasis was also its longest-lasting. It is not hard to see why. Where most ancient cities have walls and battlements, Jiaohe, 5km west of Turpan City, has sheer cliffs. This long, narrow promontory, 30m above the conflu-ence of two streams, was inhabited for 2000 years before being abandoned in the 15th century. No-one seems to know who got here first, but the Han Chinese turned it into a garrison town in the 2nd century and the forest of grey mud walls that survives dates from the late Tang Dynasty (9th–10th centuries). The paved road starting at the ticket office leads to the remains of an enormous Buddhist monastery with niches containing vandalized but discernible Buddhas.

UIGHUR KNIVES

Thousand-Buddha Caves

There are at least four sets of 'thousand Buddha caves' in Xinjiang. The ones at Bezeklik are in a cliff in a side valley, 50km east of Turpan City where the main road turns north into the mountains. There are more than 60 caves here, and the oldest of them date from the 6th century. Although thoroughly pillaged, they are notable for being built out from the cliff with adobe brick, as well as dug into it.

Artistically, there is less to see here than in Berlin Museum of Indian Art, following Albert von Le Coq's 1902 haul of statues and frescoes. The big gaps are his work. Invading Muslims had already gouged all the eyes out of the wall paintings.

Gaochang

South of Bezeklik and 46km east of Turpan are the impressive ruins of the Uighurs' first capital, **Gaochang**. The Chinese claim to have founded it as another garrison in the 1st century AD. By 450 it was larger and more powerful than Jiaohe. The Uighurs arrived in the 9th century; the Mongols destroyed the city in the 13th. Whoever named it was either unaware of its nega-tive altitude or enjoyed sarcasm: Gaochang means 'prosperous highland'.

Gaochang's most illustrious dead were buried naked and coffinless, 6km from the city in the subterranean **Astana tombs**. Tourists are shown three of the 500 tombs, dating from between the 3rd and 8th centuries, which have been excavated since 1949. One of the three contains two shrivelled corpses, one some beautiful frescoes of birds, one a box for donations. A temporary exhibition of other bodies found here inspired a rare burst of vivid detail from one official Chinese propaganda-writer:

'I saw a woman mummy that looked like a middle-age Han woman with dark red skin, well-developed muscles, high breasts, thick hair worn in a bun, and white, straight teeth... The husband, Zhang Ning, served as vice-governor of Gaochang and court general before his death in 558. His bulging scrotum showed that he had an inguinal hernia.'

A 3-km donkey-cart trip into the ruins is about ¥10 per person. There is a Uighur café at the entrance.

Some of the hotels in Turpan have grown gradually and offer rooms at a variety of prices in buildings of widely differing ages. All but the cheapest rooms have air-conditioning to combat Turpan's scorching summer temperatures, and many have satellite television with English language programming. Summer water shortages may sometimes limit the availability of showers to a few hours a day. Prices for some rooms may drop to as little as one third in the low season.

expensive

The best hotel is the **Oasis Hotel** (Luzhou Binguan), ☎ 522491, 🖶 523348 where a double with bath costs from ¥350. Both this hotel and the **Turpan Hotel** (Tulufan Binguan), ☎ 522301, 🖶 523262, 15 minutes' walk south, have several buildings arranged around green spaces, the Turpan Hotel's grape-hung cold drinks area being particularly pleasant. Double rooms in its new wing are ¥380. There's another **Turpan Hotel** (this one is Tulufan Fandian), ☎ 522147, 🖶 522336, north of the bus station, which is less appealing in location and layout, but has smart doubles in its new wing from ¥320. Enter through the gate at the right-hand end of the building to find the newer wing and reception across the car park. All these hotels, and the **Gaochang Hotel**, ☎ 523229, a little further north have suites at between ¥300 and ¥680. Walk round to the right-hand side to find the entrance, or walk through the restaurant at the front of the building if it is open.

moderate–inexpensive

The **Turpan Hotel** (Binguan) also has an older Muslim-style wing, where a triple with bath and day-long hot water costs ¥90 per bed. The other **Turpan Hotel** (Fandian) has older doubles from ¥80 per bed. The new **Yiyuan Hotel**, ☎ 522170, between the Oasis and Turpan hotels has smart doubles for ¥90 per bed, as does the **Gaochang** for ¥75. The **Jiaotong Hotel** next to the bus station, ☎ 523238, has basic doubles with bath for ¥80 per bed, and triple rooms with bath for ¥40 per bed. The **Grain Trade Hotel** (Liangmao Binguan), ☎ 522448, one block east of the centre, has doubles and five-bed rooms with bath for ¥80 per bed.

There are dorms in the older buildings of the **Turpan Hotel** (Binguan), costing from ¥20. At the **Oasis**, four-bed rooms cost ¥20. The **Turpan Hotel** (Fandian) offers four-bed rooms for ¥24. The **Jiaotong** has three-beds for ¥36, four-beds for ¥24, and larger rooms for ¥16, and the **Grain Trade Hotel** has four-bed rooms at ¥20.

All the hotels have restaurants (the Oasis claims to have six). Shun them. Instead, turn right out of the Turpan Hotel, take the first left, and choose from the half dozen friendly Uighur and Chinese restaurants competing for your custom with English menus and tables on the pavement across the road.

Ürümqi

Ürümqi (population 1.3 million) is much maligned. True, it is an ugly, industrial city with very little history. True, it calls itself capital of the Uighur Autonomous Province despite being mainly Chinese. But being Chinese, it is part of China's current boom. After the CIS's crippling shortages and inflation, Ürümqi feels like New York. People take time off work to trade warrants on the streets. There is a private department store owned by a Uighur woman Yuan billionaire. There is life after midnight, in dance halls and round *al fresco* floodlit billiard tables. There is food everywhere you look. There is Central Asia's only Holiday Inn. And when Ürümqi's urban sophistication palls, the alpine lakes and pastures of the eastern Tian Shan are a mere three hours away by bus.

Getting to and from Ürümqi

With flights to Moscow and Almaty, and rail and road links with Kazakhstan, Ürümqi has become China's gateway to the CIS.

by air

There are three flights a week to and from Almaty. CAAC (known here as China Xinjiang Airlines), flies there and back on Mondays and Fridays, leaving Ürümqi at 9.50am Beijing time and returning in the afternoon. Kazakh Airlines flies on Tuesdays, leaving Almaty at 5pm. CAAC charges ¥1660 one way, Kazakh Airlines $111. To board either plane you must at least have a Kazakh transit visa, available under certain circumstances in Ürümqi.

CAAC flies to Moscow on Fridays (¥2270), calling at Novosibirsk (¥1300), and to Islamabad on Sundays (also ¥2270). Aeroflot flies from Ürümqi to Moscow on Tuesdays for $280, with onward connections to most of the planet. You can purchase a through ticket to any Aeroflot destination in Ürümqi, and nationals of most countries can board the plane without a Russian visa. If you are simply changing planes in Moscow no visa is required, but if you wish to visit the city transit visas for between 6 hours ($18) and 72 hours ($110) can be bought at Sheremetyevo airport in Moscow. Tourist visas can also be bought if you also book accommodation. CAAC, however, will not sell you a ticket unless you already hold a Russian visa.

CAAC also flies to Islamabad on Sundays for ¥2270. You must have a Pakistani visa, and the nearest place in China to get one is Beijing.

Ürümqi is the Xinjiang hub for CAAC's domestic network, with daily flights to Kashgar (6.50pm Beijing time; ¥1220), Beijing (¥2550), Xi'an (¥2090), Guangzhou (¥3420), and regular ones to Kashgar (Kashi), Khotan (Hetian), Gulja (Yining), Korla (Kuerle), Cherchen (Qiemo) in Xinjiang, and many other Chinese destinations.

There are **departure taxes** from Ürümqi of ¥90 for international flights and ¥50 for domestic ones.

China Xinjiang Airlines (CAAC)'s booking office, ✆ 4514668 (*open 9am–9pm Beijing time*) is below the Hongshan pagoda on the east side of Youhao Nanlu, 10 minutes' walk west of the Hongshan Hotel. Payment is in renminbi cash only. Buses leave from here to the airport two hours before each flight, ¥6.

Aeroflot, ✆ 2862326 (*open 10am–1pm and 3–7pm Beijing time; closed Sund*) is south of the centre in the old building of the Overseas Chinese Hotel at Xinhua Nanlu 51. Payment is in US dollars cash only.

Kazakh Airlines, ✆ 3821207 (*open Mon–Fri 10am–2pm and 4–7pm*) has an office at Kunming Lu 31, well to the north of the city, one block to the east of Beijing Nanlu, best found by taxi. Alternatively take bus 2, and ask for the stop called Dazhaigou, one stop north of the Hotel World Plaza. Walk north and turn right into Qingdao Donglu. Kunming Lu is a left turn. Payment for all services is in US dollars cash notes of 1990 or later date.

by rail

Ürümqi is 44 hours from Lanzhou by train and 80 from Beijing. Domestic tickets are a sweat to get. Start queueing before 8am, or pay someone else to (*see* below). For trains to Almaty in Kazakhstan, *see* p.288. The station overlooks the city from the west.

by bus

Sleeper buses to **Aksu and Kashgar** leave the long-distance bus station daily at 4pm Beijing time and reach Kashgar two days later around 9am. The fare is ¥199.

Turpan buses (¥11–¥15; 4–5 hours) leave several times a day to make the 4–5 hour journey. There are also buses from the Turpan Affairs Office just north of the Erdaoqiao market, but these tend to double the prices to ¥22–¥30. For buses to **Almaty,** *see* p.289. At the long-distance bus station the window for buses to the south is no.5, and to the north is no.6. For Almaty tickets go to no. 7 and pay the ¥460, or $50 plus ¥10.

Getting Around

Get a city map from CITS, a hotel, or Xinhua Bookshop, and hire a bicycle through your hotel. Metered taxis are abundant, and cost about ¥1.30 perkm, with a minimum charge of ¥10.

Tourist Information

CITS is next to the Holiday Inn at Xinhua Beilu 51, 2nd floor. There are several competing agencies in the Hongshan Hotel, such as **CYTS** and **South Moutain Travel Service.** CYTS employs sweet young women to accost hotel guests in the corridors, but has the usual dour males in its office. The South Mountain people are friendly, but are not above upping the price of an Almaty bus ticket by $10 so as to appear to be charging less commission than the others (a further ¥10). All

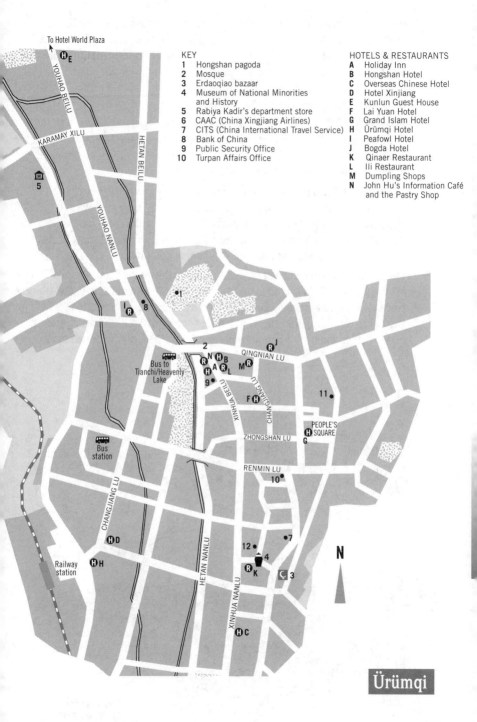

To Hotel World Plaza

KEY
1 Hongshan pagoda
2 Mosque
3 Erdaoqiao bazaar
4 Museum of National Minorities
 and History
5 Rabiya Kadir's department store
6 CAAC (China Xingjiang Airlines)
7 CITS (China International Travel Service)
8 Bank of China
9 Public Security Office
10 Turpan Affairs Office

HOTELS & RESTAURANTS
A Holiday Inn
B Hongshan Hotel
C Overseas Chinese Hotel
D Hotel Xinjiang
E Kunlun Guest House
F Lai Yuan Hotel
G Grand Islam Hotel
H Ürümqi Hotel
I Peafowl Hotel
J Bogda Hotel
K Qinaer Restaurant
L Ili Restaurant
M Dumpling Shops
N John Hu's Information Café
 and the Pastry Shop

YOUHAO BEILU
KARAMAY XILU
HETAN BEILU
YOUHAO NANLU
QINGNIAN LU
Bus to Tianchi/Heavenly Lake
XINHUA BEILU
CHANGJIANG LU
ZHONGSHAN LU
PEOPLE'S SQUARE
Bus station
RENMIN LU
CHANGJIANG LU
HETAN NANLU
XINHUA NANLU
Railway station

N

Ürümqi

companies offer car, jeep and mini-bus tours to Heavenly Lake (Tianchi), the Southern Grasslands and Turpan. All will also buy plane, train and bus tickets for you for commission of between ¥10 and ¥50. **John Hu's Information Café** opposite the Hongshan provides a reliable ticket booking service. Plane, bus, and Almaty train tickets are easy to arrange for yourself, as are trips to Tianchi, but domestic train tickets are harder. For one-day tours, shop around between the agencies and haggle.

The main **post office** and poste restante facility (*open daily 10am–8pm*) is on the west side of the large traffic island at Chan Gijiang Lu and Guangming Lu, ten minutes' walk west of the Hongshan Hotel.

The **Bank of China** (*open 10am–1pm and 3.30–6.30pm Beijing time*) is at the junction of Renmin Lu and Jiefang Nanlu five minutes' walk southwest of Renmin Square, and lets you withdraw yuan with all major credit cards. You can also cash travellers' cheques for dollars—necessary if you are going to Almaty or Bishkek. There is another branch almost opposite the main post office.

The **Public Security Bureau** is north of the northwest corner of Renmin Square, on the left hand side, corner of Jiankang Lu and Minzhu Lu. If the Chinese embassy in Almaty has only given you a transit visa you cannot extend it here (or anywhere else) but other types may be extended without difficulty. Also check here whether you need a permit before going anywhere off the beaten track.

LAKE JIAN
PEOPLES PARK
ÜRÜMQI

Opposite the Aeroflot office on the ground floor of the old building of the Overseas Chinese Hotel (Xinhua Nanlu 51), there is a gift shop which also sells a good selection of postcards and English-language guidebooks. The **foreign-language bookstore** on the third floor of the multi-storey bookshop at Xinhua Beilu 14, one and a half blocks north of its junction with Renmin Lu has a reasonable selection of novels from *Hard Times* to *Jaws*, as does the third floor of the new **Xinhua Bookstore** on the corner of Renmin Lu and Jiefang Nanlu, opposite the bank.

A Stroll Around Town

Start with the **pagoda** on top of **Hongshan** (Red Hill), north of the Hongshan Hotel, for a panorama of tower blocks, factory fumes and behind them, on a good day, the snows of the Tian Shan. Due south is the Holiday Inn. Its Western restaurant is the place to be seen for Chinese *nouveaux riches*, and its 'English Pub' has waitresses in tartan and no draught beer.

The **Museum of National Minorities and History** (*open daily 9.30–7.30*), is on Xibei Lu, ten minutes northwest of here by bike or three stops on bus or minibus 7 from the department store near the entrance to Hongshan Park. The history section upstairs in its right wing includes remarkably well-preserved bodies from various sites, including Cherchen (Qiemo), Loulan, and Hami.

For Uighurs the centre of Ürümqi town is the **Erdaoqiao market**, a covered street of food and textile stalls going from Xinhua Nanlu to Jeifang Nanlu two long blocks south of Renmin Lu. At its east end there is a working mosque. Going north again up Jeifang Nanlu you pass on the left a six-storey cube topped off with an English sign: **Rabiya Kadir's Department Store**, evidence that Uighurs are not excluded from Ürümqi's boom. Ms Kadir is a Uighur and a self-made Yuan billionaire who has made most of her money through trade with the CIS. Her department store, once the last word in Xinjiang retail, has now been eclipsed by new glass-and-chrome buildings throughout the city.

Ürümqi's official centre is **Renmin Square**, three blocks south of the Holiday Inn and three more east. This vast piece of concrete is enlivened in the mornings by communal movement-to-music and in the afternoons by kite-flying.

Around Ürümqi

Heavenly Lake (Tianchi) is an achingly beautiful alpine lake which feels light years away from Ürümqi but is actually three hours' bus ride away to the east, 1980m up in the Tian Shan. You can row on it in summer, skate on it in winter, stay beside it in tents or in the incongruous Heavenly Lake Hotel, and trek from it towards Bogda Peak (5445 m). Most days in summer buses leave for Tianchi from the entrance to Ürümqi's People's Park at around 9am Beijing time.

The **Southern Pastures** at Baiyanggou, 56km (one and a half hours) south of Ürümqi, have been described as Heavenly Lake without the lake. A designated tourist attraction, they are an area of grassy uplands overlooked by snowy mountains and used in summer by tame Kazakh herdsmen and their cattle, sheep and horses. Buses leave in the early morning and late afternoon from the east side of the roundabout on the way to the long distance bus station where Huanghe Lu meets Heilongjiang Lu, and from the entrance to the People's Park.

Private transport to both places can be arranged through agencies in the Hongshan Hotel and elsewhere.

Ürümqi (✆ 0991–)

Where to Stay

expensive

Ürümqi's **Holiday Inn**, Xinhua Beilu 168, ✆ (0991) 218788, 🖷 217422, telex 79161 XJGHP CN, is very central. It is also Central Asia's best—or least Asian—hotel, depending on your point of view. Its gleaming marble and zealously-trained English-speaking staff certainly make a change after a month or two of real Central Asia. Restaurants, bar, business centre and disco are open to non-residents for a price. They also have BBC World Service TV and MTV. The four-room Presidential suite is $285 a night, twin rooms go from $96 plus a 15% service charge and 3% tax.

The nearest competition is the not-so-central **Hotel World Plaza**, (Huanqiu Dajiuguan) Beijing Nanlu 2, ✆ 3836400, 🖷 3836399, a Hong Kong–China joint venture hotel with a similar atmosphere and topped with a revolving restaurant. Double rooms cost from ¥750, suites ¥1390, plus 18%). The **Lai Yuan Hotel** (Laiyuan Binguan), Jianshe Lu 3, ✆ 228368, 🖷 on extension 6, is 5 minutes' walk south-east of the Holiday Inn; all rooms here cost ¥760.

moderate

The best value for money in this price range is the brand new **Ürümqi Hotel** (Wulumuqi Binguan), at the beginning of Changjiang Lu and walking distance from the railway station. Doubles start from ¥336, singles from ¥196, and three-beds rooms, all with bath, telephone, television, etc., go for ¥80.

Also good is the **Peafowl Hotel** (Kongque Dasha), in Youhao Nanlu, opposite the CAAC office, ✆ 4822988, 🖷 4322943, Here, doubles with bath are ¥238, and triples with bath ¥70 per bed, all plus ¥2 per person tax.

The hotel with the grandest name in Ürümqi is the **Grand Islam Hotel**, in a fine position on the southwest corner of Renmin Square, ✆ 2828360. The staff are friendly, but they don't speak English; a twin with bath costs ¥480.

In the same direction as the World Plaza but not so far, is the cavernous and somewhat overpriced **Kunlun Guest House** (Kunlun Binguan), ✆ 4811403, 🖷 4840213, on Youhao Beilu, reached by bus 2 from the railway station. Here, a twin with shower is from ¥480.

The top foreigners' hotel was once the spruce, peaceful **Overseas Chinese Hotel**, Xinhua Nanlu 51, ✆ 2860793, ✉ 2862279, 10 minutes south of Hongshan by bus 7, where a twin room with bath costs ¥200 in the old building or ¥350 in the new.

inexpensive

The central **Hongshan Hotel**, ✆ 2824761, within easy walking distance of Hongshan and Renmin parks, has long been the most popular hotel with independent travellers, but is unfriendly and overpriced, with absurdly long queues for the common showers which are in a separate building. The rate for doubles with bath is from ¥150 and dormitory beds go from ¥25. Further east at 10 Guangming Lu is the friendlier **Bogda Hotel** (Bogeda Binguan), ✆ 2815238, ✉ 2823910 ext. 4101. Dorms here cost from ¥45 per bed, plus ¥2 government tax.

An alternative but slightly rowdy option is the huge **Hotel Xinjiang**, popular with Pakistani traders, ✆ 5852511, ✉ 5811354, conveniently located opposite the railway station, but a bus ride from the centre of things, offering dormitory beds from ¥30.

Ürümqi (✆ 0991–)   ***Eating Out***

The food is the best thing about Ürümqi. It has literally hundreds of restaurants, Uighur and Chinese, seldom expensive, open all hours. Most hotel restaurants do respectable sit-down meals for ¥20–40, or three to four times that at the Holiday Inn.

expensive–moderate

An Uighur restaurant with an excellent menu of mixed Muslim and Chinese food, the **Qinaer Restaurant** in the Erdaoqiao Market at Tianchi Lu 73, also features bursts of live Uighur pop music, and traditional dance performances by an Uighur woman. The small dance floor fills with ballroom dancing Uighurs, and foreigners are made very welcome. Expect to pay around ¥50 per head.

The **Ili Restaurant** (Ili Dajiudian), just south of the Hongshan Hotel on Xinhua Beilu announces itself to be Muslim, and offers comfortable surroundings with attentive service for upwards of ¥40 to 50 per person upwards; it's well worth it. This might be the place to try frog or snake.

inexpensive

The restaurant behind the Bogda Hotel has a menu which includes good sizzling Sichuan dishes and popular Cantonese dishes as well as Uighur ones for around ¥15 to ¥20 per meat dish. At the north end of Jianshe Lu almost opposite the same hotel is a group of Shanghai-style dumpling shops serving beef and lamb stuffed dumplings (*baozi*) for ¥0.60 to ¥0.80 each. **John Hu's Information Café** has a cheap Chinese menu and Western snacks opposite the Hongshan Hotel, and a few doors to the east the **Pastry Shop** has cakes and pizza.

To restrict yourself to hotels and restaurants, however, is a waste. For noodle-making as performance art, visit the Hongshan market near the entrance to the Hongshan Park, where about 40 Uighur food stalls compete for your custom under a giant smoke-filled hangar.

At night a further group of stalls run by people from a variety of minorities magically appears on the south side of Zhongshan Lu just east of the junction with Hongqi Lu, and stay until nearly midnight. At the Erdaoqiao market *shashlyk* and *pulau* food is available until around 8pm. Other late opening food stalls are scattered around pavements everywhere.

Entertainment

There are numerous discos and karaoke bars, including ones in the Holiday Inn and World Plaza Hotels. Under the bridge between the Hongshan and People's Parks hundreds of billiard tables entertain thousands of billiards players who never seem to pot anything.

From Ürümqi to Kazakhstan

The spotless international express no.13, complete with starched sheets, frilly tablecloths and plastic bonsai trees in every compartment, pulls out of Ürümqi's main station on Saturday and Monday nights on the newest stretch of railway in Central Asia.

The Northern Xinjiang Railway, which skirts the northern edge of the Tian Shan from Ürümqi to the Kazakh border, was only completed in 1990. The border crossing at Druzhba—the name is Russian for 'friendship'—was litmus test for Sino-Soviet relations between 1917 to 1991. Fitzroy Maclean tried and failed to get through here in 1938.

Druzhba guards the highly strategic Jungarian Gap between the Tarbagatai and Jungarian mountain ranges and between East and West Asia—conduit for countless nomad armies on their way to terrorize Chinese or Western 'civilizations'.

Most of the middle day in either direction is taken up with Chinese and CIS border formalities and with changing the wheels here, just inside the Kazakh frontier. The coaches are separated and lifted ten feet in the air by giant yellow jacks so the Chinese bogies and wider-gauge Russian ones can be swapped. Most of the travelling happens at night.

by rail

The no.13 train leaves Ürümqi every Saturday and Monday at 11 pm Beijing time. The no.14 train leaves Almaty for Ürümqi on the same days at 6.10pm Moscow time, 9.10pm local time. The train which leaves Ürümqi on Saturday and Almaty on Monday is Chinese. The one which leaves Almaty on Saturday and Ürümqi on Monday is Kazakh. The trip takes 35 hours in all.

In Ürümqi, tickets are sold only at the special window at the far end of the station's international departure lounge at the right hand end of the main building (*open 10am–3pm and 5–7pm Beijing time*). Bookings can be made up to one day in advance.

A place in a four-berth compartment on the Chinese train costs ¥588, and in luxury wood-panelled two-berth compartments with comfy chair, ¥1130. On the Kazakh train the prices are ¥505 and ¥860.

The Chinese for Almaty is *Alamutu*.

by bus

For those who prefer to travel by bus, the Almaty express leaves Ürümqi's long-distance bus station at the west end of Heilongjiang Lu daily except Saturday at 5pm Beijing time, crossing into Kazakhstan the next day. Altogether it takes 24 hours and costs ¥460, or $50 plus ¥10 one-way.

The border crossing is south of the Jungarian range at Khorgos, 40km from the Kazak town of Panfilov. Most travellers across the border here are local Uighurs visiting relatives, or on business; and for Kazaks who can't afford to enter China, an enormous Chinese bazaar has sprung up at Khorgos.

It is possible, but trickier, to get to Kazakhstan by taking a bus from Ürümqi to Gulja (Yining) for a fare of ¥103, and then covering the remaining 40km to the border by local bus (¥10–15). It's also possible to get off at Qingshuihe, before Ili but closer to the border; however, negotiations with local transport to the border are more difficult here.

Other options include taking the Almaty bus and getting off at Khorgos (about ¥150) or negotiating a cheaper price with Uighur-run buses parked outside the railway station. There is a bus which shuttles the 3km or so between the border posts (¥10). The border is open 8.30am–4pm Kazakh time, which is two hours earlier than Beijing time, except for a variable three-hour gap caused by the Chinese and Kazakh guards taking lunch consecutively (Kyrgyzstan will adopt a summer 'Daylight Savings Time' in 1996, so, in summer at least, the border lunch breaks should be simultaneous). Taxis and sometimes buses can be found on the Kazakh side. Hard bargaining is necessary.

visas

You must have the necessary visa *before* you travel; neither Chinese nor CIS visas are available at the border. Kazakh visas are available at the offices of Kazakh Airlines (*for visas open Mon–Fri, 10am–2pm only*) ✆/✉ 3821203. The office is not used to issuing tourist visas, but can do so for the same price as transit visas, as long as you have arranged visa support, a copy of which has been faxed to them separately.

If you already have another CIS visa, or if you have an onward air ticket from Almaty, three-day transit visas are available in one week ($15) or three days ($30), and you can enter Kazakhstan by bus, train, or plane. In theory having a visa for any CIS country will allow you to enter Kazakhstan for 72 hours without a Kazakh transit visa, but corrupt Kazakh border officials on the train may insist that you pay up to $65 for not having a visa, and may threaten to arrest you if you refuse. They simply pocket the money themselves and give neither visa nor receipt. No other CIS visas are available in Ürümqi.

BC

from *c.* 100,000	Mesolithic cave dwellers in Tian Shan and Pamir foothills
from *c.* 10,000	Siberian ice sheet withdraws; forerunners of Huns, Turks and Mongols inhabit Altai and Mongolian steppe
c. 2000	Aryan migrations into Central Asia
545–540	Cyrus the Great adds Sogdiana to Persian empire
329	Alexander the Great crosses river Oxus (Amu Darya Spitamen leads rebellion in Samarkand
312	Seleucus Nicator founds Seleucid dynasty
247	Parthian empire founded
138	Chang Ch'ien sets out from Chang'an
52	Chinese sign treaty with Hsiun-Nu

AD

14	Silk worth its weight in gold in Rome
78	Khan Kanishka becomes first Kushan emperor
224	Ardashir founds Persian Sassanid dynasty
484	Huns capture Sassanids' eastern empire
c. 560	Huns driven from Transoxania by Turks
570–632	Life of Prophet Mohammed
651	Sassanian empire overthrown by Arabs
654	Arabs reach Amu Darya
705	Qutaiba ibn Abbas becomes viceroy of Khorassan...
712–715	... and conquers Khorezm, Bukhara, Samarkand, Tashkent and Fergana before being assassinated by his own troops
748	Abbasids replace Umayyads as caliphs of Baghdad
751	Chinese crushed by Arabs at battle of Talas
875	Samanids take Transoxiana and cede from Abbasid empire
992	Karakhanid Turks make Bukhara their capital
by *c.* 1050	Seljuks control area from Afghanistan to Aral Sea

Chronology

1150s	Kara-Khitai overrun Seljuk empire
1156	Death of Seljuk viceroy Sultan Sanjar
1207–1210	Khorezmshahs defeat Kara-Khitai

REGISTAN SQUARE, SAMARKAND

1218	Genghis Khan's envoy to Khorezm murdered
1220	Mongols sack Urgench, Samarkand and Bukhara
1227	Genghis Khan dies
1336	Tamerlane born
by 1370	Tamerlane controls Transoxiana
1372	Urgench destroyed by Tamerlane
1398	Tamerlane's invasion of India
1405	Tamerlane dies
1449	Ulug Bek assassinated by his own son in Samarkand
c. 1500	Uzbeks cross Syr Darya; Sheibanids take control of Transoxiana Khanates of Khiva and Bukhara founded
1526	Babur, the last Timurid, takes Delhi
1598	Abdullah Khan dies in Bukhara; Astrakhanids replace Sheibanids
c. 1710	Khanate of Kokand founded
1717	Russian mission to Khiva butchered on arrival
1718	Russian garrison established at Semipalatinsk
1755	Qing dynasty reasserts Chinese rule in Tarim basin
1839	Perovsky's expedition to Khiva defeated by snow
1838–42	1st British-Afghan War
1863	British client Kashmir takes control of Yasin
1865	Russians take Tashkent
1867	Kaufmann first governor general of Russian Turkestan

1868	Kaufmann takes Samarkand and makes Bukhara a protectorate
1877	Kaufmann annexes Kokand; British set up agency at Gilgit
1878–81	2nd British-Afghan War
1881	Tekke Turkmens massacred by Russians at Geok-Tepe
1882	Russians open consulate in Kashgar
1884	Russian governor installed at MervChinese create Xinjiang Province
1885	Pandjeh incident nearly leads Britain and Russia to war
1889	Algernon Durand sets up second British agency at Gilgit
1890	British open consulate in Kashgar
1893	British invade Hunza
1895	Vakhan corridor separates British and Russian empires
1897	Muslim rebellion in Andizhan
1911	Nationalist revolution in China; Qing dynasty falls
1916	Dzhizak rebellion spreads through Russian Turkestan
1917	Russian Revolution
1918	Anti-Bolshevik coup fails in Tashkent; Bolsheviks take Kokand
1919	British withdraw from Turkmenistan
1921	Enver Pasha arrives in Bukhara
1922	Enver Pasha killed by Red Army
1924	Soviet border commission creates Uzbek and Turkmen SSRs
1926	Soviet Kyrghyzstan founded
1928	First Soviet Five Year Plan; collectivization begins
1929	Soviet Tajikistan founded
1936	Soviet Kazakhstan founded
1947	Indian independence and partition; founding of Pakistan
1949	Chinese Communist Revolution
	First Russian A-bomb tested at Semipalatinsk
1954	'Virgin Lands' campaign begins in Kazakhstan
1964–79	Construction of Karakoram Highway

ALTIT FORT
HUNZA VALLEY

1983	Sharaf Rashidov, Uzbek leader, dies
1986	Riots in Almaty as a Russian replaces Kazakh leader
1990	200 killed in rioting in Osh
	Nuclear testing stops at Semipalatinsk
1991	End of USSR; Central Asian republics become independent
1992–3	Tajik civil war contained within Afghan border area by CIS troops
1993	With exception of Turkmenistan, four Central Asian republics sign CIS charter
1993	Tajikistan and Russia sign bilateral treaty
1994	Kazakh, Kyrgyz and Uzbek presidents sign an economic partnership agreement
1995	Referenda/decree confirm presidents of Kazakhstan, Uzbekistan, Kyrgyzstan and Turkmenistan in office into the 21st century
1996	UN-sponsored peace talks attempt to end Tajik civil war, but they are followed by a fresh outbreak of fighting

ak-kalpak	traditional white felt Kyrghyz hat ark citadel
aryk	irrigation channel
ash-khana	restaurant, café
ayvan	open room on upper storey of a two-storey Khivan house, designed to catch cool breezes
basmachi	lit. bandit, brigand; also used of Muslim anti-Bolshevik rebels in 1920s
beryozka (Russ.)	state-run hard currency shop
caravanserai	inn for caravans and merchants
chai-khana	tea house
chorsu	covered market
dacha (Russ.)	suburban or rural bungalow, usually with an allotment
dervish	member of Sufi or other ascetic Muslim sect
Emir/Amir	hereditary ruler of Bukhara and its lands
ganche	traditional decorative plasterwork
girikh	abstract geometrical motif used in decorative tilework
göl	hallmark motif of Tekke Turkmen carpets
hadj	pilgrimage to Mecca
imam	Muslim priest; the Imam is the spiritual leader of Ismaili Muslims
iwan	vaulted niche or hallway, usually in a mosque or madrasa
jihad	Muslim holy war
karez	underground irrigation channel unique to Turpan
Khan	hereditary ruler of Khanate of Khiva or Kokand
khanaga	hostel for wandering dervishes
khauz	stone-lined pool; Bukhara was famous for them
kolkhoz (Russ.)	collective farm
kombinat (Russ.)	factory complex
koumis	fermented mare's milk, slightly alcoholic
kosh	adjective describing a pair of mosques of madrasas whose identical facades face each other

Glossary

Kufic	Arabic calligraphy used for monumental purposes
kurgan	mound or tower

laghman	noodle-based dish ubiquitous in Kyrghyzstan and Kazakhstan
lepeshka (Russ.)	flat, round, unlevened bread
madrasa	Islamic seminary
majolica	glazing technique named after Majorca, where Europe first came across it, and used in 14th-century Samarkand on carved brick and terracotta, turning it mainly blue; also called faience after Italian city of Faenza
marshrutnoe taxi (Russ.)	minibus which follows a fixed urban route
mazar	mausoleum or shrine
mechet (Russ)	mosque
mihrab	niche in mosque or design on carpet indicating direction of Mecca
mimber	pulpit in a mosque
muezzin	Muslim prayer leader who traditionally calls the faithful to prayer from the top of a minaret
mujahedin	Muslim freedom fighter
oblast (Russ.)	largest administrative unit within a former Soviet republic
Polygon (Russ.)	nuclear test site
pishtak	main portico of mosque or madrasa
ploshchad (Russ.)	square
plov (Russ.)	risotto-like rice dish; pilau
pravodnik (Russ.)	railway carriage attendant
Registan	lit. 'sandy place'; central square in Silk Route oases
rayon (Russ.)	sub-unit of an oblast
Ramadan	Muslim month of daytime fasting
remont (Russ.)	'under repair'; in practice this usually means closed or out of action for the foreseeable future
shashlyk	grilled meat on a skewer; kebab
squinch	clever kind of corner arch designed to support a round dome on a square base
stalactite	even cleverer downward-facing plaster decoration for a squinch, usually a miniature quarter-dome, sometimes load-bearing itself
steppe	flat, grassy none-too-fertile plain
ulitsa (Russ.)	street
yurt (*yurta* Russ.)	round felt tent used by Turkic nomads

Central Asia's history of overlapping migrations has made it a linguistic kaleidoscope.

Broadly speaking, the indigenous languages of the former Soviet republics fall into two categories. Uzbek, Kazakh, Kyrgyz and Turkmen are all Turkic tongues closely related to each other and to Turkish. Speakers of one can generally understand and make themselves understood by speakers of the others. Tajik is the odd one out; an ancient Persian language similar to those of Iran and Afghanistan.

These languages have all replaced Russian as the official language of their respective countries, and the four Turkic governments, along with that of Azerbaijan, undertook in 1993 to replace the Cyrillic alphabet with Turkey's version of the Roman one from 1995.

Meanwhile, Cyrillic remains the alphabet in general use and almost everyone can speak Russian even if they prefer not to. Very few

Language

Russians living in Central Asia speak any Turkic, however. As a result, Russian is still the only real *lingua franca* in former Soviet Central Asia.

Most Intourist offices have at least one English-speaker and students of English will frequently introduce themselves hoping to use you for practice. Nevertheless, **it is hard to overstate the value of learning at least some basic Russian before setting out.**

It is also well worth learning some universal Turkic greetings and other courtesies.

In Xinjiang the indigenous Muslim population speaks Uighur, another Turkic language similar to Kyrgyz and Kazakh, while the official language is Mandarin Chinese. You can be sure of finding English-speakers only at CITS offices and at tourist hotels and restaurants.

Pakistan's official language is Urdu, but in the Northern Areas virtually every valley has its own dialect. In major cities English is spoken widely and well, and is used on most signposts and street signs. Along the Karakoram Highway those involved in tourism generally speak good English. Most others speak a pidgin variety if at all.

Learning Russian

To become fluent in Russian is a great accomplishment. To master enough to survive and hold gesture-aided conversations is easier than you might expect. This wonderful Eurasian soup of a language has as many ingredients and nuances as Russia herself. Swimming around in it, tentacular and fiendish, are verbs with aspects as well as tenses and few clues as to their meanings. On the plus side, there is a helpful clutch of nouns taken straight from French, the fashionable language of 19th-century St Petersburg (*bagazh, garazh, park, karandash* etc), and Central Asians tend to speak a boiled-down sort of Russian anyway.

Two good self-study books are *Russian Made Simple* (Heinemann), which has you speaking the language from page one, and the more old-fashioned, grammar-based *Penguin Russian Course*. Cassettes are available to accompany both.

There is no substitute, of course, for a good teacher who is also a native speaker. Reasonably priced evening classes at three levels—beginners, 'post-beginners' and 'advanced conversation'—are run by:

The Society for Cooperation in Russian and Soviet Studies,
320 Brixton Road, London SW9 6AB, ✆ 0171 274 2282.

The going rate for a private tutor is £15–20 an hour. Approach one who has been recommended to you, or ask for a 'taster'.

If nothing else, take along the excellent *Penguin Russian Phrase Book* by Jill Norman and Pamela Davidson.

he Russian Alphabet

rinted	Symbol in transliteration	Approximate pronunciation
Аa	*a*	as in 'car'
Бб	*b*	as in 'book'
Вв	*v*	as in 'van'
Гг	*g*	as in 'good'
Дд	*d*	as in 'day'
Ee	*ye/e*	as in 'yes'
Ёё	*yo*	as in 'yomp'
Жж	*zh*	like 'sh' in pleasure
Зз	*z*	as in 'zone'
Ии	*i*	as in 'feet'
Йй	*y*	as in 'boy'
Кк	*k*	as in 'kind'
Лл	*l*	as in 'lamp'
Мм	*m*	as in 'man'
Нн	*n*	as in 'nut'
Оo	*o*	as in 'pot' when stressed; like 'a' in aloud when unstressed
Пп	*p*	as in 'pen'
Рр	*r*	as in 'red' (rolled)
Сc	*s*	as in 'sing'
Тт	*t*	as in 'top'
Уy	*u*	as in 'fool'
Фф	*f*	as in 'fat'
Хх	*kh*	like the 'ch' in Bach
Цц	*ts*	as in 'lots'
ч	*ch*	as in 'chair'
Шш	*sh*	as in 'ship'
Щщ	*shch*	as in 'fresh chops'
ъ	*(none)*	hard sign (not pronounced)
Ыы	*y*	like the 'i' in 'ill'
ь	*(none)*	soft sign (softens preceding consonants)
э	*e*	as in 'met'
Юю	*yu*	like the 'u' in use
Яя	*ya*	as in 'yard'

Russian Essentials

yes	*da*	да
no	*nyet*	нет
hello	*zdravstvuitye*	Здравствуите
goodbye	*da svidaniya*	До свидания
thank you	*spasiba*	спасибо
Do you speak English?	*Vy gavaritye pa-angliski?*	Вы говорите по-английски
I don't understand.	*Ya nye panimayu.*	Я не понимаю.
I don't speak Russian.	*Ya nye gavaryu pa- russki.*	Я не говорю по-русски.
I'm English/American. (m)	*Ya anglichanin/amerikanyets.*	Я англичанин/американец.
" " " (f)	*Ya anglichanka/amerikanka.*	Я англичанка/американка
Please help me.	*Pamagaitye mnye pazhaluysta.*	Помогайте мне пожалуйст
May I?/Is this OK?	*Mozhna?*	можно?
forbidden/impossible	*Nyelzya*	нельзя
good	*kharoshi*	хороший
bad	*plakhoy*	плохой
expensive	*dorogoy*	дорогой
cheap	*dyeshyovy*	дешёвый
fast	*bystry*	быстрый
slow	*myedlyenny*	медленный
difficult	*trudny*	трудный
easy	*lyogki*	лёгкий
hot	*goryachi*	горячий
cold	*kholodny*	холодный
last	*poslyedni*	последний

Extras

Who?	*kto?*	кто?
What?	*shto?*	что?
Where?/Where is?	*gdye?*	где?
Why?	*pachyemi?*	почему?
When?	*kagda?*	когда?
big	*bolshoi*	большой
small	*malyenki*	маленький
many	*mnogo*	много
few	*malo*	мало
old	*stary*	старый
new	*novy*	новый
excellent	*atlichny*	отличный
beautiful	*krasivy*	красивый
How are you?	*Kak dyela?*	как дела?
What is your name?	*Kak vas zavut?*	как вас зовут?
My name is...	*Menya zavut...*	меня зовут...

s/	*muzhskoy*	мужской/
men's toilet	*zhenski tualet*	женский туалет
much is...?	*Skolka stoit...?*	сколько стоит...?
ey	*dyengi*	деньги

ting Around

lane	*samalyot*	самолёт
	poyezd	поезд
	avtobus	автобус
o	*myetro*	метро
ybus	*trolleybus*	троллейбус
	tramvay	трамвай
	taksi	такси
	avtamabil, mashina	автомобиль, машина
rbike	*matatsikl*	мотоцикл
le	*velasipyed*	велосипед
opter	*vertalyot*	вертолёт
steamer	*parakhod*	параход
	parom	паром
rt	*aeraport*	аэропорт
flot office	*agenstva Aeraflota*	агентство Аэрофлота
ay station	*zhyeleznodarozhny vokzal*	железнодорожный вокзал
tation	*avtavokzal*	автовокзал
top	*astanovka avtobusa*	остановка автобуса
l station	*byenzakalonka*	бензоколонка
ms	*tamozhnya*	таможня
k-in	*registratsiya*	регистрация
iggage office	*kamera khranyeniya*	камера хранения
t	*bilyet*	билет
n	*tuda i abratna*	туда и обратно
ige	*bagazh*	багаж
lass compartment	*liux*	люкс
class compartment	*kupe*	купе
	myesta	место
ige attendant	*pravodnik*	проводник
ay	*zhyeleznaya daroga*	железная дорога
	daroga	дорога
:	*ulitsa*	улица
vard	*bulvar*	бульвар
ие	*praspyekt*	проспект
	vastochny	восточиый
	zapadny	западний
	sevyerny	северный
	yuzhny	южный

(on the) left	(na) lyeva	на лево
(on the) right	(na) prava	на право
straight on	pryama	прямо
timetable	raspisaniye	расписание
arrivals	pribytiye	прибытие
departures	atpravleniye	отправление
Where is the...?	Gdye....?	Где?
Is there a plane/train/ bus to...?	Yest li samalyot/poyezd/ avtobus do...?	Есть ли самолёт/поезд/ автобус до...
When is the next plane/ train/bus to...?	Kagda slyeduyushchi samalyot poyezd/avtobus do...?	Когда следующий самолёт поезд/автобус до...?
How long does it take?	Skolka vremeni idyot?	Сколько времени идёт...?
A ticket to..., please.	adin bilyet do..., pazhaluysta	Один билет до... пожалуйста.
Two tickets to..., please.	Dva bilyeta do..., pazhaluysta.	Два билета до..., пожалуйста.
Is there a bus to the airport/to the town?	Khodit li avtobus do aeraporta/ goroda?	Ходит ли автобус до аэропорта/города...?
Which number bus goes to...?	Kakoy nomyer idyot do...?	Какой номер идёт до...?

Accommodation

hotel	gastinitsa	гостиница
room	nomyer	номер
bathroom	vannaya	ванная
reception	priyom/foye	приём/фойе
floor lady	dyezhurnaya	дежурная
Do you have a room?	Nomyer yest?	Номер есть?
I would like a room.	Ya khotyel by nomyer.	Я хотел бы номер.
for one person	na adnavo	на одного
for two people	na dvaikh	на двоих
The... doesn't work.	... nye rabotayet.	... не работает.
tourist base	turbaza	турбаза
tent	palatka	палатка

Food and Drink

(*See also* 'Food and Drink', pp. 30–3)

restaurant	restaran	ресторан
café	kafe	кафе
tea-house	chai-khana	чай-хана
bar	bar	бар
food shop	gastranom	растроном
bazaar	bazar	базар
breakfast	zavtrak	завтрак
lunch	abyed	обед
dinner/supper	uzhin	ужин

Food	Pishcha	Пища
bread	*khlyeb*	хлеб
cheese	*syr*	сур
yoghurt	*kefir*	кефир
butter	*masla*	масло
jam	*varenye*	варенье
honey	*myod*	мёд
eggs	*yaitsa*	яица
fried eggs	*yaichnitsa*	яичница
sugar	*sakhar*	сахар
salt	*sol*	соль
salami	*kalbasa*	колбаса
sour cream	*smyetana*	сметана
fish	*ryba*	руба

Fruit	Frukty	Фрукти
apple	*yablaka*	яблоко
pear	*grusha*	груша
melon	*dynya*	дыня
watermelon	*arbuz*	арбуз
apricot	*abrikos*	абрикос
plum	*sliva*	слива
cherry	*vishnya*	вишня
grape	*vinagrad*	виноград
pomegranate	*granat*	гранат
fig	*figa*	фига
peach	*pyersik*	персик
walnut	*aryekh*	орех
orange	*apyelsin*	апельсин
lemon	*limon*	лимон

Vegetables	Ovashchi	Овощи
potato	*kartofyel*	картофель
rice	*ris*	рис
tomato	*pamidor*	помидор
cucumber	*aguryets*	огурец
pepper	*pyeryets*	перец
aubergine	*baklazhan*	баклажан
cabbage	*kapusta*	капуста
onion	*luk*	лук
carrot	*markov*	морковь
turnip	*bryukva*	брюква
lettuce	*latuk*	латук
mushrooms	*griby*	грибы

Drink	Napitky	Напитки
water	*vada*	вода
mineral water	*mineralnaya vada*	минеральная вода
tea	*chai*	чай
green/black/	*zelyony/chyorny/*	зелёный/чёрный
Indian tea	*Indiski chai*	индийский чай
coffee	*kofye*	кофе
fruit juice	*sok*	сок
lemonade	*limanad*	лимонад
wine	*vino*	вино
beer	*piva*	пиво
milk	*malako*	молоко
vodka	*vodka*	водка
cognac	*kanyak*	коньяк
champagne	*shampanskoye*	шампанское
port	*partvein*	портвейн

Menu	Myenyu	Меню
starter	*pyervye blyuda*	первые блюда
caviar	*ikra*	икра
salad	*salat*	салат
soup	*sup*	суп
bortsch	*borshch*	борщ
consomme	*bulyon*	бульон
cabbage soup	*shchi*	щи
main course	*vtarye blyuda*	вторые блюда
entrecote	*antryekot*	антрекот
mutton	*baranina*	баранина
beef stroganoff	*byefstraganov*	беф-строганов
meatballs	*bitochki*	биточки
steak (hamburger)	*bifshteks*	бифштекс
pancakes	*blinchiki*	блинчики
goulash/stew	*gulyash*	гуляш
rissoles	*katlyety*	котлеты
chicken	*kuritsa*	курица
stewed meat	*myasa tushyonoye*	мясо тушёное
plov/pilaf	*plov*	плов
trout	*faryel*	форель
carp	*karp*	карп
sturgeon	*asyetrina*	осетрина

Numbers

one	*adin*	один
two	*dva*	два
three	*tri*	три
four	*chyetyrye*	четыре
five	*pyat*	пять
six	*shyest*	шесть
seven	*syem*	семь
eight	*vosyem*	восемь
nine	*dyevyat*	девять
ten	*desyat*	десять
eleven	*adinadtsat*	одиннадцать
twelve	*dvenadtsat*	двенадцать
thirteen	*trinadtsat*	тринадцать
twenty	*dvadtsat*	двадцать
thirty	*tridtsat*	тридцать
forty	*sorok*	сорок
fifty	*pyatdyesyat*	пятьдесять
sixty	*shestdyesyat*	шестьдесять
ninety	*dyevyanosta*	девяносто
one hundred	*sto*	сто
two hundred	*dvyesti*	двести
three hundred	*trista*	триста
five hundred	*pyatsot*	пятьсот
one thousand	*tysyacha*	тысяча
one million	*million*	миллион
1996	*tysyacha dyevyatsot*	тысяча девятьсот
	dvevyanosta shyest	девяносто шесть

Time

Most people and all timetables use the twenty-four hour clock. Round hours are easy (though note the variations below). So are other times when given as minutes past the hour. However, 'quarter past' and 'half past', to Russians, are quarter or half of the following hour, which is given as an ordinal, not a numeral. Just to confuse things, times in the second half of the hour are often given as the number of minutes still to elapse before the following hour; literally, without however many minutes the following hour finds itself. In this case the hour is a numeral and the number of minutes an ordinal.

one o'clock	*chas*	час
two (to four) o'clock	*dva chasa*	два часа
five o'clock (onwards)	*pyat chasov*	пять часов
quarter past nine	*dyevyat pyatnadtsat*	девять пятнадцать
half past nine	*dyevyat tridtsat/*	девять тридцать
	palavina dyesyatava	половина десятого

eight minutes past eleven	*adinadtsat vosyem*	одиннадцать восемь
twelve-twenty	*dvyenadtsat dvadtsat*	двенадцать двадцать
twenty to one	*byez dvadtsati chas*	без двадцати час
time	*vremya*	время
What's the time?	*Skolko vremeni?*	Сколько времени?
	Kotory chas?	Который час?
morning	*utra*	утро
evening	*vyechyer*	вечер
night	*noch*	ночь
day	*dyen*	день
today	*cyevodnya*	сегодня
tomorrow	*zavtra*	завтра
yesterday	*vchyera*	вчера
week	*nyedyelya*	неделя
month	*myesyats*	месяц
year	*god*	год
spring	*vyesna*	весна
summer	*lyeta*	лето
autumn	*osyen*	осень
winter	*zima*	зима

Days

Monday	*panyedyelnik*	понедельник
Tuesday	*vtornik*	вторник
Wednesday	*sryeda*	среда
Thursday	*chyetvyerg*	четверг
Friday	*pyatnitsa*	пятница
Saturday	*subbota*	суббота
Sunday	*voskryesyenye*	воскресенье

Months

January	*yanvar*	январь
February	*fyevral*	февраль
March	*mart*	март
April	*apryel*	апрель
May	*may*	май
June	*iyun*	июнь
July	*iyul*	июль
August	*avgust*	август
September	*syentyabr*	сентябрь
October	*aktyabr*	октябрь
November	*nayabr*	ноябрь
December	*dyekabr*	декабрь

Town and Country

city	*gorod*	город
suburb	*prigorod*	пригород
housing estate	*mikrorayon*	микрорайон
village	*syelo*	село
mosque	*myechet*	мечеть
madrasa	*medrese*	медресе
church	*tserkov*	церковь
museum	*muzyey*	музей
theatre	*teatr*	театр
concert hall	*kantsertny zal*	концертный зал
nightclub	*nachnoi bar*	ночной бар
desert	*pustynya*	пустыня
forest	*lyes*	лес
mountain	*gara*	гора
river	*ryeka*	река
lake	*ozyera*	озеро
sea	*morye*	море
rain	*dozhd*	дождь
snow	*snyeg*	цнег
sun	*solntse*	солнце
moon	*luna*	луна

Some Verbs

to speak	*gavarit*	говорить
to think	*dumat*	думать
to eat	*yest/kushat*	есть/кушать
to sleep	*spat*	спать
to drink	*pit*	пить
to know	*znat*	знать
to understand	*panimat*	понимать
to look	*smatryet*	смотреть
to like/love	*lyubit*	любить
to work	*rabotat*	работать
to want	*khatyet*	хотеть
to read	*chitat*	читать
to go (*irreg*)	*idti/khadit*	идти/ходить
to come (*irreg*)	*prikhadit*	приходить
to see (*irreg*)	*vidyet*	видеть

Present tense of читать to read:

I read	*ya chitayu*	я читаю
you read (*sing*)	*ty chitayesh*	ты читаешь
he/she reads	*on/ana chitayet*	он/она читает

we read	*my chitayem*	мы читаем
you read (*plur*)	*vy chitayete*	вы читаете
they read	*ani chitayut*	они читают

Present tense of говорить to speak

I speak	*ya gavaryu*	я говорю
you speak (*sing*)	*ty gavarish*	ты говоришь
he/she speaks	*on/ana gavarit*	он/она говорит
we speak	*my gavarim*	мы говорим
you speak (*plur*)	*vy gavaritye*	вы говорите
they speak	*ani gavaryat*	они говорят

Regular verbs with the infinitive ending - ать conjugate like читать. Those with the infinitive ending - ить conjugate like говорить. Any verb in any form can be negated by prefixing it with не (nye). You can turn any spoken sentence into a question with a rising inflection at the end, i.e. by making it sound like one.

Uzbek Essentials

(also understood in Turkmenistan, Kirghizstan and Kazakhstan)

welcome/hello	*salam* or	How are you?	*Akhvollingiz kalai?*
	assalamu alaikum	well	*yakhsh*
goodbye	*khair*	hotel	*mekhman-khana*
thank you	*rakhmat*	restaurant	*ash-khana*
yes	*kha*	bread	*non/nan*
no	*yok*	water	*su*
good	*yakhsheh*	How much?	*Kanchapul?*
bad	*yoman*	Where is...?	*Khayedeh...?*

Mandarin Essentials

hello	*ni hao*	avenue	*jie/dajie*
goodbye	*zai jian*	east	*dong*
please	*qing*	nan	*south*
thank you	*xiexie*	west	*xi*
yes	*dui*	north	*bei*
no	*budui*	middle	*zhong*
Where is...?	*Zai nar...?*	upper	*shang*
How much?	*Duo shao qian?*	lower	*xia*
good	*hao*	hotel	*binguan/(da) fandian/jiuguan/luguan*
bad	*huai*	mansion (hotel)	*dasha*
How are you?	*ni hao ma?*	guesthouse	*lushe*
well	*hen hao*	hostel	*zhaodaisuo*
street	*lu*	restaurant	*da fandian/jiuguan*

There is a dearth of English language material on Soviet Central Asia, but a plethora of Great Game era books which are variously turgid, hilarious, rip-roaring and inspirational. They make expensive collectors' items but are also held by the British Library and in some cases other libraries, from which they are generally available on inter-library loan.

Selected Travel and Memoirs

Bailey, F. M., *Mission to Tashkent*, Jonathan Cape, 1946, OUP paperback, 1992. Bailey was perhaps a better spy than writer, but his is still the ultimate real-life Central Asian spy story; he was assigned by the *Cheka* in 1919 to hunt *himself*.

Battuta, *The Travels of Ibn Battuta*, tr. H. A. R. Gill, Hakluyt Society, 1958. Vivid descriptions of 14th-century Transoxiana by an indefatigable Arabian traveller.

Clavijo, Don Ruy Gonzalez de, *Narrative of the Embassy of Don Clavijo to the Court of Timur at Samarkand*, Hakluyt Society, 1859. Famous account of an extraordinary journey; Clavijo was the only European to be entertained by Tamerlane 'at home'.

Burnes, Sir Alexander, *Travels into Bokhara*, London, 1834.

Curzon, Hon. George, *Russia in Central Asia*, London, 1889. Scaremongering and superb dry wit from the man who travelled the Transcaspian railway with an india-rubber bath.

Fleming, Peter, *News From Tartary*, Jonathan Cape, 1936, Sphere Books, 1990. Fleming makes light of a gruelling caravan trek along the south side of the Taklamakan.

Graham, Stephen, *Through Russian Central Asia*, Cassell and Co., 1916. Charming, whimsical account of a walk through the idyll that was Central Asia on the eve of the Russian Revolution.

Hopkirk, Kathleen, *Central Asia: A Traveller's Companion*, John Murray, 1993. Interesting scene-setting through reference to travellers' accounts over the centuries.

Krist, Gustav, *Alone through the Forbidden Land*, London, 1939. An almost literally unbelievable adventure in Bolshevik Central Asia.

Maclean, Fitzroy, *Eastern Approaches*, Jonathan Cape, 194,9 and recently in paperback. Classic tales of high jinks on Stalin's southern frontier by the young diplomat who later founded the SAS.

Moorhouse, Geoffrey, *Apples in the Snow—A Journey to Samarkand*, Hodder and Stoughton, 1990, and Sphere paperback, 1991. Intourist-constrained but erudite travelogue.

Teague-Jones, Reginald, *alias* Ronald Sinclair, *The Spy Who Disappeared*, Victor Gollancz, 1991. Peter Hopkirk's introduction is the best thing about this diary of a British spy in Turkmenistan, 1918.

Thubron, Colin, *The Lost Heart of Asia*, William Heinemann, 1994. Perceptive, reflective account of the republics' search for a new identity shortly after independence.

Further Reading

Whittell, Giles, *Blowing Hot and Cold Through Central Asia*, Victor Gollancz, 1995. Travelling beyond the Intourist limits, Whittell follows the route of Stephen Graham (*see* above).

History and Archaeology

Allworth, Edward (ed), *Central Asia: 120 years of Russian Rule*, Duke University Press, Durham (USA) and London, latest edition 1989. Dry but authoritative, concentrating on Central Asians' responses to alien rule.

Fox, Robin Lane, *Alexander the Great*, Allen Lane, 1973, and Penguin. Definitive and very readable.

Hopkirk, Peter, *The Great Game*, John Murray, 1990, and OUP paperback. A galloping read but also a thorough treatment of this irresistible subject, based on the author's unrivalled collection of Great Game memoirs.

Hopkirk, Peter, *Setting the East Ablaze*, John Murray, 1984. Bolshevik Revolution comes to Central Asia. Another ripping yarn, mainly of espionage.

Keay, John, *The Gilgit Game*, John Murray, 1979. Personality-based account of British 19th-century manoeuverings near the Roof of the World.

Knobloch, Edgar, *Beyond the Oxus*, Ernest Benn, 1972. Archaeology, art and architecture to the 19th century. Covers Xinjiang too.

Pander, Klaus, *Sowjetischer Orient*, DuMont, Cologne, 1990. Very thorough guide to former Soviet republics' Islamic monuments, in German.

Sinor, Denis (ed), *The Cambridge History of Early Inner Asia*, CUP, 1990.

Staley, John, *Words for My Brother*, OUP Karachi, 1982. Anthropology and anecdote as well as the recent history of Pakistan's Northern Areas.

Soviet Studies

Akiner, Shirin, *Islamic Peoples of the Soviet Union*, Kegan Paul International, 1986. Exhaustive data on Soviet Muslims.

Bennigsen and Wimbush, *Muslims of the Soviet Empire*, Indiana University Press, 1986. More data.

Rumer, Boris, *Soviet Central Asia: A Tragic Experiment*, Unwin Hyman, 1989. Harvard academic allows himself plenty of spleen in dissecting the related issues of water, cotton, organized crime and the death of the Aral Sea.

Index

Mongols (*see also* Genghis Khan) **56–7**, 58, 175, 242, 283, 347
cities destroyed by: Dzhambul 280; Khŭjand 201; Merv 57, 91, 92; Samarkand 128–9; Sarakhs 90; Urgench 195–6
Mor pagoda 341
Moscow, accommodation 50
mosques 62, 68–9
visiting 40–1
motorbikes
buying in Central Asia 20
travelling by 20–1
Mughal dynasty 58, 130, 217
Muhammad Bini Atciz Az Seracksin 95
Muhammad Nazim Khan, Mir of Hunza 328
Mukanov, Sabit 297
Muradov, Ustor Shirin 171, 176
Murgab 236
Murgab river 78, 91, 93, 96, 233
museums 41
opening hours 41–2
Muslims *see* Islam
Musslahaddin Badi-uddin Nuri, Sheikh 204
Mustagh Ata 333, 334
Muynak 71–2, 197, **198–200**
Muzaffar al-Din, Emir of Bukhara 104

Nabiyev, Rakhman 225
Nadir Divanbegi 146, 173–4
Nadir Shah 144, 159, 184, 188
Nadira 218
Nadjmaddin Kubra, mausoleum of 196
Nagar 327, 328
Naizatash pass 236
Namangan 215
Nanga Parbat 317, 321
Nakshbandi sect 69, 177, 216
narcotics 26, 68
Naryn 259, **266–7**
Naryn river 215, 243, 251, 266, 269, 270
Nasir-i Khosrov 232

Nasrullah, Emir of Bukhara 159–60, 166, 205–6
Navoi, Alisher 114, 117
Nazarbayev, Nursultan 274, 283
Neanderthal Man 52
Nebit Dag 81
Nestorian Christians 92
Nevada-Semipalatinsk campaign 62-3, 284, 296, 307, 310
New Merv *see* Mary
Newbolt, Sir Henry 323
newspapers 38
Nilt 327
Nisa 53-4, 85, **87**
Niyaz-Kul, Khalif 174
Niyazov, Saparmurad, president of Turkmenistan 78, 82
Novgorod School, ikons 116
nuclear testing, at Semipalatinsk 63, 274, 284, 296, 307, 310–11
Nukus 73, **197–8**

Ob river 72
Ögödei (son of Genghis Khan) 57, 129
Old Merv *see* Merv
Old Nisa *see* Nisa
Old Urgench *see* Kunya Urgench
Omar Khan 205, 208
opening hours 41–2
opium 26
Ordzhonikidze, General G.K. 66
Osh 63, 69, **220–2**, 243
map 221
Osman Koran 115, 139
Ossipov (Bolshevik commissar) 105
Ot-Mok 269
Ottomans 115, 130
Oxus river *see* Amu Darya river
Ozero Son-Kul 265–6

packing 42
Pakhlavan Makhmud, mausoleum of 192

Pakistan (*see also* Karakoram Highway)
currency 39
tourist information 47–8
transport 17, 18, 19
visas 16
Pamirs 232–5, 333
Alai range 200, 212, 220, 237
hunting 36, 232
Pamir Gap 60, 236, 323
Pamir Highway 226, 233, 235–8
trekking 48–9, 235
Pan Chao, General 335
Pandjeh 60
Pandzhrud 154
Panfilov, General Ivan 294
Parthians **53–4**, 76, 85, 87, 92, 158
Passu 330
Pathans 318
Pattan 320
Pazyryk 70
Pendzhikent 68, **153–4**
Bunjikath 153, 154
Perovsky, General V.A. 185, 206
Persia (*see also* Achaemenids; Cyrus the Great; Nadir Shah; Sassanians; Turan) 53, 54, 55, 57, 58, 152, 159
art and architecture 184, 192, 277
Peter the Great, Russian czar 58, 80, 184, 311
petrol 21
photography 42–3
Piandzh river 67, 226, 232, 233, 235
Pik Bielukha 312
Pik Chimtarga 68
Pik Kommunisma 228, 232, 237
Pik Lenina 220, 232, 237
Pik Pobieda 242, 263, 264
Pir Sar 53, 320
Pirali 331
Pishpek *see* Bishkek
Pokrovka 261
Polat-bey (Polat Khan) 206
police 43